Studies in the Legal History of the South

EDITED BY PAUL FINKELMAN AND TIMOTHY S. HUEBNER

This series explores the ways in which law has affected the development of the southern United States and in turn the ways the history of the South has affected the development of American law. Volumes in the series focus on a specific aspect of the law, such as slave law or civil rights legislation, or on a broader topic of historical significance to the development of the legal system in the region, such as issues of constitutional history and of law and society, comparative analyses with other legal systems, and biographical studies of influential southern jurists and lawyers.

The Long, Lingering Shadow

The Long, Lingering Shadow

SLAVERY, RACE, AND LAW
IN THE AMERICAN HEMISPHERE

ROBERT J. COTTROL

The University of Georgia Press
Athens & London

Designed by Walton Harris
Set in 10.5/14 Minion Pro

Printed digitally

Library of Congress Cataloging-in-Publication Data

Cottrol, Robert J.
The long, lingering shadow : slavery, race, and law in the
American hemisphere / Robert J. Cottrol.
     p.   cm. — (Studies in the legal history of the south)
Includes bibliographical references and index.
ISBN 978-0-8203-4405-8 (hardcover : alk. paper) —
ISBN 0-8203-4405-2 (hardcover : alk. paper) —
ISBN 978-0-8203-4431-7 (pbk. : alk. paper) —
ISBN 0-8203-4431-1 (pbk. : alk. paper)
1. Slavery—Law and legislation—America. 2. Slavery—Law
and legislation—Western Hemisphere. 3. Blacks—Legal
status, laws, etc.—Western Hemisphere. 4. Slavery—History—
Western Hemisphere. 5. Race relations—History—Western
Hemisphere. I. Title.
KDZ546.C68 2013
342.708′7—dc23   2012029629

British Library Cataloging-in-Publication Data available

To the memory of my parents,
Robert W. Cottrol and Jewel G. Cottrol,

and

To my children,
John M. Cottrol II and Dora J. Cottrol,
who will inherit the future

Contents

Acknowledgments

I HAVE ACCUMULATED MANY DEBTS in the writing of this book. My prior training and writing had been in the legal and social history of the United States. I owe a big debt to a number of friends and colleagues who are students of Latin American history, law, and society and who took the time to read some of the chapters dealing with Latin America and to offer valuable criticisms and suggestions. These include George Reid Andrews, Barbara Weinstein, Jan Hoffman French, Tanya Hernandez, Paula Alonso, Peter Klaren, Cynthia McClintock, Matthew Mirow, Mieko Nishida, Seth Racusen, José Guilherme Giacomuzzi, Marcelo D. Varella, Victor Uribe, and Anani Dzidzienyo. ¡Muchas gracias e muito obrigado para todos!

This work has also benefited from careful readings from colleagues and friends who are students of U.S. history and law, among them Jonathan Bush, Charles Craver, Raymond T. Diamond, Davison Douglas, Stanley Engerman, Wendy Greene, Ariela Gross, Daniel Hamilton, James Horton, Michael Meyerson, Stephen Middleton, Jefferson Powell, Judith Schafer, Dinah Shelton, Richard Stott, and Mel Urofsky. This book has especially benefited from support and suggestions from Paul Finkelman. Others who have read the manuscript and offered valuable suggestions include Nancy Grayson, Timothy S. Huebner, and an anonymous reviewer. Also a special thanks to Don Gastwirth and Alice Beard, who provided help at a critical time.

Portions of this work have been read and discussed at the American Society for Legal History, the Law and Society Association, the Latin American Studies Association, the Eastern Sociological Society, the Triangle Legal History Seminar at Duke University and the University of North Carolina, and faculty workshops at the George Washington University Law School. I have benefited considerably from the comments made in those forums.

I have also benefited greatly from informal conversations with Latin Americans who have given me their views on race in their nations. These discussions have not risen to the level of formal ethnographic or oral history interviews, but they nonetheless helped shape my thinking on questions of race and social status in Latin America. Among the people who privileged me with their insights were Jorge Ramirez (Peru), María Magdalena "Pocha" Lamadrid (Argentina), Miriam Gomes (Argentina), Lucia Molina Dominga (Argentina), Horacio Pita (Argentina), Marta Maffia (Argentina), Romero Rodriquez (Uruguay), Eunice Prudente (Brazil), and minister Joaquim B. Barbosa Gomes (Brazil).

The George Washington University Law School has been absolutely fantastic in its support of the project, including providing me with a sabbatical during part of the writing of the manuscript and summer funding for research and travel. Fred Lawrence, Greg Maggs, and Paul Berman all served as dean of the law school at various stages of the project and gave the project their strongest support. The law school and other divisions of the university also furnished bright and skilled research assistants; special thanks in that regard to Rebecca Szucs, Jacqueline Strzemp, Ana Karruz, and Laura Valden. Finally, I would like to thank my secretary, Kierre Hannon, and James Wilson of the Faculty Support Staff and Omar Clarke of the Information Systems Staff, who provided invaluable assistance fighting the many glitches that occurred as we wrestled the manuscript from its original draft in Word Perfect to its final draft in Microsoft Word.

The Long, Lingering Shadow

Introduction

THIS BOOK IS AN EFFORT to broaden our current conversation on law and race. In the United States, the discussion on law and race has, in my view, tended to focus too narrowly on the American experience. This is perhaps understandable. The law in the United States has played a clear, undeniable role both in the construction of the American system of racial inequality and in the struggle to achieve equal rights. Any student educated in the United States — perhaps one who has simply taken the undergraduate survey course in American history or even one who only vaguely remembers the subject from high school — knows this history, at least in broad outline.

The new nation that began with a ringing declaration "that all men are created equal" quickly adopted a constitution that protected slavery, most prominently in that document's fugitive slave clause. Slavery had the law's imprimatur, an imprimatur reinforced by the Supreme Court's 1857 decision in *Dred Scott v. Sandford* — the infamous *Dred Scott* case. A cataclysmic civil war that killed more Americans than any of the nation's foreign conflicts put an end to slavery. The Constitution was amended in the wake of that conflict. The new Thirteenth Amendment permanently prohibited slavery. The Fourteenth proclaimed the citizenship and equal status of the former slaves. The Fifteenth opened political rights — voting — to all men, regardless of race. The nation enjoyed, briefly, that "new birth of freedom" eloquently proclaimed in Lincoln's Gettysburg Address. But by the end of the nineteenth century, the light of freedom was growing dimmer. Inequality was again being made part of the law of the land. State Jim Crow statutes mandating separate and stigmatizing treatment for Americans of African descent were declared constitutional by the Supreme Court in *Plessy v. Ferguson* in 1896. The stage was set for an early twentieth-century history of rigid segregation, racial violence, and disenfranchisement. The stage was also set for one of the more inspiring chapters in the legal history of the United States and indeed any nation, the struggle to use the law to dismantle the system of state-mandated inequality that prevailed in the southern states and indeed throughout the nation. That struggle would take many forms, bringing the champions of equal rights many times before the nation's courts and legislatures. The most important triumphs of the civil rights movement in the postwar era — the Supreme Court's 1954 decision in *Brown v. Board of Education,* outlawing segregation in public education; the Civil Rights Act of 1964, outlawing discrimination in public accommodations and employment; and the 1965 Voting Rights Act prohibiting discriminatory practices against minority voters — remain the foundations of modern American antidiscrimination law.

American scholars might be forgiven for thinking that the legal history of race relations in the United States is sufficiently long and difficult enough to unravel so as to demand the exclusive attention of legal historians and others concerned with issues of race and law. The sheer size of the United States, coupled with its governance under a federal system where much of the law is determined not only by the national Congress and the federal judiciary but also by different state courts and legislatures, ensures that simple statements about the law will never be easy. This is as true or perhaps more so for what the law has had to say about issues of slavery and race as it is for other topics. And legal historians have also come to realize that the legal history of race in the United States is made even more complex because it involves more than the histories of those we have come to call black and white. The law has regulated the statuses of other groups — peoples of indigenous descent, and those whose ancestors came from Latin America and Asia as well. This has also contributed to the complexity of any discussion of the role of law in the troubled history of race relations in the United States. It has also contributed to the largely inward gaze of American legal historians concerned with the topic.

This prevailing tendency to focus inward might be contrasted with the broad comparative work essayed by sociologist Frank Tannenbaum in the 1940s. Tannenbaum believed — correctly, in my view — that comparative study can tell us much not only about other societies but also about our own. Tannenbaum was concerned with law as a force that greatly influenced the treatment of slaves in different societies and had a profound impact on race relations after emancipation as well. The Tannenbaum thesis is well known to students of comparative slavery. Tannenbaum's central claim is that the law played a critical role in helping to fashion slave systems in Latin America that were more protective of the rights of slaves and ultimately more conducive to egalitarian race relations than was the case in the United States. His work remains the starting point for modern discussions on comparative slavery and race relations in the Americas, an impressive accomplishment for a work now more than six decades old.[1]

If the Tannenbaum thesis has been sharply criticized in recent decades, with historians of slavery convincingly challenging its benign portrayal of the institution in Latin America and students of race relations exploding the myth of racial democracy in the region, Tannenbaum still presents a worthy point of consideration and departure for scholars concerned with the role of law in creating and sustaining systems of racial hierarchy. Tannenbaum asked what historical sociologist Theda Skocpol has termed the "big" questions — those questions that force us to confront the fundamental differences between the society or civilization with which we are familiar and others that have developed in different or seemingly different ways. Confronted with the harsh realities of the Jim Crow America of the 1940s, Tannenbaum tried to understand those realities by contrasting the America he knew — with its color lines, its segregated schools, its Jim Crow army, its lynchings, its ubiquitous "white" and "colored" signs in front of water fountains and restrooms, train station waiting rooms, and park benches — with the seeming absence of discrimination in Latin America. He sought to explain what appeared to be the radically different developments of societies that had begun with the common institution of African slavery. He believed he had found the answer in the different ways that the law governed the lives of masters, slaves, and free people of color in what would become the United States and the different nations of Latin America.[2]

The "big" questions posed by Tannenbaum — How can we account for different patterns of race relations in the Americas, and to what extent can these differences be traced to the different slave regimes that developed in the New World and to the laws that governed those regimes? — remain critical. The black experience in the United States is a small part of a much larger history of the forced transportation and settlement of Africans in the Americas and the histories of their Afro-American and non–Afro-American descendants. Our best information indicates that less than 4 percent of Africans brought to the Americas settled in what became the United States. The experiences of Portugal, Spain, and later Latin America with African and Afro-American slavery were of a far longer duration than that of British North America. African slavery would begin in metropoli-

tan Spain and Portugal before the fifteenth century. Latin American slavery would formally end nearly four hundred years after Columbus's voy-
age to the New World with Cuban emancipation in 1886 and the abolition
of slavery in Brazil in 1888. This final emancipation occurred a generation
after Lee's surrender at Appomattox and the enactment of the Thirteenth
Amendment. Nearly 5,000,000 of the more than 10,000,000 Africans forcibly brought to the Americas (roughly 45 percent) went to Brazil alone. The
giant Lusophonic colony and nation received the largest number of Africans
from the trans-Atlantic slave trade, more than twelve times the 388,700
Africans who are estimated to have come to British North America. The
Spanish-speaking regions of the Western Hemisphere received 1,292,900
African captives. The sugar plantation economies of the Americas were
by far the biggest magnet for the African slave trade. British and French
Caribbean colonies combined received more than 3,000,000 Africans. The
pull of the sugar plantation economy was so strong that Cuba is estimated
to have imported more than 780,000 African slaves between 1790 and 1867
alone, nearly double the total number of Africans brought to the United
States between the seventeenth century and the end of the Civil War.[3]

Today, the descendants of those African captives who were forced to
come to the Americas to labor, and often perish, in the plantations and
mines of the New World inhabit every nation in the hemisphere. In some
countries, the presence of people of African descent is highly visible. In
the Caribbean, the states of Bahia and Pernambuco in northeastern Brazil,
and other parts of the Americas, large numbers of people are visibly of
African descent; in addition, African cultures have been preserved in
these regions, often influencing the language, religion, music, architecture,
and other aspects of the daily lives of most people. In other nations, the
African presence is more elusive. Descendants of Africans, some visibly
Afro-American, others regarded as white or mestizo may be found in nations such as Argentina and Chile, although most people in both countries
are largely unaware of this phenomenon and in many cases would vigorously deny it. In some nations, the business of locating Afro-Americans is
complicated by national ideologies, legacies of stigmatization, and traditional antagonisms. A substantial Afro-Mexican population lives on that
nation's Atlantic and Pacific coasts. There is an even larger population of
Mexican mestizos who do not acknowledge and in many cases are probably unaware of their African ancestry. And yet the African contribution

to what Mexicans have long celebrated as "La Raza Cósmica" remains largely unrecognized, in large part because of a national racial ideology that stresses that the nation is a biological and cultural synthesis of the indigenous Aztec Empire and the conquering Spaniards. Both groups are given a noble history in the national narrative, while the large presence of African slaves in colonial Mexico and the subsequent history of their Afro-Mexican descendants is often ignored.[4]

In many American nations, the stigma associated with black or African ancestry causes many who clearly have that ancestry to deny it. The population of the Dominican Republic is predominantly of African descent. Only a minority of the population is phenotypically white, and even a majority of that group probably has some African ancestry. Nevertheless, many Dominicans customarily define themselves as "Indios" — Indians or descendants of indigenous peoples — and not as Afro-Dominicans. Blacks have frequently used the term *Indio Oscuro* (dark Indian), while mulattoes have tended to use the term *Indio Claro* (light Indian) to describe themselves and their ancestry. This tendency has in part reflected the traditionally higher status for people of Indian descent in Latin America as well as the history of strong enmity between Haitians and Dominicans.[5]

It is this broad variety of Afro-American experiences that I want to contrast with the experience in the United States. At one time, researchers embarking on such a task believed that their comparisons were made easier by looking at Latin American societies as racial democracies free of the kinds of prejudice and discrimination that existed in the United States. Such explanations, like Tannenbaum's discussion, which played a critical part in developing the racial democracy thesis, should be seen in context. Students of race relations who accepted this thesis did so due in no small part to the stark differences between the often rigidly segregated United States of the Jim Crow era and Latin America. If, as we are becoming more and more aware, racism, racial exclusion, and racial hierarchy have been part — indeed, a strong part — of the social history of Latin America, racial barriers nonetheless took on different forms from those in the United States. Exclusions were less absolute. As historian Alejandro de la Fuente reminds us, the ideology of racial democracy that developed in Latin America after the First World War worked to prevent the rigid segregation and often total exclusion from national life that was the lot of Afro-Americans in the United States. And the law did not mandate a separate and inferior position for Afro-Americans in Latin America. Legal institutions and legal actors discriminated, to be sure, but that discrimination did not have the kind of official sanction — the formal support from the highest courts and legislatures — and the normative and physical power that comes from such support, as was the case in the United States for the first half of the twentieth century and, indeed, beyond.[6]

Like Tannenbaum, I believe that the greater rigidity, the greater tendency toward exclusion, mandated by law in U.S. race relations had its origins in the system of slavery that prevailed in the United States. Tannenbaum saw the different legal systems governing slavery in the New World as having played a critical role in this process. The law in Latin America, he noted, protected the slave's life, his right to maintain his family, and — perhaps most important for future race relations — his right to purchase his freedom through binding manumission contracts and his right to be recognized as a citizen and equal after attaining that freedom. Tannenbaum was not a student of law as such and it is not unfair to say that he presented a somewhat unsophisticated legal history in which he read the relevant codes and assumed that they accurately reflected the legal history of slavery in Latin America and the United States as well. But his essential claims have been reiterated by more knowledgeable students of comparative law, including Roman law scholar Alan Watson, who has argued that the receptivity to manumission that originated in Roman law and continued in the slave codes of the Spanish and Portuguese Empires provide a stark contrast to slave law in Anglo-American jurisdictions. That law, according to Watson and others, was uniquely hostile to manumission and, it should be added, to the rights of free people of African descent. This hostility provides the genesis of the rigidity that has historically characterized race relations in the United States.[7]

This point can be oversimplified and overstated. The history of North American slavery is long and complex. The colonial period is particularly instructive, and we will spend some time in this volume examining it. Slavery existed in every one of the English colonies that would become the United States. Slavery in the North would last for two centuries, longer than the period between the adoption of the Thirteenth Amendment and the present. It would only die a lingering death in that region after the American Revolution. The physical conditions under which slaves lived, toiled, and died and the legal regimes that governed masters, slaves, and

free people of African descent would vary greatly in different times and
places. In some colonies slaves were totally outside the protection of the
law. They could be killed by white persons with legal impunity. In other
colonies, slaves were protected by the law. In some colonies, slaves could
and occasionally did manage to successfully sue their owners for freedom.
In some colonies, particularly in the seventeenth century, relatively little
difference seems to have existed between the legal and social statuses of
Africans forced to labor on farms and plantations and the white indentured servants who toiled alongside them. At times, the laws of different
colonies treated free Negroes as citizens, making few distinctions between
their rights and the rights of others. At other times, the laws made clear
the inferior legal and social status of Africans and their descendants.
Generalizations about Anglo-American law and its supposed hostility to
manumission and citizenship for people of African descent are made difficult when the record of the English colonies that would become the United
States is closely examined.

But it is in the world of race and slavery in the United States in the
nineteenth century where scholars such as Tannenbaum and Watson are at
their most accurate, both in their descriptions of the differences between
the United States and Latin America and in their efforts to find the origins of the rigid racial exclusions that for so long dominated American
life. This is true whether we consider the slave states, the Cotton Kingdom
of the antebellum era, or the increased racial restrictions endured by free
Afro-Americans in the states that had abolished slavery. The American
caste system — the determination that people of African descent could
not be citizens or equals and that even their very freedom was an evil to
be barely tolerated, if at all — was a feature more of American slavery and
race relations in the antebellum years of the nineteenth century than the
previous centuries. Racism, discrimination, and restrictions on manumission existed in the colonial era to be sure, but these would become more
systematic and more of an integral part of a full-throated ideology of white
supremacy and a vigorous defense of what would come to be called the
"Peculiar Institution" in the nineteenth century. This ideology would argue that slavery was not merely necessary but virtuous, a positive good,
the optimal arrangement for the governance of the inferior and dependent
Negro. In antebellum America, that ideology would gain increasing support in the law. It was an integral part of Roger B. Taney's opinion in *Dred*

Scott. That opinion, in which the nation's chief justice spoke through its highest court, gave the law's imprimatur to more than a system of race-based slavery. Race-based slavery was not unique; it had been part of the Atlantic world of European expansion since the fifteenth century. What *Dred Scott* reflected was a view that found increasing support in antebellum America that not only slavery but citizenship as well was to be based on race, that the system of inequality forged in slavery was to be a system of caste, inescapable and indelible. That new legal thinking and the cultural change that supported it would also leave an indelible mark on race relations in the United States, the creation of a caste-like system of race relations that would survive long after the demise of the Peculiar Institution that helped give it birth.

Why did slavery bequeath to the people of the United States a system of racial exclusion more rigid than those found in Latin America? Slavery was certainly not more benign in Latin America — indeed, everything we know about the physical conditions that slaves endured indicates that slavery was harsher, at least in those regions whose economies were dominated by large-scale plantation agriculture, than was the case in the United States. And Latin America was certainly not free of racial prejudice: Spanish and Portuguese law had codified the legal disabilities of people of African descent long before such legislation was attempted in British North America.[8]

What was different in the United States was an ideology of freedom and egalitarianism that clashed with the institution of human bondage in a way that it did in no other slave society. Slavery had existed largely unquestioned in many societies until the end of the eighteenth century. The common law of England was somewhat unusual in that its jurists refused to sanction the institution, declaring it to be contrary not only to natural law but to the common law as well. But law and custom elsewhere in Europe and the rest of the world recognized the right of human beings to own property in other human beings. There was, to be sure, some recognition that slavery was contrary to natural law. The law recognized that slaves naturally yearned for freedom. Provisions were made to facilitate manumissions. Civil codes recognized the freedom of fugitive slaves under some circumstances. But the institution itself remained largely unquestioned, unremarkable in most societies, where inequality and restraints on liberty were generally common.[9]

But the Enlightenment, the liberal ideology that informed that historical moment, and the revolutions and constitutions, including the American, that derived from it brought new challenges for the institution of slavery. The new thinking that was informing the Atlantic world at the end of the eighteenth century was causing many people to question the institution of slavery, not in the traditional terms of whether or not an individual slave might be deemed worthy and set free but instead whether the whole practice was fatally flawed, inconsistent with the professed ideals of the new age. This new antislavery thinking — and, it should be added, African American participation in the American Revolution — helped put the northern states on the road to emancipation. That same combination of liberal thought and Afro-American participation in national wars for independence would also bring about emancipation in the former colonies of Spain. This process would be relatively rapid in some of the new nations: Mexico, for example, would abolish slavery soon after attaining independence. In other nations — Peru and Argentina are examples — emancipation would come slowly, in stages, and with significant attempts to circumvent the law's mandate to end slavery.[10]

The United States in the early nineteenth century stood alone as a slave society that also strongly proclaimed and indeed acted on liberal and egalitarian values. Brazil would become an independent empire in 1822. Its first constitution in 1824 would certainly show considerable liberal influence. But the newly independent Brazil remained an extremely hierarchical society. The empire had both a royal family and a noble class. Suffrage was restricted to substantial property owners. One's well-being frequently depended on the protection of powerful patrons. Brazil's liberalism was largely a liberalism of and for the propertied elite, confined primarily to issues of free trade and the protection of property rights. The contradiction, at least initially, between Brazilian liberalism and the practice of slaveholding was not seen by many as a particularly acute one.

But that contradiction was quickly acknowledged in the United States, even as early as the Declaration of Independence, and would grow even deeper in the nineteenth century with the expansion of democratic rights and egalitarian practices. In the land of universal (white) manhood suffrage, expanded access to landholding, education, the abolition of indentured servitude, and restrictions on the severity of punishments, slavery stood in marked contrast to the practices of the infant republic. American law, unlike the law in Latin America, had the cognitively difficult task of reconciling first race-based slavery and later race-based hierarchy with a strongly liberal national ideology and a normatively antihierarchical national culture. This was a unique, intellectually difficult, and ultimately impossible task. The law of slavery had to resolve two irreconcilable demands, that of the South's slave economy — made more robust by the spread of the Cotton Kingdom in the nineteenth century — with that of the nation's strong liberal ideology and culture. The law had to engage in a kind of cognitive dissonance that was not to be found, at least not to the same degree, in any other slave society.

Out of that dissonance would come an emphasis on race and racial difference that was stronger in the United States than elsewhere in the hemisphere. Slavery had to be justified in racial terms in a way that did not occur in other New World slave societies. To be sure, racism (a belief in African inferiority) existed throughout the hemisphere and had always provided a rationale for why Africans and their descendants could be enslaved while Europeans and the indigenous peoples of the Americas could not. But the United States in the nineteenth century took the business of making Africans and their Afro-American descendants outcasts to new levels. The racial rationale for slavery in a society that otherwise celebrated freedom meant that the barriers between black and white had to be made more rigid, less permeable. That determination meant, among other things, a greater hostility to the possibility that free people of color could exercise the rights of citizens. The slave states increasingly would pass limitations on manumission and restrictions on the rights of those blacks who were free. Even in the free states, free Negroes came to lose rights that they enjoyed immediately after the revolution, a reflection of the fact that the American nation of the nineteenth century that was expanding rights and opportunities for white people was becoming increasingly hostile to any suggestion of equality and inclusion for blacks.

The notion of race as a fixed caste line would strengthen in the early nineteenth century and would shape the world of American race relations long after emancipation. If there was an attempt to undo these caste lines during Reconstruction, they would nonetheless be firmly reconnected in the twentieth century with the establishment of Jim Crow and the elimination of black voters from southern politics. These practices were more stringent in the southern states than in the rest of the nation, to be sure, but a majority of Afro-Americans — nearly 90 percent — lived in the former slave states at the start of the twentieth century, and the South in many ways was setting the pace for the nation in race relations.

The lack of a need to reconcile chattel slavery with strong liberal and egalitarian sentiments contributed to a different style in race relations in much of Latin America. Let's be clear, racism and racial exclusion are very much a part of the culture in Latin America. Racial hierarchies exist and exist in ways that would be familiar to most North Americans. Whiteness is considered superior, blackness inferior. Groups that fall between the two extremes have an intermediate status. But there are important differences as well. Perhaps the most important of these is that race is seen not as a binary divide but as a continuum. Latin Americans make distinctions between blacks and mulattoes in ways that people in the United States generally do not. Latin American racial taxonomies owe much to colonial demography. The Portuguese captaincies that became Brazil had few white colonists. Mulattoes — children of those white colonists and enslaved African women — would come to have a status different from blacks in part to bolster the initially small ranks of those who were not African and not enslaved. Spaniards achieved much the same end through formal codification, providing legal definitions for mulattoes and other intermediate categories between black and white. Spanish colonial codes attempted to categorize every conceivable mixture of the three groups — African, European, and Indian, that inhabited Spain's American empire. Such codes sought in part to ensure divisions among the subject peoples of colonial Latin America by preventing combinations that might threaten the domination by the tiny minority of whites. This system of meticulous distinctions had unintended consequences, including helping to develop a culture of racial mobility. If there were many gradations between black and white, then improvements in one's social standing, acquisition of wealth, or education or status could also bring an improvement in one's racial designation from perhaps *negro* to *moreno* or *moreno* to *mulato* or *mulato* to *trigueño* or perhaps even *blanco*. The etiquette of race in many parts of Latin America would dictate that as a matter of courtesy, the unfortunate fact of one's African ancestry might be minimized or even overlooked in an inappropriate social setting. This stood in some contrast with the United States, where even when racial mixture was acknowledged — mulatto, quadroon, and octoroon are, after all, part of the American vocabulary — it was still within a context that rigorously divided the population into two groups, black and white.[11]

Notions of racial mobility, of course, reflect notions of racial hierarchy. The felt need to disguise, minimize, or excuse an individual's African background reflected the inferior status accorded African ancestry. It was stigmatized, certainly not as noble as a European background, even less noble than an indigenous one, especially after nationalist authors in many parts of Latin America began to celebrate indigenous heritage in an effort at national mythmaking and nation building. But racial — indeed, racist — attitudes in Latin America in some ways did not produce an exclusion from national life in quite the same way that they did in the United States. Latin America after emancipation did not have a codification of petty apartheid similar to the Jim Crow laws of the U.S. South. The Catholic Church in Latin America ensured that black and white and all the myriad classifications in between shared the experience of worshiping together and not in separate denominations as usually occurred in the Protestant United States. Marriages across racial lines were accorded an official tolerance not to be found in the United States, where such marriages were illegal in a number of states until the Supreme Court's 1967 decision in *Loving v. Virginia.* The history of popular political and social movements also illustrates an important difference in the dynamics of racial inclusion. The United States has a long history of conflict between Afro-Americans and populist movements designed to better the circumstances of working-class whites. In Latin America there has been a greater history of inclusion of peoples of African descent in working-class populist movements, even such right-wing populist movements as those led by Getúlio Vargas in Brazil and Juan Domingo Perón in Argentina.

Latin America has a history of men with some African ancestry serving as presidents or senior officials in the nineteenth and early twentieth centuries, at a time when such achievements would have been inconceivable in the United States. Nineteenth-century Mexico and Argentina had presidents who were generally believed to have some African ancestry. A few Afro-Brazilians achieved national prominence as statesmen in the nineteenth century, when the Brazilian Empire was the largest slaveholding society in the Americas. In the early decades of the twentieth century, at a time when the American Bar Association prohibited black members and more than a half century before Thurgood Marshall's appointment to the Supreme Court, Brazil had two mulatto ministers on that nation's highest tribunal, the Supremo Tribunal Federal. A mulatto, neurosurgeon Ramón Carrillo, served as Juan Perón's minister of health in Argentina in the 1950s. Both Cuba and Venezuela had Afro-American presidents, Fulgencio Batista and Rómulo Betancourt, in the 1940s and 1950s. The people of African descent who were able to move into the upper reaches of the political, economic, or social sectors of their nations usually were of mixed racial background. Their rise to prominence was helped in part by lesser prejudices against mulattoes and frequently by the ability to have openly acknowledged family connections with influential white relatives. This kind of mobility was largely impossible in the United States. [12]

These differences helped contribute to the notion of racial democracy in Latin America. They also helped to hide very real racism and racial discrimination. If the occasional mulatto might find his way into national office or become a doctor or lawyer with a largely white clientele, the situation for Afro-Americans generally remained grim. Victims of strong prejudice, they were also frequently victims of governmental policies that sought to ignore their very existence. These policies actively and openly sought through *blanqueamiento* (whitening) to replace the African- and indigenous-descended populations with new European immigrants who would transform the brown nations of nineteenth-century Latin America into white ones in the twentieth century. White immigration was encouraged with land grants and guarantees of education that were frequently denied to Afro-American and indigenous-descended populations. Discrimination in employment, particularly in the more modern industrial and commercial sectors would increase in the twentieth century to reflect the increased preference for the development of white nations. Severe discrimination often also existed in the provision of governmental services.

After the Second World War, the comparative history of race in the United States and Latin America would take an ironic turn. If the contradiction between slavery and racism and the strong liberal and egalitarian norms of the United States had historically contributed to the development of a caste-like approach to race relations, those very norms would help bring about a more thoroughgoing civil rights revolution in the United States than has occurred to date in Latin America. This revolution has included the development of a more effective body of antidiscrimination law and remedial policies, including often highly contested affirmative action measures. By way of contrast, Brazil, the Latin American nation that has been most forthright in addressing issues of the exclusion and marginalization of its Afro-American population, just began tentative steps toward affirmative action in universities and government employment in 2001. On April 26, 2012, the South American nation's highest court decided its first case on race-based affirmative action in public universities. The Supremo Tribunal Federal declared in a unanimous decision that the practice was constitutional. Throughout the hemisphere, Afro-American groups are seeking recognition and a greater inclusion in society. They are often, ironically enough, looking at the civil rights movement in the United States and the legal and social progress that it brought about as a potential model for their own struggles.[13]

It is this curious comparative odyssey that is the focus of this book. I have tried to follow the role of legal doctrine, legal institutions and public policies in helping to develop the often differing racial cultures in the Americas. The book examines Afro-American experiences in the Western Hemisphere. I should note in passing that Latin America presents other, still largely underexplored, possibilities for students of comparative race and ethnic relations. For those with an interest in indigenous populations and for legal scholars working in the area of Indian law and indigenous rights, Latin America is a particularly fruitful area for comparative exploration. Almost every country in the hemisphere has significant Indian or indigenous populations. While the study of indigenous populations as a separate and discrete group is well developed among Latin Americanists, the study of peoples who are of indigenous descent but who have joined the general population — in short, the study of people of indigenous descent as a racial group subject to the problems of discrimination in the general society — is less well developed. Similarly, Latin America presents interesting possibilities for those who might wish to do comparative explorations of immigration and adaptation. Those who have concentrated their research on Asian American populations would find much to explore and contrast in Latin America. Brazil's state of São Paulo has the largest ethnic Japanese population in the world outside of Japan. Large ethnic Chinese and Japanese populations can also be found in Peru. Significant populations of Chinese descent can be found throughout Central America and the Caribbean. Descendants of twentieth-century European immigrants are significant segments of the population in southern Brazil, Argentina,

Uruguay, and Venezuela, among other parts of Latin America. The possibilities for fruitful comparative research, perhaps involving greater collaboration between scholars interested in American studies and those interested in Latin American studies, would add greatly to our understandings in a number of fields, including the formation of racial and ethnic identities, the acculturation of newcomers, and the development of patterns of social inclusion and exclusion. *for men not women*

But in this volume the discussion will be confined largely to Afro-Americans. This is a complex enough topic. If race, as we are frequently told, is a social construct, it is one that is often difficult for North Americans to grasp in its Latin American manifestations. The range of racial classifications, the fact that some individuals have racial identities that seem to shift not only over the course of a lifetime but sometimes over very brief periods, changing with differing social contexts, puzzles *at least* the North American observer who grew up on our false but oddly settling *black* certitudes that a person can be readily classified as black or white. The fact *but is* that this received tradition is now under increasing dispute in the United *openly* States only adds complexity, challenge, and hopefully value to this com- *unacceptable* parative discussion. *than*

This volume examines the Afro-American experience in nine nations — Brazil, the United States, and seven nations carved from Spain's American empire (Argentina, Uruguay, Peru, Colombia, Costa Rica, Cuba, and the Dominican Republic). The discussion of slavery and emancipation looks at the place of Africans and their descendants in the Spanish Empire as a whole. The examination of the independent nations of Spanish-speaking Latin America looks at the seven nations, with occasional material from the histories of other countries. This discussion is less complete than the examinations of Brazil and the United States. The historiography on Afro-American life in Spanish America after emancipation is less well developed than is the comparable study of Afro-Brazilian or African American history. The primary sources are also less likely to reflect the considerable Afro-American presence in those nations than are similar records in Brazil and the United States. My efforts are not directed at doing in-depth histories of the selected nations but at using them to illustrate broader themes concerning race in the Spanish-speaking nations of the hemisphere. I believe that the seven Spanish-speaking nations combined with Brazil and the United States are helpful in illustrating a range of significant legal and social issues that have confronted peoples of African descent in the Americas.

I have chosen the United States not only because I am an American of African descent and have spent a good deal of my personal and professional lives trying to unravel the mysteries of race in our society but also because the United States has been the American society where law has played the most unambiguous role both in constructing a racial hierarchy and in the struggle to dismantle it.

I selected Brazil as the American society with the longest history of slavery. It is also the nation that received the most African slaves and today has the largest population of African descent in the Americas and indeed the second-largest African-descended population in the world, trailing only Nigeria. Brazilian slavery in the nineteenth century also presents what to many U.S. readers will be a paradox. Brazil had an economically vigorous slave regime with strong legal protections for the property rights of slaveholders. This was combined with a regime of legal equality for free Afro-Brazilians as well as actual political and social prominence for some free Afro-Brazilians. Brazil also presents another important issue for students of race relations. Like the United States, it is a huge continent-sized nation. And like the United States, Brazil is a nation of different, often contrasting regions. This statement is as true in the area of race relations as it is in others. Regional differences and their impact on Brazilian law and policy governing race form an important part of this discussion.

The seven Spanish-speaking nations were somewhat harder to select. Almost all of the Spanish-speaking nations of the hemisphere have compelling Afro-American histories, many of which remain underexplored for the postemancipation period. I believe that the countries I have chosen are important because they illustrate the range of issues that have confronted peoples of African descent in the Spanish-speaking nations of the hemisphere. The history of Afro-Americans in Argentina and its fraternal Rioplatense republic, Uruguay, illustrate the problem of marginalization and invisibilization. *Blanqueamiento,* governmental policies designed to transform the nations of Latin America into white nations through European immigration, were common throughout the region at the beginning of the last century. Latin America's leading intellectuals and governmental policy makers shared in the thinking of the age, including beliefs in scientific racism and Social Darwinism. They believed that the inferior indigenous and African elements of the national populations would not and should not survive competition with the superior European newcomers. New immigrants would create white nations, and with that would come the progress that was the promise of the new century. This project would meet with considerable success in both Argentina and Uruguay. Massive waves of Spanish, Italian, and other European immigrants would transform the two nations into reconstituted European societies. Both countries would develop inaccurate but powerful self-images as exclusively white nations with few indigenous, Afro-American, or mestizo elements. Argentina and Uruguay provide exaggerated examples of one pattern in Latin America race relations, the invisibilization of the Afro-American.

Cuba and Colombia represent the opposite end of the spectrum. Afro-Americans are quite visible in both societies. Although intellectuals and public officials in both nations at the beginning of the twentieth century also championed national whitening, it became clear early on in both Colombia and Cuba that the Afro-American populations were not going to disappear. The history of the twentieth century in both nations was in part a history of coming to grips with the Afro-American presence, including Afro-American cultures with strong African elements. Both societies were also the scenes of significant struggles against racial exclusion and of integrated working-class populist movements. Cuba has also had since 1960 a Marxist regime that has struggled with the issue of racial inequality with mixed results. Colombia since 1991 has had a constitution committed to providing land rights and a minimum of congressional representation for Afro-Colombians and yet has also had difficulty in providing protection against many forms of racial discrimination.

Peru is included in this volume because it represents two important issues that complicate and enrich our examination of race in the Americas. Afro-Peruvians live in a society that has too often ignored them or overlooked them, in part because their circumstances were overshadowed by a larger fault line in their nation — the line between those Peruvians who are still part of the indigenous culture (that is, those who are of indigenous descent, speak Quechua as a first language, and live in distinct indigenous communities) and those who are part of what we might call the Peruvian mainstream. This latter population speaks Spanish as a first language, lives in more or less modern communities, and adheres to a somewhat less alloyed version of the Catholic faith than those who are labeled *indigenous*.

As in other parts of Latin America, ethnic division — in this case, the division between those called indigenous or Indian and the other parts of the population — has served to mask very real racial divisions and patterns of discrimination in that society. The immigration of large numbers of Chinese and to a lesser extent Japanese to Peru after emancipation has also added to the complexity of any discussion of racial and ethnic hierarchies in that nation.

Costa Rica presents yet another issue, one that combines the issues of racial and ethnic exclusion. Costa Rica, like other Central American nations, has an Afro-American population largely descended from late-nineteenth- and early-twentieth-century immigrants from the British Caribbean. The Afro–Costa Rican population has historically been concentrated in and near the Caribbean port city of Limón. They were brought to work on that nation's railroads and banana plantations and have been the subject of no small amount of legal and social discrimination. English-speaking and black, they have had a difficult struggle gaining acceptance in a nation whose majority is Spanish-speaking and accustomed for much of the twentieth century to thinking of itself not only as white but also as citizens of a white nation. The black population of the Limón region would not in fact gain full Costa Rican citizenship until after the Second World War. Their struggle against marginalization and discrimination continues into the twenty-first century.

This volume also discusses the Dominican Republic. The historic enmity between Haitians and Dominicans has led to some of the most dramatic and tragic examples of racial tension and racial exclusion in the American hemisphere. This history is made more tragic and more ironic because most Dominicans share with Haitians not only the troubled island of Hispaniola but also a significant amount of African ancestry. The hostility between Haitians and Dominicans in part reflects sharp cultural and linguistic differences between the two groups and serves as a vivid reminder that race and racial difference can often reflect more than ancestry or appearance.

I look at race relations in these nine countries largely, though not exclusively, through the lens of a legal historian. A few words about this are in order. Legal history is a broad field done in different ways by different practitioners of the art. Many legal historians have greatly enhanced our knowledge of the law's development by focusing primarily and in some

cases exclusively on the evolution of legal doctrine. Mine is a somewi.
different task. I am concerned, of course, with law and legal doctrine. But
my concern is not with legal rules and doctrine alone. Instead my concern is with those symbiotic relationships between legal processes and social structure, between doctrinal evolution and cultural change, that force
a synthesis between legal analysis and social inquiry. I share Lawrence
Friedman's view that legal history must be approached "not as a kingdom
unto itself, not as a set of rules and concepts, not as the province of lawyers
alone, but as a mirror of society." This charge, this challenge that Friedman
made to the community of legal historians in the early 1970s, was directed
largely at historians of law who would be looking at one complex nation,
the United States. His approach is even more appropriate for scholars es-
saying a comparative legal history, where different political institutions,
social structures, and national legal cultures inevitably influence how law
affects social relations.[14]

At times, the role of law in constructing or dismantling patterns of racial
inequality has been clear. The slave codes throughout the Americas and the
postemancipation Jim Crow laws of the United States were clearly designed
to ensure the inequality of Afro-Americans. Similarly, court decisions such
as *Brown v. Board of Education* in the United States and Brazil's first civil
rights statute, the Lei Afonso Arinos,[15] were clearly meant to address the
issue of racial discrimination. At other times, the role of law in regulating
race relations has been more ambiguous. The United States is somewhat
unusual in historically having a body of law that formally mandated discriminatory treatment of its native-born Afro-American population after
the abolition of slavery. Yet we know that profound racial inequalities have
been a part of Latin American history and that the law in its application
if not its formal pronouncements has played a role in perpetuating that
inequality. I intend to show how this has been the case even when the law
has been nominally egalitarian.

I have tried to keep Lawrence Friedman's advice on how to do legal history in mind during the course of this study. This volume covers a great
deal of territory in a fairly short space, and it does so with one overarching
concern — the relationship between a society's broader sentiments concerning equality and the rights of individuals and the role of law in sustaining or combating patterns of racial inequality. This focus can help us to
understand the complicated relationship between law and racial inequal-

ity in the past as well as provide a guide to law's future role in helping to eradicate slavery's long, lingering shadow from the American hemisphere.

I would like to add a terminological postscript to this introduction. There has been a tendency for historians and other writers in recent decades to feel compelled to take sometimes strenuous efforts either to avoid using the word *Negro* or to preface their use of the term with an apology or perhaps to bracket the word with quotation marks when usage is unavoidable. That will not be my practice in this volume. *Negro* was the term that most black people used to describe themselves for a good portion of American history. It was used with pride by some of the most courageous people in the history of the United States. Ida B. Wells would so describe herself when she was an outspoken newspaper editor taking a brave and physically dangerous stand against lynch law and mob rule in late nineteenth century America. Carter Woodson would use the term when he founded the Association for the Study of Negro Life and History in 1915, at a time when American apartheid was becoming even harsher and when the best scientific minds proclaimed the doctrine of white supremacy and commended the virtues of Jim Crow policies. His efforts and those of his associates and successors would, over time, change the way the world viewed peoples of African descent. Thurgood Marshall and Constance Baker Motley and their associates used the term in *Brown v. Board of Education* when they asked the Supreme Court why Negroes, out of all the peoples in the American nation, were singled out for separate and stigmatizing treatment in segregated schools. Martin Luther King Jr. used the word *Negro* throughout his inspiring career and most notably when he stirred and changed the nation with his "I Have a Dream" speech during the 1963 March on Washington. The name *Negro* requires neither avoidance nor apology. It will be used in this volume with respect along with other names to describe peoples of African descent. One name that you will see frequently in this volume is *Afro-American*, used to describe both Americans of African descent and also citizens of other nations of the Western Hemisphere who are of African descent. Afro-American will be used somewhat more frequently in this volume than the currently more popular term *African American* for three reasons. First, it corresponds more closely to usage in other parts of the hemisphere — that is, the general practice is to speak of *Afro-Brazilians*, *Afro-Cubans*, *Afro-Colombians*, and so forth. Second, the term *Afro-American* also has had a long history in the study of peoples of African descent in the Americas, particularly comparative studies. Finally, *Afro-American* immediately denotes a person of African descent native to the Western Hemisphere. The term *African American* can be more ambiguous. It can certainly describe an American of African descent, but it also might describe more recent African immigrants who have come to the United States, a point that has been made by sociologist Orlando Patterson, among others.[16]

If the racial terms used in this volume require a little explanation, so do the terms indicating national identity. It is common in the Spanish-speaking countries of the hemisphere (the Brazilians seem less worried about this) to insist that those of us who are citizens of the United States not describe ourselves simply as *Americans*. The argument, quite well made and quite well taken, is that everyone in the hemisphere might reasonably describe themselves as *American* and that those of us who are from the United States should use the term *norteamericano* or *North American* to describe ourselves. The difficulty with that is that Canada and Mexico are also in North America, and the peoples of both nations have equal rights to the term *North American*. Our geographical difficulties do not end there. The inhabitants of the state of Hawaii as well as the residents of Puerto Rico, the U.S. Virgin Islands, Guam, and other U.S. territories in the Pacific are citizens of the United States, although it would hardly be accurate to call them "North Americans." There is a term in Spanish, *estadounidense*, used to describe citizens of the United States. It would probably best be translated as "United Stateser" — accurate enough, perhaps, but really just a little too clunky in its English manifestation to be really serviceable. In this volume, I generally use the term *American* to describe citizens of the United States with the occasional use of *North American* either for emphasis or distinction. I do so realizing that we do not have, nor should we claim, a monopoly on the name.

PART I

Our Bondage and Our Freedom

CHAPTER ONE

Casta y Color, Movilidad y Ambigüedad

SLAVERY AND RACE IN THE SPANISH EMPIRE

BETWEEN THE COLUMBIAN VOYAGES of the late fifteenth century and 1867, when the last slave ship from Africa landed in Cuba, nearly 1.3 million people were forcibly transported from West Africa to Spain's American empire. This migration was part of the Atlantic slave trade, the largest forced transfer of human beings in world history. The viceroyalties and *audiencias* that made up Spain's New World empire were an immense territory that extended from the southern part of the modern Argentine republic to what is today Northern California. Spanish America received nearly one of every eight of the more than ten million Africans brought to the Americas as slaves.[1] The results of that uprooting and transportation of Africans into the Americas are evident today. People who are of visible African descent inhabit every one of the republics that wrested their independence from Spain in the nineteenth century. In some of those nations, the Afro-American presence is strong. Cuba's population today has a predominance of people who would be described by most observers as black or mulatto. Afro-Cubans have had a strong impact on their nation's culture. Many of them, as well as many of their white compatriots, practice Santeria, an African form of religious worship. The persistence of Santeria is living testimony to the survival of African culture even in often harsh New World settings. At the other end of the spectrum, most Chileans are unaware — or at least were unaware until quite recently — that their nation, too, has a modern Afro-American population. A small Afro-Chilean community lives in the northern part of the country, in and near the port city of Arica. That community has become more visible in the last decade in

can you imagine of forces like this not up to combat open

+ forced subordination of women

part because Afro-Chilean community leaders in Arica have joined with Afro-American activists in other nations in a hemisphere-wide movement to combat traditional practices that have tended to make people of African descent invisible in many parts of Latin America.[2]

Most of the Spanish-speaking societies of the Americas fall somewhere between the Cuban and Chilean examples. Most of the nations of the hemisphere have visible Afro-American minorities, although few have had the cultural salience of the Afro-Cuban population. For North American observers race and the status of people of African descent in Latin American societies is often difficult to understand. If the American observer comes to one of the Spanish-speaking nations of the hemisphere, he or she usually does so with racial reflexes conditioned by race as we have traditionally known it in the United States. The very ideas that a person can be easily categorized as black or white or that remote traces of African ancestry make an individual black are artifacts of the history of slavery and racial domination as they developed and as they were struggled against in the United States. So, too, is the notion that there should be little in the way of formal recognition of racial mixture, despite the use of words like *mulatto* or *quadroon* and *octoroon* in the past and the more recent adoptions of such terms as *mixed race* and *multiracial*.

But the American observer soon finds that Latin America can be quite different. If race is a social construct, in Latin America it is often one that can be quite difficult for those with North American racial reflexes to grasp. Latin Americans readily employ meticulous vocabularies detailing every conceivable racial mixture, sometimes real, sometimes imagined. Latin American lexicons are filled with terms such as *negro, pardo, moreno, mulato, trigueño, zambo,* and others detailing presumed degrees of African, European, and indigenous admixtures. This extensive use of terms often detailing skin color has led some observers to argue that Latin Americans are perhaps somewhat obsessed with color but not really concerned with race as such. The existence in modern Latin America of racial stereotypes and governmental policies designed to favor whites and disfavor peoples of African and indigenous descent calls this view into sharp question.

In Latin America, many people of partial African descent and frequently even many people of predominantly African ancestry have often resisted any racial or color classification that would link them with their African ancestry. The reasons for this rejection are often complex and varied. It partly reflects the desire of many individuals to escape the stigma that frequently accompanies an Afro-American identity in many parts of the Americas. At times, this denial is supported by the general culture. An individual's rejection of African ancestry or of an identification as an Afro-American can at some level be comforting to those who have wanted to reassure themselves that they lived in essentially white or at least white and mestizo societies. Denial of African ancestry and redefinition of people of African descent into some other racial category historically aided in the project of national definition, a project that in many nations included writing Afro-Americans out of the national narrative. Mexican anthropologist Gonzalo Aguirre Beltrán notes that Mexican social scientists have traditionally sought to bury the considerable African and Afro-American presence in that nation's history in an effort to support a national narrative that made the Mexican nation solely a synthesis between its indigenous and Spanish roots.[3]

The effort in many Spanish-speaking nations to ignore the presence of populations of African descent as inconvenient or embarrassing has helped create a view of racial identification quite different from that traditionally encountered in the United States. Some persons with known and even visible African ancestry can be accepted, at least at some level, as white or at least not Afro-American. Racial identity in Latin America can often involve a complex negotiation involving ancestry, phenotype, social status, and family connections. Racial classification is often contextual. A racial hierarchy exists in which European ancestry and phenotype are more prized than African ones. At times, whites in Latin America allow some individuals of African descent to proclaim a whiter status than their ancestry or phenotype might dictate. This can be done out of courtesy to the individual as well to confirm national myths that one's nation contains few if any citizens of African descent. Despite this the individual who is visibly Afro-American and who claims to be white can often be the victim of race- or color-based exclusions.

After a while, the North American observer begins to get the hang of things. Latin Americans make often strong distinctions between blacks and mulattoes. People are categorized along a color continuum, not simply as black *or* white. There is a certain amount of racial or color negotiation, an effort on the part of individuals to achieve a somewhat whiter racial classification, and an etiquette that dictates that the individual attempting to do such should not be directly confronted and contradicted. African ancestry is looked down on, and in many nations there is or at least traditionally has been an effort to deny or at least minimize the Afro-American presence. The American observer begins to absorb these lessons, coming, often slowly, to an understanding of race as viewed by many Latin Americans. Just as these new realizations begin to dawn, Latin America throws a curve or two the North American observer's way. If many people with visible African ancestry try to claim that they are white or mestizo, individuals who are visibly white or mestizo occasionally will proudly proclaim a black or mulatto grandparent and identify with an Afro-American community out of familial loyalty or for cultural or political reasons. If African ancestry is disparaged and Afro-Americans are the victims of racist stereotyping, the North American researcher will nonetheless find that a surprising number of Latin American nations have had national leaders of African descent at a time when such was unthinkable in the United States. These paradoxes will often leave the American observer understandably confused.[4]

The Latin American system of racial hierarchy and racial categorization, like the system in the United States, had its origins with the enslavement of Africans and their descendants. The Spanish experience with slavery, including African slavery, far antedated that of the English settlers who would populate North America. If slavery had largely died out in England and indeed most of northwestern Europe by the thirteenth century, it was still a going concern in the Mediterranean world, which included the Iberian Peninsula. With an ability to benefit from the thriving Mediterranean slave trade, conflicts between Christians and Moors, and Portuguese raids into black Africa, the kingdoms that would ultimately be united under the Castilian Crown were home to slaves of a variety of races and ethnic backgrounds. Black slaves could be found in Valencia as early as the fourteenth century. Whatever prejudices Valencians and other inhabitants of the Iberian Peninsula may have had, it seems to have had little effect, at least initially, on the legal or social status of black Africans. Black Africans were but one of many enslaved groups on the Iberian Peninsula in the late Middle Ages. They were enslaved alongside Bulgarians, Greeks, Tatars, and Saracens as well as natives of the Iberian Peninsula who had been convicted of such crimes as adultery and robbery.[5]

The Spanish appear to have approached the business of enslaving foreign and Iberian captives with more than a little ambivalence. Slaves were used throughout the Iberian Peninsula. Historians of slavery make a distinction between domestic slavery (the use of slaves largely as household servants) and industrial slavery (the use of slaves in the principal economic activities of a society — mining or plantation agriculture have been the major examples in most slave societies). Slaves were employed in both capacities in the Iberian Peninsula. Used throughout Spain and Portugal as domestic servants and artisans' assistants, slaves also toiled in the mines of Portugal and on sugar plantations in the Azores and Canary Islands, the forerunners of the Portuguese and Spanish sugar colonies of the New World. But despite this commonplace use of slave labor, Spanish law and culture recognized slavery as an undesirable — indeed, unnatural — state and one from which the slave should have a chance to be able to gain freedom. *Las siete partidas*, thirteenth-century Castile's reception of Roman law under the direction of Alfonso the Wise, unequivocally condemned slavery as both evil and unnatural: "servitude is the most vile and most despised state that can exist among men, for man is the most noble and free creature among all the other creatures that God made."[6]

Las siete partidas's condemnation of slavery was unlike the modern antislavery sentiment with which we are more familiar. The growth of antislavery sentiment in the late eighteenth century and the ultimate triumph of abolition in the Americas in the nineteenth were in large part the products of the Enlightenment and of liberal revolutions that argued for the basic equality of human beings and also for the existence of a body of rights that severely curtailed the state's power over the citizen. *Las siete partidas*, on the other hand, was the product of a society where human inequality was presumed and where the extensive authority of the state was largely unquestioned. *Las siete partidas* premised its condemnation of slavery not on modern notions of equality and universal rights but on an empathetic understanding of the human condition. The slave was human — base perhaps, the victim of misfortune or perhaps his own malfeasance to be sure, but nonetheless a man, one of God's noblest creatures. Like all creatures, the slave yearned for freedom, but because he was made in God's image, this yearning was to be given perhaps a special solicitude. The slave had intelligence, personality, a soul. He, unlike horses or cattle, which also often wanted to escape bondage, could be set free. *Las siete partidas* made it clear that, where possible, the law should accommodate the slave's desire for freedom. While this Castilian reformulation of Roman law did not go so far as to suggest universal abolition, it did provide for seemingly generous avenues for manumission. *Las siete partidas* would provide the foundation for the law of the unified Spanish kingdom. It would also indirectly influence Portuguese and later Brazilian law. As scholars such as Frank Tannenbaum and Alan Watson have noted, *Las siete partidas* helped make the law in the Spanish Empire more protective of manumissions than the law elsewhere in the Americas.[7]

Las siete partidas provided for the protection of slave marriages. If slaves were Christian, they were to be married inside the church. Slaves could marry free persons. The children of enslaved women and free men would be slaves, but the children of enslaved men and free women would be free. Masters had to approve the marriages of slaves, but a recalcitrant master could be forced to sell his slaves to someone more amenable to the marriage. Married slaves who belonged to different masters could not be sold to distant owners, effectively breaking up the marriage. Certain aspects of family law, rules regarding adoption and legitimation, would have an important impact, particularly in the Americas. Like the Justinian Code from which it had been adopted, *Las siete partidas* recognized both adoption and the ability of fathers to legitimate offspring after birth. Whatever importance these features of traditional Roman family law might have had in Spain or Portugal, they would later have even greater significance in the Americas. Spanish and particularly Portuguese colonists in the Americas were able to formally recognize and legally protect their mulatto children by slave mothers in a way that was generally impossible in the United States. We will discuss this a bit more extensively in the Brazilian context in chapter 2.[8]

The Roman slave code before the Justinian imposition of Christianity could encompass both profound cruelty and incredible generosity to those in bondage. The Roman master had absolute power—literally the power of life and death over the slave. A master could kill a slave with impunity or set him free and elevate him to the status of Roman citizen. *Las siete partidas*, reflecting its Christian influence, set, at least in theory, strict limits on the master's powers. The law stated that masters could not kill or mutilate slaves or force slave women to act in a manner contrary to nature. Provisions in *Las siete partidas* allowed slaves to complain to the courts if masters were excessively cruel. The law specified that courts could order the forced sale of slaves who were victims of excessive cruelty and that the courts could order that slave women forced into prostitution be set free.[9]

But it was in its bias for freedom that *Las siete partidas* stood out. If the Castilian reception of Roman law had an embedded slave code, that code nonetheless recognized slavery's uneasy place in the natural order. The roads to freedom were numerous. Christians could not be enslaved by Jews or Muslims. If that did occur, the enslaved Christian was to be set free. If two persons had an interest in a slave, the one willing to set the slave free was to be preferred by the courts. A slave who married a free person with his owner's knowledge was to be set free. A slave could become free by receiving holy orders or by rendering such critical services to the Crown as informing against a man who had raped a virgin, discovering a counterfeiter, or uncovering a plot to kill the master or the king. When a slave had rendered a critical service to the Crown, he could be freed even against the master's wishes. A slave could also gain freedom by living openly as a free person for ten years in his master's community or for twenty years in a more distant location.[10]

And freedom could of course be attained through the master's generosity. Voluntary manumissions might be brought about for a mixture of motives. Some slaves bought their freedom with money gained while working in their spare time. Others were the beneficiaries of genuine affection and goodwill. The law recognized both inter vivos and testamentary manumissions. The law demanded a measure of gratitude from the manumitted slave, particularly one who had been the beneficiary of a gratuitous manumission (one not paid for by the slave's self-purchase). Freedom was a boon. Manumission liberated the slave from what the law acknowledged was a vile and unnatural condition. The manumitted slave in return had a legal obligation to show his gratitude. The manumitted slave was given a conditional freedom, *liberto* status. A *liberto* was free, but the *liberto* who was the beneficiary of a gratuitous manumission could have his freedom revoked for ingratitude. The *liberto* was required to show respect to the former master. Suing the master or defaming him or failing to come to his or his family's aid in the event of misfortune were the signs of a bad *liberto* and one whose freedom was at peril. The *liberto* who died intestate would have his property revert to the master. The rules governing *libertos* were clearly designed to maintain what we today might term a strong system of patron-client ties between *libertos* and former masters and their families after the bonds of slavery were formally severed.[11]

This notion of a strong bond between masters and their former slaves is one that we should not skip over too quickly. These bonds often extended beyond simple clientelism. The rules governing the ongoing relationships between former masters and slaves give us something of a glimpse into a world of powerful patrons — usually patriarchs, occasionally matriarchs — of extended families encompassing both the blood relatives of the family, but also frequently former slaves as well. This had been part of the law and the culture of those societies, particularly Mediterranean societies, whose languages and notions of family membership owed much to the imperial conquests of ancient Rome. Roman law recognized adoption. The Catholic Church supported paternal recognition of and legitimation of children born out of wedlock. Both contributed to the cementing of ties between *libertos* and the master's family. The church's emphasis on godfathers and godmothers who would watch over the spiritual and often the temporal lives as well of the children of favorite servants, slaves, and *libertos* could further extend the notion of family ties and family obligations. Spanish law and custom could even dictate that the *liberto*'s debt of gratitude and familial obligation might extend beyond the grave. The death of the former master would require that the *liberto* care for the master's widow and surviving children if they were impoverished. But the *liberto*'s obligations did not end with such earthly concerns. Catholic doctrine dictated that some souls would neither be directly banished to Hell nor be immediately rewarded with Heaven. They were instead to linger in Purgatory until purged of their earthly sins; they could gain a belated admittance to Heaven. Their period of suffering could be shortened by their earthly well-wishers. Good deeds done and prayers said on behalf of a soul in Purgatory could speed that soul's way to Heaven. The *liberto* as part of his obligation to show gratitude to the former master was often expected to pray for his former master or to perform an act of charity for the church to aid the spiritual journey of a deceased former master and benefactor. The manumitted slave's continued relationship with the master and the master's family often remained ongoing and deep.[12]

We shouldn't get overly sentimental here. Slavery in the Spanish Empire could be and often was a brutal business. To the extent that that brutality was somewhat tempered on the Iberian Peninsula, it was probably tempered less by legal institutions and more by the fact that slavery in Spain was largely domestic slavery. Throughout history, the great brutalities associated with slavery have occurred with the large-scale employment of slaves in economically profitable mines and on plantations. Certainly when Spanish slavery was transported to the New World with its gold mines and large sugar plantations, slavery in Spanish colonies could prove to be exceedingly brutal with life for many slaves both miserable and short. What was important about Spanish law with its receptivity to manumission and its emphasis on enduring and even familial ties between former masters and former slaves is that it did allow slave owners to bestow their generosity on a favored few. And like the Roman law from which it was derived, *Las siete partidas* and other sources of the Spanish law of slavery would allow some of the beneficiaries of a master's generosity to maintain continued bonds with powerful patrons.

What we today call race appears to have played little role in this Iberian world of masters and slaves and patrons and clients, certainly not in the thirteenth century, when *Las siete partidas* was written, or even in the fourteenth century, when black Africans began appearing in the Iberian Peninsula in noticeable numbers. Slavery was justified not on the grounds that it was deserved by inferior peoples or somehow necessary to their governance. It was explained instead as the result of personal misfortune, capture in war, satisfaction for debt, punishment for crime. Insofar as group identity had any importance in questions of slavery and freedom, religion was far more important than race. This situation would begin to change in the fifteenth century, with the expansion of sugarcane production in the Canary Islands and the Azores and an increase in the number of black Africans enslaved in Spain and Portugal. The law began to take race into account. Local ordinances sought to control the behavior of slaves and free blacks who lived in Madrid and other cities. Some local regulations curiously enough even anticipated the Jim Crow statutes of the American South in the early twentieth century. Laws forbidding free blacks from wearing clothing above their station, or carrying swords, or other conduct inappropriate to their lowly status began appearing in some locations. And yet the church and the Crown remained more concerned with religious competition with the Islamic Moors than with status regulation for the black population. Ordinances passed in Valencia and elsewhere prohibited Moorish enslavement of black Africans. Authorities feared that

Moorish masters would convert black Africans, adding them to the Islamic ranks, a prospect Spanish authorities found theologically, politically, and militarily unacceptable.[13]

But it would take the expansion of the Spanish Empire into the newly discovered lands of the Americas that would forge an indelible link between race and slavery. The expansion of the Spanish Empire into the Americas and the mixtures of the Iberian, indigenous, and African populations that resulted from that expansion would help bring about a concern for race and color far stronger than anything that had previously been known on the Iberian Peninsula. That concern, in turn, would help create a body of racial and color classifications and codified privileges and disabilities linked to race and color. Racial and color classifications that began in the early days of Spain's New World conquests still shape the lives of millions who inhabit the American hemisphere.

We are going to spend a good deal of the rest of this chapter trying to sort out the complex and often tangled strands that made up the boundaries and hierarchies of race and color in colonial Latin America. Much of what is said here will necessarily involve a great deal of painting with a broad brush, a broad brush that will invariably miss a great deal in the way of geographical and temporal nuance. Slavery in Spain's New World empire lasted from the beginning of the sixteenth century to final emancipation in Cuba in 1886. This was some 386 years, as long as the time between the 1607 English settlement of Jamestown in Virginia and the inauguration of William Jefferson Clinton as president in 1993. Slavery and exceedingly complex questions concerning the status of Africans and peoples of African descent were played out in a variety of often radically different settings.

The history of race in Spain's American empire was made even more complicated by the presence of a large indigenous population in most of the empire's viceroyalties. This was not the case throughout the Spanish Empire. Contact with Spaniards including early Spanish attempts at Indian slavery devastated many of the indigenous populations of the Caribbean. But in other parts of the Americas the indigenous populations would survive and would continue as majorities. Interactions among the African, European, and indigenous populations are a critical part of the demographic and social history of every American society. But the importance of the indigenous populations to the development of the societies that would be part of the Spanish Empire and later the Spanish-speaking nations of Latin America far exceeded the importance of the Indian populations in what would become the United States and Brazil. Spanish authorities saw what they called "la reducción de los indios" — the civilizing and converting of the indigenous populations to Christianity — as central to their mission in the New World. They would also see the Indian populations as a critical source of labor first in the *encomienda* system of labor taxation and then through systems of debt peonage in the grand haciendas. The Portuguese at least nominally saw themselves engaged in the business of trying to convert Brazil's Indian population and also attempted early on to enslave some of the indigenous inhabitants. But conditions in Brazil made the prospects of subduing and converting the Indian populations less sure. Few Portuguese came to the vast territory that was Brazil, fewer still ventured into the *sertão* (backlands), into which many Indians could escape from their Portuguese "civilizers." And Brazil lacked the kind of large Indian civilizations like the Aztec or Inca Empires that could provide an already existing social hierarchy and administrative structure that could aid in the ruling of the indigenous population. The Portuguese in Brazil would find practical difficulties that made them less able than the Spaniards to convert and rule the Indians they encountered. The English, who would come to dominate what would become the United States, were simply less interested in the Indian population. The Anglo-American settlers came to parts of North America with relatively small Indian populations, certainly nothing like the large Aztec and Inca Empires encountered by the Spaniards. And many of the Protestant denominations that developed in England were not as keen as the Roman Church on spreading their religious doctrines to others, at least not in the beginning. Although Indian slavery was attempted in some North American colonies, it simply proved less practical than the African and Afro-American alternatives. Spain was in many ways unique in its efforts to bring large numbers of Indians not only physically but culturally into its empire.[14]

From the beginning, the law had to reconcile — or at least try to reconcile — the contradictions in social status created by the blending of three races and a far greater number of cultural traditions in Spain's American empire. The law recognized the African and the African's descendants as inferior peoples, candidates for slavery. If there were still a lingering presence of European and Moorish slaves in the Iberian Peninsula at the opening of the sixteenth century, it was a dwindling one. The need to keep peace with the Moors and with other European kingdoms would limit the employment of Europeans and Moors as slaves. Here and there, an occasional European slave might be found in Spain's American colonies. Historian Kris Lane has found a Sicilian slave in sixteenth-century Quito. Others have been located elsewhere. But Europeans would not be found in significant numbers among the slaves in Spain's American empire. Spanish law, both secular and religious, would prohibit the enslavement of Indians. Spanish friar Bartolomé de las Casas would argue vigorously against their enslavement, fearful that such enslavement would thwart the Spanish church's efforts to convert the new, virgin population of the New World to Catholicism. By the sixteenth century, royal decrees were proclaimed that attempted to give legal teeth to Las Casas's religious sentiments. The laws governing the Indies prohibited enslavement of Indians. Violators were to be punished with fines and in some cases physical punishment. One provision of Spain's Law of the Indies called for the flogging of *bandeirantes* (roving bands of frontiersmen and freebooters) from São Paulo who entered Spanish territory to capture Indian slaves. The law also specified that Indian slaves fleeing Portuguese territory were to be set free upon reaching Spanish soil.[15]

Africans, increasingly viewed as barbaric and inferior as the sixteenth century unfolded, were seen as proper candidates for enslavement. Their forced labor would bring wealth inuring to the benefit of the empire while also sparing the noble Indians the indignities of slavery. The barbaric African would even benefit, having his soul saved by being brought to the New World outposts of a Christian kingdom. Despite this, a simple connection between race and social status in the viceroyalties of Spanish America cannot be easily made. The Spanish processes of exploration, conquest, and ultimate subjugation of the lands and peoples of what would be called the Americas produced a complex and often contradictory set of human relations. If the African was increasingly seen as barbaric and a worthy candidate for enslavement, the African — or perhaps more accurately, the Afro-Iberian — was often a part of the expeditions of the conquistadors, an auxiliary who was frequently armed and often either a free man or one who would gain his freedom because of valor displayed and loot gained during the expedition. If Indians were seen as a race superior to blacks and protected from enslavement, they too were nonetheless often subjected to a regime of forced labor, first through the *encomendero* system and later on the great haciendas. The former system effectively held large numbers of Indians in bondage through a system of labor taxes. The latter effectively held many Indians in bondage through a system of debt peonage. To make matters more complicated, many of the majordomos (overseers) who supervised the nominally free Indians who labored on the great estates of the Spanish Empire were men of African descent, sometimes slave, sometimes free.[16]

This use of black slaves or freemen to oversee nominally free Indians forced to labor in the mines and on the haciendas of Spain's American Empire points to the complexities of race and status in colonial Latin America. If people of African descent were considered to be members of a race that was less noble than the Indians who were native to the Americas, they were often nonetheless integrated into Spanish society in ways that Indians (at least those Indians who adhered to traditional indigenous cultures) were not. Africans, Afro-Iberians, and their descendants were counted as part of the "Republic of the Spaniards" — part of Spanish society and unlike the Indians subject to a legal regime meant to govern Spaniards and others who came from the Old World. People of African descent were expected to speak Spanish and to acquire other aspects of Spanish culture, particularly the Catholic faith. This latter expectation would often be enforced with all the rigors of the Inquisition.[17]

This idea of the person of African descent as part of Spanish society can help point us to an aspect of the cultural history of Latin America that has traditionally been somewhat understated by the region's historians: the role of people of African descent in spreading elements of Spanish culture to the indigenous population. Spaniards recognized important differences among the groups of black people who inhabited the Iberian nation's New World empire. Africans were labeled *Bozales*. Spaniards saw *Bozales* as cultural and linguistic aliens, frightening, with a tendency to run away and form dangerous *palenques* or *cimarrón* communities, rebellious reconstituted African societies in New World settings. Their labors were needed, but *Bozales* were feared both for the dangers they posed and for the possibilities that they would corrupt Indian populations, bringing with them religious notions different from if not outright hostile to the Catholic faith that the Spaniards wanted to impart. But if Africans were regarded warily, Afro-Iberians — those who spoke Castilian and were accustomed to Spanish ways — could prove valuable in the greater project of subduing, "civilizing," and supervising the vast indigenous populations that dwarfed the small communities of Spanish explorers and settlers. In many parts of the Americas, it was Afro-Iberians and later Afro-Americans who played as great and in many cases a greater role than Spaniards in spreading the Spanish language, the Catholic faith, and other aspects of Spanish culture to the indigenous populations. It should be noted that cultural exchange went in all directions. Elements of the different African, Indian, and Iberian cultures of the Americas were picked up and blended by the different peoples who came into contact with each other in the Spanish Empire. Historical archaeologist Daniel Schávelzon informs us of but one of many examples. In nineteenth-century Córdoba in northwestern Argentina, Afro-Argentine slaves who worked on cattle ranches were frequently Quechua speakers, reflecting in all likelihood a biological as well as cultural synthesis occurring in the region.[18]

The often supervisory role that Afro-Iberians and Afro-Americans had over indigenous laborers evidently played an important role in *mestizaje*, the physical and cultural mixing of the three races in Latin America. The Law of the Indies, like *Las siete partidas* before them, recognized the children of enslaved men and free women as free. The Law of the Indies specifically noted that the children of enslaved black men and Indian women would be free and subject to the *encomendero* labor tax that bound Indians for a term of years, but not life. One historian has argued that the possibility that their children would be free may have made Indian women more attractive to black men. Demographic realities — the large Indian populations and the small populations of Spaniards and men of African descent throughout much of the Americas — certainly made Indian women attractive to Spaniard and African alike. In any event, the law protected intermarriage between the indigenous population and people of African descent. Some historians have argued that the free status of the children of such unions played a major part in creating populations of free people of color in many parts of the Americas.[19]

The mixing of the three races would occur from the beginning. Few Spanish women came to the Americas during the initial phases of colonization. Spanish men had children with Indian women and women of African descent. Men of African descent had children with women of African descent and indigenous women. Colonial Latin America was a large multiracial and multicultural empire and one in which legal privileges could be and were bestowed on the basis of race and status. At times, whether one would be classified as slave or free, whether one could possess gold or carry arms without supervision or have a slave of one's own, might depend on one's racial status. The Spanish were aware that they constituted a rather small minority of the people in their American empire. At times they sought to maintain a rigid separation among the different African-descended, Indian, and mixed peoples over whom they ruled. This was to be accomplished in part through codification, the development of a highly precise system of racial classification through law. Spanish lawmakers were particularly artful at this, importing racial categories developed in Spain and adding to them classifications developed in the New World. Gonzalo Aguirre Beltrán reports on one such scheme employed in eighteenth-century Mexico. The codified categories indicated the designation and status of individuals according to the race, color, and gender of their parents:

[The offspring of a]

1. Spaniard with an Indian (woman) [is a] Mestizo.
2. Mestizo (woman) with a Spaniard [is a] Castizo.
3. Castizo (man) with a Spanish woman [is a] Spaniard.
4. Spaniard (man) with a Black (woman) [is a] Mulatto.
5. Mulatto (woman) with a Spaniard [is a] Morisco.
6. Morisco (man) with a Spanish woman [is a] Chino.
7. Chino (man) with an Indian (woman) [is a] Leap Backward.
8. A Leap Backward (man) with a Mulatto woman [is a] Wolf.
9. A Wolf (man) with a Chino (woman) [is a] Gibaro.
10. A Gibaro (man) with a Mulatto (woman) [is a] Leper.
11. A Leper (man) with a Black (woman) [is a] Cambujo (very dark).
12. A Cambujo (man) with an Indian (woman) [is a] Zambaigo.
13. A Zambaigo (man) with a Wolf (woman) [is a] Calpa Mulatto.
14. A Calpa Mulatto (man) with a Cambujo (woman) [is a] Stay in the Air.
15. A Stay in the Air (man) with a Mulatto (woman) [is an] I Don't Understand Thee.
16. An I Don't Understand Thee (man) with an Indian (woman) [is a] Step Backwards.[20]

Some of these names were attempts by Spanish authorities to classify some of the new peoples appearing in the Western Hemisphere with old names for peoples with whom the Spanish were already familiar. Other names attributed animal-like qualities to some of the peoples who resulted from the racial mixtures that were occurring in the Americas. Still other names seem to be the product of sheer whimsy. These categorizations were more than just a pedantic attempt to outline a human taxonomy of the New World. They were part of the law, codes developed in part to strengthen Spanish rule. The law created different racial categories in an effort to implement a system of castes with differing sets of legal privileges and duties. This was done as part of a divide-and-rule strategy. Spanish colonial administrators were particularly concerned with preventing the subject peoples in their American empire — the Africans, the Afro-Iberians and Afro-Americans, the Indians, and the people of mixed race — from making common cause against Spanish rule. The Spanish used the word *casta* to describe the different human categories specified by Spanish law. Although the word does not have exactly the same meaning as the English word *caste*, it does describe groups that are meant to be strictly differentiated, with different legal privileges.[21]

This legal attempt to make fine racial and color distinctions appears to have had an ironic consequence. Far from strengthening the boundaries between the different subject peoples of the Spanish Empire, the often bewildering multiplicity of racial classifications actually contributed to a culture of racial mobility and to what North American eyes often appears to be a culture of racial ambiguity in Latin American societies. One historian of Latin American slavery has even argued that the system was characterized by its "porousness." If law and custom in the United States have traditionally dictated that race is an immutable characteristic, one that is fixed at birth and one that cannot be openly and legitimately changed, Latin Americans have long had a very different view of the matter. That different view was recognized in Spain's American colonies from early on. One could improve one's racial status, and the multiplicity of racial and color categories aided that process. If whites stood at the top of the social pyramid and the black race was acknowledged as inferior to the other races in the empire, that did not end things. The Africans and Afro-Iberians who accompanied Spaniards on their missions of conquest complicated matters, as did the Afro-American majordomos who supervised Indian servants. But the complications did not end there. The Spanish Empire was often short of loyal free men willing to protect the Crown's colonies from its enemies, foreign soldiers and marauders, Indians who resisted Spanish subjugation, and the dangerous African *cimarrones* who via both example and action posed a constant threat to slave order and slave discipline. Spain thus had a great need for men able and willing to bear arms. And despite the existence of color restrictions on military service and separate military units for free men of color and white men, military service provided possibilities of mobility for free men of color. Some became officers, not only in the companies to which free men of color were frequently restricted but at times in more general military formations as well. Men who achieved status in such office further complicated the business of assigning race or color to an individual. Successful individuals — military captains, people who had struck it rich in the gold fields, and others on whom fortune smiled — could and often did aspire to a better racial status.[22]

At times, the law itself abetted the individual's quest for racial mobility. In his discussion of the multi-*casta* world that was colonial Mexico City, historian R. Douglas Cope paints a portrait of a lower-class plebeian world that was vividly multiracial despite the desire of Spanish rulers to keep the different *castas* distinct. In his words, members of the different *castas* "worked, played, begged, gossiped, argued, fought, gambled, made love" across racial lines. When marriages between members of the different *castas* were challenged on racial grounds, hearings, presided over by members of the clergy, were held to determine the proper *casta* of prospective marriage partners. At a time of profound and often untraceable mixtures of the three races and in a setting when *casta* indications on baptismal records were known to be inaccurate, priests determined the racial status of potential brides and grooms by examining physical appearance and by hearing the testimony of witnesses, usually proffered by the intended marriage partners as to the race of one partner or the other. Such proceedings permitted a measure of racial mobility. The law at times was even more explicit in its willingness to further racial mobility for a favored few. In 1795 the Spanish Crown offered the mechanism *gracias al sacar*, a device by which wealthy individuals with somewhat attenuated African ancestry could remove the stain of that ancestry and purchase a document declaring them legally white. Given the quest for racial mobility that existed in much of the Spanish Empire, it is likely that even some individuals with quite visible African ancestry took advantage of the *gracias al sacar*.[23]

The existence of this legal mechanism to better one's race is ironic in light of the persistence of the Spanish practice of *limpieza de sangre* in colonial Latin America. Originally designed in Spain to ensure that persons of Jewish or Moorish ancestry did not achieve high civil or ecclesiastical office, the practice was continued in the Americas to ensure that persons with indigenous and particularly African ancestry were also kept out of prestigious offices and schools. Spanish views on race and ancestry could be complex and frequently contradictory. Yet the law and custom did allow some to better their racial status. And even if whiteness might be beyond an individual's grasp, a free person of color might aspire to a status higher than the lowly *negro* category. Perhaps he might be recognized as a *zambo* (a mixture of the African and indigenous races) or as a *mulato* or *morisco* (with an indication of Spanish blood in his veins). Politeness itself might dictate that a successful person be accorded a status higher than "negro." And there could be important legal consequences for such. The Law of the Indies and the local codes could be quite specific in outlining legal disabilities. Whether one was "negro" or "mulato" could determine the liberties one enjoyed or the restrictions that one endured. The prospect of racial mobility was an important element of social mobility in colonial Latin America.[24]

Historians have traditionally attributed a great deal of this possibility of individual mobility despite race to the influence of *Las siete partidas* and derivative legal sources. One common explanation for the relative receptivity of the Spanish Empire to manumission and ultimately citizenship and even advancement for enslaved Africans and their descendants and the relative hostility of the American South in the nineteenth century toward manumission and a free Negro presence has been the difference in legal regimes. Spain's inherited Roman law, mediated through *Las siete partidas* and subsequent enactments, protected the right of slaves to make and enforce manumission contracts, to keep property with which to purchase their freedom. The law of slavery in the United States, derivative of the common law, which did not recognize the institution, had not developed a body of legal doctrine protecting the rights of the slave, particularly the right to manumission. This difference was the foundation of the differences between the two systems and a reason why people of African descent could be accepted as free people with some even rising to prominence in colonial Latin America, where such was not possible in the United States.

The intertwined issues of manumission, race, and citizenship in the United States are more complex than has traditionally been acknowledged in many comparative discussions. These questions will be examined at some length in chapter 3. But the students of slavery who have contrasted the law's relative receptivity to manumission in colonial Latin America with the hostility exhibited by the law in most southern states in the nineteenth century are essentially correct. These differences might be partly explained by the different legal heritages of the two societies. They might also be partly explained by significant demographic differences — the relative scarcity of free white settlers in the Spanish colonies of the Americas allowed free people of color a degree of social mobility that was largely missing in the slave states of the American South in the nineteenth century. In the American South the white population constituted a majority. This largely denied free people of color the possibility of acting as a class of intermediaries the way similar populations did in the Spanish Empire.

But more was at work. The very nature of the slave regime in the Spanish Empire played a significant part in both the development of the empire's racial attitudes and hierarchies and the empire's willingness to allow some free people of color the possibility of escape from the codified rigors of the *casta* system. This is a somewhat difficult issue to explore in part because of the sheer size of the Latin American slave experience. But it is difficult for yet another reason. Slavery in the Spanish Empire, and in Brazil as well, might be thought of as standing midway between two very different Western slave traditions — perhaps we might use the sociological term *ideal types*. One of these traditions, the one we are all somewhat familiar with, was that of the antebellum South, the Cotton Kingdom that lasted for some two generations before the American Civil War. It is important to note that slavery in the Cotton Kingdom depended to a significant extent on a justifying racial ideology. In a nation with strong democratic political practices and equally strong egalitarian social norms, the enslaved Negroes had to be made a people apart, a singular exception to the American ideology that emphasized the equality of all men. To that end, slavery's apologists in the antebellum South occupied their time writing elaborate treatises and vigorous polemics proclaiming both white supremacy and Negro inferiority. The law in the southern states would follow suit, prohibiting the education of blacks or restricting manumissions and otherwise inhibiting or attempting to inhibit the growth of a free Negro class. Educated

*graduation as tool of ruling class

Afro-Americans and successful free people of color were an embarrass-ment, a contradiction to the reigning ideology that stressed black incom-petence and lack of fitness for free society.[25]

If the slave regime that was the Cotton Kingdom with its justifications rooted in presumptions of racial difference and black inferiority might serve as one ideal type of Western slave society, ancient Rome might serve as its contrasting counterpart. Generalizing about Roman slavery is haz-ardous, even more hazardous than generalizing about slavery in the United States or Latin America. Roman slavery existed under both the republic and the empire. Records of a Roman slave code exist from as early as 200 B.C. and would still be part of the Justinian digests some seven hundred years later, in 534 A.D. This was a period longer than that between 1492 and the present, the era of recognized African and European contact with the Americas. Roman slavery encompassed household slavery as well as in-dustrial slavery and was to be found in every corner of the empire. Before Constantine's imposition of Christianity on the empire, the Roman slave code could encompass both stark cruelty and incredible generosity toward the slave. A slave favored by his master could be freed and even elevated to the ranks of Roman citizens. And yet Roman law and culture could also prescribe an excruciatingly harsh regime for the slave. The slave was con-sidered an enemy of all Roman society, an enemy who could only be made less dangerous by the most draconian of sanctions. The Roman code called for the execution of all slaves in a household if one slave had killed the master. This was to be done regardless of the guilt or innocence of the other slaves. It was also to be done before the reading of the master's will in order to prevent a slave's escaping execution by virtue of testamentary manumission.[26]

What is most important about Roman slavery for our purposes is that it did not require a theoretical justification rooted in the putative inferi-ority of slaves or enslaved peoples. In ancient Rome, slavery was viewed largely as a matter of personal misfortune and not individual or group in-feriority. Indeed, in one important respect, the ancient Romans were will-ing to acknowledge the cultural equality or even superiority of some of those whom they held in bondage. It was not at all uncommon in wealthy Roman households for Greek slaves to act as the tutors of the master's children, a sharp contrast with the American South, where even teaching slaves to read was often prohibited by statute. The Roman belief in Greek cultural superiority did not prevent the enslavement of Greeks, even those who were well educated.[27]

That Roman ability to enslave those whom they acknowledged as their equals or even perhaps their superiors stood in marked contrast to the experience with slavery in the antebellum South. The Romans were able to do so in part because theirs was a society comfortable with inequality. The Roman Empire was a strongly hierarchical society with a large slave population. Roman law recognized that subject peoples and particularly slaves sought to improve their status and allowed for the possibilities of manumission and citizenship. But the slave's manumission, even his elevation to citizenship, was seen as purely an act of generosity on the part of the master, not as an attack on slavery, certainly not as a challenge to the broader notions of hierarchy and subjugation on which the empire rested. In a society where a majority of peoples were legally unequal and subject to the domination of others, slavery required little in the way of elaborate theories of difference and inferiority. In the United States, where slavery was the exception, where the majority of the population was free, and where there was a strong ideology of human equality, defenders of the institution would have to develop elaborate justifications.

Slavery in the Spanish Empire and in Brazil represented something of a midpoint between the ideal types represented by ancient Rome and the American Cotton Kingdom. Colonial Latin America, like Rome, was part of a large empire where at least initially, a small class of citizens ruled over a much larger class of subject peoples, many of whom were slaves. Unlike Rome and like the American South, slavery in colonial Latin America was based on race. It included an ideology of African inferiority. But that ideology was not an essential apologetic needed to explain enslavement in an otherwise free society with a strong egalitarian ideology. People of African descent in Latin America were enslaved in authoritarian, often strictly hierarchical societies. They toiled with and frequently supervised unwilling laborers with indigenous backgrounds. Although white slaves had largely vanished by the end of the sixteenth century, poor white men and more frequently mestizos could be found in servile conditions, even if these conditions were not formally labeled as outright slavery. The highly structured society that was colonial Latin America had less need to come up with an elaborate justification for slavery and less need to feel threatened or embarrassed when a person of African descent achieved some success. And if the successful free person of color was a mulatto with acknowledged connections to a powerful white family, there was even less reason to regard that person as a threat to the social order.

Slavery in the Spanish Empire did not require a justifying ideology, one that made people of African descent a group apart, radically separated from all others. Consequently, the law could retain many of the mechanisms favorable to individual emancipation that were originally found in *Las siete partidas*. The world of slavery had changed, to be sure. It had expanded considerably from the rather marginal world of domestic slavery that existed when *Las siete partidas* was adopted. Race played a crucial role in slavery in the Spanish Empire, as indeed it did throughout the Americas. Still despite these significant changes, Spanish law, at least in those cases where the question was engaged, retained its view that the slave maintained her or his position as a member of the community and a member whose life and even honor and dignity were entitled to the law's protection. Perhaps nowhere is this better illustrated than in the late eighteenth-century petition for freedom brought in Guayaquil by María Chiquinquirá Díaz. Her petition for freedom was based on the claim that she was born free because her putative master had abandoned her mother before her birth. Her mother was abandoned because she had leprosy and was forced to turn to prostitution to survive. Chiquinquirá was able to base her petition in part on the doctrine that a master who dishonored a slave or forced a female slave into prostitution would lose the right to the slave and the slave would be set free. The case, as related by Ecuadorian historian María Eugenia Chaves, is instructive from several points of view. Spanish authorities had procedures to hear such cases. Chiquinquirá could present her case. There was a *procurador* or government attorney charged with presenting her case to the court. The honor of Chiquinquirá's mother was the key issue in the case, and although *mulatas* and *negras* were assumed to have less honor and sexual chastity than white women, the law would nonetheless punish the master who forced a slave — even a black slave — into prostitution.[28]

The law could be relatively enlightened and sympathetic toward freedom. At times the knowledge that the courts were open, that the master's power could be contested, that the law might provide a remedy for bondage spurred on the desire for freedom. Slaves and their free Afro-American relatives would sue slave owners, at times with a spirit of defiance that belied their lowly status. The statutes permitted a slave to bring suit and be a party to her petition for freedom. It could also allow slaves to trade masters in an attempt to get a new owner who might provide better treatment or be more amenable to manumission. Yet the law could also prescribe one hundred lashes, amputation of a foot, or even permit death sentences for slaves who attempted to escape. And there were precincts where the law's writ simply did not run or if it did, only infrequently. If statutes, courts, and *procuradores* for slaves might soften the rigors of bondage in cities where it might be hard to hide the sadism or cruelty of a particular master, the law's ability to supervise the conduct of slave owners on plantations and in mines that employed large gangs of slaves under often prohibitively harsh conditions was often minimal.[29]

In an effort to mitigate the harshness that remained part of the law and custom of slavery in the Spanish Empire, the Crown proclaimed a new *Código Negro* in 1789. The new code in many ways reiterated principles that could be traced back to *Las siete partidas*. The code moderated punishment for slaves and specified that slaves would be allowed free time and the right to keep money earned during leisure periods; both rights protected the ability of slaves to earn money to purchase manumission. The new code while not antislavery does give evidence that the Spanish Crown was conscious of the new thinking sweeping the Atlantic world at the end of the eighteenth century. That new thinking was liberal and supportive of free trade and the independence of American colonies from European nations. It was also increasingly hostile to slavery.[30]

But it was not the growth of liberal sentiments alone that would put the new nations of Spanish America on the ultimate path to abolition and the elimination of the formalized system of *castas*. These changes would occur in the nineteenth century. They would occur as by-products of a set of revolutions precipitated in part by the Enlightenment. But these revolutions originally had a very different set of beneficiaries in mind. The wars that would ultimately free the continent from Spanish domination began with the dissatisfaction of native-born whites, the Creole elites of the Spanish colonies. Their complaints against Spanish rule and mercantile restrictions would increase with the beginning of the new nineteenth century. Spurred on by both the nearby North American and Haitian examples as well as the French Revolution in Europe, complaints against restrictive Spanish rule grew louder and more frequent. Like the pamphleteers who mobilized the colonists who would form the United States, the advocates for independence in the Spanish Empire likened the restrictions of Spanish rule to slavery. The slaves listened. The rhetoric in favor of freedom was enticing. Many decided that the struggle for independence would also become a struggle for their personal emancipation.[31]

Both royalist and proindependence armies sought to enlist slaves and free men of color to fight in the wars of independence. The forces fighting for independence tended to be more successful. Their libertarian rhetoric and their greater willingness to embrace abolition and give at least lip service to republican notions of equality regardless of race made them more attractive than their royalist rivals. The wars for independence that were waged against the Spanish Empire would ultimately bring about both the abolition of slavery and the elimination of the legal distinctions that had been an inherent part of the empire's *casta* system. This would occur at different speeds and with different degrees of sure-footedness in the nations that emerged. Some, like Mexico and Chile, were able to legally abolish slavery almost immediately after independence. In both nations the slave populations were small and generally peripheral to the overall economy. Abolition might have discomfited individual slave owners, but it posed little threat to the overall political and economic equilibrium.[32]

Elsewhere, the paths to freedom and equality in the new republics were more difficult, less certain. Historians Carlos Aguirre and Aline Helg in their respective discussions of revolution and emancipation in what are now Peru and Colombia provide us with a picture of the often tangled relationship between the revolutionary liberalism that informed the struggle for independence in the Spanish Empire and the efforts of the enslaved to achieve freedom and the struggle of free people of African descent to escape the bonds of racial restrictions. Both authors tell us of societies on the eve of revolution that had large populations of free persons of African descent. Indeed, on the eve of independence, most people of acknowledged African descent in both societies were free. These populations had swelled toward the end of the eighteenth century, the result of manumissions through self-purchase, masters emancipating their children by slave women, and the free birth of the children of male slaves and free women. They had also increased through the increase of *cimarrón* communities or *palenques*. Those communities had started out as communities of escaped slaves, usually Africans. At times Spanish authorities sought to subdue these communities but often — perhaps more often than not — they realized that they needed to make peace with them, come to a modus vivendi in which the inhabitants of the *palenques* agreed not to wage war on Spanish settlements and perhaps help protect them from hostile indigenous populations or even other *cimarrones* in return for being allowed to live at peace and in liberty.[33]

Independence in Gran Colombia, out of which came the modern nations of Venezuela, Colombia, and Ecuador, brought with it an acceptance of the principles of antislavery and racial equality. The 1821 constitution of Gran Colombia proclaimed liberty and equality. But it also provided for the protection of property, which gave slaveholders some claim on retaining their rights in human chattel. The compromise between these conflicting principles was the adoption of "free womb" legislation: children born of slave mothers after July 1821 would be free but would owe a debt of service until their eighteenth year. This type of legislation was common in the postindependence Americas. Similar legislation had been passed in the northern states of the United States in the late eighteenth century and would later be adopted in the Brazilian Empire in 1871. Other legislation in the 1820s abolished the colonial system of *castas* and removed lingering restrictions on interracial marriages. Despite these measures, as Helg informs us, race and racial fears continued to shape policy in Gran Colombia. Simón Bolívar, the revolutionary leader who had played a key role in the liberation of the viceroyalty, had received considerable aid from the revolutionary government of Haiti. Yet for Bolívar, Haiti was a haunting specter, one that he feared could inspire the large African-descended population to revolt and establish a republic dominated by *pardos* (people of mixed African and Spanish descent). This fear would, Helg tells us, limit the reach of the new egalitarian measures that were adopted in the independent republic.[34]

If the path to emancipation and equality was difficult in Gran Colombia, it was even more so in Peru. José de San Martín, who led independence forces in Peru, opposed slavery and issued a "free womb" decree in 1821. The constitution of 1823 proclaimed that all free persons born in Peru were Peruvians and citizens of the nation. It also declared that nobody was born a slave in Peru and that slaves would not be allowed to enter the nation. But these measures left plenty of room for the protection of slaveholding interests. Those emancipated by San Martín's decree were to remain in bondage for a considerable time — females for twenty years, males for twenty-four. What's more, there was a significant legal loophole. While technically free, people emancipated by the decree could be sold and exported while they were in temporary bondage during their youth. Even more sinister, by the 1840s, there was a vigorous attempt to reverse the process of gradual emancipation. Slave owners in coastal areas where cotton and other crops could be profitably cultivated by slave labor began to push for a setting aside of emancipatory decrees. They argued, in a manner reminiscent of proslavery apologists in the American antebellum South, the merits of slavery as a positive good, one that conferred a benevolent, paternalistic regime on the slave. Their efforts would ultimately fail, but it would cause slavery to die a slow lingering death in Peru. A death that would not be fully accomplished until 1854.[35]

If slavery was undergoing a relatively rapid demise in some of Spain's former colonies and a lingering, contested death in others, it would thrive for most of the nineteenth century in Spain's island colony of Cuba. Along with Puerto Rico, Cuba would remain a Spanish colony until the end of the century. The sugar boom that transformed the island's economy in the early nineteenth century was partly precipitated by the loss of Saint-Domingue, Haiti, to slave-based sugar cultivation. Emancipation in Jamaica would also help boost the demand for Cuban sugar. Cuba's gain in the international sugar market would transform not only the island's economy but also its social relations. Historian Franklin Knight tells us that the relatively relaxed system of slavery that had existed in Cuba in the eighteenth century would transform radically in the nineteenth. The island's eighteenth century economy based on a mixture of tobacco cultivation and cattle raising yielded to a more robust slave-based economy based on the international demand for sugar. The slave population of Cuba would grow from some 65,000 individuals by the end of the 1780s to 370,000 in the 1860s. New Africans, *Bozales*, would populate the island in the nineteenth century. Demographic historians estimate that more than 600,000 entered the island colony between 1800 and 1867, more than the nearly 400,000 Africans who were estimated to have come to the United States between 1619 and 1865.[36]

These demographic and economic changes would have profound social consequences. The growing slave population and the African origins of the slave population would increase the fears of whites, both those who owned

slaves and those who did not, that the slaves might revolt and have critical allies from among the free population of color. Spanish authorities had
a dilemma. Cuba's free people of color, mostly of mixed race, could legally own slaves and enjoy many of the other rights possessed by the white
population. As was the case elsewhere in the Americas, they were seen by
Spanish authorities as potential allies against slave rebellion. But they were
also feared as potential abettors of rebellious slaves. Increasingly in the
nineteenth century this group would face new restrictions. But discrimination against free Afro-Cubans would be tempered by the realization
that if the loss of rights became too severe it could backfire and precipitate
the feared alliance of Afro-Cubans slave and free. Such an alliance could
destroy slavery and the wealth produced by the island's sugar economy.
Maintaining a slave society on an island with a large African and Afro-
Cuban population was a precarious enterprise. It would become even more
so as the rest of the Caribbean became free. It would become even more
problematic after abolition in the United States in 1865.[37]

Slavery would ultimately die a halting death in Cuba. Efforts at emancipation would be fought every step of the way by Cuban planters anxious
to maintain both their investment in slaves and a cheap labor force for
their sugar and plantations. Historian Rebecca Scott's research tells us that
emancipation legislation came slowly, prodded in large part by Spanish
fears of Afro-Cuban support for the island's growing independence movement. Spain was growing isolated as a slaveholding power. Abolition had
come to its former colonies and to the English- and French-speaking islands of the Caribbean. General emancipation came to the United States
in the wake of the American Civil War. Spain, along with the Brazilian
Empire, stood alone in maintaining a system of chattel slavery in the
Americas. Antislavery sentiment in Spain grew. A new liberal government
in Madrid introduced gradual emancipation legislation. A statute passed
in 1870 declared free all children born after September 1868. They would
owe service to their former masters until age eighteen. The 1870 legislation
also freed slaves over age sixty. Subsequent legislation established a system
of apprenticeship for former slaves continuing the system of unfree labor.
Final abolition would come by virtue of royal decree in 1886.[38]

Cuban abolition would bring to an end four centuries of African and
Afro-American slavery in Spain's New World empire. That system of slavery and the body of laws that supported it would be swept away by the new

legal regimes that governed the independent nations that emerged. Slavery was abolished. The new constitutions proclaimed the end of the system of *castas*. Race was deemed not to exist — or at least not to be legal grounds for discrimination. There was an exception to this new, liberal principle. Indians who had not assimilated the essentials of the Spanish language and the Catholic Church would be an exception to the new constitutional and legal orders. They were to be treated differently — for their own good, of course. But all others, the descendants of African slaves included, were citizens under the new legal regimes, citizens of equal standing and with equal rights. That was what the new constitutions and statutes proclaimed. But the legacy of the Spanish system of slavery and *castas* would persist long after emancipation. A culture of race had developed during the four centuries of slavery and *castas* in Spain's American Empire. The precepts of that culture, its values, still shape the way millions in the American hemisphere view their neighbors and themselves. African ancestry is disfavored. The person having it should somehow strive to overcome this handicap. The notion that an individual can better the race, perhaps through personal accomplishments or by marrying a member of a "better race," thus improving the status of one's children, is part of the legacy of slavery in colonial Latin America. So too is a strong concern with color gradations and an often fierce desire to escape the *negro* category. This legacy is part of the heritage that came from Spain's conquest and subjugation of a huge part of the New World. A similar legacy would also help shape the destiny of Brazil, the colony and nation that received more Africans and had a longer experience with slavery than any other society in the Americas.

CHAPTER TWO

Terra de Nosso Senhor

THE PARADOX OF RACE AND SLAVERY IN BRAZIL

YOU MAY NOT RECOGNIZE THE TITLE, but you are probably familiar with the melody to Ary Barroso's "Aquarela do Brasil." Hollywood — Disney, to be a bit more precise — changed the title to "Brazil" and gave the song a few of those June/moon/soon lyrics so beloved by songwriters and jukebox aficionados a few generations ago. But Barroso's original words had a somewhat deeper significance. His song, a Samba-based hymn to the Brazilian nation and Brazilian nationalism, placed the Afro-Brazilian at the center of what it meant to be Brazilian. Brazil the nation was the cunning mulatto, child of the black mother, land of the parading Congo king, a nation shaped by its African roots. Composed in 1939, a little more than fifty years after the abolition of slavery in 1888, "Aquarela do Brasil" became a national icon, part of a self-image Brazil wanted to project to the rest of the world and to itself in the middle years of the last century. That image was an image of racial harmony. Brazil was the land of racial democracy, the "paradise for mulattoes" discussed by nationalistic historian Gilberto Freyre, the place where the African and Afro-American contributions to the nation were given their just due. I am going to discuss that self-image and how accurately it did or did not reflect Brazilian reality a bit later in this volume, but what I want to do in this chapter is to begin a journey, a journey that can help unravel something of a mystery. How did Brazil get to this mid-twentieth-century celebration of racial harmony and what today we might call multiculturalism? Why did the Brazilian nation, including many of its leading thinkers and statesmen, come to embrace such an inclusive vision of their society two generations after the final abolition of one of the more brutal and certainly the longest-lasting example of race-based slavery in the Western Hemisphere?[1]

The path to a Brazil that proudly celebrated its African and Afro-Brazilian heritage was an uncertain one. Brazil, like the other societies of the American hemisphere, had a system of slavery based on race. Africans and their Afro-American descendants were to be enslaved. Others — whites and Indians — at times might be made to endure various forms of forced labor, but they would not as peoples be reduced to the status of slaves. We are familiar with the intertwined histories of slavery, racism, and racial exclusion in the United States, but generalizations that we might draw from that experience are often hard to translate into the Brazilian setting. By dint of its sheer size and duration, Brazil's experience with African and Afro-American slavery dwarfed that of the United States and indeed all the other slave societies of the New World. Over a period that would last from the beginning of the sixteenth century to the middle of the nineteenth, Brazil imported nearly five million African captives or roughly 45 percent of all Africans brought to the Americas in the Atlantic slave trade. This was a figure that was more than twelve times the nearly four hundred thousand Africans who were forcibly brought to the United States.[2]

Brazil's complex history with African slavery would begin in Portugal in the fifteenth century even before European exploration of the Americas. Slavery had existed in Portugal since ancient times. The Portuguese had inherited much of the Roman law of slavery. As in other slave societies, the slave was regarded as chattel for purposes of the commercial law and as a person for purposes of the criminal law. The Portuguese had experience with the enslavement of many peoples during the medieval period. As was the case throughout the Iberian Peninsula, the Portuguese had enslaved Moors as well as other Europeans. As early as 1443, King Dom Henrique authorized the importation of Africans into Portugal. Like the Spaniards the Portuguese would use Africans as both domestic servants and in early efforts to cultivate sugarcane in the Azores.[3]

By the sixteenth century the population of slaves and manumitted individuals (*libertos*) in Portugal was plentiful enough to cause authorities enough concern to enact status legislation designed to keep a potentially unruly population in check. Lisbon in 1551 had a population of 100,000 inhabitants of whom nearly 10 percent, 9950, were slaves. Decrees designed to limit association between *libertos* and slaves were enacted, including one prohibiting *libertos* from taking in slaves as boarders. Portuguese law would take on some of the Roman slave code's cruelty, calling for death by torture for slaves who killed their masters and the execution of slaves who wounded their masters. Unlike Roman law, Portuguese law, influenced by Christian doctrine, did not call for the execution of all of a household's slaves in such cases. Slaves were prohibited from carrying arms except in the presence and under the direction of their masters.[4]

Traditionally the Portuguese law of slavery had little to do with either racial justification for slavery or racial differentiation among slaves. But the world of slavery was beginning to change in the sixteenth century and that change would be reflected in how the law treated people of different races. A combination of their increased participation in the slave trade and the desire to maintain peace with the Moors led the Portuguese to curtail the use of Moorish slaves in favor of black Africans. Some Moorish slaves, along with a few white ones, would remain in Portugal well into the sixteenth century, as reflected by the fact that Portuguese officials authorized different levels of reward for the capture and return of black, Moorish, and white slaves. But slaves in metropolitan Portugal and more importantly the Portuguese Empire increasingly would be black Africans.[5]

It would take Portuguese expansion into Brazil to bring race and ideologies of racial inferiority into the business of providing a justification for designating Africans and their descendants as unique candidates for enslavement. This was a process that was worked out slowly in the sixteenth and seventeenth centuries. Portuguese planters who settled in Brazil pragmatically enough sought to enslave the indigenous population. Close at hand, many Indians came under the domination of their new Portuguese masters, who were less concerned with cultural and theological justifications for slavery than with acquiring field hands who could cultivate sugarcane and not incidentally bring great wealth to their masters. But if potential slave owners wanted and used the most readily available labor supply with scant concern for elaborate racial theories and justifications, the Portuguese Crown and the Catholic Church had other concerns, concerns that would ultimately cause would-be slave owners to look elsewhere — to Africa.

Historian Frédéric Mauro tells us that the Portuguese attempt to enslave Brazil's indigenous population was a somewhat problematic enterprise because the Brazilian Indians proved to be relatively unproductive as agricultural laborers. And yet, as he also informs us, Portuguese planters fought often fierce battles with representatives of the Crown and church for the right to keep and exploit Indian slaves. Both the Crown and the church had active policies designed to protect Indians from enslavement. Pope Paul III issued a bull in 1537 condemning Indian slavery. The Jesuits, who played a prominent role in the church in Brazil, were particularly anxious to protect the colony's indigenous population. The Portuguese Crown followed the church's lead with the enactment of decrees limiting the ability of Portuguese colonists to enslave Indians. Indians initially were to be enslaved only if taken captive in "just wars." Later on, other justifications for enslavement of Indians would be added as the colonists' demand for slaves increased and the supply of African captives was disrupted, particularly when Pernambuco and Angola fell into Dutch hands. By the beginning of the sixteenth century, the Crown, responding to the demands of Portuguese colonists for labor and the relative scarcity and expense of Africans, added cannibalism to the list of permissible justifications for enslaving Indians.[6]

The Jesuits would play an often heroic role in combating Indian slavery. The royal decrees and church pronouncements prohibiting or restricting indigenous slavery were met with hostility and frequently fierce resistance from the often lawless Portuguese colonists who saw the potential for great riches in the sugar plantations of the New World. Several Jesuits who resisted Indian enslavement were murdered. The Jesuit order convinced Pope Urban VIII to publish a bull in 1639 declaring that Catholics who engaged in the trade of Indian slaves would be excommunicated. This measure was also resisted by Portuguese colonists eager to exploit slave labor. The papal bull and Jesuit efforts to protect Indians caused the expulsion of several priests from São Paulo.[7]

The solicitude of the church and Crown for the freedom of the indigenous population was not matched by an equal antislavery fervor when it came to Africans. The view that Indians were not to be enslaved while Africans could be — the view prescribed by Bartolomé de las Casas in the Spanish Empire — was echoed in Portugal's laws and policies in the New World. Portuguese racial attitudes could be complex and contradictory. They frequently fitted the needs of Portuguese officials in different settings. African historian John Thornton's research informs us that Portuguese traders and representatives of the Portuguese Crown recognized in their initial contacts with African kingdoms in the sixteenth century that they were dealing with societies with a level of technological and organizational sophistication that matched their own. That recognition played a critical role in the ability of the Portuguese to establish trading relationships with and settlements in the powerful kingdoms of West and Central Africa. But the sixteenth century was also a time when European writers were increasingly exploring the idea that Africans were a primitive — indeed, bestial — species of humanity, in many ways scarcely meriting the designation *human* at all. Animal-like images of the inhabitants of the African continent were becoming prevalent in Portugal as indeed elsewhere in Western Europe. By 1544, French explorer Alfonse Saintonge described the inhabitants of Angola as having dog-like teeth and faces. Others disagreed with the notion of the African as animal arguing that Africans were human beings, but human beings who were products of a barbarous environment in sore need of Portuguese rescue and enlightenment. The church, which had waged a vigorous if at times unsuccessful struggle to safeguard Indians from slavery, acquiesced in the enslavement of Africans, reasoning, much like the Spaniards, that their enslavement and transportation to the Christian colonies of the Americas would help to save their souls and not incidentally redound to the economic benefit of Portuguese settlers in the new colonies.[8]

As would be the case with other New World slave societies, the image of the bestial, barbarous African would provide continuing justification for African enslavement and a harsh regime of social control designed to curtail rebellious impulses. The Jesuits endorsed African slavery as a tool that brought the barbarous African under the civilizing and soul-saving tutelage of Portuguese masters. The church's view was that masters held their slaves as a trust with a responsibility to turn them from barbarous sinners into true Christians. At least one priest went so far as to argue that masters and colonial authorities should not try to separate Africans who had been unlawfully enslaved — those who were free in their native lands and under the protection of Portuguese or other European powers — from those who were lawfully enslaved. He argued that those who were unjustly enslaved under Portuguese law were so few and the tendency of Africans to lie about their enslavement and prior conditions was so great that it was not worth the effort to separate those who were legally free from those who were properly enslaved.[9]

But Africans were to be more than the object of Portuguese efforts to save their souls and turn them into civilized, albeit inferior members of the colonial community. They were to be carefully watched and brutally punished lest their savage tendencies and penchants for rebelliousness wreak harm on their masters and other Portuguese colonists. The African slave, like the slave in ancient Rome before him, was considered an enemy to be harshly controlled. The full severity of the Roman code, with its requirement for mass crucifixion of a household's slaves in retribution for the master's murder, could not be applied in the face of Christian doctrine and the influence of *Las siete partidas*. Nonetheless offending slaves could be subject to the harshest of punishments. Flogging, branding, torture, and death were prescribed penalties for slaves who threatened the social order. This was to be expected. The world of crime and punishment in the early modern Atlantic world was a harsh one. Punishment, even for free people in Europe, was seen as having one primary purpose, to terrorize potential lawbreakers to make them obey the law. Executions for property crimes were common. Death by torture for crimes deemed especially heinous was routine. Western Europe was a place where malefactors could be drawn and quartered or crucified or boiled in oil. Portugal was no exception to this practice of harsh physical punishments. Later the kingdoms and republics of the West would begin to rethink such severity. The English Bill of Rights of 1689 and its American counterpart of 1791 would prohibit cruel and unusual punishment. The Brazilian Constitution of 1824 would prohibit floggings, branding, and torture, although the nineteenth-century Brazilian criminal code would retain these punishments for slaves. But these reforms were light-years away temporally and geographically from the world of punishment and deterrence experienced by the Brazilian slave of the colonial period.[10]

The brutality of the Brazilian slave regime and the fierce and often violent African resistance to that regime have been well documented by students of Brazilian slavery. If the racist attribution of barbaric tendencies to Africans can be easily dismissed as early modern European pseudoscience combined with a felt need for a justification for enslaving Africans, the Portuguese fear of the African as rebellious and as a threat to the system of slavery was nonetheless well founded. Brazil's small white population would remain a distinct minority both during and after the colonial period. That small white population, combined with an ever-increasing population of enslaved Africans, made conditions ripe for the fierce rebellions initiated by Africans. This resistance to slavery often took the form of efforts, frequently successful, to establish African or reconstituted African communities on Brazilian soil. These communities, *quilombos*, were an ever-present thorn in the side of colonial authorities. They not only sheltered communities of rebellious runaways, they also provided slaves who had not escaped with successful examples of slave resistance. The fiercest and most successful of these rebellious *quilombos* of the colonial era was Palmares. Surviving some sixty-five years, from 1630 to 1695 the Palmares Quilombo was, with the exception of the Haitian Revolution, the most successful slave rebellion in the Western Hemisphere. The people of Palmares would resist some seventeen punitive expeditions by Portuguese and Dutch forces designed to subdue the rebellious African Republic in Brazil. The Portuguese Crown estimated that at its height, Palmares consisted of some twenty-seven thousand square kilometers of territory and between eighteen and twenty thousand inhabitants.[11]

Palmares would be the most dramatic but by no means the only example of a massive slave rebellion rooted in African culture in Brazil's history. Life for Brazilian slaves was often a Hobbesian hell—nasty, brutish, and exceedingly short. The sugar plantations of the northeast and the mines of Minas Gerais in the colonial era as well as the coffee plantations of São Paulo in the nineteenth century exhausted the lives of their slaves at a rapid pace, continually creating demand for new African captives. This demand was made easier to fill because of the extensive slave trade between Brazil and its sister South Atlantic lusophonic society, Angola. Unlike the United States, whose slave population started with a relatively small importation of African captives and persisted and grew through natural population increase, the growth of Brazil's slave population depended on its extensive African slave trade. Brazil would continue its large and active slave trade until 1850.[12]

That African trade would mean a continual replenishment not only of Africans but African culture as well in Brazil, ultimately helping to shape and define the nation. Brazil, particularly its northeastern region, would become one the great centers of West African culture in the Americas and indeed the world. Resistance from African-oriented *quilombos* would plague Portuguese and later Brazilian authorities throughout the history of slavery in Brazil. The inhabitants of these settlements were not content simply to run away from slavery, hiding in the often difficult terrain of the Brazilian *sertão* (backlands). They sometimes challenged authorities with raids, at times making captives of free Brazilians and occasionally offering succor to fugitive slaves seeking to join their ranks. Resistance to slavery rooted in African cultures would also come to threaten the social order in some of Brazil's major cities. In the nineteenth century, Islamic-inspired revolts would strike fear into the hearts of Brazilian authorities in Rio de Janeiro and Salvador, Bahia. If the African was considered a necessity as a laborer in Brazil's plantations and mines, he was nonetheless often seen as one that was both frightening and evil. As one Brazilian historian has noted, a major theme in traditional Brazilian historiography has been an examination of how the nineteenth-century empire came to grips with African "barbarism."[13]

That fear of barbarism and rebelliousness on the part of African-born slaves would have the ironic consequence of helping to lessen racial prejudice or at least discrimination against native-born Afro-Brazilians, both mulattoes and to a lesser extent blacks. Sociologists at least since Émile Durkheim have informed us of the role that outsiders play in cementing social solidarity and lessening friction or divisions among those who are not the principal objects of society's concern. The criminal, those labeled deviant, the racial outsider, all help to bind a society, or at least its non-outsider members, closer together. This kind of social dynamic would find itself working out relatively early in Brazil's colonial history. With few Portuguese settlers available to fight rebellious Africans, Portuguese authorities would turn to people of African descent, some Africans, but mostly Afro-Brazilians in an effort to suppress African rebelliousness. The ranks of the military forces of different Brazilian captaincies would include Africans and later Afro-Brazilians because the small Portuguese population made it difficult to enlist sufficient whites, even as officers. In March 1682, the prince regent of Portugal offered freedom to blacks or mulattoes who helped to liberate formerly free individuals who had been taken captive by the inhabitants of Palmares. According to the warrant, a slave who helped liberate a captured free person would be set free, subject only to a five-year indenture with his former master. The former slave's right to freedom would be enforceable in court.[14]

The dynamics of the slave economy coupled with strong fears of African slaves would contribute to the formation of a free Afro-Brazilian population that would be less plagued by formal, legal discrimination than its counterparts elsewhere in the hemisphere. The free Afro-Brazilian population would grow considerably in the eighteenth century due to an increase in urbanization and the development of gold mining in Minas Gerais. Both cities and mines offered opportunities for freedom for the slave who was entrepreneurial, daring, or sometimes just plain lucky. As was the case with the American colonies of the Spanish Empire and indeed in slave societies throughout the Americas, cities provided slaves with opportunities to earn money. There was work to be done. It was close by. The entrepreneurial slave could sell produce and handicrafts in the market or work for artisans or on the docks in her or his spare time. Activities and potential employers were close by. There were few whites, and even fewer willing to do some of the city's more unpleasant tasks. The city provided an opportunity to earn money even if it meant adding additional hours to an already backbreaking schedule. Similarly the mines of Minas Gerais provided slaves with the opportunity to gain money. Sometimes slaves could get money by working out what was in effect a partnership with their owners. They would get to keep a percentage of the gold they found, while their owners would get the rest. Some slaves saw other possibilities. They could take the gold that the law said belonged to their masters and put it to their own uses. Other slaves saw the possibilities of selling food or providing other services to masters and slaves who were spending all of their energies on the gold fields of the prosperous captaincy.[15]

However the slave acquired it, money opened up the possibility of manumission by self-purchase. The standard form for the manumission of slaves was the *alforria*, which had been part of the Portuguese law of slavery from medieval times. The law recognized two kinds of *alforrias*. The perfect *alforria*, usually acquired after self-purchase, granted the slave unconditional manumission. The imperfect *alforria*, viewed by the law as a gift or an act of charity on the master's part, was often accompanied by conditions. Slaves who were manumitted through this means were given conditional manumissions. These could be revoked by former masters for acts of ingratitude. These included actions that might bring shame on the former master, physically attacking the former master, or damaging the former master's business interests. An *alforria* could also be revoked if the former slave had promised the former master a reward or compensation for freedom and had failed to satisfy that condition after receiving manumission. Slaves who had been granted conditional manumission were *libertos*, while their children would be full-fledged free persons.[16]

A severe shortage of marriageable white women in colonial Brazil also contributed to the growth of the free Afro-Brazilian population. There were few white women. Historians of Brazil tell us that the number of white women eligible for marriage was reduced even further by the tendency of white parents in Minas Gerais and other captaincies to ' their daughters to convents rather than allowing them to marry the often-disreputable white men who populated colonial Brazil. This shortage of white women increased the tendency of slave owners not only to have sexual relations with African and Afro-Brazilian women but also to establish families with these women. A number of slave owners freed their children and slave mistresses through wills. Others set up families, becoming husbands to their black and mulatto mistresses and fathers to their mulatto children. This was aided by Portuguese and later Brazilian law, which generally looked favorably on the adoption and legitimation of children.[17]

The continued slave trade, combined with the paucity of whites and the rise of the free Afro-Brazilian population, contributed to the development of Brazil's strongly hierarchical society. Wealthy white slaveholders were clearly the elite. Whether or not nonslaveholding whites were seen as superior to wealthy, slaveholding mulattoes is less clear. Colonial Brazil was a society with clear race and color prejudices, prejudices that would occasionally manifest themselves in formal attempts at legal discrimination — ordinances restricting public office to whites or to men of "pure blood" were frequently enacted. But these would often be overlooked because of the shortage of available white men for military offices or because a man of mixed African and Portuguese ancestry had powerful family connections or a strong patron. If class did not trump the disabilities of race for wealthy and well-connected mulattoes, it could certainly mitigate them. Further down the social ladder would be free blacks, who were less likely than mulattoes to be wealthy or have influential family connections, and the taint of their more visible African ancestry made the prejudice against them even stronger. At the bottom of the social pyramid of course were the slaves. Toward the end of the colonial period, these slaves were more and more likely to be Africans, while Afro-Brazilians were increasingly likely to be found among the ranks of the free population. Brazilian historian Rafael Marquese has argued that the very process of the massive Brazilian slave trade contributed to the increase in *alforrias* in the eighteenth century. The constant arrival of new Africans made the native-born black or mulatto someone who was no longer an outsider or a foreigner but a Brazilian. He or she was Catholic and Portuguese-speaking and had absorbed the basic etiquette of Luso-Brazilian society. And, most important, the native-born Afro-Brazilian was seen by Portuguese and later Brazilian authorities as an ally, one who could help maintain control over the ever-threatening population of African slaves.[18]

By the end of the eighteenth century, slavery had come to be such an integral part of the Brazilian economic and social structure that the system of human bondage seemed to create few dissenters. But the Enlightenment, the liberal imagination that would transform the Atlantic world in the late eighteenth and early nineteenth centuries, was also having its influence on Portugal and its giant South American colony. Toward the end of the eighteenth century, Brazilian elites, chafing under Portugal's mercantilist restrictions, began to find justification for greater autonomy, at least for themselves, in the liberal political philosophies developed in France and elsewhere in Europe. These sentiments led to abortive struggles for independence in various parts of Brazil. This rebelliousness and dissatisfaction with the colonial order at times spread beyond white elites. One rebellion, the 1798 Revolt of the Tailors in Bahia, raised the issue of racial equality as well as independence. The northeastern uprising aimed to establish a Brazilian republic and end discrimination against free Afro-Brazilians. If these struggles proved unsuccessful in separating Brazil from Portugal, they nonetheless helped increase a sense of nationalism among Brazilian elites. They also spread a sense of Brazilian nationalism to the masses, slave and free, a point noted later in the nineteenth century by Brazilian abolitionist Joaquim Nabuco. Brazilian elites hoped that independence and the liberal ideals that independence advocates were espousing would lead to freedom from the restrictions of Portuguese mercantilist rule. The Napoleonic Wars would ultimately give independence advocates their victory. The French emperor's occupation of Portugal in 1808 would force the displacement of the Portuguese Crown to Brazil. By 1815, Brazil was declared a kingdom united with Portugal. By 1822, Brazil had declared itself an independent empire, with Dom Pedro I of the Portuguese royal family as its emperor.[19]

The new empire would need a new constitution, but how would that document handle the issues of race and slavery? The liberal ideals that had produced the break with Portugal were very much in evidence in the Constituent Assembly that drafted the 1824 constitution. Emperor Dom Pedro I in his speech before the assembly in May 1823 stressed the need for a constitution that was in tune with the enlightened thinking of the early nineteenth century. Among other measures, the emperor called for a constitution that recognized the separation of powers, dividing the government into distinct executive, legislative, and judicial branches. He also called for a constitution that protected the freedom of the Brazilian people. The emperor's speech touched off a bit of controversy because Dom Pedro's call for a constitution worthy of his acquiescence was seen as an implicit threat to veto a constitution he deemed inappropriate. Many representatives attacked this threat as undemocratic, but a majority seemed prepared to allow the emperor this power.[20]

The constitution would ultimately be drafted by a small committee picked by the emperor, but the Constituent Assembly's deliberations greatly influenced the final draft. The assembly's work would range over a number of topics. The overall liberal influence on the process of constitution making can be seen in the final product, the constitution of 1824, which, among other things, specified that the empire was to be a constitutional monarchy. Citizenship was granted to all native-born free people, regardless of race. The constitutional text specifically included *libertos* in this group. All citizens were equal before the law and equally entitled to the law's protection. Citizens were guaranteed freedom from religious persecution provided that their actions did not offend public morals. Harsh physical punishment was prohibited. People were guaranteed security in their homes, due process before punishment, and the right to property and personal security. In the Constituent Assembly, a minority went even further in their advocacy of human rights, urging the abolition of the death penalty. Their efforts failed, but the attempt showed the influence of the modern Enlightenment on at least some of the members. The 1824 constitution was clearly influenced by Enlightenment ideals of equality, freedom, and human dignity. However much the new constitution was also willing to sanction a system of representation that limited political participation to a propertied few or however hierarchical the new empire's social structure might be, the acceptance of liberal ideals as constitutional norms was an impressive accomplishment as the new Brazilian nation emerged from the shadow of the Portuguese Empire.[21]

But the Constituent Assembly also had to wrestle with the issues of race and slavery and how the new empire that recognized equality and the rights of man would deal with the greatest of inequalities. Some members of the assembly recognized slavery as an evil incompatible with the liberal ideals of the new age and the new empire. Deputy Silva Lisboa condemned human bondage and called for gradual emancipation combined with moral instruction for the slave population. Others agreed that slavery was an evil, but in their view a necessary one that could not be abolished without wrecking the Brazilian economy. One deputy argued for the good of slavery by noting that it was maintained in the United States, a nation known for its justice, humanity, and moderation. Still others argued the inferiority of the slave population and the dangers of emancipation.[22]

If there was relatively little support for or debate over general emancipation, the status of free Afro-Brazilians and the rights of slaves to have access to the courts excited considerable interest among deputies debating the new constitution. Several deputies expressed the view that slaves and former slaves were entitled to representation in court. Former slaves should be provided lawyers either in cases where there was an attempt to reenslave them or in cases where an individual had been manumitted only to join the ranks of the impoverished — "the miserable classes," as a number of deputies put it. This latter concern was probably motivated by more than pure humanitarian considerations. In Brazil, as indeed was the case throughout the Americas, public authorities feared that slaves who were elderly or infirm, who could no longer work, and who had ceased to have any economic value would end up being manumitted and becoming public charges. Many jurisdictions passed legislation in attempts to prevent these kinds of manumissions or to require slave owners to provide surety for such slaves. The discussions in the Constituent Assembly concerning the rights of some former slaves for support and access to the courts seem to have been partially motivated by these concerns.[23]

If the treatment of impoverished ex-slaves concerned a number of deputies in the Constituent Assembly, no issue relating to race and slavery seemed to have concerned them more than the question of citizenship for Afro-Brazilians, both *libertos* and those who were fully free. Different proposals were put forth. A few radicals seemed to suggest that the new constitution might even include slaves among the ranks of citizens, but the majority of deputies adhered to the view that slaves, while entitled to the law's protection and to fair treatment by the courts, were not citizens. Citizenship, they argued, meant membership in the political community, or at least the possession of full civil rights, both of which were incompatible with slavery. Others wanted to create classes of citizens: Brazilians, consisting of native-born free persons, presumably a category meant to cover *libertos* and Brazilian citizens, and native-born free persons with full political and civil rights, a category that at a minimum would probably have excluded *libertos*.[24]

The final product of the Constituent Assembly's deliberations, the 1824 constitution, is more reflective of the liberal idealism that informed the document's drafters than it was of the undeniable realities of slavery and its critical place in the Brazilian economy. Slavery is nowhere mentioned in the document. Instead Title 2 of the constitution recognized citizenship for all free-born Brazilians, with a specific inclusion of *libertos*. Title 8 recognized the principles of freedom of speech and the press, freedom from religious persecution, freedom in the home from government searches, and the right to due process in criminal procedures. Title 8 also recognized freedom from ex post facto law and prohibited torture. The constitution's enumeration of rights also prohibited special privileges and recognized the equality of all citizens before the law. Beneath the grand pronouncements of the 1824 constitution was also a determination to ensure that power would remain in the hands of the slaveholding elites. Property and income qualifications for voting allowed few men who were not of the elite, slaveholding class the opportunity to participate in politics. Racial liberalism and race-based slavery, support for a government that protected individual rights and disallowed special privileges combined with political participation in the hands of an elite few — the Brazilian constitution, like the empire it governed, had more than its share of paradoxes.[25]

Those paradoxes were fully on display in the life and career of Antonio Pereira Rebouças. Rebouças, the subject of a biography by Brazilian legal historian Keila Grinberg, was a prominent lawyer, jurisconsult (legal commentator), and politician of the Brazilian Empire. His life in many ways embodied the contest that was being waged for the soul of the giant empire both in the debates of the Constituent Assembly and indeed for the rest of the nineteenth century. A mulatto, the son of a Portuguese father and a *liberta* mother, Rebouças would rise high in the legal and political cultures of nineteenth-century Brazil, yet he would always be subject to spoken and unspoken prejudices due to his race and color. An opponent of racial discrimination, Rebouças would nonetheless become a slaveholder and would defend slaveholders in court in manumission suits between slaves and their owners. Rebouças could eloquently argue against discrimination against free black and mulatto citizens of Brazil while still supporting the suppression of slave revolts and decrying what he and other free Brazilians saw as African barbarism.[26]

Rebouças's legal and political career can help give us some sense of how free Brazilians in the nineteenth century navigated their nation's cognitively difficult combination of race, slavery, and Enlightenment values. For Rebouças, liberal values, a rejection of discrimination based on race or color, a revulsion against African culture, and an acceptance — and, indeed, participation to a point — in the system of slavery all were part of what for him was a coherent way of looking at the world and one that was by no means singular in the Brazilian Empire of the early nineteenth century. This worldview was shaped by the dynamics of a slave society, which, although based almost from the beginning on the enslavement of Africans and their descendants, had social and demographic currents that made race as such less important than it would be in a society like the United States. The very harshness of Brazilian slavery had ensured that there would be a continuous importation of new Africans, to replace those who perished in the stark conditions that prevailed in the *fazendas* of Bahia, Rio, and São Paulo, the mines of Minas Gerais, and other Brazilian venues. These Africans would be culturally distinctive and not infrequently frightening not only to whites but also to native-born Afro-Brazilians. The society that had emerged by the early nineteenth century was one where slaves were often predominantly African. It was also one where African cultures and particularly the Islamic cultures of West Africa were often seen as providing a distinct challenge to Luso-Brazilian Catholicism.[27]

This fear of the African could help to normalize native-born Afro-Brazilians, particularly mulattoes such as Rebouças. His history can do much to shed light on the complex web of race, color, culture, class, and clientelism in nineteenth-century Brazil. Rebouças began as an outsider to the elite world of practitioners of law and state affairs, the world of the *bacharel* in which he would attain preeminence. His status as a mulatto contributed to this and throughout his career would lead to charges that he sympathized with slave rebellions or that he sought to re-create a revolution similar to the much feared one that had occurred in Saint-Domingue. But race was not the only reason Rebouças was an unlikely candidate for this elite world of law and governance. The Brazilian bar and the *bacharel* class more generally were dominated by the sons of the elite, young men who had the time and money to study law, philosophy, and political economy at Portugal's Coimbra University. Rebouças had neither and instead taught himself the law while working as a clerk in a notarial office. In 1821, he was admitted to the practice of law with all the privileges normally reserved for graduates of the Portuguese university. By 1823, in part because of his support for the cause of independence, Rebouças met with Emperor Dom Pedro I, was appointed to a government position, and was made a knight of the Order of the Cruzeiro. His public career was under way.[28]

It is easy, too easy, to see historical figures' public life and policy positions simply as an extension of their personal biographies, social background, and struggles for achievement and recognition and as the sum total of their personal alliances and animosities. We would like to believe — and, indeed, should believe — that more goes into the stands public figures take on the issues of their times. This would be especially important in any effort to analyze Rebouças, a complex man of both strong ambition and profound learning. And yet Rebouças's constitutional vision clearly owed much to both the harsh realities of social prejudice with which he was familiar as well as the potentialities for equality and mobility that the 1824 constitution promised. Rebouças firmly resisted encroachments on the legal equality promised by the 1824 constitution. The struggle over who could be an officer in the National Guard was particularly revealing of Rebouças's views of the links between law, race, and civilization. As a member of the Chamber of Deputies, in 1832 he opposed a measure that would have prevented *libertos* from receiving commissions in the National Guard, a militia controlled by the central government and used for internal security. Rebouças denounced the measure as "unjust, incendiary, impolitic, and unconstitutional." He noted that *libertos* had aided in the struggle for independence. More revealingly, Rebouças cautioned his fellow deputies that they were following the dangerous example of the French in Haiti. By excluding *libertos* and other free people of color from the rights of citizenship, the French had set the stage for an alliance between the African slaves of that island and the free people of color, who he argued should have been the allies of the French.[29]

Rebouças's support for the rights of *libertos* curiously enough was tempered by a concern for the traditional proprietary and dignitary rights of their former masters. Title 2 of the 1824 constitution, which specifically included *libertos* in the ranks of the Empire's citizens, had raised a thorny legal issue. If native-born *libertos* were citizens, as the text of the constitution proclaimed, could they be reduced to slavery for ingratitude, as had been the tradition in Portuguese law? A number of jurisconsults argued that applying the traditional doctrine would be contrary to the spirit of the 1824 constitution and that it would also violate Article 179 of the Criminal Code, which made it a crime to reduce a free person to slavery. Rebouças argued that the original provisions in the *Ordenações Filipinas* allowing the courts to return the ungrateful *liberto* to a state of slavery still applied despite the code and the constitution. If Rebouças was an advocate for the rights of the *liberto*, it was an advocacy that would not stray too far from the law's traditional demands for fidelity to a generous master.[30]

Still, Rebouças's fight to allow *libertos* to earn commissions in the National Guard put the Bahian deputy at odds with a number of his liberal peers, who were prepared to restrict the rights of manumitted men as a means of reinforcing the social order in which racial boundaries were important, even if they had few explicit legal manifestations. Rebouças's dissent in this area is not at all hard to understand. His fight for a broadly inclusive vision of citizenship was one that validated his own being — that of the self-made man of color who was able to use the law's lack of formal restrictions, his own talents, and a bit of good fortune in securing powerful patrons to rise in a society even when social prejudices were strongly arrayed against him. It was a formula that had worked well for Rebouças. His talents and political connections would ultimately bring him into the ranks of the empire's political elite. He had a grand mansion that included a magnificent library of nearly three thousand volumes and was the owner of seven slaves who acted as his house servants. And most important, he was admitted to the Brazilian Empire's highest courts despite his race and his not being a graduate of the law faculty at Coimbra. A successful free man of color in a society that practiced African slavery, Rebouças's life embodied the contradiction that was the Brazilian Empire.[31]

Of the slaveholding societies of the Americas, Brazil had what was in many ways the most incoherent response to the challenge that the Enlightenment posed to African and Afro-American slavery. If we consider those societies in which slaveholding was a largely unchallenged practice in the middle of the eighteenth century — Brazil, the Spanish Empire, the northern and southern colonies that would become the United States, the British Caribbean, and Saint-Domingue — all of them with the exception of Brazil would ultimately fashion responses to the new thinking concerning human equality and unalienable rights in ways that were at least internally consistent. The northern states of the United States would begin the process of abolishing slavery after the American Revolution. They would also opt, at least initially, for citizenship and equality for their emerging free Negro class, although many states would retreat from this racial egalitarianism in the nineteenth century. We will discuss this history in further detail in chapter 3. The nations formed after the successful wars for independence from the Spanish Empire would also move to abolish slavery, recognizing that it was incompatible with the liberal thinking that had helped to bring about independence from Spain. The new nations also recognized the equality of citizens of all races before the law, even if that recognition masked significant racial inequalities and discriminatory practices. Cuba and Puerto Rico did not have successful nineteenth-century liberal revolutions. They would remain colonies of Spain until the end of the nineteenth century and would continue as active participants in the Atlantic slave trade and as slave societies for most of the century. The southern states of the United States would ultimately develop a full throated ideology of Negro inferiority and dependency in order to justify racial slavery in a nation that prided itself on its democratic and egalitarian character. The slaves of Saint-Domingue themselves overthrew the hemisphere's most brutal and most lucrative slave system. Britain in the nineteenth century would become the principal opponent of the African slave trade and abolish slavery in its empire in the 1830s.

Brazil would follow none of these paths. In the nineteenth century, slavery would expand in Brazil from the sugar plantations of Bahia and the mines of Minas Gerais into the coffee *fazendas* of São Paulo. Brazil would have a liberal constitution that would explicitly extend citizenship to Afro-Brazilians, including *libertos*, and yet that document would have nothing to say concerning slavery itself. The efforts of some deputies in the Constituent Assembly to abolish the institution were rejected, but the 1824 constitution contained no specific guarantees for slaveholders beyond a generic provision protecting property rights. Insofar as slavery received legal protection, it rested in statutes, particularly the penal code and code of criminal procedure. This might be contrasted with the U.S. Constitution, with its specific, if somewhat euphemistically phrased, references to slavery found in clauses discussing fugitive slaves, apportionment of congressional representation, and the Atlantic slave trade. The wealth of Brazil rested on its slave economies. The empire's political order to a large extent depended on the loyalties of its free Afro-Brazilian citizens. The fundamental and also lesser laws of the land were steeped in the thinking of the Enlightenment, limited government, recognition of basic human rights, restrictions on the severity of punishment, and freedom of religion. The African was feared as a barbarous savage who would, as he had in Haiti, bring the horrors of servile rebellion. And yet Africans would continue to be brought to the new empire in the nineteenth century, including nearly eight hundred thousand after Brazil signed an 1831 treaty outlawing the Atlantic slave trade. More significantly the fear of the African did not extend — or perhaps did not extend with as much force — to the African's children, particularly those of mixed ancestry. The African could be feared and yet the mulatto Rebouças could be a respected jurisconsult, adviser to the emperor, and a supporter of the slaveholding order. The Brazilian Empire and its approach to the issue of slavery, how it could be reconciled with a liberal order and also how it could be maintained in a society that gave little legal support for notions of racial inferiority, was complex and often contradictory. Slavery would persist — indeed, thrive — throughout most of the nineteenth century, yet it would do so without the recognition of the inevitability and desirability of abolition that occurred in some slaveholding societies or the development of an ideology of racial exclusion that occurred in the American South. Brazilian slavery would remain incoherent and sui generis in the American hemisphere.[32]

There was a sharp dissonance between the liberal norms that informed the constitution of 1824 and such progressive reform measures as the Penal Code of 1830 and the Code of Criminal Procedure of 1832 and the harsh realities of Brazilian slavery. That dissonance would attract increasing opposition to slavery throughout the course of the nineteenth century. The Brazilian Empire would see this opposition early on from many who played a role in securing the new nation's independence and first constitution. Most prominent among these was José Bonifácio, adviser to Dom Pedro I and a key architect of the 1824 constitution. Bonifácio from the beginning of the empire's independence argued that slavery was incompatible with the liberal state they were trying to establish. Bonifácio's opposition to slavery also introduced early on what would become an important subtext in the Brazilian antislavery argument: slavery was wrong not only because it violated liberal and enlightened norms, not only because it was a crime against the African and the Afro-Brazilian. It was also bad policy because it hindered the new nation's development of Brazil. Brazil's future, Bonifácio and others would argue, lay not in importing, subjugating, and possibly civilizing the savage African. It lay instead in encouraging greater European immigration, having the vast and rich land of Brazil come under the cultivation and enterprise of civilized and industrious Europeans, allowing Brazil to join what we today might call the First World community of nations, Europe and the United States. Bonifácio's argument would be echoed by other nineteenth-century Brazilian abolitionists, including, later in the nineteenth century, one of the nation's leading antislavery advocates, Joaquim Nabuco.[33]

Antislavery pressure would also come from the outside. Britain, which had been a major supplier of Africans to New World slave societies, became, in the new, enlightened nineteenth century, the chief foe of the African trade. It spurred the Brazilians to pass legislation in 1831 outlawing the nation's participation in the slave trade. Brazilian authorities and traders largely ignored the law, declaring it to be "for English eyes" — that is, necessary to maintain good relations with the Atlantic's naval superpower. That superpower was patrolling the seas in search of pirates violating the new international norm against slaving. But the law was not one that would be enforced by Brazilian authorities. They were not prepared to interfere with the vital commerce in Africans so necessary to the nation's sugar and coffee *fazendas*, or its lucrative mines in Minas Gerais. The law would hopefully just reassure the pesky English, allowing the trade and the nation's slave economy to continue. It would do so for some nineteen years until the English forced a stronger anti-slave-trade treaty on the unwilling Brazilians.

If the 1831 law produced little in the way of direct enforcement, it did contain one provision that would provide a vehicle that would allow antislavery lawyers to attack the institution and come to the aid of some of those held in bondage. The statute declared free those Africans illegally brought to the country after the enactment of the 1831 legislation. The legislation enabled slaves to petition for freedom and a number of pro-abolition lawyers represented slaves in such actions. One such attorney, Afro-Brazilian Luiz Gama, was particularly adept at using his legal skills in the antislavery cause. Born in 1822, the son of a free African mother and a Portuguese father, he was betrayed by his father, who sold him into slavery at age eight. He was able to regain his freedom at age eighteen by proving his free status. He gained a position as a secretary to the provincial police in São Paulo due to the friendship of his patron, a provincial delegate. He later became a lawyer through self-study. He would become a specialist in actions or petitions for liberty, representing Africans who had been brought illegally to Brazil after 1831. This kind of petition for liberty found an increasing number of Brazilian lawyers willing to represent complaining slaves in the 1850s and 1860s. The law seemed relatively straightforward. The African trade was illegal. The statute specified that illegally imported Africans were to be set free. But the law and the legal mind in nineteenth-century Brazil were anything but straightforward. The petitioning slaves were, after all, Africans, the very people whose barbarism and savagery inspired great fear in many Brazilians. Were they to be simply set free, turned loose on Brazilian society? Such a result could wreak havoc on the social fabric — and not coincidentally, the financial interests of powerful slaveholders. That would not do. A number of jurists hit on a solution. The freedom of the illegally enslaved Africans would be recognized, but they would not be precipitously set free. No, they would be paroled to their masters instead. Under that parole they would theoretically be trained for their place in free Brazilian society. As a practical matter, they would continue to be slaves. Only after strong pressure from Britain did the Brazilian government finally agree to emancipate all illegally held Africans in 1864.[34]

But if some jurists would seek to avoid the antislavery mandates of the law, others toward the end of the 1860s came to embrace the law as a tool that could help further the ends of abolition. Increasingly members of the bar were finding the contradiction between the nation's liberal ideology and its practice of large-scale slaveholding an embarrassment and one that they hoped to eliminate. Petitions by slaves for freedom provided an important vehicle that allowed members of the bench and bar to work for the antislavery cause. As Grinberg's research indicates, antislavery lawyers and jurists were significantly aided in this task by the surprisingly unsettled nature of much of Brazilian law. In the nations that inherited their legal systems from the common law of England, judges were strongly constrained by precedent — the requirement to defer to decisions made by higher courts and indeed to take as persuasive authority decisions made by peer courts in other jurisdictions. In legal systems that had been influenced by the codification movement of the early nineteenth century, extensive codes governing both civil and criminal matters played a role in reigning in judicial discretion. These constraints were largely absent from the Brazilian context. Brazil was not an inheritor of the common law legal system. And yet the extensive codification that had occurred on much of the European continent and indeed in the former colonies of Spain in the Americas had not occurred in Brazil in part because the Portuguese and Brazilian Crowns had escaped Napoleonic conquest and the imposition of the Napoleonic Code. Brazilian jurists were instead advised to look to the *lei da boa razão*, which might in this context be translated as the rule of good reason, the jurist's best judgment. This approach often left Brazilian jurists with multiple sources of law — Roman law, canon law, concepts of natural law, the writings of legal scholars, and customary law — from which to fashion their decisions. As antislavery sentiment increasingly became the conventional wisdom among the *bacharel* class that supplied the nation's jurists and advocates, legal decision making increasingly favored slaves over masters in cases where freedom was at stake.[35]

The pressures to end slavery would grow as the nineteenth century unfolded. And yet the dependence of the large planters on slave labor and their influence on the Brazilian government would increase their determination to hold onto their human property. Emancipation in the United States in the wake of the Civil War left Brazil as the only independent American nation that still permitted legal slavery, heightening the sense of isolation among liberal thinkers. That sense of isolation also increased their determination to bring about emancipation and bring the Brazilian nation more in tune with the modern age. Demographic realities and acts of rebellion on the part of the slave population also contributed to the ever-more-tenuous hold that slave owners had on public opinion and their human property. It became harder and harder to control slaves and their inclination to escape bondage in a society where race or color was less and less an indication of slave status. In the American South race could provide an easy marker of slave or free status, one that could be simply translated into a legal presumption. Ninety-five percent of the Afro-American population was enslaved. The law was simple. If an individual was a Negro, he was presumed to be a slave. He would have the burden of proving otherwise. No such easy presumption could be employed in Brazil where an Afro-Brazilian was as likely and indeed more likely to be free rather than slave. As early as 1850, the free Afro-Brazilian population outnumbered the slave population. The first national census, conducted in 1872, showed a free Afro-Brazilian population of 4.2 million, dwarfing the slave population of 1.5 million and outnumbering the white population of 3.8 million. The simple equation of African ancestry and slave status so easy in the American South was impossible in Brazil.[36]

And Brazilian slaves seemed to realize particularly toward the latter decades of the nineteenth century that their owners' grasp on their lives was becoming increasingly fragile and tenuous. The closing of the African trade was the occasion, as it was in the United States, for a growth in an interregional slave trade, moving slaves to the more productive and lucrative coffee *fazendas* of São Paulo. As had been the case in the United States, this new trade brought with it greater forced family separations, despite the law's attempts to limit such. This would in turn bring acts of rebellion, escapes from slavery, with fugitives blending into free populations or escaping to *quilombos* with the threat of still further rebellion. The separation of family members also brought about increased instances of slaves attacking and killing their masters. Ironically enough, this new slave rebelliousness seemed to have coincided with a relaxation of the rigors of the criminal law as applied to slaves. Legislation in 1857 permitted slaves who had killed their masters the prerogative of mercy in extenuating cases. This change was part of a broader evolution in thinking that saw legal reform and greater restraint on the disciplinary powers of masters as a way of heading off large-scale slave rebellion.[37]

The new atmosphere would increase the pressure on the institution of slavery. The passage of "free womb" legislation in September of 1871 would be the first recognition by the national government that slavery would ultimately have no place in the Brazilian nation. The legislation took a very conservative approach to ending human bondage in the Brazilian Empire. Lei Rio Branco, named after José Maria da Silva Paranhos, the Viscount of Rio Branco, the statute's parliamentary sponsor, provided for the freedom of children born of slave mothers after September 28, 1871. Children born to slave mothers after that date would have *ingênuo* status.

They would be forced to labor for their masters as indentured servants until the age of twenty-one. Brazilian abolitionist Joaquim Nabuco criticized the legislation, calling it "imperfect, incomplete, impolitic, unjust and absurd." He correctly observed that it would have allowed the continuance of unfree labor for generations. A girl born a slave on September 27, 1871, would, under the legislation, have remained a slave for life. Had she had a child sometime between the age of thirty and forty, from 1901 to 1911, that child would have remained an *ingênuo* well into the 1920s or even the early 1930s.[38]

If the legislation was conservative in guaranteeing slave owners long-term rights to hold slaves or to at least maintain property rights to unfree labor, the legislation did import one protective feature that had long been a part of Spanish but not Portuguese or Brazilian slave law: it protected the slave's right to a *peliculum,* or property that might be ultimately used in the purchase of an *alforria.* Although Brazilian courts had previously recognized the right to an *alforria* in special cases, usually involving military service to the state, the recognition of a legally enforceable right to self-purchase in the 1871 legislation was an indication of the growing strength of antislavery sentiment.[39]

That sentiment would find perhaps its clearest and most systematic expression in the writings of antislavery advocate Joaquim Nabuco. Nabuco's 1883 tract, *O abolicionismo,* would touch on many of the critical themes regarding race and slavery in the nineteenth-century Brazilian Empire. Nabuco's argument was one that went beyond abolition as a humanitarian measure. Abolition, he argued, was necessary to Brazilian progress. It was a measure that would transform the empire from a land of servile subjects to one of free citizens, and a nation of free citizens that would have an increased number of industrious European immigrants among its ranks. Nabuco's tract also showed his sensitivity to the ever-present fear of slave insurrection that was an indelible part of the culture in nineteenth-century Brazil. In his volume he cautioned slaves against insurrection, arguing that such would be both cowardly and criminal. Abolition was just, Nabuco argued, but it must be the product of a reasoned national consensus that produced legal change.[40]

Nabuco's discussion of slavery hit on two critical racial themes that would resonate even more strongly in the Brazil of the twentieth century. Like many Brazilians of the nineteenth century, Nabuco saw a greater

European presence in Brazil as essential to modernization and progress. Yet he also proudly contrasted what he saw as the absence of racial discrimination and the integration of people of color in Brazilian society with the stark practice of racial exclusion in the United States. Providing an early version of the notion of Brazil as a racial democracy, Nabuco argued that the Negro in Brazil was not an outsider but was instead an integral part of the Brazilian nation. He noted that African and slave ancestry was prevalent in Brazil and was not a mark of distinction and a cause for exclusion, as it was in the United States.[41]

The efforts of Nabuco and other abolitionists would finally come to fruition. Spurred on by slavery's increasing lack of viability — only a minority of Afro-Brazilians remained slaves, those who were legally enslaved increasingly were simply running away, and Brazil remained the lone slave-holding society in the Western Hemisphere — the Parliament enacted Lei Áurea in 1888, finally abolishing Brazilian slavery. Princess Isabel, in the absence of her father, Dom Pedro II, signed the legislation in May of that year, appropriately enough with an ornate golden pen. Four long centuries of Brazilian slavery, four centuries that brought four million souls from Angola, the Congo, Ghana, and the Bight of Biafra to new lands called Bahia, Pernambuco, Rio de Janeiro, Minas Gerais, São Paulo, and, yes, Santa Catarina and Rio Grande do Sul as well, forever linking the South American nation with the peoples and cultures of West Africa, had come to an end. The Brazilian Empire would fall to a republican coup the following year. One of the causes of that coup was diminished support for the monarchy on the part of planters dissatisfied with the royal family's abolitionist sympathies.[42]

What legacy did the world of race and slavery that dominated colonial and imperial Brazil leave to the Brazilian republic that would emerge in the twentieth century? This is a harder question to answer than is the analogous question for the United States. We are accustomed when speaking of race in the United States to trace patterns of racial exclusion back to the era of slavery. Racial exclusion had its origins in the American system of slavery. Jim Crow and other measures that made Afro-Americans in the United States a people apart not only socially but often legally as well can be traced to that system of slavery. As I hope to show later on, the story is not as simple and straightforward as we often think, but our tendency to link American slavery and later patterns of racial exclusion and subordination in the United States is essentially correct. In Brazil, the history and linkages are a bit more complicated. Slavery in Brazil — including the existence of a legally dependent category of manumitted individuals, *libertos* — certainly contributed to a Brazilian social structure where people of African descent were more likely to be found toward the bottom of the Brazilian social pyramid. Race and color prejudice were clearly a part of the culture of the Brazilian Empire, as were strong fears of Africans and African culture. *Branqueamento* (the desire to whiten Brazil through European immigration) was championed by even the leading antislavery statesmen and thinkers of the Empire, even before it became a well-articulated national policy in the early twentieth century.

And yet these prejudices, these preferences for Europeans and abhorrence of Africans and African culture, did not translate into categorical exclusion, at least as it would be known in the United States in the nineteenth and early part of the twentieth century. Successful mulattoes like Rebouças and Gama could and did have influence, sometimes at the highest level of Brazilian law and politics. The free Afro-Brazilian was fully acknowledged to be a citizen despite the fact that his nation practiced one of the more vigorous and indeed cruel brands of African slavery in the Americas. And like Rebouças there were people of African descent who could simultaneously decry racial discrimination while also defending Brazil's system of African slavery.

The paradoxes — or what to our North American eyes seem to be the paradoxes — of nineteenth-century Brazilian racial culture can in part be explained by demography. Colonial and imperial Brazil had too few white people to permit the kind of racial exclusion that would develop in the United States. Students of slavery have long known that societies engaged in the business of large-scale slaveholding — plantation agriculture, mining, and similar enterprises — need a large class of free nonslaveholding or small-scale slaveholding people to maintain a certain social equilibrium. The police and military forces that protect the slave society from external enemies and, even more important, from the internal threats posed by the slaves have to be drawn from this population; they cannot come exclusively or even principally from the minority of people who are large slaveholders. Also, many of the important economic tasks required by slave societies — the production of food, the work of artisans, and similar activities — are often left to free individuals, allowing slave owners to employ their slaves in what are seen as more lucrative production of cash crops or the extraction of valuable minerals. The relative absence of a class of free nonslaveholding yeoman white farmers and artisans such as existed in the American South doubtless contributed to a greater tolerance for the free Afro-Brazilian.

But something more than sheer demographic necessity was at work. The very hierarchical structure of Brazilian society, its rigid and undemocratic class structure, the power of Brazilian elites and the tendency of people in the lower strata of the social pyramid to defer to those above them also played a role in muting racial exclusion. As we shall see in the next chapter, much of the impulse for racial exclusion in the United States seems to have been a by-product of the nation's democratization and the often competitive relations that developed between poorer whites and the free Negro class that emerged after the revolution. That kind of democratization was not a feature of the social or political life of the Brazilian Empire. Power was held in the hands of a small, elite class of large landholders and slaveholders. That class had the ability to bestow favors and open the corridors of wealth and power to a privileged few like Rebouças and to maintain their hold on a society where personal contact and clientelism played a strong role in determining an individual's chances in life. This helped to lessen the likelihood of categorical racial exclusion despite the very real race and color prejudices that existed.

The experience with race and slavery in the nineteenth-century Brazilian Empire and, indeed, the preceding three centuries as a Portuguese colony would set the stage for patterns of race and racial domination in the twentieth century. Color differences between blacks and mulattoes would remain important, even making the notion of an "Afro-Brazilian" people somewhat problematic. Racial prejudices against Afro-Brazilians would remain strong, and the burden of the legacy of slavery would be a crippling one for many well into the twentieth century, even though there would be highly successful Brazilians of African descent. Brazilian law would erect no formal racial barriers to inclusion, but the Brazilian state would come to equate the Afro-Brazilian with an atavistic past to be overcome through extensive European immigration. The republic, now called the Old Republic, that would follow in the wake of Dom Pedro II's empire would be a long way from Ary Barroso's celebration of the African in Brazil.

CHAPTER THREE

Race, Democracy, and Inequality

ORIGINS OF THE AMERICAN DILEMMA

NO EVENT BETTER ILLUSTRATES THE DIFFERENCE between the Brazilian Empire and the young American republic than the *Dred Scott* case. Applauded and reviled at the time it was handed down, Chief Justice Roger B. Taney's opinion has vexed generations of students of the Supreme Court and the American Constitution. Most modern commentators agree that the decision was a bad one with bad consequences. It strengthened the South's "Peculiar Institution" and probably hastened secession and Civil War as well. Modern legal scholars also see the case as a vehicle against which to judge various strategies of constitutional interpretation. Is the Taney opinion an argument against a jurisprudence that too slavishly follows the original intentions of the Constitution's authors? How should Taney have come to grips with the evil inherent in the original Constitution, a document that recognized and protected chattel slavery despite its otherwise robust concerns for human liberty?[1]

We will return later to *Dred Scott*, but two elements of the Taney opinion are important for what they had to say about race and citizenship in the United States. First, Taney's opinion endorsed a robust view of the rights of citizens. Citizenship meant equality, a freedom from legal discrimination, and an untrammeled enjoyment of those rights specified in the Constitution and that were part of the Anglo-American heritage. Second, according to Taney, people of African descent, slave or free, native- or foreign-born, could not be citizens. A brief passage captures both Taney's robust view of the rights of citizens and his belief in the United States as an exclusively white republic:

It would give to persons of the negro race, who were recognized as citizens in any one State of the Union, the right to enter every other State whenever they pleased, singly or in companies, without pass or passport, and without obstruction, to sojourn there as long as they pleased, to go where they pleased at every hour of the day or night without molestation, unless they committed some violation of law for which a white man would be punished; and it would give them the full liberty of speech in public and in private upon all subjects upon which its own citizens might speak; to hold public meetings upon political affairs, and to keep and carry arms wherever they went.[2]

Dred Scott was the clearest expression of a view unique to the law of the United States. Throughout the Americas differing legal regimes supported systems of slavery based on race. Taney's opinion took American law a step further. It endorsed race-based citizenship. This perspective was far removed from the view of the Brazilian Empire. Dom Pedro I's empire could house both an often cruel brand of African slavery and a constitution that proclaimed citizenship and equality for all free Brazilians. The South American colossus could also be home to men like Afro-Brazilian statesman Antonio Rebouças. Some have argued that Taney's opinion was the logical and inevitable result of the system of race-based slavery that had developed on the North American continent. Others have contended that it stemmed from a unique hostility to manumission and citizenship embedded in Anglo-American law. Still others have argued that the Constitution itself inexorably led to Taney's exclusionary vision, that Taney was simply expressing the Framers' vision that the new nation was to be exclusively a republic of free white men. These views rest on a somewhat problematic foundation. The path to Taney's jurisprudence of exclusion was tortured and difficult, filled with roads not taken, detours, near misses, and influential advocates for alternative visions. It was not primarily the product of the colonial experience with African and Afro-American slavery. Nor was it, as Taney insisted, largely the result of the worldview that informed the men who wrote and ratified the Constitution. It was, ironically enough, more related to the greater democratization and heightened egalitarianism of the United States in the antebellum era and how the nation would handle the tensions inherent in a society that celebrated freedom and equality while also practicing slavery and racial inequality.

This chapter will explore the path the American nation took toward Taney's racially exclusive vision. It will also look at the struggle waged against that vision. That struggle, which included a cataclysmic conflict, the American Civil War, would meet with partial success — the abolition of slavery and the adoption of the principle of racial equality into the Constitution. This chapter will spend some time looking at the law of slavery in the United States. It will do so with a somewhat narrow focus. The concern here is with how American law and the broader culture generally came to support a doctrine of racial exclusion. This is part of the multiple definitions of slave treatment that Eugene Genovese once suggested to comparative historians as falling under the category of "access to freedom and citizenship." All of the slave societies of the Americas had strong racial and color prejudices, especially toward people who were visibly of African descent. The antebellum United States was unique in that it was the slave society that put up the most in the way of legal obstacles to manumission. It also offered the most explicitly racial defense of holding human beings in bondage. The law in antebellum America was also singular in preventing free Afro-Americans from enjoying the rights of citizens.[3]

And yet this focus on race and slavery in antebellum America can leave us with an incomplete — indeed, distorted — picture of the development of race as both a social and legal phenomenon in American history. It is easy to see why the nation's historians have traditionally made the Cotton Kingdom (the five decades after the War of 1812) their major focus. The politics of slavery and sectional conflict that played out in that brief era provided the prelude to the U.S. Civil War. It was also an era in which American racial attitudes including strong patterns of racial exclusion crystallized.

But that focus on the last half century of American slavery has served to obscure a larger history, that of the two centuries of slavery before the Cotton Kingdom. What the law and the broader culture said about slavery and race during those two centuries was complex, often contradictory. At times, the law's protection of slavery was clear; at other times, less so. Race mattered, but not in the all-consuming way suggested in Taney's opinion. At certain times, in certain places, the law protected manumission; at other times not. The law at times treated free people of color as citizens with rights and duties similar to those of other citizens. At other times the law limited the privileges of free Afro-Americans, although rarely with the rigidity that would occur in the nineteenth century. If we want to understand how race became the critical dividing line in American culture and if we want to understand how the law in antebellum America became uniquely hostile to Negro citizenship, this is a history we must engage.

If we were to turn back the calendar some three centuries before 1857 and Taney's opinion, we would find little in English law or custom that might have caused us to predict either an opinion like Taney's or the robust pattern of racial exclusion of which it was a part. Spain and Portugal had well-developed slave codes and were home to thousands of African slaves even before they embarked on the business of New World conquest and settlement. This was not the case with England. Africans were largely unknown there before the seventeenth century. The common law was distinctly hostile to slavery, which had withered away in medieval times. By the sixteenth century even villeinage, a status roughly comparable to serf status, was largely a distant memory.[4]

English jurists of the early modern period frequently saw the common law and English custom as reflections not only of the law of England, but that of nature as well. They did so with respect to slavery. As early as 1569, in what is known as Cartwright's case, an English court ordered a Russian slave who had been brought to England freed on the grounds "that England was too pure an air for slaves to breath in," that his very presence in the kingdom had freed him. Cartwright's case and the more well known eighteenth-century decision by Lord Mansfield in *Somersett v. Stewart*, provided a basis for slaves brought to England to petition for release by means of the writ of habeas corpus.[5]

But if English jurists deciding the fate of slaves brought to England felt free to proclaim their freedom and slavery's incompatibility with the common law, the opening of English settlements in the Americas would bring about a modification of the law's hostility toward slavery. New statutes in the colonies permitted slavery. The new laws would be enforced by English jurists and English courts despite the common law's abhorrence of slavery. The common law would yield to England's status as a major slave-trading power.[6]

But even as English law came to recognize slavery in the Americas and to enforce property rights in human beings, the core principle that slavery violated both common and natural law remained a part of legal doctrine. Jurists and legal commentators recognized that the enslavement of human beings, even radically different ones like Africans, could not be justified. Eighteenth-century English legal commentator William Blackstone took issue with the different justifications for slavery. He noted that slavery was considered absolutely contrary to English law and that frequent justifications, such as the taking of captives in just wars or the fiction that slaves had sold themselves and were along with their children bound to a master and his heirs in perpetuity, were illogical and did not serve to provide justification for human bondage. Blackstone also stressed that the race or religion of the enslaved individual did not provide a justification for slavery.[7]

Nonetheless the colonies developed a body of law governing slavery and the status of peoples of African descent. This legal transformation began in Barbados early in the seventeenth century. There the law was refashioned to accommodate the wishes of planters, who saw the possibilities of great wealth in the cultivation of sugar. The law was transformed to allow these planters to work, often to death, gangs of Irish and African laborers who would cultivate the lucrative but deadly crop.[8]

The law of slavery would spread to North America. This body of law was statutorily based, enacted by local legislatures. It was responsive to local conditions and would change over time with shifting needs. In a sense this mirrored American law more broadly in the seventeenth century. The full-blown, refined common law of England did not migrate easily to the rough American colonies. The common law required learned jurists and advocates skilled in winding their way through the often obtuse system of writs embedded in the forms of action that characterized much of the day-to-day life of the law in early modern England. It also required practitioners who could understand a little Latin and Law French and had access to the reporters and treatises on which much of common law decision making rested. The common law required a honing of what Elizabethan jurist Sir Edward Coke called the lawyer's "artificial reasoning," a reasoning based on the education and training that was perhaps common to Coke's peers, but rare in the frontier colonies of seventeenth-century America.[9]

Law in this setting was informal, lawyers rare. Courts and legislatures were often combined. Disputes were brought before presiding officers who knew little of the subtleties of the common law or indeed of any other legal system. The function of the courts was to keep the peace and to resolve disputes when more informal methods failed. In such a system the consistency and predictability normally found in more settled legal systems was often absent. Decisions by courts were more likely to reflect a community's rough sense of justice and the immediate needs of powerful persons than to follow the complexities of the common law.[10]

If the technical skills of the common law were uncommon in the new colonies, American lawmakers were nonetheless aware, at least in broad outline, of the demands of English law, including an awareness of the problematic nature of slavery. If the laws enacted in seventeenth-century America are any indication, colonial lawmakers consciously sought to reconcile their desire for cheap African labor with the common law's prohibition against slavery. Two examples are illustrative. New England Puritans made an early, legalistic effort to justify slaveholding in the face of disapproval of both the common law and Deuteronomy's prohibition against man-stealing. In the 1640s, they would pass legislation authorizing the enslavement of those allegedly taken captive in "just wars." The introduction of slavery in seventeenth-century Virginia appears to have been somewhat less sure-footed. The first Africans bought and sold in Virginia were bought and sold without the benefit of a statute. Some of those who came to the colony early in the seventeenth century were treated as indentured servants. They worked for a number of years and were set free. Only later, in the 1660s, did Virginia law come to formally recognize a slave status. Interestingly enough, that change in status was initially justified less on racial grounds than religious ones. The Africans, so the rationale went, were to have their souls saved by being brought to Virginia. There they could be saved through conversion by Christian masters. To the embarrassment of colonial authorities many masters refused to convert their slaves for fear that their conversion would cast doubt on the legality of their continued enslavement. To allay these fears, the Virginia Assembly passed legislation in 1667 indicating that slaves would not be set free by virtue of conversion.[11]

The efforts of colonial legislatures to codify a body of rules that would govern this new experience with race and slavery would be greatly influenced by a unique aspect of American slavery. The North American continent was the site of a successful effort to build a system of industrial slavery based on the labor of enslaved Africans in a society with a white majority. This effort created a body of racial dynamics appreciably different from those found in the colonies of Spain and Portugal. Plantation slavery in Latin America took place against a backdrop of small white populations ruling over larger populations of conquered indigenous peoples and enslaved Africans. Population dynamics produced intense pressures to allow for possibilities of racial mobility and an acceptance of free people of color into the dominant society. The law accommodated these pressures.

Population would also play a critical role in developing cultural and legal norms governing race and slavery on the North American mainland. The English colonies from the beginning were conceived as white settlements, re-creations in many ways of English society. They received far fewer — less than 4 percent overall — of the victims of the African slave trade than the more vigorous plantation economies of the Caribbean and Brazil. And unlike the Spaniards, the English had little desire to rule over large indigenous empires. They were content for the most part to keep Indians outside their settlements. Colonial governors successfully encouraged white settlement in order to ensure the economic and military viability of colonies. A majority of the population in the American colonies was white, even in those southern colonies whose economies rested to a significant degree on plantation agriculture and slave labor. Only South Carolina in the early decades of the eighteenth century would have a black majority.[12]

Colonial America's white majority was brought about in part through vigorous recruitment of English, Irish, and other white indentured servants. They were not slaves; still, they were not exactly free laborers as we might use the term today. Before the nineteenth century, most English laborers spent a considerable portion of their working lives under legal compulsion to work for a master. Apprentices, journeymen, and servants were frequently under strict contractual obligations to work for their masters for a specified period of time. They were not free to leave their employment even if they encountered harsh conditions or saw better prospects elsewhere. Persons so bound could be subject to cruel and demeaning treatment, including corporal punishment. The situation for indentured servants in the American colonies could be even direr. Some were individuals convicted of what we today would consider rather petty crimes and offered the choice between the gallows and transportation to the Americas. Others were the poor of England or Ireland, unable to find land. Indenture contracts usually promised land and the tools to make a new start once the requisite term of years had been fulfilled.[13]

The demography of slavery and servitude in colonial America would help to create a world of interracial contact that in many ways was surprisingly more open and fluid than that which was to be found later in Taney's era. Historians of race relations, particularly relations between blacks and white servants, have noted the remarkably free level of interracial association among the unfree classes in colonial America. In the towns and cities of the North there was an often raucous street life attended to by servants, apprentices, and slaves. Town officials in northern colonies left frequent records of their complaints of the exuberant and riotous tumult caused by "boys and Negroes" attesting to the frequent multiracial mingling of the lower classes in bondage.[14]

This sort of interracial association was also present in the Chesapeake region, comprising the modern states of Maryland and Virginia, and in North Carolina. It seemed to take place even in the face of efforts by colonial authorities to use the law to curtail it. Historians of slavery in colonial Virginia generally agree that until the latter part of the seventeenth century, the legal and social distinctions between the black and white servants who labored in the colony's tobacco fields were often slight. Many of the blacks, at least initially, were treated like indentured servants. Many of the whites seemed to have seen little reason to make racial distinctions. The two groups worked together and frequently hatched plots to escape bondage together. White indentured servants and blacks frequently had sexual relations with each other. Mulatto children with white mothers appear to have been common well into the eighteenth century. The ability of the two groups to freely associate with each other was probably helped because initially many of the blacks were not Africans but "Atlantic Creoles" — persons of African descent with a familiarity with European languages and cultures gained in Europe or the Americas. This familiarity doubtless made them somewhat less alien and frightening to the white servants who toiled beside them.[15]

The law would take time to adapt to this new phenomenon of interracial association. Winthrop Jordan and other historians have made the case for an English predisposition toward antiblack prejudice. The record in Virginia and other colonies indicate a trek toward a body of law designed to foster racial separation that was uneven and tentative. It was dictated more by the evolving needs of the emerging slave system than by ancient prejudices. The English of the seventeenth century were a broadly intolerant people, eager to celebrate what they termed the rights of Englishmen and also convinced that those rights belonged peculiarly to them. Their subjugation of the Irish was ruthless. For the English, the division between English and non-English was probably, at least initially, of as great a concern as the distinction between black and white. Over time, the English concern with providing stricter regulation for those who were not English would change into a concern with making sure that the law enforced distinctions between black and white. By the end of the seventeenth century, a number of developments began contributing to a greater tendency to make legal distinctions between whites held to terms of service and blacks, who were increasingly being treated as slaves. Owners of plantations were becoming more and more aware that white labor, even the labor of indentured servants, was more expensive than that of Africans, who could be purchased for life. The demand for Africans as unskilled laborers on the region's farms and plantations grew. Increasingly white indentured servants were looked to for skilled labor and to oversee plantations. This new set of labor demands also meant that slaves brought into the mainland colonies would increasingly be Africans and not the Atlantic Creoles that had come earlier in the seventeenth century.[16]

The fear that black slaves and white indentured servants might make common cause provided yet another reason for lawmakers to make racial distinctions. As Edmund Morgan has argued, Bacon's Rebellion of 1676 frightened Virginia authorities with the possibilities of broad-based interracial revolt by the unfree laboring classes. That experience prompted legislation designed to curtail the easy intimacy that had existed between the two groups. Morgan informs us that Virginia authorities, fearing the possibility of both servile unity and servile insurrection, deliberately used the law to create a sense of racial separation between the two groups. The law began to prescribe harsher punishments for blacks and whites. A 1705 act illustrates the law's new direction. It provided for the dismemberment of unruly slaves. It also confiscated property owned by slaves, often a critical precursor to manumission. The act specifically protected the property of white indentured servants.[17]

With the development of a system of slavery rooted in racial distinctions, the law began to define race and slave status. It made more efforts to prevent racial commingling. Virginia led the way early in the eighteenth century with statutes prohibiting interracial marriage and sexual relations. The colony also enacted statutes providing legal definitions of the races and the inheritance of slave status. Whether a child was born slave or free was determined by the mother's status. Racial classifications could be some-what more complicated. In light of the rather strict rules of "hypodescent" (the "one drop rule" that would develop later in American history), the law approached the issue of how to classify the children of interracial unions with some degree of ambivalence. Some children of mixed unions were classified as mulattoes, others as whites. The early statute recognized three races, white, Indian, and "Negro and mulatto." That third category is significant. It indicates that while whites fairly early on recognized a difference between Negroes and mulattoes, the difference never attained the kind of legal or cultural salience that it attained in other parts of the Americas.[18]

It is harder to make broad generalizations about the law of slavery in colonial America than colonial Latin America. The law could be and often was incredibly harsh. In some of the southern colonies the slave was outside the law's peace, or protection. The killing of a slave was a mere trespass, an interference with the owner's property rights, nothing more. If done by the owner, it was no offense at all. Virginia law in the early eighteenth century made promiscuous use of outlawry — a common law status that put an individual totally outside the law's protection allowing an individual to be killed by anyone with impunity — as a means of controlling runaway slaves. Dismemberment was a common punishment for slaves in Virginia before the Revolution. The colony also denied benefit of clergy — the common law's device for relaxing the excessive use of the death penalty — to blacks slave and free. The northern colonies were different, by and large extending the law's protection to the slave.[19]

The often harsh and hierarchical world that was colonial America was in many ways less race-conscious than Taney's Jacksonian America. Race and racial discrimination were, to be sure, part of the law and culture. Blacks were for the most part in bondage, but then again, many whites spent a significant portion of their lives in servitude before finally becoming fully free men and women. Slavery in the century and a half between its introduction on the North American continent and the American Revolution took place in an environment that was largely unapologetic about hierarchy, servitude, and slavery, early seventeenth-century efforts to find a justification for slavery notwithstanding.

This largely unquestioned acceptance of hierarchy and servitude coexisted with a tolerance for manumission and possibilities for equal rights for free Negroes that would become more strained in the nineteenth century. If Spanish law provided specific protection for the manumission contract and the slave's ability to sue for its enforcement, the courts in some colonies also allowed slaves to sue their owners to enforce manumission agreements despite the absence of a generalized source of law like *Las siete partidas* specifying the contractual rights of slaves.

The legal status of free Afro-Americans before the revolution varied. At a time when citizenship was not formally defined, it is probably best to approach the question of free Negro citizenship by looking at how hostile or receptive a colony's laws might be to manumission and the rights granted free Afro-Americans. Virginia's Eastern Shore in the seventeenth century was the home to a small, free, and somewhat prosperous African American community. A few purchased bondsmen of their own, African slaves, and even some white indentured servants. In the relatively racially fluid atmosphere that still existed at the turn of the eighteenth century, an individual's legal rights seem to have been remarkably independent of race. A few blacks in bondage in Virginia were able to successfully bring suits for freedom. There are indications that a few propertied black men may have voted or served on juries at the end of the seventeenth century. The pattern of multiracial association of the unfree laboring classes common in the seventeenth century seems to have persisted several decades into the eighteenth despite the efforts of the law to create stronger barriers between blacks and whites.[20]

Racial dynamics were considerably different in South Carolina. There, the colony's population was nearly two-thirds black, and the law and custom regulating slavery and race often bore a greater resemblance to patterns found in parts of colonial Brazil and the Caribbean. South Carolina's earliest slave code was taken from the draconian Barbadian code. As was the case elsewhere, a legal regime that permitted cruel treatment of slaves was not necessarily hostile to black citizenship. Unlike other colonies, South Carolina in the first decades of the eighteenth century lacked a large population of white indentured servants or recently freed indentured servants who would supply the essential free nonslaveholding class critical to the survival of plantation slave societies.

South Carolina law responded to this need. In the early decades of the eighteenth century, the colony's code gave a surprisingly broad body of rights to free Negroes. Black men who met the requisite property qualifications could vote. Free Negroes served in the militia. Because the colony bordered on Spanish Florida, had a majority slave population, and was close to hostile Indian groups, authorities were anxious to secure the colony's defenses. Even slaves could participate in the colony's defense and gain freedom by killing invaders in time of war.[21]

Population dynamics were different in the North. Thousands of slaves lived in the Middle Atlantic and New England colonies. Their history has to be taken into account in any overall discussion of the history of American race relations. The proportion of slaves in the overall population of the North was small, never exceeding some 5 percent of the total. Nonetheless, cities like New York, Newport, and Philadelphia all had relatively large concentrations of slave populations, as did southern Rhode Island. The law was less strict in part because of the small numbers. Northern colonies were less preoccupied with slaves and their potential threat to a colony's security. If the law in Virginia was concerned that slaves and indentured servants might combine and threaten the hegemony of planters, slavery in northern venues rarely raised similar concerns. The law could be draconian, as was the case with New York's alleged Negro Arson plot of 1741. But that was an exception. For the most part the social control of the slave population was seen as less a question of warding off threats to the overall society and more a matter of keeping the peace, often broken by slaves, servants, and other members of the rowdier classes.[22]

Some slaves in the North were able to secure their freedom through self-purchase. Urban areas, with their multitude of small jobs and short distances between potential employers, offered slaves the best possibilities for earning money and eventual freedom. At least some slaves in the North appear to have been able to appeal to the courts for enforcement of manumission agreements. Free Negroes were subject to legal discrimination, but it was not particularly systematic. In New England, free black men were barred from the militia and required to labor on public works projects as a substitute. Nevertheless, black men from those colonies served in expeditionary forces during the French and Indian War and were generally permitted to own arms. Free Negroes who met the requisite property qualifications were not explicitly barred from voting, and it is likely that a few did.[23]

The law took notice of race. We can find cases and statutes specifying legal disabilities for persons of African descent, slave and free. At times, the law might be a friend to the slave who sought manumission. At other times, it was hostile. A Virginia act of 1723 prohibited manumission except in cases where the slave had performed meritorious service for the colony. We can find class legislation restricting the rights of free Afro-Americans and yet also locate prominent free Negroes in the colonial era who seem to have exercised the rights of citizens and to have received a general acceptance from whites while doing so. The law varied over time and place, reflecting the highly localized character of American law in the colonial period.[24]

The development of laws governing race and status took place against the background of a world in which slavery was largely unquestioned. If the common law early on had pronounced slavery illegal, the institution nonetheless thrived throughout the American colonies. By the middle of the eighteenth century, the holding of slaves was rarely challenged. The yearning of slaves for freedom was recognized. Individual slaves were set free. But there were few broader antislavery stirrings. The Quakers in Pennsylvania to be sure had early on come around to the view that the practice violated God's law and should not be part of the law of their earthly commonwealth, but they were not able to turn this new revelation into law, at least not immediately.[25]

It would take the American Revolution to cause large-scale public questioning of slavery. It would also cause American law to begin to focus on questions of race and citizenship in ways that had not generally occurred before. The revolution that began with Jefferson's ringing declaration proclaiming the equality of all men helped generate for the first time strong, public antislavery sentiment. That sentiment would in turn help create a free Negro class with sufficient numbers to be a significant social category and not an anomaly as had been the case in most colonies. Between the 1770s and 1810, the free black population of the North went from an insignificant few hundred persons to a size of fifty thousand. The revolution helped create this class in different ways. As was the case in the republics carved out of the Spanish Empire, a number of black men gained their freedom by fighting with the forces struggling for independence. This was particularly true in New England. Although Afro-Americans from that region made up only 5 percent of the new nation's total black population, they were 50 percent of the black men in the American forces.[26]

The Afro-American role in the revolution played a major role in weakening northern slavery. But slavery would also be weakened by the new sentiments brought about by the revolution. What had begun as a fight to reaffirm the traditional rights of Englishmen had for many broadened into a greater struggle for human rights. The very rhetoric of the revolutionary era pamphleteers with their constant comparison of the colonists' plight to slavery and the likening of British rule to the chains of bondage doubtless caused some to reexamine the previously unquestioned practice of holding men and women as slaves. Many observers came to recognize slavery's incompatibility with the liberal spirit of the new age.[27]

In wake of the revolution, many in the new nation began to act on these new ideals. State supreme courts in Massachusetts and Vermont moved boldly, taking seriously declarations in their new state constitutions proclaiming all men free and equal. They rendered decisions abolishing slavery on the grounds that it was incompatible with the new constitutional principles. Other states — Connecticut, Rhode Island, Pennsylvania, New Jersey, and New York — passed gradual emancipation statutes freeing children born after the enactment of the legislation, usually after they served terms of indenture well into their twenties. There was a danger in these emancipations. Northern slave owners who owned the labor of black children who were to be freed in their twenties had a wasting economic asset, one that could be made much more valuable by sale to purchasers in the slave states. This occurred, although it was often prevented by legislation and by adverse public sentiment. If the progress of northern abolition was gradual and at times halting, it was nonetheless the first large-scale emancipation in the Western Hemisphere, a testament to the power of the ideals generated by the American Revolution.[28]

This new antislavery sentiment would also spread to at least the Upper South. Thousands of slave owners, inspired in part by the ideals of the new age, manumitted their slaves. Virginia in 1782 passed legislation specifically permitting manumission, removing restrictions passed earlier in the century. In Maryland a 1796 Act Concerning Negroes provided for relatively liberal procedures for manumission, including the right of slaves to petition courts in disputed cases.[29]

Virginia jurist St. George Tucker, in his "On the State of Slavery in Virginia," captured the conflicting sentiments of some antislavery Virginians in the postrevolutionary era. Tucker saw profound evil in slavery and its utter inconsistency with the ideals of the revolution. He captured the tragic irony of race in the United States in ways that would remain prophetic for generations to come: "Whilst America hath been the land of promise to Europeans and their descendants, it hath been the vale of death to millions of the wretched sons of Africa."[30]

These sentiments did not lead him to support immediate abolition. Like Jefferson, Tucker had a vision of Virginia as a republic of free white men where Negroes could not be citizens and indeed would be tolerated only in very small numbers, if at all. He proposed that Virginia end slavery through a gradual emancipation scheme that by his calculations would have taken a century to complete. Tucker argued that his proposal would ultimately end slavery while also protecting the property rights of masters. He went further. People emancipated by his scheme or by voluntary manumissions would not be citizens: "Let no negro or mulatto be capable of taking, holding or exercising any public office, freehold, franchise or privilege or any estate in lands. . . . Nor of keeping or bearing arms. . . . Nor of contracting matrimony with any other than a negroe or mulattoe; nor be an attorney; nor be a juror; nor a witness in any court of judicature, except against, or between negroes and mulattoes . . . nor capable of making any will or testament."[31]

Tucker proposed these stark restrictions in an effort to further his dream of a white republic. Writing in 1805 with fears that the Haitian rebellion that had traumatized slave societies throughout the Americas might be replicated in Virginia, Tucker wanted to promote free Negro emigration. Realizing that large-scale expatriation to Africa was impractical, Tucker proposed a regime of severe legal restrictions for free Negroes that would prompt many to emigrate voluntarily, perhaps to the western frontier but in any event away from settled white society.

Tucker's essay also discusses how the new debate over slavery helped bring about legal change. Virginia law changed both in response to the critics of slavery and probably in response to the internal doubts of slaveholders as well. Tucker tells us how the law began to change. A 1788 statute specifically placed slaves within the law's protection making it an unlawful homicide to kill a slave without legal justification or excuse. Benefit of clergy was extended to slaves. The outlawing of runaway slaves, placing them totally outside the law's protection, was prohibited. Slaves were allowed counsel in criminal cases. These ameliorations of the criminal code had significant limitations. A white person, even a master, could be prosecuted for the murder of a slave. But as a practical matter, it would be hard to bring such a case to trial. Distinguishing between murder and the master's right to discipline his slaves would be difficult, and most authorities would have been reluctant to look into such a case. Even in those egregious cases that might cause authorities to prosecute, the most likely witnesses, other slaves, were forbidden by law from testifying against whites. Slaves could have defense counsel, but Afro-Americans slave or free were barred from juries. If the rigors of Virginia's slave code were softened somewhat after the revolution, the law still left considerable room for harsh treatment.[32]

Tucker's proposal to deny free Negroes the rights of citizens reflected Virginia law. But surprisingly, Virginia was something of an exception. The libertarian sentiment that put the northern states on the path to emancipation and that brought about tens of thousands of private manumissions in the Upper South seemed to have taken place with an amazing openness to the possibility of free Negro citizenship. We know this best by looking at black suffrage. Virginia, South Carolina, and Georgia were alone in restricting the vote to white men. All the other states drafted state constitutional provisions or suffrage statutes allowing free black men to vote. There were property qualifications, to be sure, and these kept the number of Afro-American voters relatively small in the late eighteenth century. But it is significant that the founding generation had made a determination that property and not race would determine who would be enfranchised.

This was no accident, no slip of the drafter's pen. There was strong opposition to black suffrage. Measures designed to limit the vote to white men were proposed, debated, and defeated. In Massachusetts, a proposed state constitution containing a provision restricting the ballot to white men was defeated in a 1778 referendum. The state constitution adopted in 1780 had no such restriction. In 1785, New York's Council of Revision rejected proposed legislation limiting the ballot to white men. Pennsylvania's constitution of 1790 had no racial restrictions on voting.[33]

Perhaps it is not so remarkable that northern states permitted Negro suffrage. The black populations were small. Slavery was being abolished. The former slaves had done their part and then some in the war for independence. So what if a few got to vote? Why write restrictions into the new constitutions so clearly contrary to the spirit of the new age? That is an understandable explanation of what went on in the emerging free states.

What is somewhat harder to explain is that this same unwillingness to write explicit racial restrictions existed in the slave states as well. Delaware and Maryland were slave states. Delaware allowed black men to vote. Black men who were born free could vote in Maryland, although those who were manumitted could not. Ira Berlin informs us that in Maryland, one black man was actually a candidate for the House of Delegates in 1792. Kentucky also permitted black suffrage in this period. Black voting rights would be lost in these states early in the nineteenth century.[34]

North Carolina and Tennessee in the late eighteenth century are particularly important to any discussion of Afro-American citizenship in antebellum America. Both states allowed free black men to vote and would continue to do so well into the nineteenth century. The original eighteenth-century constitutions of both states allowed free black men to vote. Both states also allowed free Negroes to serve in the militia well into the nineteenth century. North Carolina law also extended to free Negroes another privilege normally reserved for whites, immunity from having slaves testify against them in court. If the law supported slavery, it was less inclined to demand racial exclusion than it would later in the state's history.[35]

This relative absence of racial exclusion would also find its way into national law. Provision 4 of the Articles of Confederation granted the free inhabitants of each state the privileges and immunities of free citizens of several states including the right to enter and leave each state. A proposal that would have allowed only free whites to be recognized as citizens was defeated. The Constitution protected slavery through its Fugitive Slave Clause but did not distinguish between free blacks and free whites in the apportionment of representatives.[36]

This eighteenth-century equality thesis can be pushed too far. The law discriminated. In northern states a number of cities and towns passed ordinances requiring free Negroes to post bonds and prove their free status before moving into a new town. The Militia Act of 1792 restricted membership in the militia to white men. Congress enacted legislation restricting postal employment to white men. Considerable social prejudice existed, and free black people often had to wage a difficult struggle to exercise their rights. The right of Afro-American men to vote in Massachusetts was firmly established because black merchant Paul Cuffee and other free Negroes petitioned the courts and state legislature in the 1780s. Prejudice and discrimination existed, but the absence of official legal discrimination in the nation's fundamental charters in the first generation after the revolution was remarkable. There were conscious, albeit contested, decisions not to make racial exclusion a part of those laws that defined the rights of the American people.[37]

That would change in the nineteenth century. The relative racial liberalism of the late eighteenth century would increasingly yield to a new less tolerant racial climate. This process would accelerate after the War of 1812, finding its way into the nation's politics and the nation's laws. Race had an importance in antebellum America that was rarely if ever matched elsewhere in the hemisphere. There would be many reasons for this. It is hard to sort out the different combinations of economic and demographic pressures and cultural and social influences that help give race this paramount importance. The demography of American slavery and the American slave trade certainly played a critical role. Relatively few Africans came to the United States. By the nineteenth century, most American slaves were American-born. This would have a profound cultural impact that would affect relations both between masters and slaves and between blacks and whites. A smaller, Creole slave population would mean less pronounced cultural differences between whites and blacks. Religion would also play a role in lessening black and white cultural differences in the United States. The Protestant denominations of the United States were less receptive to the kind of blending of traditional African religions with Western Christianity than was the Catholic Church in Latin America. The conversion of Afro-Americans to the American Protestant version of Christianity would be another reason for the break with the African past.

This cultural convergence would influence both the law of slavery and how the law treated race. Historian Thomas Morris makes a convincing argument that the softening of the law of slavery coincided with and was related to the cultural convergence that occurred in the South after the American Revolution. Both master and slave were born on American soil. Slaves spoke English and increasingly were Christian. It became more difficult for slave owners and other whites to adhere to the earlier legal vision of a slave population totally outside the law's peace. The law's protection would, at least nominally, be extended to the new American-born slaves in ways that had not been done for their African-born parents or grandparents. That the Americanization of the slave population coincided with the Enlightenment and the rise of antislavery sentiment only heightened the development of the idea of more humane treatment of slaves as both a legal and cultural norm.[38]

The Americanization of the slave population and the existence of the American South as a slave society with a majority population of free non-slaveholding whites would also shape the dynamics of racial exclusion. In Brazil, the free Afro-Brazilian could draw nearer to the dominant white population in part because their shared Luso-Brazilian culture provided a boundary between them and the African-born slaves. A Brazilian-born free mulatto like Rebouças could feel little identification with the African slaves in his midst and share many of the fears of his white contemporaries concerning potential African rebelliousness or barbarism. Culture in that context did not erase racial barriers, but it did mitigate them.

With perhaps the exception of French-speaking parishes in Louisiana, culture or cultural affinity played less of a role in creating bonds between whites and Afro-Americans in the American South. The smaller African presence in the nineteenth-century U.S. slave population would serve to decrease the relative emphasis on cultural differences between blacks and whites and to increase the attention paid to racial or supposed racial differences. Fear of slave rebelliousness was always present, but that fear was generally not focused on a fear of African rebelliousness. In other parts of the Americas, such rebelliousness was capable of creating reconstituted African societies that challenged the European and Brazilian empires. South Carolina's Stono Rebellion and the wars between the United States and the Seminole nation were among the more serious of the American slave rebellions. They paled in comparison to the century-long struggle waged by Brazilian slaves in sixteenth-century Palmares, or the Haitian Revolution at the end of the eighteenth. White southerners, unlike white Brazilians of the nineteenth century, were less likely to see free Afro-Americans as a people with whom they shared a common culture that created a bond against African slaves. Instead, they were more inclined to see free Negroes as a people whose shared racial identity with the enslaved population made their loyalty suspect and their possibilities for making common cause with slaves great.[39]

A different body of family law and a different culture of familial relations also contributed to stronger patterns of racial exclusion in the United States than in Latin America. If the slave master had an ability to formally

MAN's ability, NOT (woman's

acknowledge, adopt, and legitimate his slave children in Latin America, U.S. law and culture provided even a willing master with fewer possibilities for the formal recognition and protection of their slave children. Legal adoption was largely unknown in the United States until the 1850s. American law, like English law before it, did not provide mechanisms for legitimation of children born out of wedlock. Anglo-American culture, unlike the cultures of Spain and Portugal, did not provide much tolerance for open and acknowledged "second families" with enforceable claims to support and estates. If the mulatto child of a slave owner in Latin America could be adopted, legitimated, and brought into the dominant society, the possibilities for such in the United States were considerably less. This inability to formally recognize and care for such children contributed to strong patterns of racial exclusion in the United States. It also contributed to the American notion of caste that black and white were hermetically sealed categories with family connections across the races rarely acknowledged or given legal weight.[40]

The racial dynamics of the new century would bring a new vigor to racial exclusion and the call for yet more racial exclusion. Part of this is easy to explain. Slavery's economic importance was increasing. The transformation of the South's economy brought about by the cotton revolution would bring a new vitality to slavery. It would greatly increase the demand for slave labor, particularly after the closing of the African slave trade in 1808. The heightened demand for slave labor would ultimately draw slaves from urban areas, reducing the number of slaves able to hire themselves out and ultimately purchase their freedom.[41]

This vitalization of the Cotton Kingdom would coincide with a broader democratization of American life. Where once suffrage had been the province of gentlemen with property, the vote would be granted to all men or at least all white men. If many whites before the revolution were indentured servants, the law increasingly in the nineteenth century looked with disfavor on indenture contracts. State criminal codes were being amended to make punishments less severe. The new nation was a leader in limiting capital punishment. In a number of states, common schools were being established, providing education for the children of the poor. Ordinary men through jury service had a tremendous influence on the legal process. Above all, an ideology of classlessness was developing in antebellum America, a rejection of traditional notions of aristocrats and betters.

The sharp contrast between this egalitarian ideology and the growing use of slave labor, forced anew the question of the morality of slavery. If the revolution had forced southern statesmen into an apologetic, prudential defense of the institution, the new economic realities would produce a more muscular defense of slavery. Slavery was not evil! It was a positive good, the best way to order relations between the inferior Negro and the superior white race. Race had long been part of the justification for slavery, but in a colonial America where people were accustomed to sharp differences in status, unfree labor, and the frequent degradation of the poor and unfortunate, race did not require emphasis as a rationale for enslavement. In the Cotton Kingdom, however, the situation was different. The proslavery ideology became even more robust, with apologists arguing not only that the institution was essential to the progress of southern whites but also that it provided the most humane order for the treatment of blacks. This view was often romanticized, forming the basis for a myth of a South of benevolent masters and contented slaves that would linger in American historiography and popular culture well into the twentieth century.

One proslavery apologist, South Carolinian James Hammond, argued that not only did slavery not contradict the new egalitarian order, it was instead its very foundation. Hammond's "mud sill" theory, that the subordination of African Americans elevated and equalized all whites, provides an important insight. It gives a clue why so many nonslaveholding whites in the South and elsewhere felt a stake in both slavery and white supremacy. In the popular democracy that was nineteenth-century America, that psychological stake would play a critical role in constructing the new less hospitable racial atmosphere. At a time when state constitution law was decided by referenda or popularly elected delegations, that popular stake in white supremacy would have critical and often devastating effects.[42]

This new atmosphere was not sympathetic to the growth or even presence of the free Negro population. Legislation limiting both the ability of masters to manumit their slaves and the ability of those who were manumitted to remain in residence was passed in a number of states. Southern propagandists stressed the degraded conditions of free blacks, contrasting their conditions unfavorably with that of slaves. Free blacks were a troublesome presence. The white South feared their making common cause with slaves. Their very existence contradicted the southern justifi-

cation for its departure from the nation's liberal norms. Cases where free
Negroes thrived or even survived contradicted the idea that blacks were
uniquely dependent and best suited to a benevolent, paternalistic form
of slavery.[43] *[handwritten: women best suited for the house]*

Southern law reflected this new ideological turn. If Upper South states
in the late eighteenth century were willing to countenance manumission
and the growth of a free Negro class, the new states of the Cotton Kingdom
were hostile to both. With the exception of Louisiana, the laws of the new
states admitted in the nineteenth century largely reflected this hostility.
Legislation in the new western states usually restricted manumission, requiring that slaves who were set free leave the state shortly thereafter or
risk reenslavement. The American Colonization Society was formed in
1817 to promote the expatriation of free Afro-Americans to Africa.

Manumissions nonetheless continued, particularly in urban areas. In
Maryland the need for labor allowed some slaves to negotiate terms permitting them to hire themselves out and ultimately purchase their freedom.
These agreements usually included agreed-upon prices for self-purchase
and agreements to continue in service for a period after manumission. They were enforceable in Maryland courts. That was the exception.
Throughout the South, slaves who were able to negotiate manumission
agreements had to depend on the honesty and goodwill of their owners
to honor them. Research by economic historian Shawn Cole indicates that
the lack of legally enforceable manumission contracts in the United States
probably contributed to a significant reduction in the number of manumissions occurring in the nineteenth century.[44]

The law's hostility to manumission was mirrored by the erosion of
rights previously enjoyed by free Negroes. Most states passed legislation
preventing blacks from testifying against whites or owning firearms. Some
slave states went further, requiring free Negroes to register on an annual
basis in order to remain. Many southern states, especially the new western
ones, passed legislation prohibiting free Negroes from settling in the state
altogether. A Mississippi case, *Heirn v. Bridault and Wife*, provided a stark
statement of that state's law:

> Free negroes . . . are expressly prohibited from coming into this State and on
> ten days' notice, are required to leave the State. . . . [T]hey may be caught or
> captured, by warrant, . . . sold into slavery for life. . . .

. . . [F]ree negroes . . . who are here in violation of our laws and policy, are entitled to no such rights. They are to be regarded as alien enemies . . . and without the pale of comity.[45]

Free black men voted in North Carolina and Tennessee until the mid-1830s. Disenfranchisement in both states illustrates how the contradiction of slavery in a liberal society and the psychological needs of many nonslaveholding whites combined to strip free Negroes of their status as citizens. In Tennessee, a constitutional convention called by Democrats in 1836 passed a measure to eliminate property qualifications for white voters. A proposal to limit the vote and militia service to white men also passed. It was controversial. It passed by a vote of thirty-three to twenty-three, an indication that even with the rising proslavery, anti-Negro ideology of the nineteenth century, many could nonetheless envision Afro-American citizenship. The North Carolina constitutional convention the previous year even better illustrates the mixture of motives that informed delegates debating the issue of black suffrage. The delegates appear to have been split at least in part along geographic lines. Delegates from the eastern parts of the state, where there were large slave populations, tended to favor disenfranchisement, while delegates from western districts with relatively few slaves and few blacks tended to be less sympathetic. Advocates of disenfranchisement argued that Negroes were not part of "the people" and that allowing free Negroes to vote degraded poorer whites. Supporters of black suffrage argued that allowing free Negroes with sufficient property to vote would cause them to align themselves with whites in the effort to control the slave population. The debate reflected geographic and partisan differences, with Democrats supporting disenfranchisement and Whigs opposed. The measure narrowly passed, sixty-seven to sixty-two.[46]

As race became more important, the law had to devote more attention to defining each individual's racial category, a process that at times proved tricky. Courts and other bodies would develop elaborate genealogical and behavioral tests to make racial determinations. In a society where citizenship and a strong body of rights increasingly depended on race, the law could do no less.[47]

Slavery's role in increasing racial exclusion in the South is clear. But it is important to note that the trend toward a white republic was a national one, occurring in northern and western states as well. This history is more complicated. It cannot easily be accounted for by lingering northern links to slaveholding interests, although that is a part of the story. The history cannot be easily subsumed under some kind of "consistency of northern racism" thesis, for as we have seen, the initial constitutional impulse in the northern states was to define the rights of citizens without reference to race. If the development of racial exclusion in the North is difficult to explain, it is nonetheless important. Anyone attempting to come to grips with race in the United States, particularly within the context of a comparative history, must look at the nation as a whole. The South as a region played an obvious and dramatic role in the formation of the nation's racial culture and the legal regulation of race. The overwhelming majority, more than 90 percent, of Afro-Americans lived in the South in the decades before the Civil War. But the South had no monopoly on the use of law to promote white supremacy.

Racial tensions increased in the North. In the 1820s and 1830s, vicious antiblack riots occurred in cities with significant free Negro populations. Day-to-day life became harsher for Afro-Americans. White workingmen frequently succeeded in closing all but the worst jobs to blacks. Jim Crow made its debut in the cities of the North as a growing number of public facilities were either closed to African Americans or open only on a segregated basis. States established common school systems but restricted their entry to white children, forcing black children into separate and unequal facilities. In Boston, black parents so feared violence against their children if they attended the new common schools with white children that they initially petitioned in the 1820s to have the Boston School Committee set up separate schools for black children.[48]

Things would get worse. Some new states passed legislation prohibiting Afro-American settlement altogether. As was the case in the South, the new, more strident antiblack sentiment often found its clearest expression in democratic moments — efforts to broaden the franchise or in other ways expand rights for poor and working-class white men. In a number of states, as property requirements for suffrage were being eliminated for white men, black men were denied voting rights that they had previously exercised. If late-eighteenth-century constitutionalism could countenance free Negro citizenship, the era of Jacksonian democracy was significantly more hostile. All the states that were admitted to the Union in the nineteenth century, with the exception of Maine, denied suffrage to black men.[49] *what about women*

The politics of black suffrage in the early nineteenth century provides a good window into the struggle over racial exclusion in the North. New York and Pennsylvania are particularly illustrative. Both states enfranchised black men in their postrevolutionary constitutions. Black voting in Pennsylvania seems to have been sporadic at the beginning of the nineteenth century. Black men did not vote or voted only very rarely in Philadelphia, which had a large Afro-American population. A few black men may have voted in rural areas where their numbers were too small to have any political effect. An 1837 decision by the state's supreme court held that free Negroes were not citizens and not entitled to vote. The decision in *Hobbs v. Fogg* echoed the growing tendency in the Jacksonian era to read free Negroes out of the body politic and the term *the people*. The opinion employed reasoning similar to the kind Taney would use in *Dred Scott* a generation later, stating in part that the degraded condition of the Negro as slave precluded black suffrage and citizenship: "Our ancestors settled this province as a community of white men, and the blacks were introduced into it as a race of slaves; whence an unconquerable prejudice of caste, which has come down to our day, insomuch that a suspicion of taint still has the unjust effect of sinking the subject below the common level. Consistently with this prejudice, is it to be credited that parity of rank would be allowed to such a race?" Pennsylvania's Reform Convention the following year wrote a white-only suffrage provision into the state constitution.[50]

If black men rarely voted in Pennsylvania, they voted in noticeable numbers in New York. Like other northern black voters, they generally supported the Federalists and opposed the Republicans, the ancestors of the modern Democratic Party. This was due in part to Republican ties to the slaveholding South. Patron-client ties with former masters or other influential whites probably also played a part in developing ties with the Federalists. This early black voting pattern would help to exacerbate racial tension in New York and other northern states. New York state elections were hard fought and closely won or lost at the beginning of the nineteenth century. Federalists and Republicans were busy attempting to register every voter they could. Federalist charges that Republicans were illegally registering unnaturalized Irish immigrants were countered by

Republican charges that Federalist masters brought their slaves to the polls. Republicans made scapegoats of black voters, charging that they were responsible for Federalist victories. They were also able to combine race and class resentment in their appeals to poorer white voters, particularly immigrants. Historians tell us that between 22 and 33 percent of white men were unable to vote due to the state's property qualifications before the constitutional convention of 1821. A constitution that left the bottom quarter of white men disenfranchised while also allowing some black men to vote was ripe for racial demagoguery, and the Republicans were more than up to it. In the constitutional convention of 1821, buoyed by their newfound strength and the weakening of the Federalists, Republicans proposed the elimination of the existing requirement of ownership of $100 worth of property for white voters and the disenfranchisement of Afro-Americans. They were not entirely successful. Property qualifications for white voters was eliminated. The property qualification for black voters was raised to $250.[51]

women not disbussed

Partial disenfranchisement in New York, total disenfranchisement in most other states, and persistent discrimination throughout the North led to a strenuous struggle on the part of African Americans in cities to gain or in some cases regain lost rights. Shrewd or fortunate political alliances sometimes helped. Blacks in Rhode Island had been disenfranchised in 1822 but regained the vote in 1842 as a consequence of the Dorr Rebellion and a political alliance between blacks and the state's dominant Whig Party. Efforts by Boston's blacks persuaded the state legislature to repeal the ban on interracial marriage in 1843. Five years later, members of Boston's Afro-American community sought to use the provision of the Massachusetts constitution declaring all men to be free and equal to strike down all of the marks of caste or racial discrimination existing under state law. Articulating an advanced vision of constitutional equality, members of the city's black community filed suit against the system of segregation in Boston's common schools. In *Roberts v. City of Boston*, abolitionist Charles Sumner, who was assisted by Robert Morris, one of the nation's first black attorneys, argued that the act of state-mandated segregation set up a constitutionally impermissible caste system. Massachusetts chief justice Lemuel Shaw rejected the argument, although less than a decade later, in 1856, the Massachusetts legislature outlawed segregated schools. The issues first raised in *Roberts* later resurfaced in two landmark U.S. Supreme Court cases, *Plessy v. Ferguson* (1896) and *Brown v. Board of Education* (1954). The Massachusetts legislature would ultimately outlaw segregated schools in 1856.[52]

The fight to eliminate the discriminatory property requirement for black voters in New York would continue until the passage of the Fifteenth Amendment. The history of that struggle is important not only in its own right but also for the broader light that it might shed on egalitarian sentiment in the North. Two referenda to equalize suffrage requirements were held in the state before the Civil War. In the 1846 referendum, roughly 28 percent of the voters supported equalization. In 1860, equal suffrage was supported by 36 percent of the electorate. Geography played a big role in determining whether or not a white voter supported equal suffrage. The 1846 referendum received only 15 percent support in New York City and less than 14 percent in the city in 1860. It garnered majorities upstate.[53]

The New York referenda and similar referenda in other states during and immediately after the Civil War suggest that there was perhaps more support for formal equal legal rights for blacks than is commonly supposed. The geography of support for equal rights in New York suggests that in the major cities where a majority of Afro-Americans lived, racial conflict contributed to a desire to prevent free Negroes from having the rights of citizens. The cities were places of intense conflict between blacks and the poor and working-class white populations, even though — or perhaps especially because — they lived near each other. There were many causes for these conflicts. Historians have convincingly discussed economic competition, rival political mobilizations, and status anxiety as motivations for these conflicts. It is likely that in some cases religious conflict might be added to the mix, since the Afro-American population was Protestant and an increasing percentage of working-class white people in a number of cities were Irish and Catholic. In any event, racial antagonism in the North was often at its fiercest in cities with large working-class white populations whose circumstances were not appreciably better than those of their black neighbors. The New York referenda suggest that in areas with smaller black populations where there was less perceived competition for jobs or status that more whites were willing to adhere to the republic's earlier vision of equality regardless of race. It also incidentally did not hurt that the voters in Upstate New York saw black voters as potential political allies, like them, likely voters against the Democrats.[54]

Black voting rights would only survive in New York and New England in the antebellum period. Voting was important. The loss of black suffrage was the clearest indication of the nation's shifting constitutional sensibilities. Those who framed the national and state constitutions in the era immediately following the revolution were reluctant to link race and citizenship, however strong their private prejudices might have been. Their heirs in the more egalitarian nineteenth century succumbed to a populist impulse that held that democratic governance would be the exclusive province of white men. Disenfranchisement — the reading of free Negroes out of the body politic — was the result. The struggle over suffrage, however, does not tell the complete story. As legal historian Paul Finkelman has reminded us, although blacks were disenfranchised in all but six states in 1860, there were pronounced differences between the legal rights of free Negroes in the North and those in the South. First, the law in northern states presumed a black person to be free, the reverse of southern law. Free Negroes generally had the right to live in or travel through northern states without the need for passes or other special documents. Most northern states allowed blacks to testify against whites and to bring suits in their own names. Northern states by and large made provisions for the education of black children. Afro-Americans in northern states met with few legal restrictions in their choice of profession. Blacks in northern states could own firearms, a right that was often of critical importance in light of the constant threat of mob violence. And free Negroes in the North were usually able to combine with white supporters to petition for rights.[55]

If the revolutionary war generation had crafted a constitutional order that by and large accepted the possibility of free Negro citizenship, the Jacksonian generation was far more hostile. The southern states had come to reject the possibility altogether. Free blacks in that region had little claim on the rights of citizens and indeed only a very minimal claim on the most basic of human rights. While only a handful of states in the Northeast gave political rights to Afro-Americans, a much larger group gave blacks a wide array of civil rights.

The two conflicting visions can be seen in Chief Justice Taney's majority opinion and Associate Justice Benjamin Robbins Curtis's dissent in *Dred Scott*. Both men made an appeal to history. Taney argued that the late eighteenth century was a racially unenlightened era unlikely to make citizens of Negroes:

It is difficult at this day to realize the state of public opinion in relation to that unfortunate race, which prevailed in the civilized and enlightened portions of the world at the time of the Declaration of Independence, and when the Constitution of the United States was framed and adopted.

They had for more than a century before been regarded as beings of an inferior order, and altogether unfit to associate with the white race, either in social or political relations; and so far inferior, that they had no rights which the white man was bound to respect.[56]

Curtis offered a very different view of the history of the founding era:

At the time of the ratification of the Articles of Confederation, all free native-born inhabitants of the States of New Hampshire, Massachusetts, New York, New Jersey, and North Carolina, though descended from African slaves, were not only citizens of those States, but such of them as had the other necessary qualifications possessed the franchise of electors, on equal terms with other citizens. . . .

[O]n the 25th of June, 1778, the Articles of Confederation being under consideration . . . , the delegates from South Carolina moved to amend this fourth article, by inserting after the word "free" and before the word "inhabitants," the word "white" so that the privileges and immunities of general citizenship would be secured only to white persons. Two states voted for the amendment, eight states against it, and the vote of one State was divided . . . and the strong implication from its terms of exclusion, "paupers, vagabonds and fugitives from justice," who alone were excepted, it is clear, that under the Confederation, and at the time of the adoption of the Constitution, free colored persons of African descent might be, and, by reason of their citizenship in certain States, were entitled to the privileges and immunities of general citizenship of the United States.[57]

The Taney opinion and the Curtis dissent represented more than just two conflicting ways of reading the historical record. Taney, a Maryland Democrat, represented the Jacksonian tendency to view the nation as a white republic, one with strong rights for white men and no possibilities of citizenship for blacks. Curtis from Massachusetts, on the other hand, was part of a northeastern Whig political tradition that was able to both compromise with slavery and yet be willing also to support citizenship and suffrage for free Negroes.[58]

Taney's exclusionary constitutional vision would find its clearest expression in the constitution of the Confederate States of America. The document combined the individual rights guaranteed in the U.S. Constitution with strong and explicit protection for slavery. The Confederate Constitution among other provisions specified that no "law denying or impairing the right of property in negro slaves shall be passed." Confederate vice president Alexander H. Stephens left little doubt that Confederate constitutionalism closed any possibilities for emancipation and citizenship found in its eighteenth-century predecessor:

> The prevailing ideas entertained by [Jefferson] and most of the leading statesmen at the time of the formation of the old constitution, were that the enslavement of the African was in violation of the laws of nature; that it was wrong in principle, socially, morally, and politically. . . .
>
> [O]ur new government is founded upon exactly the opposite idea; its foundations are laid, its corner-stone rests, upon the great truth that the negro is not equal to the white man; that slavery — subordination to the superior race — is his natural and normal condition.[59]

The Confederacy's defeat and the ratification of the Thirteenth Amendment in 1865 would bring a formal end to both slavery and pro-slavery constitutionalism in the United States. But the legacy of the effort to secure slavery in a land that otherwise prized freedom would long haunt the reunited republic. That strong contradiction would bequeath to the American nation a legacy of exclusion, a caste like character to race relations rarely matched elsewhere in the hemisphere. It would also forge a unity among African Americans and an effort to fight racial exclusion that was also rarely matched in other parts of the hemisphere. The effort to preserve the antebellum legacy of exclusion and the struggle to eliminate it would define American race relations for more than a century after Lee's surrender at Appomattox put an end to the War of the Rebellion.

PART II

A White Man's Country

CHAPTER FOUR

Blanqueamiento

BUILDING WHITE NATIONS IN SPANISH AMERICA

SEÑORA MARÍA MAGDALENA LAMADRID, "Pocha" to her friends, is a fifth-generation Argentine. On August 22, 2002, at 10:00 in the morning, she went to Ezeiza Airport, Buenos Aires's principal airport for international travel. She was planning to attend a conference in Panama honoring Martin Luther King Jr. When she presented her documents to airport officials, she was told that her passport must be a forgery. One official told Pocha, who was then fifty-seven years old, that because she was black, she could not be Argentine. She was detained for six hours, three of them in a holding cell. Airport officials asked her if she spoke Spanish. When they found she did they asked if she were Peruvian. Finally after having taken her fingerprints and having her citizenship verified by the police, airport officials were satisfied that Pocha — whose family has been in Argentina longer than probably 70 percent of the nation's population — was indeed an Argentine. They apologized. Their apologies did not make up for the indignities she suffered or her trip, which was ruined. She had missed her flight and was unable to get another in time for the conference. Later airport officials would claim it was not Pocha's race that made them suspicious but recent changes to the Argentine passport that caused their concern. But Pocha's memory is clear. The officials would not believe a black woman could be an Argentine. She must be a foreigner, perhaps from Peru or some other nation, but certainly not Argentina.[1]

Pocha's ordeal is part of a larger and often not very well-understood story of the role of race in much of Latin America in the twentieth century. Our earlier discussions of the system of *castas* and the intricacies of racial hierarchy and racial mobility in the colonial era are a foundation for this later history, but they only provide a start for an understanding of the complex and frequently contradictory worlds of racial identity and racial exclusion that would be an integral and often ignored part of the histories of many of the nations of the hemisphere in the twentieth century. This history has much to do with a concept — an aspiration, really — called *blanqueamiento,* an idea that grew in popularity in the closing decades of the nineteenth century. The idea was simple. The nations of Latin America could join the ranks of modern, Western nations — what we today might term the First World — through the whitening of their populations. This was to be achieved through massive European immigration. Pocha's Argentina was the most successful practitioner of this policy. Between 1880 and 1914, it would receive more European immigrants than any other country in the hemisphere except the United States.[2] The sheer size of that immigration helped realize the ambitions of the advocates of *blanqueamiento*. It overwhelmed the nation's Creole population — a term that will be used in this context to indicate Argentina's early-nineteenth-century population, peoples of varying mixtures of Spanish, African, and indigenous descent. Massive immigration contributed to the twentieth-century invisibility of the earlier populations of indigenous and African descent. This was the hope of advocates of national whitening. The inferior peoples, the legacies of the colonial era with its large Indian and Negro populations, were to be overwhelmed by their betters, the new immigrants. These immigrants would help transform the backward societies of the hemisphere into modern European nations that could take their rightful place in the coming progressive age.

Blanqueamiento would meet with different levels of success in different nations. Both Argentina and Uruguay met with such overwhelming success in attracting European immigrants that they developed inaccurate but nonetheless powerful images of themselves as white — indeed, European — nations, free from a twentieth-century indigenous or Afro-American presence and in the minds of many little in the way of an indigenous or Afro-American past.[3]

Elsewhere, advocates of *blanqueamiento* found that demography could be a stubborn thing. In many nations — Mexico, Peru, Cuba, Colombia, and Venezuela, to name some but not all — there proved to be too many descendants of the indigenous populations, the formerly enslaved Africans, or both for there to be any realistic chance that these nations would become white nations, certainly not in the sense that the nations of Europe

were white nations and not even in the sense that the United States, with
its small Indian population herded onto reservations and its disenfranchised and rigorously segregated Negro minority, was a white nation at
the beginning of the twentieth century. It would not be for a lack of trying.
But in many nations the overwhelming populations of African and indigenous descent combined with an inability to attract a sufficient number
of European immigrants would frustrate the would-be architects of *blanqueamiento*. In many countries, national leaders would attempt to make
something of a virtue out of a necessity. If *blanqueamiento* could not be
achieved, the nation would instead come to celebrate *mestizaje*, the blending of the peoples who had come together to produce the national population. In Peru, Mexico and elsewhere in the hemisphere, the nation could
celebrate the national history as the felicitous union of the worthy Spanish
and Indian races, the noble Aztecs or Incas combined with the courageous
conquistadors. Often conspicuously absent from these commemorations
was any mention of an African or Afro-American contribution. The Afro-
American population was to be considered part of the nation's colonial
past, a relic of the age of slavery and *castas*, a bit of atavism best left to
those with an antiquarian bent. The revolutions that had brought forth the
new nations had brought with them the abolition of slavery and constitutions proclaiming the citizenship and equality of all. Considerations of race
and racial inequality were out of place. Such would do a disservice to national unity and national harmony. And too much attention paid to the descendants of African slaves and their social standing in the nations of the
Americas might reveal the embarrassing truth that they were still present
in large numbers not only in the remote colonial past, but in the twentieth-
century present as well. There had been strong prejudices since the colonial era that the African race was an ignoble one, inferior to the Indian as
well as the white. Those ancient beliefs would be buttressed by the new scientific racism of the late nineteenth and early twentieth centuries. This new
way of thinking would make it even more critical to make the descendants
of Africans less visible in Latin America. In nations with large indigenous
populations, the ideology of *mestizaje* would often contribute to making
the Afro-American invisible, just as the ideology of *blanqueamiento* would
do so in nations that had acquired large white populations.[4]

We will be concerned with *blanqueamiento* and to a somewhat lesser
extent *mestizaje* in this chapter. This chapter will look at those nations

where it largely succeeded, as well as those where it failed. The concern will be with *blanqueamiento* both as a racial ideology and also as a set of social practices. It was viewed as a project of critical importance by many Latin American statesmen. It was part of the process of nation building. *Blanqueamiento* would play a critical part in many countries in defining who was part of the nation and who was not. But *blanqueamiento* was more than an ideology or set of social attitudes. It was also public policy. It would find its way into the legislation and at times even the constitutions of a number of Latin American nations. Many Latin American nations had statutory and even constitutional provisions that explicitly prohibited immigration by persons of African descent. National censuses would also be enlisted in the effort to create white nations. Officials in a number of nations found that the census was a tool that could be manipulated to demonstrate that their nations were white, or at the very least nations with little or no Afro-American presence. In some nations, *blanqueamiento* could take other forms. Where the Afro-American presence was strong — indeed, undeniable — the criminal law could be mobilized to suppress expressions of African culture or threatening signs of racial solidarity among Afro-Americans. Cuba provides an important example. Even early in the twentieth century, it was probably clear to all but the most exuberant exponents of national whitening that blacks and mulattoes would remain a significant part of the Cuban population. But if the Afro-Cuban would remain, Afro-Cuban culture could be cleansed of its barbaric Africanisms. Witchcraft and Santeria were to be outlawed, or at least have their public manifestations suppressed. If Afro-Cubans were to remain a significant part of the Cuban population, their religious and other cultural practices could at least be made to conform to Spanish norms. In those nations where a physical *blanqueamiento* could not be achieved, law and public policy could at least force the Afro-American to abandon African practices and conform to European norms. And the law, or at least state-sanctioned action, could be used — and used quite ruthlessly, as we will see — to prevent Afro-Cubans from coming together as a group to protest racial discrimination.[5]

It should be stressed that race in the nations that were the heirs of Spain's American empire was more complex than the simple story of *blanqueamiento* or *blanqueamiento* combined with *mestizaje* might suggest. As a pure matter of the ideology of race, the story seems straightforward enough. African descent was a mark of inferiority, an indication that an individual by virtue of ancestry or blood could be presumed inferior to those of indigenous or European descent. If the law on at least a nominal level recognized the descendants of Spaniards, Indians, and Africans and the innumerable mixtures of the three groups as citizens, theoretically equal and entitled to the same body of rights, the racial ideology of the day posed a strong challenge to these egalitarian legal norms. Afro-Americans were subject to often rampant discrimination, and not just in immigration laws and policies. Race frequently determined where an individual could live or the kind of job at which he or she might be employed. People with visible African ancestry, along with others from the poor and working classes, were frequently the victims of police brutality and rather summary justice at the hands of the criminal courts. Afro-Americans even found, at times, some of the more desirable public spaces — parks, theaters, and public libraries — closed to them, although rarely with the systematic rigor and legal mandate found in the Jim Crow South of the United States.

But race was just one of several considerations that might determine social relations or even an individual's social standing. Culture might mitigate racial prejudice. In nations whose large Indian populations continued to speak indigenous languages and worship traditional gods, a Catholic, Spanish-speaking Afro-American, despite his stigmatized race, might be seen as more a part of society's mainstream than an Indian still following traditional tribal customs. Connections to powerful white families could also lessen the effects of racial prejudice, as could patron-client ties to powerful political figures. The racial ideology was clear. Africans and their visible descendants had tainted blood, a mark and a presumption of inferiority. But actual practice could be less clear, at least in some cases. Societies in Latin America were often characterized by strong social hierarchies and authoritarian governance during episodes of both democratic and authoritarian rule. In such settings, class position and personalistic ties, combined with notions of racial mobility that had been part of the culture from the earliest times, might allow some individuals with acknowledged African ancestry to gain a measure of acceptance, even prominence in ways that could confound and contradict the prevailing racial ideology. During the era of *blanqueamiento*, racism could be found and found in abundance. But that racism also took place against a background in which class distinctions were significantly sharper and more openly acknowledged than was the case in the United States. This phenomenon probably helped contribute to a racial integration of poor and working-class populations in many parts of Latin America at the beginning of the twentieth century in ways that would have been hard to imagine in the United States in the same era. It can also help us understand why a surprising number of individuals of mixed racial backgrounds but with known and acknowledged African ancestry were able to attain positions of prominence in parts of Latin America despite national ideologies emphasizing whiteness and whitening. The story of *blanqueamiento*, how it developed as an ideology and the twists and turns that characterized its actual implementation is a complicated one serving at times as a vivid reminder that national ideologies and day-to-day practices can often be at odds, especially in an area as complex as race relations.[6]

The nineteenth century dawned in Spanish America with the promise of the elimination of the racial and *casta* restrictions that had been integral to Spain's rule. But as the century unfolded, political leaders and leading intellectuals began to encounter new ways of thinking that were more in tune with the eighteenth century than with nineteenth-century ideals of emancipation and universal citizenship. Scientific racism, particularly scholastic efforts to proclaim the inferiority of Africans and their unique suitability for slavery, had been around for hundreds of years but began to take on new importance in Latin America, especially among forward-thinking intellectuals and statesmen. Progressives believed that science harnessed to pragmatic thinking was the key to the great advances of the age — the telegraph and the telephone, the steamboat and the locomotive, new ways of powering factories, the electric light. These scientific developments had brought immeasurable benefits to the nations of Europe and North America and could do the same in Latin America.

And why not in the biological and social sciences as well? New ways of thinking were abroad in the nineteenth century. They posed challenges for the new constitutional orders that had developed after independence. But these new ways of thinking held the promise of improved societies, societies stocked with better breeds of people. Social Darwinists were urging that Darwin's theories on natural selection should be applied to the social sphere. Life, they argued, was a Darwinian struggle, and unfit or inferior species should be allowed to perish to prevent the perpetuation of inferior breeds and to provide more room and resources for superior ones.

The eugenics movement would take Social Darwinism a step further. The movement's leading lights argued that human abilities were inherited and not the result of education or environment. The state should take active steps to improve the human race by limiting the reproduction of inferior peoples and also to preserve the genetic purity of superior ones, particularly those of Northern European stock. European and North American advocates of eugenics argued that modernity and progress were linked to a nation's racial traits. Northern Europe and the United States were centers of science and progress precisely because they were dominated by peoples of northern European ancestry. The nations of Latin America were backward precisely because they were mongrel nations inhabited by too many of the descendants of Africans and Indians. From the 1880s to the 1930s, many intellectuals in Latin America would find support for their notions of racial restrictions in European social theories like eugenics that asserted, among other things, the innate inferiority of the nonwhite races.[7]

But Latin American supporters of eugenics had a problem, a serious one. Many of their nations simply had too many people of African and indigenous descent to allow eugenics, at least of the North American or European variety, to work. The prevailing wisdom among eugenic theorists stressed the unavoidable inheritability of genetic traits, good and bad. Translated into racial terms, such ideas would mean that the march of progress envisioned by the advocates of *blanqueamiento* was doomed: the backward traits of the Indian and the Negro would remain. Progress would be thwarted. And what was even worse, many of the elite statesmen and writers who advocated the whitening of their nations were aware that their own family trees or those of their peers housed an indigenous or Afro-American ancestor, perhaps several. By European or North American lights, they too, like the societies they led, had an indelible mark of inferiority. A new way of looking at the problem, one more congenial to Latin American realities, would have to be found.

So nationalistic intellectuals and statesmen began to rethink and refashion many of the prevailing racial theories of the day. The notion that there was a hierarchy of races, that whites were at the top of that hierarchy and the descendants of enslaved Africans and the conquered indigenous populations were at the bottom, was not challenged, nor was the idea that the state had a responsibility, through active intervention, to better the racial stock of the nation. But the logic of eugenics as it had been received from Europe and North America had to be revised. If the Europeans and North Americans proclaimed that any mixing of the races was degenerate and would pass along the dysfunctional characteristics of the inferior races to the offspring, Latin Americans came to see the problem in a different light. Successive interbreeding would improve the nation's racial stock. The superior traits of the Europeans would prevail over those of the weaker Negro and Indian populations. Over time the inferior races, particularly the blacks and mulattoes, would disappear, losers in a Darwinian struggle in which even a minority of superior European genes would prevail and create a new national population. It was an adaptation of eugenic theories that fitted comfortably with the demographic realities in many Latin American societies and with traditional Latin American notions that the African and indigenous races could be improved through mixture with the white race.[8]

Bolstered by the scientific racism then common in the Western world, Latin American intellectual and political leaders developed ideologies and policies that they believed if properly followed would be the engines of progress and modernity in their nations. The quest for racial improvement was made a national priority throughout the hemisphere. It was hoped that both *blanqueamiento* and *mestizaje* would over the long run accentuate the European elements of their populations and diminish the black and Indian elements. Both ideologies would contribute to a new body of myths concerning race in the Americas. It would render Afro-Americans all but invisible in some societies, even in societies that retained significant regional and national Afro-American populations. But *blanqueamiento* and *mestizaje* would come to do more. It would contribute to a myth that race had all but ceased to exist in many Latin American societies. This notion was part of the view that *mestizaje* had done its work, producing a "cosmic race" with everyone sharing in Spanish and Indian ancestry. Proponents of this myth would often go on to assure curious observers that what appeared to be racially linked social inequalities were really class differences or perhaps the result of cultural differences caused by Indians who insisted on clinging to traditional ways. They were not the results of racial discrimination or exclusion. *Blanqueamiento, mestizaje,* and the myth that race had essentially ceased to exist, would also contribute to another myth, the idea that the different societies of Latin America had solved the problem of race, that they were free from racial discrimination, that they were racial democracies. In the early twentieth century, this view could be strengthened by the contrast with the United States and the kind of formalized — indeed, codified — system of apartheid, Jim Crow, that existed in much of the American nation. That myth would add to the complexity of race in many of the countries of the hemisphere. Open, sometimes raw racism would coexist with a relative lack of formal racial barriers and open familial relationships across racial lines. National policies designed to render Afro-Americans invisible would seemingly be contradicted by Afro-Americans who became leaders in the cultural and political lives of their nations. These tensions would often be resolved in very different ways in different Latin American societies.

No nation more closely followed this blueprint for national transformation than Argentina. In 1845, about one hundred years before Pocha was born, Argentine officials would have had little difficulty recognizing her as a daughter of the Argentine republic. Eighteenth-century Buenos Aires was a major point of entry for victims of the African slave trade, many of whom moved from there to the large farms and cattle *estancias* of the vast Argentine pampas. Others went to the sugar plantations of Tucumán or to the mines of Chile and Bolivia. Some would stay in Buenos Aires, working as domestic servants, or in the shops of artisans or in the warehouses and docks along the Río de la Plata. Buenos Aires would continue to receive a significant number of enslaved Africans well into the 1830s despite the passage of a "law of the free womb" in 1813. Final emancipation would come late to Argentina. Despite an 1853 constitutional provision freeing slaves, final emancipation would have to wait until 1861, when the province of Buenos Aires joined the Argentine Confederation and agreed to abolish slavery.[9]

Africans and Afro-Argentines were commonplace in nineteenth-century Argentina. At the beginning of that century, roughly 30 percent of the population of Buenos Aires consisted of people who were visibly of African descent. In many parts of the interior the percentages were even higher. Afro-Argentines were particularly conspicuous in the ranks of the nation's military forces. The slow pace of abolition gave officials the opportunity to raise troops for the nation's wars. Slaves would be conditionally manumitted, granted *liberto* status, but only if they enlisted in the Argentine ranks. Many did and were pressed into frontline service, often with high casualty rates. This military tradition would continue even after general emancipation, with large numbers of Afro-Argentines fighting in the 1865–70 War of the Triple Alliance against Paraguay.[10]

Nineteenth-century Afro-Argentines were aligned politically with Federalist dictator Juan Manuel de Rosas. Rosas saw free Afro-Argentines as part of his political constituency, one that included the Creole masses of all races. The identification of Afro-Argentines with Rosas was close, and later in the century, that alliance would become a rallying point for many who sought a white Argentina. Rosas, his Unitarian enemies would later argue, was a brutal dictator held in power by his appeal to the savage masses, the Negroes, the Indians and mestizos, and the wild gauchos. These must be replaced, replaced by immigrants from Europe, immigrants who would bring civilization to both Buenos Aires and the pampas. No figure was more adept at arguing that the Creole masses who supported Rosas were barbarians who imperiled the future of Argentina than Domingo Faustino Sarmiento. Sarmiento, a Unitarian politician and one of late-nineteenth-century Argentina's leading essayists and intellectuals, served as president from 1868 to 1874. He urged his vision of a modern, progressive Argentine nation on his fellow countrymen. Sarmiento's vision of the nation depended on a massive European immigration that would whiten the population. Immigration was a means to "correct the indigenous blood with new ideas ending the Medievalism" of the country. *Blanqueamiento* by immigration would bring modernity to Argentina and Argentina to modernity. It would provide the nation with a white population capable of taking part in the modern progressive age.[11]

Sarmiento's advocacy of increased European immigration was already part of national policy. The constitution of 1853, which had abolished slavery, made clear its support for European immigration: "The federal government shall foster European immigration; and may not restrict, limit or burden with any tax whatsoever, the entry into the Argentine territory of foreigners who arrive for the purpose of tilling the soil, improving industries, and introducing and teaching the arts and sciences."[12]

Argentina's efforts to attract European immigrants would meet with considerable success. Between 1880 and 1930 the nation received a net migration of 3.8 million immigrants, greater than 1.6 times the population of the nation in 1880. This was not mere happenstance. It was instead the result of concerted efforts by the Argentine government. The largest group of immigrants came from Italy. Argentine elites would come to view Italian immigrants as the bearers of Western civilization, but this too was in part an effort at making something of a virtue out of a necessity. Many of the nineteenth-century advocates of *blanqueamiento* initially were convinced that Argentina's Latin heritage, while not as backward as the nation's African and indigenous strains, was nonetheless also an impediment to progress. Northern Europeans were seen as key to a modern, progressive future. Because Argentina proved less able to attract Northern Europeans than North America, the advocates of a European Argentina came to adjust their expectations and their ideology accordingly.[13]

Argentina's success in attracting European immigrants fit in nicely with the vision laid out by the champions of national whitening. The ideology of the day dictated that the Afro-Argentine, along with the other inferior peoples native to Argentina (the Indian, the mestizo, the gaucho), would give way to the new immigrants. Even before the start of the twentieth century there had already developed a robust tradition of heralding the disappearance of the Afro-Argentine, supposedly killed off in the wars of the nineteenth century, particularly the conflict with Paraguay, and the yellow fever epidemic of 1871 among other calamities. The vanishing of the Afro-Argentine was aided by census officials seemingly determined to help the disappearance along by erasing Afro-Argentines from national population statistics. Late-nineteenth-century officials, anxious to aid the *blanqueamiento* project, appear to have reclassified individuals who might have more accurately classified as black as *pardos* or mulattoes while also reclassifying many mulattoes as white or *trigueño*, a racially ambiguous term. Essayists and editorial writers cheered the disappearance along, part of a kind of national boosterism heralding the emergence of a new, European Argentina.[14]

The Afro-Argentines did not exactly disappear. Still, they and the Argentine nation fulfilled the fondest wishes of the champions of *blanqueamiento*. In the twentieth century, they became all but invisible, largely erased from the nation's consciousness and memory even if they were not entirely gone from the streets of Buenos Aires and the other highways and byways of the nation. This would occur in part for obvious demographic reasons. In Argentina, *blanqueamiento* and *mestizaje* would work much as their champions had hoped. The waves of Italian and other European immigrants buried the Afro-Argentine population. The Afro-Argentines would become but a small part of a population base significantly larger than the nineteenth-century population in which they had been so visible. And Afro-Argentines married and had children with the new immigrants. Those children, or the children of those children, would be defined as white or at least not as black or mulatto or some other readily identifiable Afro-Argentine category. But something more than demography played a role in the disappearance of the Afro-Argentines. The national insistence that Argentina was a European nation, the insistence that the Negro and the Indian belonged to a past forever gone, became a powerful myth that helped define the nation. And yet even today, Argentines whose faces betray more than a hint of African ancestry are not hard to find. Throughout the twentieth century, historians and journalists documented the Afro-American presence in the Argentine nation, long after their supposed disappearance. Mestizos who clearly have indigenous ancestry are even more common. More than a few of these also have quite visible African ancestry as well. But like Pocha, many of these people are also often regarded as strangers in their native land. In the twentieth century the national ideology and the national culture dictated that they be ignored, discounted, or redefined. Their continued presence could not be allowed to contradict the belief in a European Argentina.[15]

How did Afro-Argentines adapt to a society that, in the early decades of the twentieth century, was increasingly identifying itself not only as white but also as fundamentally European? How did they carve out a livable social space in a nation that their ancestors had helped to build and defend but that was by the beginning of the twentieth century anxious to ignore their very existence? Our information on Afro-Argentine life in the early part of the twentieth century is fragmentary. It can be augmented by looking at Afro-American life in Argentina's more-than-fraternal twin, Uruguay, during the same time period. Taken together, the two countries give us something of a composite picture of how Afro-Americans in both Rioplatense republics interacted with the white Creole elites and the Italian and other newcomers who dominated political and economic life in both countries. We can also make some educated guesses about Afro-American employment and housing patterns, education and political allegiances, and the ability of Afro-Argentines and Afro-Uruguayans to preserve a measure of their cultural heritage in two nations that emphasized their European cultures and populations.

Cook
9
infanticide

Like Argentina, Uruguay would receive a massive European, predominantly Italian, immigration at the end of the nineteenth and start of the twentieth centuries. Between 1880 and 1930, Argentina's eastern neighbor attracted some 580,000 European immigrants, most of them from Italy. It was a smaller immigration than the nearly 4 million Europeans who arrived in Argentina. The 580,000 European immigrants who came to Uruguay were met by a Creole population of some 520,000 people, as opposed to the nearly 4 million immigrants who encountered Argentina's Creole population of 2.4 million. Afro-Uruguayans would remain somewhat more visible than their Argentine counterparts. Some researchers attribute this greater visibility to a larger Afro-Uruguayan population. Others argue that both Afro-Rioplatense populations are roughly equal but that Afro-Uruguayans are more visible against the numerically smaller population of the eastern republic.[16]

In any event, Uruguay, like its neighbor across the Río de La Plata, would emphasize its white and European nature and downplay any Afro-Uruguayan presence. As was the case in Argentina, the census was enlisted in the cause of national whitening. Late-nineteenth and early-twentieth-century censuses seem to have engaged in a severe undercounting of the Afro-Uruguayan population in order not to disturb the national belief in the essentially European nature of Uruguay. The government also engaged in an often strident propaganda campaign designed to convince the population that theirs was indeed a white republic. Statements by governmental leaders as well as public celebrations and elementary school textbooks emphasized Uruguay's white population and how the nation's whiteness separated it from other republics in the Americas. Official statements and educational texts also emphasized that the country's democratic order and its generous provisions for public education and social welfare were made possible because the Oriental Republic was a nation made up of civilized Europeans and not the unfortunate descendants of Africans and Indians so prevalent in other parts of the Americas. The combination of a white population, a generally democratic polity, and relatively generous welfare and educational provisions led many national leaders to refer to Uruguay as "the Switzerland of South America" in the first half of the twentieth century.[17]

Afro-Uruguayans remained a part, albeit often a marginal part, of the Oriental Republic. Discrimination could be strong, stable employ-

women?

ment hard to find. The best jobs open to Afro-Uruguayans often were in the lower ranks of government service, a pattern similar to the one that prevailed in Argentina, where some of the more financially secure Afro-Argentines seem to have been those who could gain low-level government employment, probably the most prominent of these being the famous *negros del congreso* (doormen and servants) in the nation's Congress. These positions were often gained as a result of political patronage and were usually kept through loyalty to the prevailing political parties. The need to attract European immigrants led officials to provide more in the way of free public education in Uruguay than was the case in many other South American nations, and many Afro-Uruguayans were at least incidental beneficiaries of this policy. But poverty and the need to contribute to the often meager incomes of their families caused many Afro-Uruguayan children to forgo school and go directly to work. Still relatively high levels of education among Afro-Uruguayans helped support one of the strongest Afro-American presses in the hemisphere. It could also produce a high degree of frustration as a number of Afro-Uruguayans discovered that even a good education often provided little relief from and indeed often exacerbated employment discrimination.[18]

In both Argentina and Uruguay, national whitening, Europeanization, was an official project supported at the highest national levels. And yet despite official sanction and often strong popular prejudice, neither nation would experience the kind of rigid racial exclusion that would be found in much of the United States at the beginning of the twentieth century. There was no body of laws prescribing segregation. Afro-Americans attended schools with the children of immigrants. Afro-Argentines and Afro-Uruguayans lived in the same neighborhoods in *coventillos* or tenements with poor and working-class whites, particularly Italian immigrants. The two groups often intermarried. The port neighborhoods of both Buenos Aires and Montevideo were venues for the exchange of cultures. Afro-Argentine characters became stock figures in the *sainete* puppet plays produced by Italian immigrants in Buenos Aires's La Boca neighborhood. That quintessential Rioplatense art form, the tango, came out of the synthesis of the African-descended *candombe* and *milonga* with European forms of musical expression brought by the immigrants.[19]

Even strong governmental policies emphasizing European immigration and the invisibilization of Afro-Americans were not applied with total consistency. In the twentieth century, Argentina would receive a small group of African immigrants from the Cape Verde Islands. Most Cape Verdeans settled in the province of Buenos Aires and gained their livelihood in the maritime industries. Afro-Uruguayans seeking to escape the Oriental Republic's discriminatory application of the nation's conscription laws would also find refuge in Buenos Aires. A few Afro-Argentines would find their way to national prominence despite the official emphasis that the South American republic was a white nation. In the 1920s and 1930s, during what has been described as the "golden age" of Argentine cinema, José Agustín Ferreyra, a mulatto, was one of the nation's leading film directors. In the early 1950s neurosurgeon, Ramón Carrillo, also a mulatto, served as minister of health during the first administration of Juan Domingo Perón. But despite these exceptions, the thrust of public policy in Argentina and Uruguay for most of the twentieth century was clear. These were nations whose self-images were very much bound up with the notion that they were white nations, extensions of Europe, and as a result of their populations very much separated from the other nations of Latin America. It was a separation very much fueled by their successful efforts at repopulation, repopulation with massive waves of European immigrants.

Other countries tried to achieve similar results. Throughout the hemisphere, national Congresses passed legislation designed to foster desirable, European, immigration and prohibit or severely discourage immigration of peoples deemed undesirable, peoples of African or Asian descent. The process would begin fairly early in the nineteenth century. As early as 1862, the Costa Rican government enacted a legal ban on immigration by persons of African or Asian ancestry. Venezuela would place a similar ban in its constitution of 1906. Other nations enacted like-minded measures. Anxious to attract European settlers, many political leaders in Latin America set about the business of trying to make their nations more attractive to prospective immigrants. Land bounties, exemption from conscription, and improvements in education were all attempted in an effort to attract more European immigrants. In a number of American republics, efforts were made at constitutional reform, including strengthening guarantees of religious freedom in an effort to attract immigrants, particularly immigrants from the Protestant nations of Northern Europe.[20]

The desire to attract European immigrants existed throughout the hemisphere. But plans to create new, white nations in the Americas were often thwarted. They could be frustrated by demographic realities. They could also run counter to dominant economic and political interests. Peru's history in the second half of the nineteenth century and in the early decades of the twentieth provides a good example of a largely unsuccessful effort at national whitening, a failed effort, it should be added, that nonetheless helped push the Afro-Peruvian to the margins of the Pacific nation's society and consciousness almost as surely as did the more successful efforts in Argentina and Uruguay.

Like their counterparts in Argentina and Uruguay, national leaders in Peru were anxious to transform the national population through large-scale European immigration. Their concern was largely with Peru's large indigenous population, which was seen as backwards, uncivilized, and an overall impediment to national progress. The nation's political and economic leaders also had another concern. The long effort to end slavery that had finally resulted in national abolition in 1854 left the owners of the large sugar and cotton haciendas in the nation's coastal regions scrambling for laborers to replace the former slaves. Newly emancipated Afro-Peruvians were reluctant to continue as simple laborers on the plantations on which they had been enslaved, a reluctance that was matched by recently emancipated Afro-Americans elsewhere in the hemisphere. And there were emerging stereotypes of Afro-Peruvians as violent, prone to crime, and a menace to the peace of society at large. If this new stereotype of the former slaves was often in direct contradiction to the more benign portrait of slavery and Afro-Peruvian character that had been offered by slaveholders in the decades before final emancipation, similar changes in the image of Afro-Americans would occur with the abolition of slavery elsewhere in the hemisphere, including the United States. In any event, Afro-Peruvian resistance to a return to the bottom rung of plantation labor, coupled with a new, somewhat more threatening image of Afro-Peruvians as a group, would add a new element to the Peruvian racial mix, one that proved to be unwelcome to national leaders looking to create a whiter nation. Peru would receive large numbers of immigrants — not the European immigrants eagerly sought by the nation's leaders, but Chinese immigrants brought to the Peruvian nation to perform some of its harder and more disagreeable tasks.[21]

Chinese immigrants actually began arriving before general emancipation in 1854, but the numbers brought in would increase significantly after final abolition. Like the earlier trade in slaves, the "coolie trade," which brought in large numbers of Chinese, was not a voluntary immigration. Many Chinese laborers were forced into contracts that brought them to labor in Peru. Between 1849 and 1874, some 100,000 more or less forced Chinese immigrants came to Peru, a significant number in the Peruvian nation whose population numbered only 2.5 million at the beginning of the period. The Chinese helped build Peru's railroad network and also labored on the haciendas that had previously employed Afro-Peruvian slaves. In something of a reversal of fortune, Afro-Peruvian overseers supervised Chinese laborers on the cotton and sugar plantations that had employed Afro-Peruvian slaves before general emancipation.[22]

The addition of large numbers of Chinese immigrants served to further complicate already complex strains of racial ideology, racial alliances, and day-to-day etiquette of racial interaction in late nineteenth-century Peru. The hoped for whitening of the nation through European immigration was not taking place. The Peruvian government had made efforts to attract immigrants from Europe, but to little avail. Land could not be offered to immigrants in the rich coastal lands that housed the large sugar and cotton haciendas. These were already owned by wealthy planters. The government made an effort to attract European settlers to the unsettled Amazon regions, but there were few takers for what many saw as wild and dangerous territories. A society, "La Sociedad de Inmigración Europea," founded in 1873 to attract European immigrants met with little success. To perhaps a greater extent than was the case in the slave era, and certainly to a greater extent than advocates of a more European Peru wanted, race in Peru in the latter half of the nineteenth century would be governed by relations among the groups that were not white, groups that Peruvian elites felt were largely undesirable and inferior elements of the national population.[23]

Relations between Afro-Peruvians and Chinese immigrants seem to have been particularly strained. Chinese laborers often complained of harsh treatment at the hands of Afro-Peruvian overseers. Conflict between the two groups frequently turned violent. Anthropologist Denys Cuche, who did pioneering work on Afro-Peruvian studies in the 1970s, has argued that the conflict between Afro-Peruvians and Chinese could be attributed to several different points of friction. The newly freed Afro-Peruvians at times treated their Chinese workers as they had been treated — harshly. They feared competition for jobs with Chinese laborers. Often there was sexual competition between the two groups — the coolie trade inevitably brought in far more men than women, and Chinese men sought partners among Afro-Peruvian, Indian, and mestizo women. Cuche also argues that their position as overseers gave some Afro-Peruvians a chance to take out pent-up frustrations on a group weaker and more vulnerable than they. Cuche notes that the violence at times reached epic proportions, with hundreds being killed in fierce battles between the two groups. He also notes that the Indian population often would find itself caught between the two groups, at times supporting the Chinese, at other times allying with the Afro-Peruvians.[24]

Conflict between the two groups was doubtless also exacerbated by cultural and nationalistic differences. From the Cantonese-speaking parts of South China, the immigrants were cultural and linguistic aliens, strangers to Peruvians of all races. With little reason to feel any loyalty to Peru, many Chinese laborers saw an alliance with Chilean forces as a way to escape bondage during the 1879–83 War of the Pacific. Afro-Peruvians, on the other hand, supported the national war effort, believing that their demonstration of loyalty would increase their overall acceptance by the Peruvian population, including the nation's leaders.[25]

Peru's history in the half century or so following the abolition of slavery in 1854 can help us understand much about the intellectual history of race as an idea in Latin America and much about the effort in many parts of Latin America to render national Afro-American populations invisible. With its large Indian and mestizo populations, its influx of Chinese immigrants, and its still quite visible Afro-American population, Peruvian intellectuals and governmental officials could not, unlike their counterparts in Argentina and Uruguay, essay an effort at national mythmaking that denied the very existence of the non-European races in the Inca homeland. The Indians and mestizos, the blacks and mulattoes, as well as the Chinese were too visible, even in the nation's capital, Lima, to make that credible. And yet the idea that European civilization and European culture would prevail also remained, despite the nation's somewhat problematic demography. Peru was not immune to the Darwinian ideas that were influencing scientific thought in the rest of the world and greatly influencing immigration policy elsewhere in the Americas. But Peruvian intellectuals were beginning to modify these ideas, partially influenced by the nation's repeated failed efforts to encourage European immigration. Peruvian writer Eugenio

Larrabure y Unánue was a vigorous advocate of the Peruvian approach to handling the problem of a nation beset with the inferior races. The races would mix. They would absorb the superior civilization brought by the Spaniards and other Europeans. He explicitly criticized the United States and the Jim Crow policies that were appearing in the American South by the beginning of the twentieth century. These would only ensure the continued perpetuation of the Afro-American population as a separate group, one that if kept apart would develop a sense of unity, a sense of unity that would not redound to the nation's benefit. The Peruvian way, which would contribute to the ultimate disappearance of this, the most dangerous of the inferior races, was, Larrabure argued, superior to the North American policy of segregation.[26]

Larrabure's views reflected a broader consensus among Peru's elites at the beginning of the twentieth century that Afro-Peruvians were not only an inferior race but a dangerous one that the nation would be well rid of. Many Afro-Peruvians believed that military service, loyalty to the nation, and support for popular political leaders might earn the group a measure of acceptance. That formula may have helped some individuals gain a degree of relief from the rigors of racial prejudice as they were developing in Peru at the beginning of the last century. But increasingly Afro-Peruvians as a group were being thrust toward the margins of their nation's society. They were increasingly identified with crime. Although Afro-Peruvians did not live in racially segregated neighborhoods, they were often forced to live in the more marginal and dangerous communities in Lima and other locations. They were consistently featured as violent desperadoes in the more lurid popular literature of the day.[27]

As was the case elsewhere in the hemisphere, the Peruvian census helped to hide the size and condition of the nation's Afro-American population. In 1918, the census eliminated the *zambo* (mixed African and Indian) category, thus eliminating one significant element of the Afro-Peruvian population from the nation's official records. The 1940 census, the last census in the twentieth century to indicate race, showed an Afro-Peruvian population of twenty-nine thousand, or 0.47 percent of the national population. That census did not show the considerable percentage of the mestizo population that had some African ancestry. Race was a matter of self-identification on the 1940 census, and few people who were not predominantly black would have been inclined to identify themselves as

Afro-Peruvians. After 1940, official statistics no longer reflected race, although Peruvian records did keep track of the indigenous population by indicating linguistic groups. This was similar to the practice of census officials in other nations with large indigenous populations, like Mexico and Guatemala. The reasons for changing census and other records of official statistics so that they simply reflected ethnic differences and not racial ones as well were probably varied. An emphasis on ethnicity rather than race certainly fit in with the official ideology that *mestizaje* was working, that the "civilized" people of the nation were blending, and that the only remaining racial or ethnic issue was that of the Indian population that had not yet assimilated into the dominant Spanish culture. Eliminating racial categories was also a way of hiding or minimizing the continuing presence of an Afro-American population. Indeed, given the racial norms of the first half of the twentieth century and the frequent reluctance of many people of partial African ancestry to identify with the stigmatized Afro-American population, many officials may have seen the elimination of the racial question from the census as a way of providing a measure of relief for peoples of partial African or indigenous descent, a way of allowing them to put behind them the troublesome question of race.[28]

Whatever the motive, the elimination of race from the census fit in well with the ideology of a nation that, like others in the hemisphere, wanted the Afro-American to disappear. Peru in the twentieth century would develop a myth that the Afro-Peruvian population had essentially ceased to exist, although Afro-Peruvians would remain quite visible in the southern coastal plantation regions where their ancestors had toiled for so long as slaves and in Lima and other Peruvian venues throughout the twentieth century and indeed into our own twenty-first century. They would remain in many cases visible but unacknowledged, an often marginal people in the land of their ancestors.

If Peruvian national leaders hoped that their nation's Afro-American population would fade into demographic irrelevance, officials in other nations in Latin America were faced with the unwelcome prospect of an Afro-American population renewed through immigration. Throughout Central America and the Caribbean, large plantations or industrial concerns, frequently owned by North American corporations, pressured Latin American governments to ignore or bend national law and allow the admission of low-wage black workers from the English-speaking Caribbean.

In Costa Rica, Cuba, the Dominican Republic, Panama, and Venezuela, the desire of political leaders to create white societies often clashed with the wishes of foreign-owned enterprises for cheap labor, usually supplied by English-speaking Afro-Caribbeans. In Venezuela, the industrial sector annually imported some six to ten thousand black seasonal laborers from the Antilles despite strict legislation against black immigration. Thousands of black laborers were brought to Panama by the United States to labor on the Panama Canal. The presence of English-speaking black laborers became a major source of controversy in Panama early in the twentieth century. Antipathy toward West Indian laborers spurred the passage of legislation in 1926 requiring all Panamanian enterprises to employ workforces that were at least 75 percent native born.[29]

Efforts to keep black West Indians out of Panama were reflected in a number of provisions of that nation's 1941 constitution. The concern over West Indian immigrants is clear. The document prohibited the immigration of non-Spanish-speaking blacks along with what it termed "the yellow race" and "the races originating in India, Asia Minor and North Africa." The 1941 constitution also placed racial restrictions on citizenship. Birthright citizenship was denied to the children of those who were prohibited from immigrating, although a provision permitted the president at his discretion to grant citizenship to the children of prohibited immigrants provided those children were, in effect, native Spanish speakers. The wording of these constitutional provisions reflected Panamanian racial and cultural concerns as well as something less than an undiluted effort at racial exclusion. Under a strict reading of the 1941 constitution, Spanish-speaking Afro-Americans from other parts of the hemisphere were not prevented from immigrating to Panama. The provisions seem to have been clearly aimed at blacks from the English-speaking Caribbean. The term used to restrict black immigration was *la raza negra* (the black race), a term that would presumably be problematic if applied to mulattoes or other persons of partial African ancestry. The 1941 constitution reflected the plurality of interests and viewpoints that informed Panamanian politics in the 1930s and early 1940s. The desire to limit Panama's Afro-American population clashed with the existence of politically significant Afro-Panamanian population, both the descendants of Panamanian slaves and more recent West Indian immigrants. The desire to impose racial limitations on new immigration was complicated by nationalist strains of thinking concerned with the preservation of Spanish language and culture in the face of a large population of English-speaking immigrants and the large North American presence in the Canal Zone. The constitution reflected these overlapping concerns.[30]

Black immigrants from the English-speaking Caribbean were common throughout Central America at the end of the nineteenth and beginning of the twentieth centuries. Despite legislation passed in 1862 prohibiting immigration by people of African descent, a number of Afro-Caribbeans began arriving in Costa Rica's port city of Limón in 1872. Blacks and mulattoes had lived in Costa Rica in the colonial era as slaves and free people of color, but by the middle of the nineteenth century, that group had dwindled into insignificance. The new West Indian immigration would help create the modern Afro–Costa Rican population. Many of them would earn their livelihoods working on the railroads and in agriculture. The Central American republic's distaste for immigrants of African ancestry clashed with the demands of the United Fruit Company and other businesses for labor. The black, Protestant, and English-speaking immigrants presented a sharp contrast to the Central American nation's early twentieth-century self-image as a nation that was white, Catholic, and Spanish speaking. Like other nations, Costa Rica was actively promoting its own version of national whitening by encouraging European immigration. The clash between the unwelcome Afro-Caribbeans and Costa Rica's self-image as a white nation, combined with episodes of intense competition for jobs between the black immigrants and the Central American nation's white and mestizo populations, led to some of the most explicit efforts to use law to enforce racial subordination in postemancipation Latin America. Before the Second World War, the Costa Rican government placed restrictions on the ability of the West Indian population to become naturalized Costa Rican citizens. Even West Indian children born in Costa Rica had to be naturalized in order to become citizens. Special legislation made the naturalization process difficult for West Indians and their children. In the early decades of the twentieth century, thousands of people born of West Indian ancestry in Costa Rica were essentially stateless. They were not British subjects as their parents or grandparents had been, but they were denied Costa Rican citizenship as well. Their stateless status frequently made them the victims of discriminatory legislation designed to reserve better jobs for Costa Ricans.[31]

Efforts at legal discrimination did not end with Costa Rica's naturalization policies. Before the Second World War, there were repeated attempts to pass legislation restricting the rights of the West Indian population, whether immigrant or native, foreign or naturalized. In 1915, legislation was proposed that would have prohibited Costa Rican women from marrying black or Asian men. The measure failed but was an indication of the substantial hostility against nonwhite immigrants. The impulse toward restrictive racial legislation would grow even stronger in the 1930s. Faced with the depressed economy and the demands from low-skilled workers, identified largely as mestizos by Afro–Costa Rican researcher Diana Senior Angulo, Costa Rican lawmakers were besieged with demands for legislation that would prevent West Indian competition with Costa Ricans. Legislation was passed preventing West Indian workers from obtaining jobs on the Central American nation's Pacific Coast. There were repeated efforts to tighten racially restrictive immigration laws and to reserve jobs for Costa Ricans. The government's efforts in this regard seem not to have satisfied many Costa Rican citizens, as evidenced by repeated petitions to the nation's courts complaining that the United Fruit Company was still hiring black West Indians instead of Costa Ricans.[32]

Substantial change would not come for Afro–Costa Ricans until after the Second World War. That nation's 1948 revolution and the victory of José Figueres and the Partido Liberación Nacional would bring with it a liberalization of naturalization procedures. During Figueres's administration and that of his successor, Otilio Ulate, the majority of West Indians would become citizens. Despite this liberalization the national self-image of Costa Rica as a white nation, with the Afro–Costa Ricans of Limón as less-than-welcome outsiders, would remain.[33]

If black immigrants found a less than cordial welcome in Costa Rica, antiblack sentiment in the Dominican Republic would take on an even more sinister turn. The long-standing enmity between Dominicans and Haitians, coupled with the relative wealth of the Dominican side of the island of Hispaniola and the poverty of the Haitian side, created a volatile situation. Haitian laborers came to the Dominican Republic, some as guest workers, others to stay, enticed by the prospect of better lives. The welcome was often harsh. The Dominican self-image was interlaced with anti-Haitian sentiment. To be Haitian was to be black, to be black was to be Haitian. Dominicans, even those with predominant African ancestry, would define themselves as something other than black or mulatto — usually as the descendants of Taíno Indians — in order to escape the stigma associated with being Haitian. Although the Taíno Indians had largely been killed off within fifty years of Columbus's landing in 1492, the myth of Taíno ancestry held and indeed still holds a strong appeal for many Dominicans.

That myth certainly held a strong appeal for Dominican dictator Rafael Leónidas Trujillo, a mulatto who shared the anti-Haitian prejudices of many of his compatriots. Trujillo was particularly active in promoting the myth that Dominicans were descended from Taíno Indians, requiring that it be taught as history in the nation's schools. His anti-Haitian sentiments could be far more dangerous. Trujillo had a sociopathic personality and a willingness to engage in wholesale slaughter. In 1937, acting on his orders, the Dominican Army murdered some twenty-five thousand "Haitians" living in the Dominican Republic, many of them second- or third-generation Dominicans of Haitian ancestry. Trujillo used anti-Haitian prejudice as a way of consolidating power, giving the Dominican people a common enemy against whom he would be the protector. If Trujillo was willing to go far beyond other Latin American national leaders in stoking and acting on antiblack sentiment, he also shared their desire to increase white immigration. His efforts would meet with little success. Dominicans would continue uneasily to share the small, troubled island of Hispaniola with the people of Haiti.[34]

Throughout the hemisphere, national leaders used immigration policy, national censuses, textbooks in public school systems, and in Trujillo's case mass murder in order to promote their vision of a European future for their nations. Even when they reluctantly realized that that European future would remain more aspiration than reality, intellectual and political elites in countries with large indigenous populations were often able to write Afro-American minorities out of the national narrative and frequently the national consciousness as well. A European future, largely free of African and Afro-American influence, had been an aspiration of many national leaders in Cuba as well after the Caribbean nation obtained its independence from Spain. Cuban officials looked to Spain as a prime source of new settlers. As was the case elsewhere in the hemisphere, the Cuban government promulgated a set of policies, land grants, and tax relief measures designed to encourage Spanish immigrants. The efforts to encourage European immigration would meet with considerable success. Between 1902 and 1929, nearly one million Spaniards immigrated to Cuba, more than had arrived during the preceding four centuries of Spanish colonial rule.[35]

But demography again would complicate the business of national whitening. Cuba at the beginning of the last century had a large Afro-Cuban population, the legacy of the extensive nineteenth-century slave trade to the island. The island's late participation in the slave trade had helped keep alive a vibrant African culture in the nation. That surviving African culture was even less welcome than the presence of a large Afro-Cuban population. African culture smacked of witchcraft. African religious custom and ritual exemplified the very barbarism that those who envisioned a white Cuba wanted to stamp out. Cuban officials would use the criminal law to declare that African practices constituted witchcraft, a set of practices that merited the severe sanction of the criminal law. Afro-Cubans might escape those sanctions but only by firmly rejecting or at least keeping hidden practices that reminded authorities that there was still an uncomfortably large number of people on the island whose view of this world and the world to come owed at least as much to Africa as to Spain. The size of the Afro-Cuban population, combined with the strength of African culture among a large segment of that population, doubtless added a particular urgency to the need for European immigration in the minds of many.[36]

That perceived need for greater European immigration was part of a growing atmosphere of racial conflict in the early years of Cuban independence. That conflict was in part an outgrowth of the system of slavery on the island as it had developed in the nineteenth century. The events discussed in chapter 1, the island's sugar boom, its late and intense participation in the African slave trade, helped heighten racial and cultural conflict. Harsh race relations were in part the results of an expanding slave economy. Cuba's slave economy was expanding at a time when the other Spanish-speaking societies of the hemisphere had begun or in some cases completed the process of emancipation. Slavery's persistence in Cuba ensured that Spanish authorities and Cuban slaveholders were preoccupied with the issue of slave rebellion at a time when leaders of the independent republics of Latin America, whatever their concerns about their Afro-American populations, had put such fears behind them. This contributed to a degree of racial tension in nineteenth-century Cuba that was considerably stronger than in other parts of Spanish America.[37]

Racial tension would be somewhat softened by bonds that had been forged among blacks, whites, and mulattoes during the island's war for independence against Spain. Afro-Cubans had played a prominent part in the war. Some rose to the rank of general in the independence forces. One of these generals, Antonio Maceo, who died during the war, would become an enduring national icon through a variety of different Cuban regimes, down to the present. Revolutionary leader and intellectual José Martí proclaimed his vision of Cuba as an inclusive republic with an equal place for blacks, whites, and mulattoes. Still, the legacy of the racial divisions of the nineteenth century were strong. The new racial sciences of the early twentieth century would add to these divisions, as would occupation by an American army more rigidly segregated than the nation it served. After independence, the desire to whiten Cuba and suppress any signs of Afro-Cuban race consciousness would become more intense.[38]

In an early-twentieth-century atmosphere where national leaders emphasized that Cuba should have a future that was white and European and one in which the Afro-Cuban was regularly disparaged and the object of often intense discrimination, Afro-Cubans increasingly sought rescue in concerted political action. In 1908, the Partido Independiente de Color (PIC) was founded to fight the growing racism in the new republic. The party's leaders were middle-class Afro-Cubans, veterans of the war for independence. They organized along racial lines to combat the very real existence of racial inequality despite Cuba's formal legal guarantees of equality for all.[39]

The party's platform urged a variety of class and racial reforms, including free education at the primary, secondary, and university levels; trial by jury; abolition of the death penalty; and land reform; among other measures. The party also challenged the policy of national whitening. Its newspaper criticized the policy of subsidizing European immigration, calling the policy an effort to destroy Afro-Cubans. The PIC instead called for free immigration for people of all races, stating that education rather than race should be the basis for admission to the nation. The PIC's demonstration of Afro-Cuban independence increasingly disquieted Cuban authorities. At first, authorities attempted to harass the independent political party. They argued that the party was an attempt to overthrow the Cuban government. Even the specter of the late-eighteenth-century Haitian Revolution was invoked to stoke fears of Afro-Cuban rebelliousness and savagery. In 1910, the party was formally outlawed. In that same year, white vigilantes began organizing to combat the Afro-Cuban party. Many members of the party were imprisoned. By 1912, there was a full-scale "race war" designed to suppress the PIC. White vigilantes and government police and soldiers participated in widespread racial violence, including the lynching of party members designed to eradicate the PIC.[40]

Racial tensions and efforts at racial reform would continue to be a major part of Cuban political and social life long after the violent suppression of the PIC. Despite strong desires to turn Cuba into a white republic through European immigration, the island nation would experience black migration from the British West Indies and Haiti. Brought to Cuba to harvest the nation's sugarcane crop during periods of labor shortage, a number of these immigrants would stay, adding their numbers to the Afro-Cuban population and at times increasing racial tensions. Both black and foreign, they would often be subject to deportation in times of economic hardship. In the 1920s and 1930s, Afro-Cubans made noticeable gains in levels of education and employment in the professions and governmental sectors, although the evidence is that they lagged significantly behind their white compatriots. If racial prejudices remained strong in Cuba in the interwar years, there were developments that somewhat softened the earlier emphasis on national whitening. Throughout the region, national leaders were reconsidering their indigenous or Afro-American populations and their contributions to national cultures. Part of this was simple necessity. the indigenous or Afro-American populations were simply too large to ignore. Their contributions to the national culture, at least on a reasonably safe symbolic or folkloric level, could scarcely be denied and indeed might be celebrated as an indication of that which was unique in the national culture. In Cuba, this was aided in part by the work of Fernando Ortiz, one of a number of Latin American scholars who after the First World War were giving a serious reconsideration to the importance of African cultures in the Americas.[41]

General efforts at political reform seem to have spurred a greater awareness, at least on a nominal level, that racial discrimination was inconsistent with the broader ideals of the Cuban republic. What historians have termed the Revolution of 1933 was a catalyst for reforms in a number of areas, among them women's suffrage and labor reform. Although the revolution was short-lived, ending in January 1934, its effects would linger. The regime of Fulgencio Batista y Zaldívar that would emerge as the de facto successor government paid lip service to social reform including supporting the reform constitution of 1940. That constitution had a provision explicitly outlawing discrimination on the grounds of sex, race, color, or class. It also had a provision that prohibited parties organized along racial lines.[42]

The provision in Cuba's constitution of 1940 represented at least the nominal triumph of the ideal of the equality of all before the law regardless of race. We know from subsequent Cuban history that there was often a wide gap between that ideal and actual racial practices in Cuba. But that would be true in other parts of the hemisphere. The idea that citizens, regardless of race, were equal before the law would gain support and find its way into the constitutions and ordinary legislation in a number of American nations during the middle and latter years of the twentieth century. But that idea had to contend with strong racial prejudices, prejudices that had been honed through national racial policies after independence just as surely as they had been cultivated by the racial policies of the Spanish Empire during the colonial era. Throughout the hemisphere, censuses and immigration policies would contribute to patterns of racial identity and racial inequality in the Spanish-speaking nations of the Americas just as surely as the system of *castas* embedded in the Law of the Indies had done in the *audiencias* and *viceroyalties* that had preceded them.[43]

Like the system of *castas*, policies designed to whiten the nations of the hemisphere left a mixed and sometimes perplexing legacy to the peoples who would live in nations that remained stubbornly multiracial and multicultural despite the fondest wishes of the architects of national whitening. If *blanqueamiento* and *mestizaje* dictated a clear racial hierarchy, they nonetheless also continued and indeed perhaps enhanced notions of racial mobility and racial improvement that had begun in the colonial era. The stigma associated with African ancestry in many nations, the higher status granted not only to those who were white, but to mestizos — even dark mestizos who claimed that they were not black — created a scramble on the part of many to escape the *negro* label. That scramble, to be sure, had been present from the earliest days of the colonial era. Escaping from blackness in the era of *castas* and slavery could mean escape from legal

disabilities, perhaps slavery itself. But even in the twentieth century in nations with constitutions that proclaimed the equality of all, many would
still feel the need to deny or minimize their African background. As anthropologist Peter Wade informs us, the process of escaping black status
might take many forms, including marriage with people of other races or
moving away from localities traditionally associated with Afro-American
communities.[44]

In some ways, this notion that individuals could and indeed should try
to escape their Afro-American identity may have represented the greatest
triumph of *blanqueamiento*. That notion represented for many a conquest
of the spirit in the twentieth century just as sure as slavery represented a
physical conquest in the colonial era. This new conquest of the spirit would
take many forms. Acceptance of the notion that the race of one's children
could be bettered through intermarriage was one. Denial of African ancestry, even in cases where African heritage was phenotypically inescapable,
was another.

Yet with the exception of immigration law, *blanqueamiento* was essayed
largely without the use of a formal body of discriminatory legislation of
the sort that underlay the system of Jim Crow that shaped the world of inequality and racial exclusion in the United States. It was also accomplished
with less of the kind of racist/populist politics that historically played such
a critical role in making the black population a caste apart in the United
States. This absence of formal barriers, the occasional presence of prominent Afro-Americans in the histories of a number of Latin American nations, even the participation of Afro-Americans in working-class populist
movements — Venezuela's Acción Democrática, Costa Rica's Partido de
Liberación Nacional, and as we shall see in chapter 5 Brazil's right-wing
populist movement led by Getúlio Vargas — have all contributed to the
difficulty of the North American observer trying to explain race in Latin
America. Explanations that were popular early in the twentieth century
that saw the relative absence of formal barriers in Latin America as evidence of racial harmony and racial democracy now can clearly be seen
as overblown. And yet the relative inclusiveness found in Latin America
compared to the more rigid legal exclusions that existed in the United
States in the first half of the twentieth century stand as sharp reminders
of the power of law to shape social status and social relations. The effort
to whiten the republics that had come out of the former Spanish Empire

left an inconsistent legacy. That effort helped to strengthen the hierarchical ordering of the races, and yet it also helped to foster a culture that at times denied the very existence of race. It fostered patterns of racial exclusion and yet also allowed personal ties and agreed-upon fictions to permit some individuals, despite race, to gain access to the highest levels of society. These contradictions and inconsistencies would be found throughout the Spanish-speaking nations of the hemisphere. They would also be part of the twentieth-century history of the vast, multiethnic, and multiracial nation of Brazil.[45]

CHAPTER FIVE

No País do Futuro

BRAZIL'S JOURNEY FROM NATIONAL WHITENING TO "RACIAL DEMOCRACY"

LONG BEFORE PRINCESS ISABEL took a golden pen and signed the law that ended Brazilian slavery, even before the Viscount of Rio Branco sponsored the law of the free womb, the dream of a white Brazil settled by industrious and intelligent Europeans and freed from the problematic presence of large Afro-American and Indian populations was a strong one. José Bonifácio, a key architect of the 1824 constitution, had framed his opposition to slavery in part on the grounds that a large enslaved population posed a barrier to European immigrants and the progress that they would bring. Brazil's great abolitionist, Joaquim Nabuco, echoed similar concerns in his antislavery tract, *O abolicionismo*. As early as 1850, at a time of growing international pressure to end slavery and the slave trade, the Brazilian Parliament took steps to encourage European settlement, passing a statute that provided for generous land grants to immigrants. The same statute also denied land title to residents of *quilombos*, many of whom came from families that had lived in those settlements for generations.[1]

Branqueamento (the desire to whiten Brazil) would become national policy starting in the Velha República (Old Republic), formed in 1889. The republic differed from its imperial predecessor. The law of the empire protected slavery but in most other major respects was silent on the question of race. The law of the republic was different. It would outlaw slavery. Nevertheless, constitutional and statutory provisions would make clear the desire of the republic's leaders to transform Brazil into a white nation. The law governing immigration would explicitly discriminate on the basis of race, encouraging white immigration and specifically prohibiting the entrance of Africans and Afro-Americans. As was the case in Spanish

America, this new regime of legal discrimination was supported by the scientific wisdom of the day, a scientific wisdom that informed elite Brazilians that their nation's progress was imperiled by the frightening predominance of Afro-Brazilians in the modern, progressive republic, the country of the future, they hoped to form.

This desire to whiten Brazil would have far-reaching consequences. With the exception of Argentina, Brazil would receive more European immigrants than any other country in Latin America. Immigration would bring to the lusophonic nation a range of ethnic and racial diversity matched in few other societies. Brazil's two southernmost states, Rio Grande do Sul and Santa Catarina, would receive a massive influx of German immigrants, so much so that before the Second World War, German was often heard in the region more frequently than Portuguese. Even today, many citizens in the two states, many who are now third- or fourth-generation Brazilians, still speak German at home particularly in cities with names like Blumenau and Novo Hamburgo. Arabs, Jews, and Turks from the Middle East also found new homes and livelihoods in São Paulo and other states. They are frequently called "Turcos" regardless of their religion or ethnicity because their families came to Brazil when their native lands were provinces of the Ottoman Empire. They were joined by large numbers of Italian and Japanese immigrants who came to São Paulo. Today, Brazil has the largest ethnic Japanese population in the world outside of Japan. We will examine a little later in this chapter the peculiar dynamics that permitted the settlement of large numbers of Japanese in a twentieth-century Brazil that was desperately working on national whitening.[2]

And of course, the Afro-Brazilians remained. They were to be found throughout the nation. The demands of different regional slave economies and the opportunities that were available for free Afro-Brazilians in the nineteenth and earlier centuries combined to help spread the descendants of enslaved Africans throughout the giant Brazilian Empire. Even the War of the Triple Alliance played a part in bringing Afro-Brazilian soldiers and their descendants to the southern state of Santa Catarina. Large-scale European immigration would make Afro-Brazilians somewhat less visible in the South, just as large-scale European immigration would make Afro-Argentines and Afro-Uruguayans less visible in their nations in the twentieth century. But they would remain. Afro-Brazilians would be more visible in states like São Paulo and Rio de Janeiro, venues where coffee cultivation had employed large slave populations in the waning years of the Brazilian Empire. Italian and Japanese immigrants were specifically brought to replace slave laborers as slavery became less and less viable and in response to strong hopes that a better breed of workers would help build a better nation. Afro-Brazilians at the beginning of the twentieth century would remain most visible in the northeastern states of Bahia and Pernambuco. Land of the large sugar *fazendas* and home to most of the Africans who came to Brazil, those states would remain an Afro-Brazilian country. Most of the region's people were at least partially of African descent — there was even a term for the whites of the region, *branco da terra* (white of the land or white of Bahia), an acknowledgment that those who were called white in that region likely had African blood, in some cases a considerable amount. While they might be seen as white in Bahia, they might not be viewed as such elsewhere in Brazil.[3]

Bahia and other parts of the Northeast at the beginning of the twentieth century were more than places where large numbers of Afro-Brazilians lived; African culture thrived there. African gods were worshiped. The recently emancipated slaves, along with Afro-Brazilians whose families had been free for generations and indeed more than a few whites, petitioned these gods to intercede and cushion them from the hardships of daily life. Sometimes they petitioned the gods and spirits of West Africa directly using their ancient names; sometimes they openly used the names of the Catholic saints with the silent understanding that they were petitioning African deities. These petitions for a good portion of the twentieth century created more than a little alarm on the part of Brazilian authorities. Despite provisions in the 1891 constitution that eliminated the Catholic Church's role as the state church and guaranteed freedom of religion, African religious practices were not viewed as legitimate forms of worship. They were seen as exercises in superstition and fetishism, evidence of African barbarism and Afro-Brazilian gullibility, perhaps even criminality. Even worse, the contagion of African religion could and did spread to whites — not only the whites of Bahia, Pernambuco, and Rio, who had had centuries of cultural and indeed racial mixture with Africans and Afro-Brazilians, but even some of the new immigrants. In Rio Grande do Sul, immigrants from Germany and Italy could be found attending Afro-Brazilian religious ceremonies, much to the consternation of local authorities. These practices, whether engaged in by Afro-Brazilians or whites, even recent arrivals from Europe, detracted from the modern, civilized, European image that Brazilian leaders wanted to project for their nation. For a good part of the twentieth century, state and national authorities would use the penal law to suppress religious practices based on African traditions. Arrests were made, trials held, and defendants convicted for practicing Candomblé, Batuque, and other forms of African worship despite constitutional guarantees of religious freedom.[4]

Even in Bahia, with its strong Afro-Brazilian presence, African religious practices were subject to persecution. In 1902, state officials went so far as to outlaw Candomblé drumming even in secular carnival processions. Some scholars have argued that Bahian elites might have been particularly anxious to suppress African-based forms of religious expression. In a nation that at the beginning of the republican era was emphasizing a future that was white and European, many elite members of Bahian society were painfully aware that they were linked to a Brazilian past with deep African roots. These *brancos da terra*, known to have African ancestors, perhaps still in touch with their Afro-Brazilian relatives, were undoubtedly often quite embarrassed by public expressions of African culture. And they were even more embarrassed by relatives black, white, and mulatto who would occasionally let slip the mask of European culture and visit an Afro-Brazilian religious ceremony or seek a cure or intervention from the spirit world proffered by an Afro-Brazilian shaman.[5]

The Penal Code of 1890 would provide a legal mechanism for suppressing many Afro-Brazilian religious practices. A number of its provisions, found in a section titled "Crimes against Public Health," were undoubtedly aimed at practices that advocates of a modern, progressive, scientific Brazil saw as superstitious and indeed dangerous. These provisions were part of a larger trend in Western nations at the end of the nineteenth century to regulate practices, particularly medical and quasi-medical practices that were seen as dangerous to health and safety. But whatever the motivations, these provisions, or the way they were enforced, would hit practitioners of traditional Afro-Brazilian religions particularly hard. The code prohibited the practice of medicine without legal certification as well as the administering or prescribing of natural folk remedies. It also outlawed the practice of spiritism or magic as a means of curing illnesses or arousing sentiments of love or hate. In one sense, the legal architects of the new Brazilian Republic were simply continuing the pattern established in the empire's constitution of 1824. The fear that African religious practices were barbaric and would undermine European civilization in Brazil had long existed, as the use of the criminal law to suppress these practices.[6]

African forms of worship were more than an area of concern for the criminal law; they would also serve as a catalyst in the development of a homegrown Brazilian school of scientific racism championed by pioneering medical anthropologist Raimundo Nina Rodrigues. Rodrigues, a physician by training, became a professor at the medical faculty of Bahia. He helped establish the field of psychiatry in Brazil and was the first Brazilian scholar to do systematic ethnographic studies of Afro-Brazilian life in his native Bahia. His studies of Afro-Brazilian religious practices served to reinforce his convictions that Afro-Brazilians were innately primitive, incapable of truly absorbing a modern, sophisticated, Western religion like Roman Catholicism.[7]

Rodrigues's views were informed in part by his observations but also in great part because he was an avid follower of evolutionary theories that were migrating from the biological sciences to the newly developing social sciences toward the end of the nineteenth century. One strain of social thought likened the social scientist to the physician. Both were charged with ferreting out and eliminating the pathological, whether it was found in a biological or social organism. Only by doing so could the organism remain healthy and competitive. It was a point of view particularly well suited to Brazilian nationalists preoccupied with the question of whether or not their nation would achieve the greatness that they believed was Brazil's national destiny. But the prevailing wisdom of the day argued against Brazilian progress. Students of the rise and fall of great civilizations assured their readers that the two principal determiners of human advancement were race and climate. Brazil's tropical climate argued strongly against any great progressive breakthroughs. And the nation was plagued with too many Negroes, Indians, and *mestiços*. The hoped-for future of progress and modernity was problematic, perhaps impossible.[8]

Rodrigues concluded that a regime of rigid racial separation, more rigid than any previously known in Brazilian life, was the only way to preserve the nation as a part of the civilized, Western world. His writings proclaimed that not only blacks but *mestiços*, a term that in this context is best translated as mulattoes, were inferior and incapable of absorbing modern civilization, including the Catholic faith. He argued vigorously against any notion of Afro-Brazilian equality with whites. Egalitarianism, Rodrigues informed his readers, was based on a dangerous sentimentality out of touch with scientific realities. It was a false notion that had been spread by abolitionists in their quest to end slavery. Rodrigues even went so far as to argue that the very notion of a Brazilian people was a myth, one that existed perhaps as a matter of law and politics but an anthropological and sociological myth nonetheless, totally unjustified by social reality and biological difference. Rodrigues used this notion of innate biological and social difference to argue for separate legal regimes for civilized and uncivilized Brazilians. Uncivilized Brazilians, by which he meant almost all blacks and most mulattoes, should not be governed by national legislation meant to govern white people; instead, he urged permitting each state to adopt its own codes to govern the dangerous Afro-Brazilian population.[9]

The Bahian physician's racism was all the more ironic because Rodrigues, like many people from the region, was of mixed African and Portuguese ancestry. His belief in Negro inferiority was probably shared by most Brazilian intellectuals and governmental leaders at the beginning of the twentieth century. It was part of the conventional wisdom of the Western world at the time. And yet Rodrigues's policy prescriptions, his segregationist tendencies, and his support for a formal, separate legal regime that would govern Afro-Brazilians more harshly than whites met with little support among Brazilian officials. There were many reasons for this. The dynamics of race as they had existed in the nineteenth-century slaveholding empire would carry over into the free republic of the early twentieth century. The scarcity of whites that had allowed some free Afro-Brazilians, particularly mulattoes, to enter into positions of influence and privilege in the nineteenth century would continue, at least in some regions, into the twentieth. Powerful patrons and family connections would continue to allow a few Afro-Brazilians into governmental offices, law and medical faculties, and major enterprises even as doctrines of white supremacy and the felt need for national whitening grew stronger.[10]

Like their counterparts in the former Spanish colonies of the hemisphere, Brazilian leaders took the scientific racism and Social Darwinism of the day and refashioned them to meet the needs of the nation that they wanted to lead into the new century. Blacks were inferior, most mulattoes only somewhat less so; and these basic truths need not be contested. But could these truths be allowed to doom the great nation that Brazil was obviously destined to become? No! Evolutionary theory had to be modified, reconsidered in light of Brazilian realities. The proper way of viewing the Afro-Brazilian was not as a permanent liability, a source of recessive traits that, as Rodrigues feared, would inevitably hold the nation back. Instead, the Afro-Brazilian's backward traits would be absorbed and transformed by successive waves of white immigrants. These European immigrants, like the Portuguese before them, would absorb the Afro-Brazilian over time eliminating his backward traits and ultimately the Afro-Brazilian himself. Progress would come. The Afro-Brazilian would eventually disappear, absorbed in the new waves of immigration. A bright future awaited the Brazilian nation.

Republican Brazil would act quickly to put this dream of a European future into effect. One of the republic's first enactments was a decree governing immigration promulgated by provisional president Manuel Deodoro da Fonseca in 1890. The decree was designed to encourage European immigration of the right sort. It prohibited the immigration of persons with criminal backgrounds. It also prohibited immigration by members of the indigenous populations of Africa and Asia. Fonseca's decree also provided for subsidized transportation of European settlers to Brazil and also for the subsidized sale of houses and plots of land to immigrant families. The 1890 decree also specified mechanisms that allowed immigrants to complain of fraud or mistreatment. It was a set of benefits not being offered to native-born Brazilians, particularly the recently enslaved Afro-Brazilians.[11]

Fonseca's decree was clearly written in conformity with the conventional racial thinking of the era. Even before the end of slavery and the establishment of the republic, planters in the rich coffee-growing regions of Rio de Janeiro and São Paulo had begun to explore European immigration as an alternative to the waning and increasingly problematic institution of slavery. In congresses organized by planters, delegates discussed alternatives to slave labor. Many planters expressed preferences for industrious white immigrants over what they saw as indolent native Brazilians. They labeled the Afro-Brazilians laboring on their plantations a "decrepit race," one they would gladly replace with superior immigrants. Theirs was not necessarily a preference for Europeans, who might have been more skilled or better educated than the enslaved Afro-Brazilians they were soon to replace. Their preference was racial. It was based on the raw belief that the Europeans provided a better stock with which to populate both *fazenda* and nation. Many of the Europeans brought by the planters to replace their former slaves were illiterate peasants, possessing few if any skills not already possessed by the recently emancipated Brazilians. Nonetheless, the Europeans were white, members of the presumably superior race. They also possessed one other advantage over the newly freed Afro-Brazilians. Immigrants did not possess memories of the harsh treatment endured under slavery and the desire to escape the *fazendas* in which so many had suffered so egregiously. The planters believed that without such memories, the European immigrants would be a more willing and indeed more pliable labor force.[12]

Fonseca's 1890 decree was part of a broader pattern of legal and political efforts designed to further the dream of a white Brazil. In 1889, the Congress enacted legislation that granted automatic naturalization to European immigrants. Several provisions of the 1891 constitution also supported automatic citizenship for immigrants. The state of São Paulo was especially aggressive in promoting immigration. Opening offices in European capitals, officials from the coffee-growing state actively recruited European settlers. State funds were appropriated to pay for the transportation of immigrant families. The incentives did not end there. Paulista officials promised prospective immigrants housing along with subsidized food and hospital care. The southeastern state also offered cash grants for European immigrants and exemptions from military service for their children. The aggressive promotions worked. Between 1890 and 1914, some 1.5 million Europeans would cross the Atlantic and make São Paulo their home. It was a success that Brazilian officials hoped could be replicated throughout the nation.[13]

Paulista officials, like their counterparts in other states and in the national government, crafted laws and policies designed to increase the European population. They also wanted to reduce the size and visibility of the population of African descent. European immigrants were preferred, but even Asian immigrants would come to be seen as preferable to the population of former slaves and free people of color of early Republican Brazil. In 1892, Congress passed a statute relaxing the ban on Japanese and Chinese immigrants. Between 1908, when Japanese immigration began, and 1968, nearly a quarter of a million Japanese would settle in the South American nation, primarily in São Paulo. The Japanese government subsidized their transportation to Brazil and arranged for employment on plantations and the housing of entire families. Japanese immigrants would prove to be particularly efficient agricultural laborers, demonstrating skills that Japanese immigrants would show in other parts of the Americas, particularly the West Coast of the United States and Hawaii. Their skill brought support for continued Japanese immigration from Brazilian politicians anxious to strengthen the coffee economy, which in the early decades of the twentieth century was the main source of the nation's wealth.[14]

If Brazilian leaders would come to accept Japanese immigration, restrictions against the immigration of people with African ancestry would be enforced with a singular rigor. They were applied not only to Africans but to peoples of African descent from the Americas as well. Brazil's exclusion of immigrants of African descent was, interestingly enough, even more rigorous than that of the United States during the height of the Jim Crow era. Immigration legislation passed by the U.S. Congress in 1921 and 1924 had quotas for immigrants according to geographic origin. The American legislation effectively excluded immigrants from Africa and Asia but allowed immigration from nations in the Western Hemisphere without quotas. This would, during the course of the twentieth century, permit hundreds of thousands of Afro-American immigrants to enter the United States from the Caribbean and other parts of the hemisphere. Such would not be the case with Brazil.[15]

Brazil's immigration policy and the increased European presence in the nation would serve to feed the kind of scientific racism that had led Brazilian leaders to embark on the national project of *branqueamento* in the first place. Intellectual and political leaders were encouraged by the success that they were having in attracting European immigrants. It was possible. Europeans would come, despite the scientific views of the day that claimed that Brazil was doomed to be backward. *Branqueamento* was working. Brazil could become a modern, European republic. As would be the case in other American nations, the census would play a role in the cause of national whitening or at the very least in minimizing the nation's Afro-American population. The process began with the census of 1890, the first one conducted by the new republican government. Brazil's first census in 1872 indicated four racial or color categories: *branco* (white), *preto* (black), *pardo* (mulatto), and *caboclo* (Indian). The 1890 census substituted the term *mestiço* for *pardo*. While *pardo* had traditionally meant that the individual had a mixture of African and European ancestry, *mestiço* was more ambiguous, subject to translation as either *mulatto* or *mestizo*, an individual with European and indigenous ancestry. Officials explained the change as necessary to secure popular cooperation with the census. Because of the stigma attached to African ancestry, they argued, people were more likely to respond to the ambiguous term *mestiço* than to the more clearly Afro-Brazilian identification *pardo*. Research by sociologist Mara Loveman indicates that while that official reason may partly explain the terminological shift, it is also likely that the change was made to help minimize the size of the Afro-Brazilian population in order to help promote European immigration.[16]

The 1900 and 1920 censuses would go even further in hiding the lusophonic republic's racial makeup. Neither census contained racial statistics on the Brazilian population. Although scholars dispute the extent to which that omission was part of a conscious effort to hide Brazil's large Afro-American population, it clearly proved to be convenient for national leaders anxious to project a European image of the South American nation. The 1920 census was also notable for publishing an introductory essay by writer Oliveira Viana. In the essay, "O povo brasileiro e sua evolução," Viana detailed his views on the inevitable whitening of the Brazilian nation and the ultimate vanquishing and disappearance of the inferior Afro-Brazilian and indigenous populations. It was a transformation eagerly sought after by many of Brazil's leaders at the beginning of the last century.[17]

Like Viana, many Brazilian political and intellectual leaders believed that the transformation was being brought about through immigration. The new immigration and the continued public and private propaganda emphasizing the superiority of immigrant laborers would take its toll on employment opportunities for Afro-Brazilians. For many Afro-Brazilians, employment prospects would be worse in the liberal republic formed in 1889 than they had been in the nineteenth-century empire. Slaves in the empire had, of course, guaranteed employment, whether or not they wanted it. But free Afro-Brazilians also had something of an advantage. The small white population in most parts of the nation allowed free Afro-Brazilians to fill positions as free laborers, artisans, petty traders, and minor government officials. This was not true throughout the nation. Even in the nineteenth century, the southern state of Santa Catarina had a large population of European immigrants and a small Afro-Brazilian population. In that state, free Afro-Brazilians frequently had severe difficulties securing regular wage labor and were forced to work in the informal economy. Employers simply preferred the new European immigrants.[18]

The kind of employment discrimination that was informally exercised in Santa Catarina in the nineteenth century would spread to other states after national abolition and the arrival of more European immigrants. São Paulo would lead the nation in reflecting the new wisdom that the Brazil of the future and particularly the more modern sectors of its economy had little if any place for the Afro-Brazilian. The southeastern state would receive roughly half the immigrants who came to republican Brazil. Even before the beginning of the twentieth century, it was clear that Paulista employers preferred the new immigrants to native-born Afro-Brazilians. An 1894 listing of occupations in the city of São Paulo indicated that over 80 percent of the occupations in the modern, urban sector of the economy were held by foreign immigrants. These jobs involving manufacturing, skilled trades, transportation, and commerce would over the course of the twentieth century transform the coffee-producing state into an industrial powerhouse, one that would ultimately place the South American nation among the world's ten largest economies. But even before the twentieth century began, a pattern was being set. Afro-Brazilians would find it difficult to enter into these modern industrial and commercial enterprises. European immigrants would be preferred. In São Paulo at the beginning of the twentieth century, even many civil service jobs, usually the mainstay of the Afro-American middle class in other countries, were often closed to Negroes: state regulations prohibited the employment of Afro-Brazilians as prison guards and in the state police force. Afro-Brazilians would often find steady employment scarce. Some survived on casual labor. Many families could survive only if mothers and daughters could find employment in domestic service.[19]

The color line in early republican Brazil could and did extend beyond the workplace. In a number of cities in São Paulo and elsewhere, there was a strong push for a physical segregation of the races. Some restaurants simply refused to serve Afro-Brazilians. In Campinas in the state of São Paulo, "White only" signs were frequently seen in front of theaters and other public places. Afro-Brazilian newspapers complained of discrimination in hospitals, restaurants, and retail stores. Advertisements for apartments would openly state, "No people of color accepted," or "Foreigners preferred." And the desire to keep Afro-Brazilians both out of sight and out of mind could take other forms. In Rio de Janeiro between 1902 and 1906, authorities undertook the renovation of the city designed to transform the nation's capital into "a Paris in the tropics." A large visible Afro-Brazilian population was inconsistent with this hoped for European makeover. More than seven hundred buildings in the central parishes home to thousands of Afro-Brazilians were destroyed. The residents were moved to locations that were less desirable and less visible.[20]

At times, the color line would be enforced by local police, often with dubious legal authority. Oral testimonies from Afro-Brazilians alive at the beginning of the last century document a system of forced racial separation in public spaces in the state of São Paulo. Afro-Brazilians were prohibited from entering certain public gardens, public squares, and streets. Violators were arrested and imprisoned by police. It would probably be stating it too strongly to say that these instances of enforced segregation were the same as Jim Crow in the American South or apartheid in South Africa. These actions did not have the support of the formal law. Arrests usually came because whites complained that an Afro-Brazilian had entered a public space customarily reserved for whites. Statutes did not prescribe separate facilities for black and white, nor did they forbid Afro-Brazilians from gathering in certain neighborhoods or enjoying specific public spaces. The constitution of 1891 and its state counterpart did proclaim the equality of all before the law. The custom of evicting and imprisoning Afro-Brazilians who intruded into areas customarily reserved for whites was almost surely selectively applied. The wealthy, well-dressed mulatto, perhaps even an occasional black man or woman who was clearly of the "better classes," was probably, given the dynamics of Brazilian social structure, allowed into the otherwise restricted public garden or fashionable avenue.[21]

But for poor black people, the ones whose race and class clearly put them at the bottom of the social pyramid, the public exclusions were real and at times unyielding. The theoretical equality proclaimed by state and federal constitutions and the absence of statutes prescribing segregated facilities meant little to a poor Afro-Brazilian imprisoned and perhaps maltreated by police officers determined to keep him in his place and out of the city's more desirable public spaces. He would have little ability to challenge such state actions. Few attorneys would champion his cause. Even if one might, even if a solid legal argument could be mustered that the police officers' actions were contrary to the spirit of the new constitutions and not sanctioned by any formal, written statute, what judge was likely to agree with the black petitioner? The judge would come from society's up-per classes. He was likely imbued with the conventional wisdom of the day, Afro-Brazilians, especially poor ones, along with other inferior peoples should not be allowed to disturb their betters in the enjoyment of the quiet gardens and walkways that provided a sanctuary from their daily manage-ment of public and private affairs. Nor should they be allowed to disturb the new Brazilians, immigrants who represented the nation's future and who might not want to associate with their Afro-American inferiors. The Brazilian legal culture, with its emphasis on judicial autonomy and "the law of good reason," had changed little with the establishment of the republic. An Afro-Brazilian petitioner contesting police-enforced segregation was unlikely to prevail, however strong his legal argument. In any event, the oral histories do not indicate that any such cases were brought.[22]

If Afro-Brazilians were unlikely to find the courts willing to protect them from extralegal action by authorities, that judicial reluctance would have been reflective of the new constitution adopted in 1891. That con-stitution was hardly concerned with vindicating the rights of the poor whatever their race or color. Modeled after the U.S. Constitution and ti-tled "Constitution of the Republic of the United States of Brazil," the new constitution adopted a scheme of federalism similar to that of the United States, creating states and state governments out of the old imperial prov-inces. The 1891 constitution differed in one important respect from its North American model. It was specifically designed to keep large segments of the Brazilian population from voting. At a time when less than 15 per-cent of the adult population was literate, the constitution prohibited indi-viduals who were illiterate from voting. The provision preventing illiterates from voting was followed by another that kept the franchise from beggars. Both provisions probably kept all but a handful of former slaves from vot-ing. Less than 8 percent of the Afro-Brazilian population was literate. This would have made the kind of racial disenfranchisement that emerged in the United States in the Jacksonian era and that would reemerge toward the end of the nineteenth century unnecessary. Political control was to be kept firmly in the hands of the better classes. The new constitution had an equality provision. It stated that "all were equal in the presence of the law." But that provision was more concerned with extinguishing the formal titles and privileges of the old imperial nobility than with establishing a legal regime mandating equal treatment of Brazilian citizens. That equality would have been a weak reed on which to hang a lawsuit alleging racial discrimination, particularly before judges with considerable discretion and little inclination to grant relief.[23]

Wherever Afro-Brazilians turned at the start of the last century, they might hear talk of the great nation, "the country of the future," that Brazil would become. They would also find clear signs that many who were proclaiming the impending greatness of the South American republic envisioned a future in which Afro-Brazilians would have little or no part. The best jobs, the ones that paid well and were tied to the economy of the future, the economy that involved commerce and industry and new technology — these were held by white Brazilians or even more glaringly white foreigners. Afro-Brazilians had difficulty finding homes or apartments in good neighborhoods. At times there were efforts to move them out of the downtown areas of major cities. Even entering a public park might be cause for arrest and imprisonment. The new century, this age of progress about which the leading intellectuals and great statesmen waxed so enthusiastic, was turning out to be a time of repeated racial insult and increased racial exclusion.

At times, racial exclusion was the result of quasi-official policy. In the state of São Paulo, a number of schools either openly refused to admit black and mulatto children or placed onerous conditions on their admission and attendance. At other times, racial exclusion could be the all but inevitable consequence of the ideology of the age and the attempt to put it into practice. This would occur with public education. From the beginning of the republic, the nation's high illiteracy rate worried liberal advocates of reform. Even during the empire, forward-looking statesmen saw that national progress would be linked to a literate, educated population. The 1871 law of the free womb called for the education of *ingênuos* born to slave mothers. By the end of the nineteenth century, republican leaders were alarmed at a large illiterate population consisting of ex-slaves, other poor Afro-Brazilians, and immigrants, many of whom were unable to understand basic Portuguese. Support for public education grew. Education was in the hands of state authorities. It was often not provided, particularly in poor rural areas with large Afro-Brazilian populations, but efforts to provide primary education and basic literacy would meet with some success in other areas, including the cities of Rio de Janeiro and São Paulo.[24]

Afro-Brazilian community leaders often took the lead in combating discrimination in education. Their actions frequently involved establishing schools designed to provide remedial education for adults as well as primary education for children. These schools often had a somewhat precarious existence, suffering from few financial resources and few qualified personnel. Nonetheless, they reflected two important trends in Afro-Brazilian culture after abolition. One of these was that Afro-Brazilian community leaders tended to share the broader national belief that education would provide the key to progress and, in the case of Afro-Brazilians, inclusion in the nation's future. Second, the development of independent Afro-Brazilian schools reflected a willingness on the part of Afro-Brazilians to organize along racial lines for mutual support and self-improvement. One study indicates that in the city of São Paulo alone between 1897 and 1930 there were some eighty-five Afro-Brazilian civic organizations organized around social, educational, and mutual aid interests.[25]

Undoubtedly the most important of these civic organizations were the magazines and newspapers written and read by Afro-Brazilians. Like the Afro-American press in other parts of the hemisphere these periodicals played a variety of different roles. They were community boosters, documenting the accomplishments of blacks and mulattoes that the white press frequently preferred to ignore. The publications served as a counter to the frequent negative stereotyping of Afro-Brazilians that would have been found in the general press, and in government reports and school textbooks. These publications were sources of information on African and Afro-Brazilian history at a time when few educated Brazilians regarded that history as worth remembering. And they were a source of protest and a vehicle through which Afro-Brazilians could assert their claim to the rights presumably guaranteed them in the new republican order that was Brazil in the Old Republic. São Paulo would lead the way with the highest number of Afro-Brazilian newspapers in the nation in the early decades of the twentieth century, but there would also be Afro-Brazilian newspapers in Recife, Rio de Janeiro, Porto Alegre, and other venues. These papers would often give a voice to those who would otherwise remain voiceless. They would also often provide evidence of injustices that would otherwise have remained undocumented.[26]

The press and the other Afro-Brazilian social organizations partly reflected some new realities. In the new republican Brazil, race was gaining in relative importance in determining an individual's or a group's social position. In the empire, particularly in the early nineteenth century, the large enslaved African population had actually served somewhat to lessen the racial boundaries between whites and free, native-born Afro-Brazilians. The two groups shared similar cultures. They also often shared a fear of the African and of slave rebellion. They were linked by familial ties and patterns of patronage and clientelism. Race could be important. Even successful Afro-Brazilians like Antonio Rebouças had to fight against racial exclusion. Some, like attorney Luís Gama, realized that race could put their very freedom at peril even though they were born free under the empire's laws. But through the ties of culture and clientelism, the vital role that the free Afro-Brazilian played as the intermediary class between master and slave in the days of the empire had provided a social space for the free Afro-Brazilian. That space was less certain in the early decades of the republic. This was especially true in the state of São Paulo, with its large immigrant population. The distinction between free and slave had been abolished. A future was being envisioned in which the black and even the mulatto with visible African ancestry were destined to disappear. Cultural differences were still important, and the Afro-Brazilian — less visibly African, more Catholic, less inclined to invoke the African spirits, and more European in speech, dress, and musical taste — might gain a measure of acceptance denied the individual who was more incorrigibly African. But the new emphasis on race still cautioned that Afro-Brazilians, even the somewhat more acceptable mulattoes, were still viewed as posing a threat, by their very existence, to the long-range health of the nation.

And yet race and social position remained complicated. The new racial ideology dictated that the Afro-Brazilian should become more marginal and less visible in the new forward-looking republic. But that ideology had to contend with the realities of the old racial culture, one in which class and family connections could modify, sometimes profoundly, the limitations of race. Perhaps nowhere is this better illustrated than in the career of Pedro Augusto Carneiro Lessa. In 1907, when the desire to transform Brazil into a European nation was at its zenith, Lessa became a minister on Brazil's highest court, the Supremo Tribunal Federal. He was a mulatto. His photograph indicates a man with quite visible African ancestry. Born in 1859 in Minas Gerais to Colonel José Pedro Lessa and Dona Francisca Amélia Carneiro Lessa, he became a successful lawyer in São Paulo. He had graduated from that city's Faculdade de Direito in 1883 and received a doctorate from the same institution in 1888. His political inclinations were republican and antislavery. In 1891, he was nominated to the post of chief of police for the state of São Paulo and was elected deputy of the state's constituent congress. He was one of the principal drafters of the state constitution. After the drafting of that constitution he left politics and decided to return exclusively to the practice of law and to legal scholarship. In 1907 President Afonso Pena nominated Lessa to the Supremo Tribunal Federal. On the Tribunal he was especially noted for his work in constitutional law and in the area of habeas corpus.[27]

Lessa's career at the forefront of the Paulista and national bars provides a vivid illustration of how class and color complicate any discussion of race in early republican Brazil. Class distinctions were strong. Political power was held by a wealthy few. Most of the population lacked the vote because of the literacy requirement of the new constitution. Even those who could vote had to exercise the franchise with great care. The ballot was not secret. Employers and political bosses knew for whom their clients voted. Rural bosses, *coronels*, took great pains to see that their political wards voted the right way. The situation was only slightly less blatant in the great cities. In that atmosphere, one's well-being would depend on the goodwill of powerful men who controlled private employment and public offices great and small. In that atmosphere, a well-connected mulatto such as Lessa could overcome the stigma of race and rise to high office. Few would want to exclude or offend the son of a powerful or well-to-do family, even if he were a mulatto. Historian Carl Degler has written that one way to understand race in Brazil is that the South American nation always permitted a "mulatto escape hatch," allowing talented people of mixed race to rise into the upper classes and thus escape the disabilities and stigma of Afro-Brazilian status.[28] Lessa's biography and those of others indicate a phenomenon somewhat stronger than Degler's mulatto escape hatch. It indicates that one legacy from the nineteenth-century empire is that some mulattoes were already so well integrated into the nation's elite that they could secure leading positions in politics, in the bar, and on the bench despite a national ideology that was increasingly hostile to the Afro-Brazilian.

That official ideology would begin to change after the First World War. Brazilian intellectuals and politicians would come to question the premises of scientific racism — notions of the biological superiority of the white race and the inherent inferiority of those of African descent. These changes would come slowly. They would not be accompanied by an end to *branqueamento*, nor would government agencies or private firms abandon discriminatory practices. Still, ideological change would be a first step in an effort to redefine the Brazilian nation and what it meant to be Brazilian. The First World War itself would play a major role in causing Brazilian intellectuals and indeed writers and scholars elsewhere to rethink the previously agreed upon conventional wisdom that science could be used to prove the superiority of the white race. The war disrupted European immigration to Brazil. That disruption provided some increase in employment opportunities for Afro-Brazilians in enterprises that had previously been closed to them. But it was the slaughter in the trenches of Western Europe between 1914 and 1918 that began to cause some major rethinking. It traumatized those who had earlier on been champions of the idea of the inevitability of progress and the leading role that men of Western European descent would play in bringing about a bright, new future. This disillusionment had set in throughout the Western world. It caused some profound rethinking in Brazil. Brazil had played only a small part in the war. With traditionally strong ties to two major belligerents, France and the United States, and in the face of U-boat attacks on Brazilian shipping, Brazil declared war on Germany in 1917. The Brazilian Navy patrolled the South Atlantic. The army sent a few small units to France and Italy during the conflict. But if Brazil's military participation was small, the horrible example of modern science run amuck in the killing fields of Western Europe prepared Brazilians to think that the progressive future that they saw for their country lay not in trying to simply become an outpost of Europe but instead to celebrate that which made them distinctly Brazilian.[29]

That new thinking, that search for a new way to define Brazil and its people, paved the way for Gilberto Freyre, who would become one of the nation's most influential social commentators, certainly in the first half of the twentieth century and indeed beyond. The Bahia-born Freyre would play a critical part in causing his nation to rethink race and the role of the Afro-Brazilian in the nation's history and culture. Freyre's work on race in Brazil would be deeply influenced by his university studies in the United States. He did his undergraduate work at Baylor University in Texas and while there came upon a site where a black man had just been lynched. The incident would profoundly impress him. It would convince him that violence and racial exclusion were integral parts of race relations in the United States. It would also start to convince him of the relative harmony and goodwill that he believed were a part of relations among the races in Brazil. He continued his studies at New York's Columbia University, enrolling in an interdisciplinary social science program under the supervision of anthropologist Franz Boas. Boas's work on race and culture was challenging and in many quarters vanquishing the premises of scientific racism that had prevailed before the First World War. Boas stressed that what appeared to many to be racial differences were in fact differences in culture, learned behavior, learned behavior that could be unlearned or redirected. Working with Boas, Freyre did a master's thesis on nineteenth-century Brazilian social life. The thesis would lay the foundation for much of Freyre's later work.[30]

Scholars have debated whether Freyre should be labeled an historian, a sociologist, or an anthropologist. He was all these things and something more — a vivid writer who could capture the popular imagination and present the educated Brazilian public with a compelling and appealing portrait of their nation. Brazil's African and Indian backgrounds, he told his readers, were not things to be ashamed of, to be denied or somehow swept under the rug. Instead, they were what made Brazil, Brazil. It was the blending of the three races made necessary by the shortage of white women in the colonial era and made possible by the racial tolerance of the Portuguese that had created the Brazilian nation and the Brazilian people. In his epic history, *Casa-grande e senzala* (*The Masters and the Slaves*), Freyre set the tone for what would be a significant rethinking of race and nation on the part of many Brazilians. Published in 1933, it detailed Freyre's view that Brazil's history was a set of intimate encounters among the three races. Those encounters created a new race, the Brazilian race. The *mestiço* was the prototypical Brazilian, born of the nation's four centuries of slavery. Freyre endorsed the idea that Brazil was a "racial democracy." That idea did not originate with Freyre. Joaquim Nabuco had endorsed the concept, although he too did not use the precise term in *O abolicionismo*. Historian George Reid Andrews notes that Brazilian writers and intellectuals had been debating the issue of racial democracy since the 1880s. But Freyre, with his combination of vivid writing and fortuitous timing was able to catch the imagination of Brazilians and later a wider international audience with the notion of Brazil as a racial democracy. The outline of the thesis was simple enough. Racial mixture had created a "Brazilian race." That new race took from the best elements of the nation's three races. The civilization, the laws, the language, the religion—all of course came from the Portuguese. But the Africans and the Indians contributed as well. Their contributions were less substantial than those of the Portuguese, to be sure, more in the way of colorful folkloric customs than great achievements in law or science, literature or the arts. But they were part of the national culture and that should be acknowledged. Racial harmony would be the Brazilian way. Brazil would proudly acknowledge that it was a biological and cultural blend of the three races while of course stressing that it was the Portuguese who played the predominant role in shaping the national civilization.[31]

Freyre's writings matched the national mood. *Branqueamento* was proving to be more difficult than its advocates had initially thought. The southern states, to be sure, had whitened—significantly so. But the Northeast remained hopelessly Afro-Brazilian, and large indigenous populations dominated in the Amazon regions. Business leaders also found that European immigrants could be something of a two-edged sword. They were white and contributed to the hoped-for Europeanization of the southern states, and hopefully ultimately the nation, but the European immigrants brought with them traditions of union activity and political radicalism that posed a threat to good order and to business interests. Labor organizing and strikes dampened the enthusiasm of Brazilian employers for recruiting European laborers. Business leaders did not want to deport the immigrants that they had brought to the nation, but they feared the arrival of potentially radical European immigrants in greater numbers. The immigrant recruitment program was discontinued in 1927. In 1931, the federal government placed restrictions on immigration into Brazil. A federal decree also restricted the employment of foreign nationals in commerce and industry.[32]

But the biggest boost to Freyre's writings and the acceptance of his ideas of racial democracy and a recognition of the role of the Afro-Brazilian in the nation's culture would be the fall of the Velha República and the rise to power of Getúlio Vargas. Vargas was a man of many sides, some might even say contradictions. He was a populist whose career began in the southern state of Rio Grande do Sul. He would first gain national power by virtue of a military coup that toppled the Velha República. He would later be a constitutional president elected by Congress, still later the nation's dictator, and later still a democratically elected president after his dictatorship had been overthrown. Vargas had a large working-class constituency throughout the nation including many Afro-Brazilians. He would sponsor far-reaching protective labor legislation that would despite its lofty language fall far short of providing much in the way of benefits to Brazilian workers. He was an admirer of Mussolini's Fascist government, yet he would lead his nation to war against Nazi Germany and Fascist Italy.[33]

Vargas's contradictions were on full display when it came to the issue of race and the position of Afro-Brazilians in the Brazilian nation. Vargas, who initially came into office in 1930 and would later become dictator in 1937, certainly supported policies that would make Afro-Brazilians a less prominent part of the nation's population. Article 121 of the constitution of 1934 contained language allowing immigration restrictions that would guarantee the "ethnic and civil integration" of new immigrants. The 1934 constitution also mandated eugenics education in the public schools. Vargas also insured that eugenics indoctrination was part of the training of recruits in the army. In 1937, Vargas signed a decree abolishing all political parties, including the racially conscious Frente Negra Brasileira, which had organized in 1930 and was officially registered as a party in 1936. Under Vargas, census officials continued policies designed to show that *branqueamento* was working, that the Afro-Brazilian population was indeed in the process of disappearing. Frequently this was done with scant if any supporting evidence. The 1940 census was ballyhooed with an elaborate report extolling the new Brazilian race. It was an indication of the triumph of the new mixed Brazilian race and a barometer for how "Negroes and Indians are continuing to disappear, both in the successive dilutions of white blood and in the constant processes of biological and social selection." Closer inspection calls this 1940 report into some question. No censuses were conducted in 1910 or 1930, and information regarding race or color was not collected in the 1920 census. There was evidence from São Paulo that the number of Afro-Brazilians was actually increasing, although many of them were being reclassified as white in official statistics. But official Brazil was not inclined to question its own statistics. The new Brazilian race and the disappearance through blending of the inferior elements, these were good things, indications that Brazil was making progress, progress under Getúlio Vargas.[34]

However, Vargas was also a Brazilian nationalist, one who realized that his country was multiracial and perhaps destined to remain so. He could share in the fervent hopes of the architects of *branqueamento* that the inferior races would ultimately disappear yet also agree with Gilberto Freyre that the Negroes and the Indians and of course, most particularly the *mestiços* were part of the national patrimony, critical elements of a Brazilian Brazil. Vargas would use the mass media and the schools to promote this vision. A daily radio program, *Hora do Brasil*, promoted the virtues of a *mestiço* Brazil, as did the public schools. The government controlled primary and secondary school curriculum and texts. Primary school teachers were instructed to explain that the Brazilian people were a combination of the whites (who contributed language, customs, and religion), the blacks (who brought gentleness and a spirit of self-sacrifice), the indigenous (who contributed a love for liberty and an attachment to the earth). The curriculum would continue in secondary school with the assignment of Freyre's *Casa-grande e senzala* as a classic and required text. Freyre's study among other things informed students that Brazilian slavery was milder because of the Portuguese ability to accept and intermarry with other races and cultures.[35]

During the Vargas era, there would be something of a new openness concerning race. This was reflected in the 1934 constitution. It contained a revised equality provision that unlike the first republican constitution specifically indicated that racial distinctions were contrary to the nation's supreme law. It would have little practical effect. The provision was generally worded, with race included along with sex, class, profession, and other characteristics that were not to be the basis of legal distinctions. The provision certainly contained no hint as to how it was to be enforced, especially in light of a judiciary that had broad discretionary powers and little inclination to hear claims alleging racial discrimination. Race was, interestingly enough, absent from a provision of the 1934 constitution specifying equal pay for equal work. That provision mentioned age, sex, nationality, and marital status as illegitimate grounds for salary discrimination but was conspicuously silent on race. Still the provision mentioning racial equality was explicitly added to the constitution. It represented a shift in thinking from its counterpart in the 1891 constitution, an indication that at least on a normative level some ground had been gained in the 1930s by those who saw Brazil as a more racially inclusive nation.[36]

Not everyone shared in that more racially inclusive vision. Political leaders in São Paulo believed that race and modernity, including industry and economic progress, were inextricably linked. Paulistas — or at least the white economic and political elite — saw their region's identity in sharp contrast to the Northeast. São Paulo was the future — scientific, progressive, European. The Northeast was the past — backward, superstitious, African. When Vargas first assumed office in 1930, the São Paulo state government declared war on the central government because Vargas appointed a "backward" man from the Northeast as interim governor. For eighty-three days starting on July 9, 1932, troops from São Paulo struggled with federal troops. The conflict was characterized at the time as a fight of the "white man's culture" against the populism of Vargas's *dictanegra* (black dictatorship). Vargas and the central government prevailed. The refashioning of Brazil into Vargas's image of a racial democracy would go forward.[37]

Vargas went further to promote the idea that racial democracy and a harmonious mixture of the races provided the true keys to Brazilian identity. He ordered the state of São Paulo to admit two hundred black recruits into the Civil Guard, the state's police force, ending a previous policy of strict racial exclusion. The *gaúcho* dictator became the first president to visit an Indian village, symbolically including the nation's indigenous population in his envisioned Estado Novo. Vargas would also employ public proclamations, assigned curricula in schools and universities, and press releases to the national media to promote his vision of racial inclusiveness. He was especially supportive of expressions of the popular culture that furthered the notion of a multiracial Brazil where all lived in harmony. Afro-Brazilian culture, particularly music, would be brought out as evidence of the Afro-Brazilian contribution to Brazil's culture, and of the nation's appreciation. It was in this new atmosphere that Ary Barroso's sentimental samba, "Aquarela do Brasil," extolling the Afro-Brazilian past gained national popularity. In many respects, Afro-Brazilians under Vargas would gain a position somewhat similar to the position indigenous peoples were gaining in countries like Mexico, Peru, and Ecuador in the interwar years. They were to become folkloric symbols of the nation. Their lives and contributions would be seen as entertaining and exotic but rarely the occasion for serious inquiry concerning their actual social conditions or inequalities.[38]

Racial democracy proved to be an illusion, but like most illusions, it was a seductive one, with just enough of a touch of truth to make it seem real. Afro-Brazilians, whether they might be classified as black or mulatto, might find themselves subject to discrimination when they sought a job, or an apartment, a meal in a restaurant, or even the chance to sit on a park bench. Vargas's government might support Afro-Brazilian musicians but continue to suppress Afro-Brazilian religious practices. The 1937 constitution, which unlike its 1934 predecessor was wholly written under Vargas's direction, gave Vargas dictatorial powers. It also eliminated the mention of race that had been present in the 1934 constitution. Racial discrimination would be prevalent in many parts of the nation. But discrimination was not the whole story. Well-connected mulattoes, even on rare occasions well-connected black men, might rise to the highest levels of Brazilian society. Pedro Lessa would be followed on the Supremo Tribunal Federal by another mulatto, Hermenegildo de Barros. Barros, whose portrait on the tribunal's official website shows a man even more clearly of African descent than Lessa, was nominated to the court in 1919. A specialist in personal injury law, Barros presided over plenary sessions that led to the Constituent Assembly that authored the 1934 constitution. Examples like Lessa and Barros have caused some students of Brazilian society to argue that in Brazil, "money bleaches." There is a certain amount of truth to this. As has been the case in Spanish America, race and color classifications in Brazil have always involved a certain amount of negotiation over an individual's ancestry, phenotype, and social position. In Brazil, categories such as *white*, *black*, *mulatto*, *mestiço*, and an impressive array of intermediate and combined categories are perhaps even more flexible than their counterparts in Spanish America and the United States. These categories in Brazil were less the creations of formal law, like the system of *castas* in the Spanish Empire or the laws prescribing racial disability in the United States; instead, the Brazilian racial and color categories owed more to custom and tradition. Under those circumstances, whether an individual with relatively dark skin was classified as black or mulatto or whether an individual with known African ancestry but relatively light complexion was classified as mulatto or white might have a great deal to do with his or her wealth and social position. In previous generations, this notion that "money bleaches" was offered as evidence for the racial democracy thesis. Today, this reasoning can be seen in a more problematic light. The very notion that "money bleaches" is a recognition of an existing racial hierarchy, one in which the Afro-Brazilian is inferior. The inferiority of blacks and mulattoes is recognized as a general matter, but exceptional individuals are allowed at some level to rise above their inferior status. Men like Lessa and Barros and others in similar circumstances were known to have African ancestry, recognized as mulattoes and not whites. They were allowed, in their cases spectacularly so, to rise despite living in a time of very real and indeed increasing racial prejudice. Their cases were not typical. But they could and did serve to mask the great racial inequalities that were part of Brazilian life.

The illusion of racial democracy was always helped by the ability of Brazilians to contrast the relative harmony of race relations in Brazil with the harsh manifestations of raw racism that often occurred in the United States, particularly in the South. That contrast had played a pivotal part in forming Freyre's views. Educated Brazilians were well aware of the extent of racism, of the absurdities and horrors that were a part of daily life in the segregated United States. The contrast could only serve to confirm many Brazilians in their belief in the essentially benign and just nature of the Brazilian ordering of racial affairs and the danger of following the unfortunate example of other nations, even one they admired like the United States. That lesson would soon be brought forcibly home to a number of Brazilians who got to see American-style Jim Crow up close and up front.

It has been largely forgotten in the United States, but Brazil played a rather substantial role in the Second World War. The Vargas government, in part responding to pressure from the United States and also popular pro-U.S. sentiment in Brazil, broke relations with the Axis governments after the attack on Pearl Harbor and the German and Italian declarations of war on the United States. In August 1942, in the wake of German U-boat attacks on Brazilian merchant ships, Brazil declared war on the two European Axis powers. Northeastern Brazil, particularly Natal, capital of the state of Rio Grande do Norte, became a staging area, the logistical base for the American invasion of North Africa. The northeastern city was the site of Parnamirim Airfield, the largest American airbase outside the United States. The Vargas government provided ports and airfields for what was a major antisubmarine warfare effort in the South Atlantic conducted by the U.S. Navy and Army Air Corps. These efforts were augmented by the Brazilian Air Force and Navy. Brazil's participation did not end there. Brazilian officers came to the United States to learn American military operations. A Brazilian general studied American armor tactics by observing the training of the all-black 761st Tank Destroyer Battalion at the rigidly segregated Camp Hood in Texas. A Brazilian Air Force Fighter Group helped guard the Panama Canal. And most significantly in 1944, after the fall of Rome, Brazil sent a twenty-five-thousand-soldier expeditionary force to Italy. The force, consisting of the 1st Brazilian Expeditionary Infantry Division, attached to the U.S. 5th Army, the 1st Fighter Group, which had previously helped guard the Panama Canal, and various supporting units. The Brazilian Expeditionary Force took part in the bloody fighting in Northern Italy from Rome to the Po River Valley over some of the roughest terrain and against some of the most determined opposition in the European Theater. It would receive the first surrender of a Wehrmacht division in Italy.[39]

The Brazilians who fought in Italy and those who worked with the U.S. Army and Navy in Brazil, Panama, and the United States came away from the experience impressed with the military skill of their American allies. The U.S. armed forces also left another impression. They were rigidly segregated. At home and abroad, Brazilians got to see Jim Crow in action. The Army and its Air Corps maintained a strict, indeed meticulous segregation between the races. Separate units, mess facilities, latrines, barracks, and servicemen's clubs were the rule. Black troops in the Army Air Corps in Brazil would have been, for the most part, confined to service units. The pilots, maintenance personnel, radar operators, and other skilled technicians would have been white. The navy mainly confined Negroes to duties as mess attendants or officers' servants.[40]

Those Brazilians who fought in Italy observed an equally rigorous segregation. The U.S. 5th Army included a number of all-white divisions. It also had the black 92nd Division and the Japanese American 442nd Regimental Combat team. The Brazilian Expeditionary Force fought in the same sector as the 92nd. The U.S. Army's segregationist policies didn't end with separate units, and separate facilities for soldiers of different races. Even whole blood and plasma at aid stations and field hospitals were labeled "White" and "Colored." Brazilians have often pointed out that while segregation prevailed among their American allies, that the Brazilian Expeditionary Force was a model of racial democracy in action. The Brazilian division had black, Indian, mulatto, Japanese, and white Brazilians — no segregated units, no separate facilities. The racial discrimination that existed in the Brazilian Expeditionary Force seemed trivial compared to the gross imposition of the rigors of Jim Crow adapted from the American South to the U.S. Armed Forces. The experience would only confirm Brazilians in their belief in Brazilian racial democracy and the essential benevolence and good sense inherent in the Brazilian ordering of race relations.[41]

World War II would, interestingly enough, bring some increase in ethnic tensions. These would not be directed at the Afro-Brazilians and Indians, the objects of the concern of the architects of *branqueamento* earlier in the century. Instead, the war would cause suspicion to fall on some of the immigrants or children of immigrants who had been brought to Brazil to improve the nation's racial makeup. Ethnic German and Japanese communities would fall under suspicion. This would also happen to a lesser extent with Italian communities. The large ethnic German populations of Rio Grande do Sul and Santa Catarina were viewed with particular alarm. They frequently spoke German, not Portuguese. They sent their children to German-language schools. They had been subject to intense Nazi propaganda before the war, propaganda that said that their loyalties were to their race, not to the *mestiço* nation of which they happened to be citizens. Rio Grande do Sul and Santa Catarina bordered on the Axis-friendly nation of Argentina. The Vargas government would move during the war to close down the German-language schools, to force ethnic Germans and others to speak Portuguese, and in other ways attempt to make the immigrants who were once seen as the nation's salvation but were now viewed as a threat more Brazilian.[42]

Ethnic Japanese also came under suspicion. Even in the late 1930s, the Vargas government began closing Japanese cultural and language schools. By 1941, the government ordered the closing of Japanese-language newspapers. Although Brazil would not declare war on Japan until June 1945, the Japanese population experienced restrictions. There would not be a mass internment of Japanese Brazilians similar to the one that occurred on the West Coast of the United States, but Japanese families were prohibited from living in sensitive areas, areas that could potentially jeopardize Brazilian or U.S. military activities or Brazilian industrial activity.[43]

The wartime experience, their having taken part in the defeat of the Axis, and the founding of the United Nations, all helped to increase a certain pride in being Brazilian. Their ability to contrast the largely easy and nonconfrontational approach to race that characterized relations among Brazilians with the rigors of American segregation all helped confirm Brazilians in their views that their nation had found the path to racial democracy and indeed racial harmony. The new postwar democratic constitution of 1946 prohibited the publication of material that incited racial prejudice, a partial reflection of the view that harmonious race relations was essential to civil peace and public order. By midcentury the belief that Brazil was a racial democracy had become conventional wisdom for many not only in the South American nation but in other parts of the world as well. The contrast with the horrors of the Nazi Holocaust, Jim Crow in the United States, and the strengthening and codification of apartheid that was occurring in postwar South Africa, all served to reinforce the view of a harmonious racially democratic Brazil. Freyre would continue to write in that vein, extolling the virtues of racial mixture and resulting harmony, Brazilian style. The postwar translation of his writings into French and English would provide a large international audience for his views, which had also become the official viewpoint of the Brazilian government. The 1946 publication of *Slave and Citizen: The Negro in the Americas* by North American sociologist Frank Tannenbaum would also help persuade an international audience of the essential accuracy of the racial democracy thesis and doubtless help reinforce that view among educated Brazilians as well.[44]

There were a few events that occurred in the 1950s that might have disturbed this comforting view. In 1950, African American dancer Katherine Dunham was refused admission to a hotel in São Paulo because of her race. The high-profile incident, which received some international attention, embarrassed many Brazilians. Congress passed a statute in 1951 outlawing racial discrimination including discrimination in public accommodations. Named for its sponsor, Afonso Arinos de Melo Franco, a member of the Chamber of Deputies, the statute would have little effect on discriminatory practices that were often prevalent in Brazil. The statute at first glance appeared to be strongly worded. It provided for criminal penalties for acts of racial discrimination. But the Brazilian legal system had structural weaknesses that made the statute a virtual dead letter. Long delays in the resolution of cases, the strong tradition of judicial autonomy even from what would be constraining sources of legal authority in other legal systems, and the lack of willingness of public authorities to take cases of racial discrimination seriously, all combined to thwart the aims of Afonso Arinos and other supporters of Brazil's first national civil rights legislation. Afro-Brazilian civil rights attorney Hédio Silva Jr. has indicated that between the statute's adoption in 1951 and its replacement with an antidiscrimination provision in the constitution of 1988 there were only nine final judgments and only one violator was fined under Lei Afonso Arinos.[45]

Another disturbing development for those committed to the notion of a racially fair and democratic Brazil was that it was often not bearing up well under close scrutiny by social scientists who were less nationalistic and less romantic than Gilberto Freyre. The United Nations Educational, Scientific, and Cultural Organization (UNESCO) was beginning to give race in Brazil a somewhat closer scrutiny. Social scientists working for UNESCO assumed the essential truth of the racial democracy thesis, as Columbia University anthropologist Charles Wagley noted in the introduction to one 1952 study: "Brazil is renowned in the world for its racial democracy. Throughout its enormous area of a half continent race prejudice and discrimination are subdued as compared to the situation in many countries. In Brazil three racial stocks — the American Indian, the Negro and the European Caucasoid — have mingled and mixed to form a society in which racial tensions and conflicts are especially mild, despite the great racial variability of the population."[46]

But despite this reiteration of the conventional wisdom concerning Brazilian racial democracy, social scientists working for UNESCO found deep-seated racial prejudices and patterns of racial inequality in Brazilian society. Brazilian sociologist Florestan Fernandes would go even further arguing that Brazilian society often masked striking racial inequalities under a veneer of cordiality. Fernandes, who came from São Paulo, would go on to document extensively the world of racial inequality in the center of the modern Brazilian industrial and commercial economy. Fernandes would attribute this inequality in part to the legacy of slavery, particularly the social disorganization, illiteracy, and family breakdown that might be traced to the slave experience. But Fernandes also blamed inequality on very real contemporary discrimination and prejudice. Fernandes was blunt: racial democracy was a myth, one that served to mask very real discrimination and structural disadvantage that limited opportunities for Afro-Brazilians. It was a view sharply at variance with the Brazilian establishment's self-image. It was most unwelcome.[47]

But official Brazil continued as before. Racial democracy and racial mixture were to be celebrated. Brazil was a model the rest of the world could emulate. Racial discrimination did not exist. Such racial inequalities as existed could be explained as a by-product of class inequalities. Embarrassing incidents like the Katherine Dunham case would be taken care of by progressive statutes like the one authored by Deputy Arinos. The earlier dream, the one that dominated so much of public debate and policy in Republican Brazil's infancy, *branqueamento*, was largely dead. Immigration — of the right sort — would still be permitted, even encouraged in some instances, to be sure. African and Afro-American immigrants would still be barred. But as was the case in other parts of the Americas, demography proved to be a stubborn thing. The Afro-Brazilian presence was simply too large to remain unacknowledged. Even manipulation of the census could only change this reality at the margins. Brazilians, even the rightist-populist Vargas, had learned these lessons between the two world wars. By the postwar era, official Brazil and the elites who controlled the nation's businesses, schools, government offices, and universities had come to find that the ideology of racial democracy was a comforting substitute for the earlier policy of *branqueamento*, a policy that proved to be impossible to achieve. Racial democracy burnished Brazil's international image and the image that many Brazilians had of their own nation as well. It could allow control of the nation's important institutions to remain firmly in charge of the better classes, classes whose ranks were filled almost exclusively from the nation's white population. Racial democracy could also confine uncomfortable questions concerning race and inequality to academic treatises authored by a small number of dissident sociologists. In the early postwar era, the illusion of racial democracy served official Brazil well. The illusion would remain strong and largely unchallenged for most of the rest of the century. It would begin to receive strong challenge only after the dismantling of a set of legal and social practices that helped give credibility to the idea of Brazilian racial democracy, American Jim Crow.

CHAPTER SIX

Jim Crow

THE HOUSE THE LAW BUILT

LATIN AMERICAN STATESMEN such as Brazil's Manuel Deodoro da Fonseca and Argentina's Domingo Faustino Sarmiento spent much of the latter part of the nineteenth century pondering how to turn their nations into European societies. They hoped to do so in part through laws that promoted European immigration and legal measures that suppressed African and indigenous cultures. White supremacists in the United States after the Civil War had another set of concerns. The United States already had a white majority. What survived of African culture was largely invisible to most whites and if noticed at all was more likely to be seen as peculiar Negro folkways, not remnants of African traditions. Some parts of the South, the old slave states, had large concentrations of blacks, a few regions even had black majorities. But the nation as a whole was overwhelmingly white — close to 90 percent if the censuses were to be believed. But that numerical dominance did not bring sufficient comfort to American advocates of white supremacy. It was better than the alternative, to be sure. One strain of proslavery apologetics before the War of the Rebellion had couched its argument in terms of fear of Negro domination, concerns that emancipation and egalitarian treatment could turn parts of the South into another Haiti, with all the potential for savage mistreatment of whites and the resurgence of African barbarism that had occurred in the former French colony.[1]

But the concern of white supremacists in the United States had less to do with the possibilities of black majorities than with how to maintain white domination, a superiority that would have to be regularly reaffirmed, preferably on a daily basis. To achieve that end, white supremacists would fashion a legal regime mandating strict separation and formal definition of the races that would be unique in the postemancipation Americas. Called by the somewhat whimsical name "Jim Crow" after a character in an antebellum minstrel show, it would come to dominate race relations in the American South for the first six decades of the twentieth century. Rigid segregation, "Colored" and "White" signs on water fountains and park benches, on railway waiting rooms and public toilets, would be the order of the day in southern states, as would a system of separate schools extending from primary grades to university-level education. Voting would be restricted to white people. Government officials would openly support lynchings and race riots as means to enforce white supremacy and black subservience. The Jim Crow system would be at its strongest in the South, where statutes and court decisions formally proclaimed a legal doctrine designed to ensure the separate and unequal status of the Afro-American population. But Jim Crow was by no means restricted to the former slave states. It would infect the nation as a whole. School segregation existed in a number of states in the North and West. Sometimes it existed by virtue of informal discrimination, sometimes by legal mandate. It is significant that the lead case in *Brown v. Board of Education* involved legally mandated school segregation in Topeka, Kansas. Kansas was not a southern state, nor had it been a slave state before the Civil War. Segregation was nationwide. Discrimination in employment, housing, public accommodations, and the provision of government services existed throughout the nation. The federal government would follow suit, maintaining a rigid segregation of black and white soldiers in the American armed forces through two world wars.[2]

But Jim Crow was at its most intense in the South. At times, segregation in the American South was exercised with a rigidity and rigor that would rival apartheid in South Africa. This chapter will focus on legal segregation in the South and the role of national law, particularly as determined by the U.S. Supreme Court, in abetting the South's regime of petty apartheid. In doing so, we will regrettably spend less time than we should on the history of racial exclusion in the North. That story is important and until relatively recently had been too often neglected by historians of American race relations. There is an important history involving state civil rights statutes and judicial decisions concerning race in the North. At times, that body of law was relatively successful in combating certain kinds of racial discrimination, at other times not. By and large the northern states did not try to reverse the verdict of the Civil War and the constitutional amendments that followed in its wake. Black suffrage, once established in the North and West by the Fifteenth Amendment, would remain largely unchallenged. It would over time change the politics of race in the northern and western states. It would, slowly, transform the Democratic Party. That party had been the agent of disenfranchisement and racial exclusion in the Jacksonian era. It had provided strong opposition to the Civil War amendments. But in the twentieth century, the party of Jefferson and Jackson would eventually come to grips with black voters and indeed ultimately come to rely on their support.

If a certain measure of formal legal equality would be achieved in the northern states after the Civil War, those states nonetheless remained places where there were often strong racial antagonisms and strict exclusionary barriers. The antagonisms between working-class white people and the emerging free Negro class that began to crystallize in northern cities after the War of 1812 would continue. They would be inherited by new groups of European immigrants and Afro-American migrants later in the nineteenth and twentieth centuries. Those antagonisms would contribute to the marginalization of Afro-Americans in the cities of the North and West. Black workers would have a tense and often hostile relationship with organized labor. That hostility would help bring about large-scale exclusion of black workers from many industrial and skilled occupations. This is an important topic for any comparative discussion of race relations in the Americas. National efforts to whiten the nations of Latin America brought the native-born Afro-American populations of Havana and Caracas, São Paulo and Montevideo, into close contact with immigrants from Italy, Spain, Germany, Poland, and other European nations. Afro-American workers in these and other Latin American cities would often experience a considerable amount of discrimination in the workplace. The new immigrants and their children would be preferred for skilled trades, industrial employment, managerial jobs, and positions that required dealing with the public. In São Paulo and other cities there were even efforts designed to keep most Afro-Brazilians from using the more desirable public spaces. Yet despite evidence of often strong discrimination, working-class Afro-Americans in urban Latin America appear to have been less marginalized than their counterparts in the industrial cities of the United States. They had a less antagonistic relationship with trade unions and working-class

populist movements, even populist movements led by such right-wing figures as Brazil's Getúlio Vargas and Argentina's Juan Domingo Perón. There
was less residential segregation by race. And despite very real racism and
discrimination, there appears to have been a greater willingness to associate across racial lines in the great urban centers of Latin America than in
the cities of the United States. Why these differences existed has important
potential for comparative exploration.[3]

But the concern in this chapter is largely with the South and with Jim
Crow. This is so because at the turn of the last century, when the system of
Jim Crow was beginning to take root, nearly 90 percent of the U.S. Afro-
American population lived in the South. An understanding of Jim Crow is
critical to an understanding of race in the United States in the twentieth
century. Jim Crow was the most unambiguous effort to use the law to enforce racial domination in the Americas after emancipation. The American
civil rights movement was forged in the struggle against Jim Crow, as indeed was much of American civil rights law. Finally, it was the contrast
with the United States and its codified racial exclusions and rigid racial
definitions that helped reinforce Latin American beliefs that their societies
were racial democracies, free from the strident discrimination found in the
southern states of the "Colossus of the North."

Jim Crow statutes would begin appearing relatively late in the South's
history. The move toward legally mandated segregation in railroad cars
and other public facilities began with tentative first steps in the 1880s and
1890s, first steps that were often somewhat controversial. The system of
public segregation would pick up steam toward the end of the 1890s and
in the first decade of the twentieth century, but the apartheid that seemed
so much a part of southern life by the 1920s and 1930s did not appear at all
inevitable when the first efforts at legal segregation began. How might we
account for this development of a system of formal, legal segregation at the
end of the nineteenth century, particularly when it appeared to be a new
and not totally welcome innovation among southern whites? Southern historian C. Vann Woodward, writing in the mid-1950s, argued that Jim Crow
was a relatively recent feature of southern life. In his seminal *The Strange
Career of Jim Crow*, Woodward argued that Jim Crow was not an integral
part of southern culture, that it had been created to a then-unappreciated
extent by a body of laws passed by southern state legislatures toward the
end of the nineteenth century. Woodward also noted that Jim Crow actu-

ally owed its origins more to laws and customs that had developed in the antebellum North than to those of the slave South.[4]

Woodward's work was in part an effort to rebut the arguments of those who claimed that segregation was such an integral part of the culture or folkways of the American South that any effort to use the law to dismantle American segregation would invite social disaster. Writing at a time when *Brown v. Board of Education* was being argued and decided, at a time when the desegregation of the armed forces was still a fresh memory, and when the battles against segregation on municipal and interstate bus lines were just beginning to be waged, Woodward was in part providing a usable past in the struggle against Jim Crow. That that usable past was coming from an historian who was himself a white southerner only increased its value as a statement about law and southern culture and the possibilities for change.

And yet another historian, Ulrich Bonnell Phillips, also a son of the South from an earlier generation, may have come closer to the mark when he argued that the desire for white domination provided continuity in southern history: "And, above all, as to the white folks, a people with a common resolve indomitably maintained — that it shall be and remain a white man's country . . . is the cardinal test of a Southerner and the central theme of southern history."[5] Phillips in some ways brings us closer to the critical question concerning Jim Crow. What is important about Jim Crow is not whether the statutes mandating segregation that appeared at the end of the nineteenth century were new legal developments. What is important is how they were linked with the South's and the nation's prior history of racial exclusion. If the antebellum South saw relatively little need for status legislation before the Civil War, it was because 95 percent of the region's black population was enslaved. The Negro's inferior status was clear and unquestioned. The white South wondered if that previously agreed upon castelike inferiority could survive emancipation?

Even before Lee's surrender, there was a fierce debate over what would be the status of the newly freed Negro population. If the American political order and federal and state constitutions had carved out a robust set of rights for American citizens in the antebellum era, the Civil War's aftermath raised the question of how far those rights would be extended to the former slaves. With the war's end, the defeated South quickly indicated that it intended to permit the freedmen only a very restricted freedom. The former slaves would not be citizens. Their rights would be strictly curtailed. They would only be grudgingly granted the limited liberties enjoyed by free Negroes in the southern states in the decades immediately preceding the Civil War. In 1865, southern states began passing legislation known as the Black Codes. While these codes recognized the nominally free status of the former slaves, they also imposed severe legal disabilities on blacks. The codes restricted public meetings, imposed curfews on Negroes, and prohibited blacks from owning firearms. Ensuring a continued supply of plantation labor immediately after emancipation was a common concern in the Americas. The Black Codes attempted to provide former slave owners with a large labor supply by forcing former slaves to sign labor contracts or face the alternative of imprisonment and forced labor for vagrancy. In many ways, the Black Codes represented a postwar codification of the Jacksonian constitutional vision articulated by Taney in *Dred Scott*. Blacks could not be citizens and could only be free under the most restrictive of legal regimes.[6]

The defeated South's initial attempt to acknowledge only the narrowest kind of emancipation was unique in the Western Hemisphere. *Libertos* had, of course, been subject to legal restrictions in many parts of the Americas. Legal requirements to perform continued labor and to demonstrate continued fidelity and a willingness to come to the aid of a former master in distress added to the burdens of the recently manumitted in many slave societies. But the Black Codes went further, providing for severe restrictions for former slaves and those blacks who had been free before the war as well. The codes were a reflection of the unique importance of race in the nineteenth-century U.S. slave regime. Notions of white superiority and African degradation played a role in all of the slave societies of the Americas. But these notions played a part in creating a regime of racial exclusion in the antebellum South that was largely unmatched in other parts of the Americas. Elsewhere in the hemisphere, free people of African descent had been recognized as citizens long before general emancipation. Emancipation had also taken an evolutionary path in other parts of the Americas. In most American societies, the relative absence of a large free white population, the diminished importance of the slave economy, or the decreased viability of the slave system led to increases in free Afro-American populations. These conditions also brought about the gradual integration of those populations into (usually the lower ranks of) free society. Indeed, in Brazil and other parts of Latin America, free people of color were often the backbone of the free nonslaveholding class. The American South was different. Emancipation was cataclysmic. It struck a severe blow to the South's prewar determination to maintain not only slavery but also its regime of racial exclusion, one of white domination and black degradation. The Black Codes were the tools used to preserve as much of the old order as could survive northern victory and national emancipation.

Ironically, this attempt to deprive the former slaves of the rights of citizens would have important unintended consequences. The reaction against the southern effort to maintain the old order would play a key role in the enactment of the Fourteenth and Fifteenth Amendments and the civil rights legislation of the Reconstruction era. For the first time, the doctrine that people of different races could be citizens and were equal before the law would become an explicit part of the U.S. Constitution. Champions of racial equality would no longer have to rely, as the abolitionists had, solely on the argument that freedom and equality were implicit in the Declaration of Independence and were required by natural law. Advocates of equal rights would not be forced to rely, like Justice Curtis in his dissent in *Dred Scott*, on the existence of black suffrage in the postrevolutionary era as evidence that the Framers recognized the possibility of Negro citizenship. Equality and citizenship were now explicit parts of the nation's fundamental charter. *Dred Scott* was decisively repudiated. In ways that we can only measure indirectly and inaccurately, the Civil War gave the American republic not only a new birth of freedom but the opportunity for many whites to reconsider the move toward racial exclusion that had intensified in Jacksonian America. The enlistment of some two hundred thousand Negroes in the Union forces, the fight against the Slave Power, the gratitude and aid rendered by southern slaves to the advancing federal armies, all helped change attitudes. Many white northerners, including some who had not been antislavery and even others who had previously seen the wisdom in white supremacy began to look at race and rights in a new light.[7]

The reconsideration began even during the Civil War. Although the Lincoln administration was more conservative on issues of race and slavery than many Republicans had hoped, it nonetheless, at times with considerable prodding, began moving the nation's laws away from the rigid exclusionist doctrine of the antebellum years. Lincoln's attorney general, Edward Bates, issued a formal opinion stating that free Negroes were citizens of the United States, directly contradicting Taney's opinion in *Dred Scott*. The Lincoln administration and Republicans in Congress, greatly aided by the absence of delegates from the rebellious slave states, also supported emancipation in the District of Columbia, legislation that permitted free blacks to act as parties and witnesses in federal court, the establishment of schools for black children, and a statute prohibiting discrimination in the municipal streetcars of Washington, D.C. If Lincoln and the Republicans had not gone to war as champions of emancipation and equality, the unfolding of the conflict was increasingly turning Lincoln and the Republican Party more and more into such. Even before the war's end, some observers realized that the likely end of slavery brought about by the Emancipation Proclamation in the rebellious states and the institution's resulting lack of viability in the loyal slave states would not be enough. Emancipation would have to be accompanied by an ability to define and protect the rights of the newly freed Negroes. Opponents and supporters of the Thirteenth Amendment debated the proposed provision as one that would go beyond simple emancipation and allow Congress to pass legislation defining and enforcing the rights of the recently freed population.[8]

Republicans would use Section 2, the enforcement provision of the new amendment, to pass the Civil Rights Act of 1866 over President Andrew Johnson's veto. This legislation was designed to counter the southern Black Codes. Among other provisions, the statute declared that all persons born in the United States were citizens and provided for equal enjoyment of civil rights for all persons regardless of race. In part because even many supporters of the legislation questioned whether the Thirteenth Amendment gave Congress sufficient power to enact the statute, supporters of equal rights in the Thirty-Ninth Congress passed and sent the Fourteenth Amendment to the states. Although the Fourteenth Amendment was designed to accomplish a number of different goals, two of its purposes would profoundly affect and alter the American law of race and caste. First, the Fourteenth Amendment would finally end the dispute concerning Negro citizenship. Its language clearly established that every person born in the United States was a citizen of the nation.

The second provision that would fundamentally alter the American law of race was the Equal Protection Clause. That clause generated more controversy than any other provision of the amendment. Critics saw that it would profoundly alter the status of blacks and whites and indeed others before the law. It would do so in the recently rebellious South, but it would also do so in the Unionist states of the North and West. Opponents, mostly Democrats, argued vigorously against the measure, some claiming that it would permit interracial marriages, others that it would force associations between black and white. Their arguments failed. The Fourteenth Amendment passed both houses of Congress in 1866. By 1868, enough states had ratified the amendment for it to become a part of the Constitution.[9]

The enactment of the Fourteenth Amendment was part of a larger process of profound legal change that can rightly be described as a constitutional revolution. The very dynamics that had tied American slavery to a rigid regime of racial exclusion unique in the hemisphere contributed to a constitutional revolution with regard to race and status that was also unique in the hemisphere. All of the former slave societies of the Americas enacted constitutional and statutory provisions prohibiting slavery and proclaiming the equality of all before the law. The United States between the end of the rebellion in 1865 and the passage of the Civil Rights Act of 1875 went considerably further. It instituted a comprehensive legal regime designed to dismantle not only the antebellum slave system but the race-based system of caste that had provided an ideological and cultural underpinning for the South's "Peculiar Institution." The Thirteenth, Fourteenth, and Fifteenth Amendments were supplemented by legislation designed to clarify and enforce the new, hard-won constitutional change. The first of these statutes, the Civil Rights Act of 1866, made it clear that its purpose was to give the newly emancipated slaves the same rights that were ready enjoyed by white persons. These rights included the right to testify and act as parties in court and the right to make and enforce contracts. Other legislation went further still. The Enforcement Act of 1870 allowed federal officials to prosecute state officials and private parties who violated a citizen's civil rights. The Civil Rights Act of 1875 prohibited discrimination in public accommodations.[10]

Abolition was different in the United States. It would be accompanied by a comprehensive legal regime designed not only to prevent a de facto return to slavery but also to promote the political rights of the freedmen and the economic and educational advancement of the recently emancipated black population as well. Nothing this comprehensive existed in the other former slave societies of the hemisphere. There were a number of reasons that American abolition took this more comprehensive — indeed, radical — turn. Emancipation in the United States was a product of the Civil War, and champions of Negro freedom realized that the South, which had fought so hard to prevent the end of slavery, would not give up its efforts to maintain some semblance of the system that they had struggled so hard to maintain. The postwar Black Codes, if nothing else, demonstrated this. Many in the North sought to enfranchise and empower the former southern slaves as a way of giving political power to the one population in the South that had clear Unionist loyalties. Black voters would provide a necessary counterbalance to the former rebels, who were regaining their place in the Union and with it their previous political rights. But something more was at work. The American tradition of strong individual rights augmented by a profound egalitarianism in the culture was a source of strength for those who argued that emancipation had to mean something more than the simple end of slavery. It could not simply mean the highly constricted freedom granted the free Negro in the antebellum South or even the somewhat more generous but still circumscribed liberty afforded blacks in the northern states before the great conflict. It had to be the robust set of freedoms that had come to be associated with citizenship in the American republic. These rights would be protected by comprehensive legislation. There was also a determination that the recently emancipated Negroes would also be prepared to play a role in protecting their own liberties. To achieve that end, the Freedmen's Bureau would establish schools designed to educate the former slaves. Reconstruction in the United States was the most comprehensive program in the hemisphere to turn former slaves into participating citizens.[11]

And most important, during Reconstruction, federal authorities acted to enforce the grand pronouncements of the new constitutional provisions and civil rights statutes. The right of black men to vote was enforced, guaranteed by the presence of federal troops and prosecutors from the newly formed Justice Department. Southern politics changed dramatically. Black men were in the state legislatures, the U.S. House of Representatives, and the U.S. Senate. South Carolina and Louisiana had Afro-American lieutenant governors. One of these, P. B. S. Pinchback of Louisiana, even served as acting governor for a brief period. During Reconstruction the first public schools for either black or white children were established in the South. In New Orleans there was even, in the early 1870s, a brief, highly controversial experiment with integrated public schools.[12]

The U.S. Supreme Court initially seemed inclined to give a reasonably broad reading to the Civil War amendments. Two early cases, *Strauder v. West Virginia* and *Yick Wo v. Hopkins*, illustrate the willingness of the Court to take the Fourteenth Amendment's equal protection language and use it to examine closely state-sponsored racial discrimination. *Strauder* involved a statute that restricted jury service to white men. The Court pronounced the statute repugnant to the Fourteenth Amendment. The Court's decision suggested the need for a broad (what today might be called penumbral) reading of the Civil War amendments. This was important. None of the Civil War amendments specifically addressed the issue of racial discrimination in jury selection. The Court could have sidestepped the issue by giving a narrow technical interpretation of the amendments that denied that they necessarily applied to the selection of jurors. Instead, the *Strauder* opinion, authored by Justice William Strong, stressed that the three Civil War amendments should be read broadly with the idea that they had a common purpose in mind, to give the newly emancipated slaves the same rights as the white population.

In some ways, *Yick Wo* may have been even more significant than *Strauder*. *Yick Wo*, which interestingly enough involved Chinese immigrants rather than Afro-Americans, dealt with a more subtle kind of discrimination. Authorities in San Francisco refused to give licenses to Chinese immigrants who wanted to operate laundries. The statute under which the authorities operated said nothing about race. There was no language restricting licenses to white people or prohibiting Chinese or others from obtaining licenses. Nonetheless, no Chinese applicant could get a license. The Court ruled for the Chinese complainants. This case was of paramount importance because it required the Court to look at the actual behavior of state actors instead of merely reading statutes. This decision potentially made the Fourteenth Amendment's Equal Protection Clause a tremendously powerful tool for those suffering state discrimination. The demands of the clause could not be thwarted by a statute that on its face appeared not to discriminate.

But if the Supreme Court's decisions in *Strauder* and *Yick Wo* suggested that the Civil War amendments might provide a shield against state discrimination, other developments were working to weaken the legal protections that had developed in postbellum America. Reconstruction would come to an end in 1877 with the withdrawal of federal troops from the South. The recently freed Negroes of the region would theoretically retain the civil rights gained in the previous decade, but they would be forced to look to increasingly hostile state governments to protect those rights.

The Supreme Court would play a major role in restricting the federal government's ability to protect the civil rights of Afro-Americans. If the Court in the 1870s and 1880s was willing to be reasonably far-reaching when it examined discrimination by state governments, it took a very narrow view of Congress's ability to protect people against private acts of racial discrimination. In 1875, Congress passed comprehensive civil rights legislation outlawing discrimination in inns, theaters, and steamships — what we today would call public accommodations. In the *Civil Rights Cases,* the Court declared that the newly enacted amendments did not give Congress the power to enact this legislation. The Court held that the Thirteenth Amendment simply abolished slavery and that the Fourteenth Amendment did not give Congress the authority to prevent discrimination by private parties such as the owners of theaters or steamships. Justice John Marshall Harlan, a former Kentucky slaveholder, issued a telling dissent:

> I do not contend that the Thirteenth Amendment invests Congress with authority, by legislation, to define and regulate the entire body of the civil rights which citizens enjoy. . . . [S]ince slavery . . . was the moving or principal cause of the adoption of that amendment, and since that institution rested wholly upon the inferiority, as a race, of those held in bondage, their freedom necessarily involved immunity from, and protection against, all discrimination against them, because of their race, in respect of such civil rights as belong to freemen of other races.[13]

The Court's earlier decision in *United States v. Cruikshank* was perhaps of even greater importance. That case involved a white mob's attack on a group of black men in Louisiana who were attempting to vote. Members of the mob were charged with violation of the constitutional rights of the victims, including their right to peaceable assembly and their right to bear arms — black men frequently went to the polls armed in the nineteenth century, a precaution against mob attack. The defendants were charged under the Enforcement Act of 1870, which made it a crime for private individuals to use force to deprive citizens of their civil rights. The Court ruled that because the members of the mob were private individuals, the federal government had no jurisdiction over their actions. The Fourteenth Amendment did not authorize Congress to pass legislation protecting one citizen from another. The Court went on to say that citizens had to look to their state governments, not the federal government, for protection of their rights against infringement by private parties.

If the *Cruikshank* Court saw the often fine distinction between state and private action, that distinction would become more academic than real to southern blacks in the 1880s and 1890s. White rule would be reestablished in the South to a great extent by means of private extralegal violence, frequently with the approval and not very clandestine assistance of local officials. The Ku Klux Klan played a key role in this reign of terror. With bullet and torch, rope and whip, the Klan threatened black voters, killing some and driving many more away from the ballot box. While black voting would not be completely eliminated in this period, it was severely weakened. White rule returned to the South. Fewer and fewer blacks dared vote. The number of black officeholders diminished. Historians of the American South have called this retreat from Reconstruction and the return of white rule *the Redemption*. By the 1890s, southern state governments were firmly in the control of white voters and white politicians. There was still, at the beginning of that decade, a question of what direction state governments might take with respect to race. Law and custom had changed, profoundly so, in the previous decades. Emancipation was irreversible. The Civil War amendments remained even if federal authorities no longer actively protected the rights of blacks. There were still a significant number of Negro voters, even if their numbers were diminishing. Blacks, too, had changed. They had experienced liberation. Men had voted and for a time had exercised real political power. Black mothers and fathers had sent their children and often themselves to school — first the schools established by the Freedmen's Bureau, later schools run by the states. The "Redeemed" southern state governments would have to confront these new realities.

Jim Crow would become a tool with which southern state governments were able to reinstate the antebellum order of white supremacy and racial exclusion that had been severely damaged with emancipation and Reconstruction. This system of segregation would turn Negroes into a group of American untouchables, ritually separated from the dominant white population in almost every observable facet of daily existence. Jim

Crow prescribed an etiquette of discrimination. It would not be enough for blacks to be second-class citizens, increasingly denied the franchise and other rights. Instead black subordination had to be reinforced by a reaffirming ritual dictating separate seating on public accommodations, separate water fountains and restrooms. Separate seats were to be found in courtrooms, along with separate Bibles with which to swear in black and white witnesses. The list of separations would become ingenious and endless.[14]

Jim Crow did not appear overnight. Indeed at the close of the nineteenth century, many whites as well as blacks argued that rigid separations were errant nonsense. Some critics in fact cited such ideas as separate park benches, railroad cars, and Bibles for courtroom witnesses as the kind of absurdities that would cause right-thinking people to reject segregation. Their arguments were to no avail. What critics of Jim Crow cited as a reductio ad absurdum would in fact become the mandate of the law in many states in the South and in a few states in other regions as well.[15]

This system of state-mandated segregation would gain the support of the nation's highest court in 1896. That year the Supreme Court handed down its decision in *Plessy v. Ferguson.* The case originated in Louisiana. In 1890, the legislature passed a statute requiring separate railroad cars for whites and blacks. The statute specified that the facilities were to be of equal quality. It also prescribed fines or imprisonment for passengers who sat in the cars reserved for members of the other race. The law did permit one exception. Servants attending children could sit in cars reserved for those of the other race. This exception was made to accommodate black nannies of white children. It was an affirmation that blacks and whites could be in close proximity only when the white person's dominance and the black person's subservience were unquestioned.

Plessy began with Homer Adolphus Plessy of New Orleans on June 7, 1892. He attempted to ride in the first-class coach reserved for white passengers. When told that he must move to the coach reserved for Negroes, he refused and was arrested. Plessy's life can tell us a great deal about race in the United States. That Plessy was ordered to the Jim Crow section and barred from the white one tells us much about the differences in racial identity in the United States and much of Latin America. Plessy was an octoroon — that is, someone who had one-eighth African ancestry and seven-eighths white ancestry. He was an illustration of the American phenomenon known as the "one drop rule," the notion that any traceable African ancestry makes a person an Afro-American. It was in part a by-product of the explicit use of law to assign rights and restrictions on the basis of race. Students of American racial classification are aware that the rule, like any social norm, is more complex than its most simple formulation. Racial classification laws were by and large the result of state statutes that varied over time and place. Students of the subject have located individuals who at various times and places were recognized as white despite known African ancestry. States differed as to what fraction of African ancestry made an individual a Negro. The most severe statutes, the ones that imposed Negro classification on an individual for the most attenuated of links to an African ancestor, appear to have been a product of twentieth-century legislation, a necessary tool designed to make the discriminations mandated by Jim Crow law work.

But even with these qualifications, we can make some broad generalizations about law and racial classification in the United States. First, remote African ancestry has been viewed as a matter of both law and custom as making an individual black. Second, despite some resistance to the idea, the American practice has been to view race as a binary divide — a person is either black or white. Terms like *mulatto, quadroon,* and *octoroon* have cropped up from time to time, but they lacked the resonance that analogous terms had in Latin America. People of mixed race, particularly those with favorable family connections, often enjoyed greater advantages than people who were viewed as black. But these advantages were more limited than the advantages often enjoyed by mulattoes in many parts of Latin America. The law in the United States dictated that an individual's liberties and limitations would be determined by race and that people of mixed ancestry would largely be classified with the dominated Negroes and not the dominating whites. *Plessy* would become a vivid illustration of that rule.[16]

Homer Plessy's Louisiana was in many ways a hybrid of the American and Latin American views on racial identity. It was also a telling example of how legal rules over time could come to alter racial identities and racial boundaries. Before the Civil War, the state had a distinct class of French-speaking mulattoes, *gens de colour libre,* who did not regard themselves as black. With U.S. annexation and Louisiana's increasing adoption of American law, particularly American law with respect to slavery and race, the group was legally classified with the free Negro population. Despite this, lingering Latin cultural influences in Louisiana allowed this group, with considerable support from the French-descended white population, to carve out a separate status different from free Negroes in the rest of the South. Some members of this group voted, quite openly, even though it was illegal. Some were large slaveholders. Others participated in slave patrols. There are even a few cases of members of this group who formally married white persons, despite the fact that this was technically illegal. Some men from this population even formed military units and offered their services to the Confederacy, although they switched sides and joined the Union ranks with the Federal occupation of New Orleans in 1862.[17]

After the Civil War, this group increasingly was treated simply as part of the African American population. Plessy, who was from this group and who by all accounts was not visibly of African descent, was not merely protesting his assignment to the colored coach. He was protesting his assignment to the colored race. Historian Rebecca Scott's research informs us that the *Plessy* litigation should be seen against a broader background of anticaste activism that had been particularly well developed among Louisiana's *gens de colour libre*. Plessy's complaint was in large part a complaint against the system of legally required racial classification, a system necessary to the emerging world of Jim Crow restrictions. If the law could classify him as colored, Plessy reasoned, it could do so at great injury to his reputation. Such classification would also provide the law's support for caste or caste-like divisions. Plessy and his associates used discrimination on the railroad to launch a test case against racial classification and Jim Crow restrictions. In the Supreme Court, Plessy's attorneys, led by New Orleans lawyer Albion Tourgée, argued that segregation stigmatized blacks and was contrary to the egalitarian promise of the Civil War amendments.[18]

The majority opinion authored by Justice Henry Billings Brown rejected that claim. Brown's opinion saw segregation as reasonable regulation, a valid exercise of the state's police power. The Massachusetts-born justice dismissed the argument that mandatory segregation stigmatized blacks:

> We consider the underlying fallacy of the plaintiff's argument to consist in the assumption that the enforced separation of the two races stamps the colored race with a badge of inferiority. If this be so, it is not by reason of anything found in the act, but solely because the colored race chooses to

put that construction upon it. *Formism* . . . . The argument also assumes that social prejudices may be overcome by legislation, and that equal rights cannot be secured to the negro except by an enforced commingling of the two races. We cannot accept this proposition. If the two races are to meet upon terms of social equality it must be the result of natural affinities.[19]

Harlan provided the lone dissent, arguing that racial distinctions were anathema to the recently amended constitution:

The white race deems itself to be the dominant race in this country. . . . But in view of the Constitution, in the eye of the law, there is in this country no superior, dominant, ruling class of citizens. There is no caste here. Our Constitution is color blind and neither knows nor tolerates classes among citizens. . . . [A]ll citizens are equal before the law. . . . The law regards man as man, and takes no account of his surroundings or of his color when his civil rights as guaranteed by the supreme law of the land are involved.[20]

Plessy gave a green light to the segregationist statutes that had been passed in the latter part of the nineteenth century. Still, *Plessy* upheld a statute that specified that the facilities provided passengers of both races had to be equal. The new century would provide new opportunities to test *Plessy*'s separate but equal doctrine. Segregation was on the rise. What started in the last decades of the nineteenth century as tentative steps to separate the races in a few areas would, by the early part of the twentieth century, become a full-fledged effort to subjugate and stigmatize the South's black population. That effort would be accompanied by the virtual repudiation of the Civil War amendments and the egalitarian sentiment that helped bring about their enactment. Along with increased segregation came increased disenfranchisement. Blacks would largely disappear from the voting rolls in southern states. In those states Negroes would become politically irrelevant, disenfranchised, victims of a new brand of politics that effectively reestablished white domination in the region. That white domination was maintained through the often vicious politics of race-baiting.

The reestablishment of white domination in southern politics was accomplished with and maintained by an incredible level of illegal violence. Mob murder — lynching — was condoned and in fact celebrated by some of the most eminent public figures in the region. Newspaper editors wrote

apd fn nomen?

editorials justifying these murders. Governors and senators delivered speeches praising the handiwork of mobs, proclaiming lynching a necessary tool for dealing with blacks who forgot their place. Federal officials ignored these crimes. The Supreme Court's decision in *Cruikshank* had largely ended the federal government's role in protecting black citizens from private terror. Besides, there was a new politics in this new century. Whites totally dominated the politics of the new South. They had an unchecked political power in the region. Few politicians outside the region, even those somewhat sympathetic to the ideal of equal treatment, were inclined to challenge the ruling order in the South.[21]

Historians of the Afro-American experience have rightly termed the beginning of the twentieth century the "nadir" of American race relations, a time — at least after the Civil War — when race relations and protection of the rights of black citizens hit rock bottom. In *The Strange Career of Jim Crow*, Woodward offered some insight as to why the American nation as a whole was willing to turn its back on the egalitarianism of the Reconstruction era and permit the South to institute a regime of strict racial exclusion. The nation's new imperial adventures in the new twentieth century helped bring about something of a national reconsideration on the issues of race and racial equality. The nation was coming into new colonial contacts with nonwhite peoples in Hawaii, the Philippines, and Latin America. These new contacts created a new sympathy for the South and its desire to maintain rule by white men. It might also be added that waves of immigrants from Southern and Eastern Europe and also China and Japan gave influential people outside of the South new skepticism concerning the concept of equality before the law.[22]

These explanations can help us to understand why the Fourteenth and Fifteenth Amendments were becoming virtual dead letters in the South. But something even more fundamental was at work. A good portion of the public, particularly those who shaped the nation's opinions, the men and women of law and letters, those who dominated the intellectual life of the nation, were helping to give the country a case of buyer's remorse over the Fourteenth and Fifteenth Amendments. The newly emerging historical profession was rendering a very severe judgment on the nation's recent past. The generation that had supported abolition in the 1850s, had fought the Rebellion in the 1860s, and had later supported Reconstruction at the end of that decade was passing from the scene. Their lives and their works were being judged by a new generation of university-trained historians at the beginning of the twentieth century.

The most prominent of these, historian William A. Dunning, taught at Columbia University in New York City before the First World War. Dunning would provide a vivid picture of Reconstruction that dominated the thinking of most Americans for most of the twentieth century. In Dunning's view, Reconstruction was a "tragic era" — to use the title of a book by one of Dunning's disciples, Claude Bowers — it was a time when a vengeful North imposed its harsh rule on the South. Part of that imposition was the forcing of Negro equality down the throats of the white people of the region. This was accompanied through unparalleled corruption and military brutality. The return of white rule to the South was an unmitigated blessing, even if it was occasioned by the illegal work of the Ku Klux Klan. This view was spread not only by Dunning's writings but by his many students who came to dominate historical writing on the subject for at least the first half of the twentieth century. This view was also spread in textbooks as part of the general education of students in high schools and universities. It was also impressed on the public in the form of popular culture. Thomas Dixon's virulently racist novel, *The Clansman*, helped popularize this point of view, as did director D. W. Griffith's 1915 film, *Birth of a Nation*, which was based on the Dixon novel. This viewpoint probably reached its zenith in popular expression with the 1939 film *Gone with the Wind*.[23]

This discussion of how historians and artists came to view Reconstruction is important to our discussion of legislatures and courts and how they dealt with the constitutional demands of the Fourteenth and Fifteenth Amendments. Our sense of history, particularly recent history, informs our understanding of the past, to be sure. But our historical sensibilities do more — they invariably influence the way we think about contemporary issues. For American legislators and jurists at the beginning of the twentieth century, this "tragic" view of Reconstruction inevitably shaped their views of the Reconstruction amendments. Some argued forcefully that Reconstruction was evil and that the Fourteenth and Fifteenth Amendments were mistakes. Some even went so far as to propose their repeal. Others, less radical, argued that the amendments, the products of what they believed to be cynical power politics, could not have really intended to provide a robust guarantee of equal rights for blacks.

Perhaps nowhere is this link between historical understanding and the practical statecraft of racial exclusion better illustrated than in the writings and policies of Woodrow Wilson. The twenty-eighth president had been a scholar of considerable renown at Princeton University before embarking on a political career that would ultimately lead to the White House. A pioneer in the disciplines of political science and history as they were emerging in their modern academic forms at the end of the nineteenth century, Wilson was an acknowledged expert in American history and constitutional law. In 1892, he authored *Division and Reunion*, a text designed to provide a broad survey of nineteenth-century American history for college students and general readers. The Virginia-born Wilson presented a history of slavery and Reconstruction that essentially reiterated the major themes of the South's antebellum and postwar apologists. Slavery, he informed his readers, was by and large a humane — indeed, indulgent — institution. If its very existence was regrettable, it was nonetheless a reasonable and practical way for the South to come to terms with the presence of a large Negro population unfit for the responsibilities of citizenship. Reconstruction was a mistake — indeed, a tragedy. Wilson was willing to concede that many of the Reconstruction measures were partially provoked by the Black Codes, but nonetheless, he believed, the southern Negro was incapable of exercising the vote wisely. He was, during Reconstruction, the unwitting pawn of unscrupulous northern adventurers. The restoration of white rule signaled the return to politically sound constitutional government.

Wilson's writings were more than the academic musings of the New Jersey university's favorite professor. His views on race, his acceptance of the traditional southern view that assumed Negro incompetence and dependence, would not remain confined to his historiographical efforts. The twenty-eighth president would bring his historical sensibilities, including his views on race, to the White House. Early in his administration, Wilson used his presidential powers to bring Jim Crow to the federal government. His administration restricted Negro enlistment in the navy to ratings as mess attendants or officers' servants. Previously, black men had been able to enlist in the Navy's general service. The Wilson administration also brought segregation to the federal civil service. Government jobs, particularly in Washington, D.C., had been a source of steady income and relatively fair treatment for some black workers since the Grant administration. Wilson, responding to voices in his administration who argued that it would demean white civil servants to have to be in close contact with black ones, ordered the segregation of lunchroom, bathroom, and other facilities and placed limitations on the hiring of Negroes. The South's system of petty apartheid would be played out on a national stage.[24]

It was not only historical sensibilities that were furnishing intellectual support for Jim Crow. The newly emerging social sciences were also providing support for those who were calling for separate and unequal treatment of the races. If Social Darwinism provided a scientific underpinning for the advocates of *blanqueamiento* in Latin America, it would also play a role in strengthening the emerging Jim Crow order at the beginning of the twentieth century. Scientific racism had a long history in the United States. It had been a staple of proslavery apologetics before the Civil War. The felt need to justify racial domination along scientific lines would increase with the coming of the twentieth century, a reflection of the new prestige accorded scientific thought and particularly Charles Darwin's theories on evolution, conflict among species, and natural selection. These theories helped transform the biological sciences and, as was the case in Latin America, had no less profound an effect on social thought and the emerging social sciences. Scholars in academic disciplines such as sociology, economics, and law readily adopted or attempted to adopt evolutionary models to their fields of study.

Pioneering English sociologist Herbert Spencer would add the notion of survival of the fittest in adapting Darwinian theory to the study of social relations. It was, he argued, Nature's plan that the best, the fittest survive and that the weaker species perish. Why shouldn't that be applicable to the social world as well as the biological? Why shouldn't weaker peoples or races perish in the great evolutionary competition that was life? This was a strongly held view in the United States and indeed most of the Western world at the beginning of the twentieth century. No less a figure than Supreme Court justice Oliver Wendell Holmes, for example, was quite sympathetic to the eugenics movement, a movement that sought to improve the population by limiting the reproduction of those deemed inferior.[25]

Many adherents of Social Darwinism in the United States, like their counterparts in Latin America, saw Afro-Americans in particular as an inferior people destined naturally to lose and perish in the competition between the races. In their view, the new industrial society of the twentieth century had no place for the inferior Negro. If blacks had had a place in the simple agrarian South of the nineteenth century, they were surplus and dysfunctional in the modern twentieth century. Left to their own devices, they would be unable to survive. Like their counterparts in Latin America, many American social commentators predicted the disappearance of Afro-Americans from the South and the nation in the not too distant future. One disciple of Darwin, William Graham Sumner, was tremendously influential in legal circles. An early president of the American Sociological Society, he argued in his 1906 book, *Folkways*, against any attempt to remedy racial inequality through legal measures. Sumner argued that racial prejudice was an indelible part of American culture and could not be eradicated by legal change. He also challenged the very notion that equality before the law was sound policy.[26]

In the years before the First World War, a time called the Progressive Era by many historians, the social and intellectual climate was not supportive of constitutional challenges to racial discrimination. Yet the Civil War amendments were still there, unerased despite the new atmosphere. The main pillars of the constitutional revolution of the 1860s survived — battered, despised in many quarters, but still a part of the Constitution. The Supreme Court was strongly influenced by the segregationist climate of the times. But the Court was also faced with the stubborn survival of the Civil War amendments. They had not been repealed. There was a body of case law, including the recently decided *Plessy*, that indicated that these amendments could not be completely emptied of all meaning. How would the Court strike a balance between the prejudices of the day, shared by most of its members, and the demands of the still new amendments — amendments that were crafted in a very different day? The Court would find ways to thread the narrow needle between the facial demands of the Civil War amendments and the burgeoning racial exclusions of the new era. The Court did so in ways that usually gave little in the way of relief to victims of racial discrimination.

The Court was willing, to a degree, to enforce claims made under the Thirteenth Amendment's prohibition of slavery. Something of a consensus had developed that slavery's day had passed. Even those who romanticized the antebellum South's Peculiar Institution were willing to concede that it was perhaps wrong, inefficient, the cause of cataclysmic sectional conflict, and out of place in the progressive New South that they wished to build.

And yet despite the general acceptance of this view and the existence of the Thirteenth Amendment, forced labor had by no means disappeared from the southern states. The sharecropping system that developed in much of the South at the end of the nineteenth century left many poor black share-croppers with little money. They were often perpetually in debt. The common pattern was that black families would work on a small portion of a plantation, often the plantation on which they or their families had been enslaved before the Rebellion. The plantation owner would extend credit to the family for seed, tools, food, and other essentials. The family was to pay the plantation owner back with a portion of the crop. Naturally, the plantation owner had the records of how much had been lent, and not surprisingly, black sharecroppers frequently found no matter how much they managed to pay to the plantation owner at the end of the year or at harvest time, they still owed more. They had a legally binding debt and were often forced to continue working. Naturally, credit would be extended for next year's crop, increasing the family's indebtedness. In many southern localities, sheriffs and sometimes even local courts forced the black family to continue working on the plantation to pay off the debt.[27]

Peonage was illegal. In 1867, Congress had passed an antipeonage stat-ute. In 1904, the Supreme Court considered a case that raised a constitu-tional challenge to the Reconstruction-era legislation. The case *Clyatt v. United States* involved an appeal to the Supreme Court of the conviction of a white defendant Samuel M. Clyatt, who had been charged with forc-ing two black men to work for him. Clyatt had had the two men forcibly returned from Florida to Georgia under warrants for larceny and forced them to work for him to pay off their debts. The Supreme Court rejected Clyatt's central argument that the Thirteenth Amendment did not give Congress the authority to legislate against the actions of private individu-als. Clyatt's attorneys asked for a ruling that would have, in effect, said that if a private individual subjected someone to involuntary servitude, only the state government and not the federal government would have had the authority to declare such action a crime and to prosecute alleged offend-ers. It would have applied the limitations of the ruling in *Cruikshank* to the Thirteenth Amendment. Needless to say, in the atmosphere of the early twentieth-century South, such a ruling would have greatly strengthened the system of peonage. With the passage of peonage statutes left solely to unsympathetic state legislatures and their enforcement left to local sheriffs

beholden to plantation owners, mill operators, and other commercial interests, the Thirteenth Amendment could have become a virtual dead letter. The decision in *Clyatt* and other early twentieth-century peonage cases
helped prevent that. Despite these decisions, many large southern land-
owners managed to continue practices that kept many southern Negroes in
conditions of virtual and actual peonage well into the 1940s. And the harsh
system of convict labor that prevailed in many southern states left much in
the way of a forced labor regime in the Jim Crow South throughout much
of the twentieth century.[28]

If the Court was willing to take a somewhat robust view of the protection guaranteed by the Thirteenth Amendment, it was also quite protective of segregation and the right of state governments to erect a wall of
separation between black and white. The Court's reasoning was that the
police power — the authority to regulate in matters of safety, health, and
morals — gave states broad powers to regulate in matters of race relations,
including legislation that mandated segregation. One of the more important cases in this area in the first decade of the twentieth century was *Berea
College v. Kentucky*. Berea College had admitted black and white students
since the nineteenth century. In 1904, the state of Kentucky passed legislation forbidding schools from educating black and white students at
the same facility. Berea College was a corporation and hence had the legal status of a person. The college was indicted for failure to comply with
the mandatory segregation statute. It was convicted and sentenced to pay
a thousand-dollar fine. Berea College officials ultimately appealed the
ruling through the Kentucky state courts and then to the United States
Supreme Court.

Berea College presented issues that went beyond the "separate but equal"
doctrine that had been proclaimed in *Plessy*. *Plessy* dealt with legally enforced segregation on public transportation. Those facilities presumably
had separate and equal sections for black and white patrons. *Berea College*
involved the power of the state to require that a private institution maintain segregation. Here there was not a question of separate facilities; instead, there was an issue of state-mandated total exclusion. There was one
Berea College, and even though the statute said that a private institution
might build a separate facility for Negroes, that of course was extremely
unlikely. If the state could enforce segregation on private schools, it could
exclude Afro-Americans from many educational opportunities. The argu-

ment in *Berea College* and the Court's decision in the case were not framed in terms of the Fourteenth Amendment and the issue of equal protection. Instead, the case was argued on the issue of the property rights of Berea College and its officials. At the beginning of the last century, the Supreme Court was particularly concerned with protecting property rights and the right of individuals to have broad freedom to make contracts against state interference. Attorneys for the college argued that the Kentucky statute restricted the college's property rights.

The Supreme Court's decision rested on interesting ground, somewhat removed from the issues of equal protection and stigmatization that had been so central in *Plessy*. The Court held that because Berea College was a corporation and as a corporation was the creation of a state statute, the state could have broad power to regulate the conduct of a corporation, broader power than it might for an individual. The Court acknowledged that such a statute might be unconstitutional if applied to an individual on the grounds that it might violate the individual's property rights or freedom to contract. The Supreme Court indicated that it was only upholding the statute as to corporations and not individuals. The Court noted that the Kentucky Court of Appeals had indicated that the statute would be applied only to corporations, not individuals. Of course, it should also be added that the Court's holding that a corporation could be prevented from educating black and white students in the same facility in effect sanctioned a ban on most likely forms of integrated private education. Almost all schools of any appreciable size are likely to be run by corporations. The Court's distinction in *Berea* was of little importance in the field of education.

The traditional distinction between law and equity in Anglo-American jurisprudence proved to be one device that allowed the federal courts to avoid rigorous enforcement of the Fourteenth and Fifteenth Amendments. In civil cases, successful legal claims usually bring monetary damages as compensation for the harm suffered. But successful equitable claims usually require courts to supervise the behavior of defendants. Equitable remedies can involve injunctions (prohibiting a party from performing an injurious act) or specific performance (requiring a party to perform a beneficial one). Equitable remedies are considered extraordinary, usually available for continuing injuries when it is believed that monetary damages will not be adequate to right the wrong done to a complaining party.

Even though equitable remedies are considered extraordinary remedies, American courts at the beginning of the twentieth century had a long history of using their equitable powers as a tool with which to police labor unions. The labor injunction proved to be such a powerful tool in constraining the actions of organized labor that one historian of labor law has argued that it shaped the whole direction of the U.S. labor movement.[29]

The Supreme Court showed no similar willingness to use its equitable powers to enforce the Fourteenth and Fifteenth Amendments. Instead, the Court used a supposed reticence to exercise those powers to allow state officials to violate what even the Court acknowledged to be the mandates of the Civil War amendments. In a 1914 case, *McCabe v. Atchison, Topeka, and Santa Fe Railway Company*, the Court acknowledged that a railroad's failure to provide a sleeping car for black passengers when one was provided for whites was a violation of the separate but equal doctrine. Nonetheless, the Court declined to order that the railroad, operating under Oklahoma's Jim Crow railroad statute, provide a sleeping car for black passengers on the grounds that an equitable remedy would be too extraordinary in such a case. The early-twentieth-century Court proved equally reluctant to use its equitable powers to enforce the Fifteenth Amendment's requirement of equal voting rights. In a 1903 case, *Giles v. Harris*, Justice Holmes wrote an opinion in which the Court refused to compel an Alabama registrar of voters to register black men on the grounds that exercising equitable jurisdiction over the Alabama registrar would enmesh the Court too closely in the state's political affairs.

There were a few bright spots in the Court's racial jurisprudence before the First World War. The NAACP, which was founded in 1909, achieved an early victory in the 1916 case of *Buchanan v. Warley*, getting the Court to strike down a Kentucky statute that prohibited whites from selling residential property to blacks in white neighborhoods. The statute was struck down on the grounds that it interfered with freedom of contract, not that it contradicted the Equal Protection Clause of the Fourteenth Amendment. In another case decided in 1915, *Guinn v. United States*, the Court struck down Oklahoma's grandfather clause, exempting men descended from those eligible to vote before 1866 (that is, white men) from the state's literacy test.

The Supreme Court would largely frame its acquiescence to Jim Crow in somewhat neutral language, recognizing the constitutional principles of equality before the law and Negro enfranchisement embedded in the Fourteenth and Fifteenth Amendments. But if the Supreme Court would recognize these principles and couch its reluctance to enforce them in discussions of procedural and practical difficulties in implementation, state courts were often far more candid about what they saw as the law's primary task — enforcing white supremacy. There were, of course, southern jurists in the Jim Crow era who tried, within the context of their society and culture and their own prejudices, to render justice as they saw it to Afro-Americans. This was especially important, often a matter of life and death, in cases involving black defendants charged with harming white victims. One need only think of the extraordinary moral and physical courage demonstrated by Alabama judge James Edward Horton. Horton was the presiding judge in the retrial of Hayward Patterson. Patterson was one of the Scottsboro Boys, nine black youths who were tried in Alabama on false charges of having raped two white women. To say that the atmosphere was explosive exhausts all powers of understatement. The youths were almost lynched immediately after arrest. They were saved only by the intervention of the National Guard. Patterson and seven others were convicted and sentenced to death at a first trial in 1931. The convictions were overturned by the Supreme Court in the case of *Powell v. Alabama* on the grounds that the youths had had inadequate counsel. A jury convicted Patterson in the second trial. Horton, looking at the flimsy evidence against Patterson, set aside the jury verdict. His courage would cost Horton his political career.[30]

The kind of courage exhibited by Judge Horton was rare. It is much easier to find raw racism in the appellate court reporters of the various southern states. Judges in the highest courts of many states clearly recognized that the law was designed to protect a system of caste and privilege and they were quite frank in acknowledging such. The Georgia Court of Appeals, in declaring that it was actionable defamation to label a white person a Negro, was blunt in its recognition that the law regarded black and white as two separate castes, one superior and the other distinctly inferior: "It is a matter of common knowledge that, viewed from a social standpoint, the negro race is in mind and morals inferior to the Caucasian. The record of each from the dawn of historic times denies equality. . . . The distinction and inequality is recognized in Holy writ."[31]

On another occasion, a justice on the Florida Supreme Court openly acknowledged that a statute restricting the carrying of pistols was only meant to be enforced against blacks: "The original Act of 1893 was passed when there was a great influx of negro laborers in this State . . . for the purpose of disarming the negro laborers and to thereby reduce the unlawful homicides that were prevalent in turpentine and saw-mill camps and to give the white citizens . . . a better feeling of security. The statute was never intended to be applied to the white population and in practice has never been so applied."[32]

A breaking-and-entering case examined by the Louisiana Supreme Court in 1907 recorded a remarkable clash in closing arguments by defense attorney and prosecutor over the likely guilt of the black defendant. Defense attorney offered as proof of defendant's innocence the fact that he had not been lynched. He argued that because the victims were white, the defendant would surely have been killed by a vengeful white mob if he were guilty. The prosecutor countered that because the white people of the state had gotten rid of "Negro domination" — that is, Reconstruction-era government — lynching was no longer necessary, and "every man, white or black, was entitled to a fair and impartial trial." The Louisiana Supreme Court saw no appeal to racial prejudice in the district attorney's remarks.[33]

I cannot say whether an exhaustive, perhaps quantitative analysis might find these kinds of remarks typical for southern courts in the Jim Crow era. Certainly the judges in these cases did not seem to be at all self-conscious or demonstrate any fear that in some way their remarks would be taken as evidence of illegal or unconstitutional activity in their courtrooms. They recognized they had little to fear in the way of rebuke from higher authority. The egalitarian promise of the Civil War amendments lay dormant. The system of white supremacy that they were designed to prevent lay largely undisturbed.

Jim Crow made the United States unique in the American hemisphere. Throughout the hemisphere Afro-Americans faced often strong prejudice after emancipation. The efforts to turn the mestizo nations of nineteenth-century Latin America into the hoped for European nations of the twentieth century brought new racialist ideologies into many American nations. These new ideologies would combine with traditional Spanish and Portuguese notions of racial hierarchy to give many parts of Latin America a more strident emphasis on race and European background. But this new, or perhaps more accurately, revitalized emphasis on race did not produce a formal body of legislation like the Jim Crow laws of the United States. Social exclusion along racial lines existed. Statutes in many Latin American countries prevented the immigration of people of African descent. West Indian immigrants in Central America faced legal discrimination before the Second World War. But no Latin American nation established a regime that mandated extensive legal discrimination against native-born Afro-American citizens. Why did the United States take such a radically different path?

There is a link between racial exclusion as it existed in the antebellum South and the Black Codes and Jim Crow, the two postwar efforts to maintain or reestablish white supremacy under law. Simply put, American law developed a formal regime separating white and black into superior and inferior castes after emancipation because it had done so during slavery. The law did not do so in Latin America because despite the harshness of many slave regimes and the existence of race and color prejudices there, Latin American law had come to recognize free Afro-Americans as citizens. That difference alone might be considered sufficient to explain why Latin America and the United States took significantly different paths after emancipation. Yet a focus solely on race in the different slave regimes might cause us to overlook other important issues critical to an understanding of the peculiarly American pattern of legal exclusion.

The political and social dynamics that had caused many white southerners who were not slaveholders to support the region's Peculiar Institution and to feel a strong psychological stake not only in slavery but in a complementary system of racial subordination, would intensify with the return of white rule to the South. Historians of race relations and the American South have long considered the unrealized possibilities of a broad interracial coalition of the southern dispossessed — the poor, the tenant farmers, black and white — to be the great road not taken in American history. This theme was a major preoccupation of southern historian C. Vann Woodward, whose initial scholarly effort, *Tom Watson: Agrarian Rebel*, told the story of a southern populist who initially sought to build that elusive interracial alliance in the last decade of the nineteenth century only to become an accomplished and vicious practitioner of the politics of race-baiting by the first decade of the twentieth. The South's already strong culture of racial exclusion would be enhanced by white fears of economic competition with blacks and a competitive politics in which the recently emancipated Negro was welcome only as a scapegoat. The law responded to and reflected these political realities.[34]

The course of abolition in the United States would also play a role in sustaining support for a regime of radical racial exclusion. Unlike the other nations of the Americas, the United States would experience emancipation in such a way that the very manner of slavery's abolition would remain a source of sectional conflict in the nation for a good century after the adoption of the Thirteenth Amendment. In most of Latin America, by way of contrast, the abolition of slavery represented a national triumph — the victory of the forces that had struggled for independence against Spain and their Enlightened decisions to set their new nations on the path to emancipation. Mexicans and Chileans could view with satisfaction their early emancipations after independence. Colombians and Venezuelans could take pride in Bolivar's liberation of slaves. Cubans of all races could identify with the role of Afro-Cuban general Antonio Maceo in his nation's struggle for independence. Brazilians could be convinced of their national good fortune and good sense in having achieved a gradual and peaceful emancipation during the course of the nineteenth century. These sentiments could form a basis for national unity and consensus, even on the part of those who subscribed to national whitening. Slavery could be acknowledged as an evil, happily dispensed with even as the nation was preparing for its progressive European future. This perspective of course required some selective recounting of national histories. The strong, century-long fight to avoid total abolition in Brazil would have to be downplayed, as would strenuous efforts to evade legal emancipation in Peru, Argentina, and other Latin American nations. But still Latin Americans who reflected on slavery and its importance in the history of their nations could see, if albeit somewhat inaccurately, abolition as the product of national consensus, a reflection of the influence of the Enlightenment in their societies in the nineteenth century.

No such agreement could exist in the United States, not even one based on faulty memories. Abolition and the subsequent enfranchisement of Afro-Americans would remain in southern memory as symbols of defeat and northern domination long after the South's defeat sealed the doom of its Peculiar Institution. If white domination had been more vigorously exercised in the South than in other regions before the war, the drive to keep the South a white man's country would only intensify after the conflict.

Novelists and historians would enlist in the effort to justify the region's nationalistic effort of 1861 to 1865. The Old South's myth of the benevolent master and the contented, simpleminded slave would be renewed and enhanced. Reconstruction would be portrayed not as an effort to bring democratic rule to the South. It would be depicted instead as placing the South's virtuous white citizenry under the rule of primitive Negroes and their northern white manipulators. Redemption, disenfranchisement, and Jim Crow were seen as necessary corrections of a series of tragic errors. Over time, this perspective on the South's past would help convince many whites from the region and elsewhere of the wisdom of the Jim Crow legal regime.

That regime would shape the lives of Americans, black and white, in ways that still form our notions of racial identity and racial association. It would have the force of law and custom in the American South for most of the twentieth century and would only meet serious challenge and its ultimate demise after the Second World War. It was a systematic effort to define racial privilege and racial burden through law that was unique in the American hemisphere. The battle against Jim Crow would shape the struggle for racial justice in the United States for much of the twentieth century.

PART III

From Emancipation
to Equality

CHAPTER SEVEN

An American Sea Change

THE LAW'S POWER AND LIMITATIONS

NO EVENT BETTER ILLUSTRATES the determination of Americans in the first decade of the twenty-first century to turn their backs on the twentieth-century legacy of Jim Crow than the election of Barack Hussein Obama as president on November 4, 2008. Many Americans, including many who indicated that they had not voted for him, expressed satisfaction at the election's outcome. The Tea Party movement, disagreements over health care legislation and Afghanistan, and strong dissatisfaction with a stubbornly depressed economy and the partisan bickering to which every president is heir, these would come in the future. But on that Election Day, in November most Americans were pleased. A number of commentators expressed the view that the election was a harbinger of a new day for the American republic, an indication that the nation had finally put race behind it. Some went so far — prematurely, in my view — as to herald a new "postracial America," one in which the old divisions no longer mattered. Others demonstrated that they had forgotten a major component of the nation's racial history. They asked, "Why is Obama being proclaimed as the nation's first black president? His father was one of the Luo people of Kenya, it is true, but his mother was after all a white American. Shouldn't he be considered multiracial?" In any event, most Americans recognized him as the nation's first black president and, if the press reports and polling data are accurate, seemed to have taken no small measure of satisfaction from the nation's accomplishment.[1]

And it was not only in the United States that the election was applauded. Heralded around the world, the election was cheered as evidence of a new day in the United States. The news was proclaimed with banner headlines by the world's newspapers. More important, in the still young twenty-first century, the election of the American nation's first black president was greeted with great enthusiasm by the talking heads of the world's insatiable television news services. But the enthusiasm spread far beyond the headlines and sound bites proffered by professional pundits and journalists. It could be found around the world. In Kenya, birthplace of Obama's father, enthusiastic crowds carried the Stars and Stripes through the streets of Nairobi. There was an air of popular enthusiasm for the election throughout the world, partly a reflection of the unpopularity of the outgoing Bush administration, partly a reflection of the amazement that the United States, of all places, would elect a black president.[2]

For many, the image of the American nation had remained frozen in time. The United States was the home of Jim Crow, a nation of violent racists, the land of racial oppression. The stereotype in its crudest form was woefully out of date. By the time Obama had gained his substantial electoral and popular victory over Arizona senator John McCain, the United States had already changed in ways that would have made it unrecognizable to Americans who had lived through the Jim Crow years of the early and middle parts of the old century. Profound changes had occurred in the last three decades of the twentieth century. Progress came at an often agonizingly slow speed. It took decades to eliminate many racial barriers. But change did come. And when it did, it came in profound ways, ways that at times made the extraordinary seem commonplace. Change came to everyday life. Most Americans forget how pervasive discrimination once was. Every black man driving a bus, every black woman working as a department store clerk, every African American wearing the uniform of a navy petty officer, every black bricklayer and firefighter, police officer, hotel clerk, and telephone operator represents a hard-won victory over previous policies, official and unofficial, that once barred Negroes from working in many of the nation's occupations great and small.[3]

But it was not just the barriers to the nation's ordinary jobs that fell. The last three decades of the twentieth century brought an unprecedented opening of professional and educational possibilities for African Americans. Black students enrolled in previously all-white universities, in many cases in universities that had been previously segregated by law. Black faculty members would also begin appearing in noticeable numbers in these universities, although Afro-American representation in most academic disciplines remains quite low. Black officers, including flag-rank

officers, in the previously segregated armed forces had become common-place by the end of the twentieth century. By the end of the last century, black men and women were to be found in large law firms and the execu-tive offices of major corporations — not in numbers that corresponded to the black portion of the population at large, but present and present in suf-ficient numbers so that the Afro-American found in such position could not be dismissed as freakish or idiosyncratic.

In the last four decades it was not simply a matter that black people gained access to the great and small jobs from which their parents and grandparents had been barred for most of the twentieth century. The possibilities for public office opened up in ways that were previously un-thinkable, or at least unthinkable since Reconstruction. By the end of the twentieth century, the number of blacks in public office had increased significantly. There were five black members of the House of Representa-tives in 1965. By 2008, that number had increased to forty-one. The Vot-ing Rights Act of 1965 dramatically changed the politics of the American South. Office seekers who had been practitioners of the art of raw race-baiting either crafted more subtle appeals to racial prejudices or, like for-mer Dixiecrat presidential candidate Strom Thurmond and former Ku Klux Klan member Robert Byrd, worked to add Afro-Americans to their electoral coalitions. A few bold black politicians managed to run for and win statewide office as governor or senator, broadening their appeal be-yond the black electorate and garnering the support of white, Latino, and Asian American voters. By the 1980s, black cabinet officials became rou-tine, advising presidents of both parties. Obama's predecessor, George W. Bush, despite having won only a small percentage of the black vote in the 2000 and 2004 presidential elections, made the unprecedented move of appointing two Afro-Americans, Colin Powell and Condoleezza Rice, as secretaries of state. The once unthinkable had become unremarkable.[4]

How did this change come about? The United States in the last three decades of the twentieth century had, to an amazing degree, managed to leapfrog ahead of a number of Latin American nations — and indeed, mul-tiracial and multiethnic nations in other parts of the world — in the vex-ing and difficult business of constructing a more racially inclusive society. As we shall see in chapters 8 and 9, by the 1980s, more and more Afro-American civil rights activists and community leaders in Latin America would come to point to the United States as an example of racial inclusion and civil rights progress. Why did this occur in the United States when so little in the nation's previous history suggested such a future for the American Republic?

The answer lies in part in the nature of racial restrictions as they had historically developed in the United States. Jim Crow gave African Americans a clear target unmatched elsewhere in the hemisphere. Patterns of racial exclusion existed throughout the Americas. African ancestry was stigmatized from the Río de la Plata to the Saint Lawrence. But it was only in the American nation that the disadvantages of being labeled a Negro were reinforced — indeed, mandated — by law. Not only did the law dictate that race would govern and constrain every conceivable aspect of an individual's public and private behavior, it also dictated that the burdens of race would be inescapable. The stain of Negro ancestry would linger for generations; indeed, it would persist as long as it could be traced. There was to be no escape for the individual known to have African ancestors. Long-standing notions of racial mobility combined with support from powerful benefactors might soften the effects of racialist ideologies in parts of Latin America. Well-connected mulattoes, even a few individuals probably more accurately described as black, might reach prominent positions in the government, the armed forces, or the arts. Even ordinary Afro-Americans in Brazil or Cuba or Peru might find that although they were the victims of persistent discrimination or demeaning racial stereotypes were inescapable, they too were part of the popular sectors, the ordinary folk, of their nations. Like the mestizos who were counted as their betters or the immigrants who were supposed to replace them and by doing so improve their nations, people of African descent in Latin America generally lived in barrios filled with other poor and working-class citizens. Their children attended, sometimes all too infrequently, schools with children of other races. They served in army regiments with men who took pride in being labeled *white* or *mestizo* but who nonetheless served alongside and sometimes took orders from men whom society called *negro* or *mulato*.

But black people in the United States faced an unambiguous caste line. Jim Crow provided an in-your-face brand of discrimination. It constantly challenged any claim that Afro-Americans might have to equality, to citizenship, at times even to humanity itself. Jim Crow was designed to provide Negroes with a sense of their own inferiority and of the superiority of the whites that they encountered. All too often it did just that. But it did something more. It provided a clear target in the battle against racial exclusion. The basic outline of the story of the American civil rights movement in the twentieth century is well known. There is only enough time in this chapter to touch briefly on some of its major landmarks — the fight against legally mandated school segregation culminating in the Supreme Court's decision in *Brown v. Board of Education*, the battle to desegregate public facilities in the South, the struggle to register black voters in southern states, and the passage of landmark civil rights legislation in the 1960s.

The American civil rights movement was an epic struggle. It transformed the nation. Jim Crow showed the sinister power that the law had to restrict and demean a people. It created or at the very least greatly exacerbated a culture of racial exclusion. But the civil rights movement demonstrated the law's liberating power. As the law changed, the nation changed, and for the better. At the beginning of the last century, the law reflected and was fed by a racist culture that in turn was strengthened and structured by law. But the law, particularly since the 1960s, has played a significant role in helping to dismantle that culture of racial exclusion. It did so by prohibiting certain kinds of behavior. That prohibition required something more than legislative enactments or judicial decisions. It required tools to enforce the new, more egalitarian legal order. As those tools developed, they had a profound effect on American race relations. If the law cannot eradicate private prejudices, it can at least prohibit discrimination in public life. At one time, few people realized how powerful a tool that was. But the American nation's short history since the 1960s suggests that that ability to break down formal barriers in public life — the desegregation of schools, prohibitions on discrimination in the workplace, even the everyday mingling of the races on municipal buses and at lunch counters, in movie theaters and in amusement parks, has been accompanied by often profound changes in attitude about race and the propriety of racial discrimination. The civil rights movement and the legal change it brought stands as testimony to the transformative power of law. Yet the movement's aftermath also shows that the past is a stubborn thing. History can impose burdens on a society long after its members have felt the desire to move on. If the Jim Crow laws and the racial attitudes that brought them forth are now a thing of the past, the legacy of those laws and of the more complex patterns of racial exclusion that existed in the North as well as the heritage of slavery constitute a past that is still very much with us.[5]

It was the very belief that a system that mandated exclusion by law had to be challenged with law that gave the civil rights movement its focus for most of the twentieth century. That belief had deep roots among African American activists as well as white champions of equal rights. Historians debate what point we should fix as the start of the civil rights movement. Some would place the beginning of the modern movement with the decision in *Brown*; others would set the date with the increased black assertiveness and the greater federal sympathy for civil rights that came with the New Deal and the Second World War. Still others would place the beginnings with the founding of the National Association for the Advancement of Colored People (NAACP) or perhaps its predecessor, the Niagara Movement, before the First World War.[6] Strong claims can be made for all of these beginnings, but a more accurate historical memory would place the start of the civil rights movement much earlier, at the very beginning of the American republic. Paul Cuffee's fight for the vote for black men in Massachusetts in the 1780s was an early example, as were the effort to desegregate the Bay State's schools in the 1840s, the failed attempt to retain Negro suffrage in Pennsylvania in the 1830s, and Frederick Douglass's successful efforts to convince his friend Abraham Lincoln to abandon colonization and to support, however hesitantly, Afro-American citizenship. The fight against legal restrictions began early. Historian Ira Berlin accurately captures how the American egalitarian ethos and a resentment of increasing restrictions in the Jacksonian era helped give the struggle for equal rights its antebellum genesis: "Freedom was more than the negation of slavery. Black people had drunk deeply from the republican culture that had surrounded them for more than a century. Perhaps no Americans more fully understood the rights of citizens than those who had been forced to protest their exclusion."[7]

Founded in 1909, the NAACP was the heir of a civil rights movement that was already more than a century old. Like its nineteenth century predecessors, the organization focused on a uniquely American question, one that had ironically been framed by Chief Justice Roger B. Taney in the antebellum *Dred Scott* decision: in a republic that celebrated robust traditions of individual rights and popular governance, could citizenship survive the law's concerted effort to restrict, to exclude, to demean?

That question, that focus, would put the NAACP and ultimately other organizations on the path to directly challenging Jim Crow and the legal

grab him by the pussy

regime that supported it. The steps were faltering at first. In the early decades of the twentieth century, everything argued against the NAACP's notion that the firm grip of racial exclusion could somehow be loosened by
resort to the courts. The Fourteenth and Fifteenth Amendments were mor-
ibund, products of another age, one that had clearly receded. The courts
were hostile, and politicians were more likely to be elected on anti-Negro
platforms than as supporters of civil rights. The best minds in the nation
were endorsing theories of eugenics and racial inferiority. The prospects for
relief from the courts or the legislatures were slim, perhaps nonexistent.[8]

And yet the NAACP did move from these slim prospects to its triumph
in *Brown,* which would usher in the modern era of civil rights law. That
it was able to do so was a reflection of profound legal and social changes
that would occur after the First World War. Perhaps the most important
of these changes was the slow movement of scientific opinion away from
previous notions of the inherent superiority and inferiority of different
races. The change in thinking came in often painful stages. World War I
indirectly contributed to the new thinking. The war brought about the first
mass intelligence testing of the American public. The War Department
administered IQ tests to the nearly four-million-man national army that
had been mustered for the conflict. At first the tests seemed to confirm
the wisdom of the scientific racists. Recruits of Northern European ancestry scored higher than those of Southern and Eastern European ancestry.
Whites scored higher than blacks. Everything seemed to be in order.[9]

But the intellectual ground was shifting away from the biological deter-
minists. Perceptive analysts of the army's standardized tests noticed something curious. Negroes from northern states had higher test scores than
whites from the South. That information aided in the process of rethinking race and ability that was going on in American social science in the
interwar years. If what we now call the social sciences were inextricably
intertwined with biology and notions of biological determinism before the
First World War, increasingly after that conflict disciplines such as sociology and social anthropology were separating themselves from biologically
based explanations of human behavior. Students of these disciplines were
becoming convinced and were convincing others that culture and social
environment played critical roles in influencing human behavior. They
were also increasingly becoming convinced that cultural differences were
largely responsible for different patterns of behavior among different racial

groups. Anthropologist Franz Boas of Columbia University, who played such a critical role in the intellectual development of Brazilian social historian Gilberto Freyre, was leading the battle. With his ability to draw on extensive and meticulous ethnographic research, Boas's views were gaining more and more acceptance among behavioral scientists. Thanks to the efforts of Boas and others, by the 1930s the scientific racism that had been the conventional wisdom of educated people before the First World War was increasingly falling into disfavor in scientific circles in the United States.[10]

If the science of race was changing, so was the demography of race. The First World War is commonly taken as the start of what historians have called the Great Migration, the movement of large numbers of Negroes from the rural South to the industrial cities of the North and West. As had been the case in Latin America, the First World War disrupted the flow of European immigrants to the United States, as did restrictive immigration legislation after the war. The need for labor during the conflict caused northern factories to hire black workers, often for the first time. The migration, which would continue after the war, created new political and social dynamics. Racial tensions would increase in northern cities. There was a period in the latter decades of the nineteenth century where a measure of racial justice and racial peace had been achieved in a number of northern venues. Anti-Negro discrimination remained strong. Most blacks could only find marginal employment and could only live in rough, undesirable neighborhoods. Nonetheless, the antagonisms of the antebellum period that had led to race riots and the frequently successful efforts at disenfranchisement were somewhat muted after the Civil War. In a number of states, Republican legislators, fortified and prodded by a recently enfranchised black electorate, managed to pass state legislation ending legal segregation in public schools. These legislators also passed state laws, not enforced with any great vigor, to be sure, prohibiting discrimination in restaurants, inns, and public transportation. Some white northerners took a certain pride in having fought for the Union and the end of slavery. Some even took no small measure of satisfaction in fair dealing toward the Negro. Black men could vote; a few even got elected to minor offices. Occasionally, a black man might manage to get a job as a policeman, or a black woman might with luck find employment as a school teacher. Most of all, there wasn't that horrible record of violence, of bloody lynchings, of bodies, sometimes burnt beyond recognition, hanging from trees or lampposts, as there was in the South. Like Latin Americans who could look North to the United States and see their societies as racial democracies because they lacked the codified and explicit discriminations found in the American South, many whites and indeed quite a few blacks in northern states could look south and see their states as centers of somewhat fair treatment and reasonability on racial matters.[11]

The Great Migration challenged that comfortable vision. As the Negro population increased in northern cities the comfortable consensus that had developed in many parts of the North became severely strained. Vicious race riots occurred in a number of northern cities in the 1920s. With the increase in the black population also came an increase in residential seg- regation. Afro-Americans would ultimately be more segregated in the cit- ies of the North in the twentieth century than had been the case in the nineteenth. But still, despite increased tensions, the Great Migration would play a major role in making the civil rights revolution possible. The new residents of New York, Chicago, Detroit, Philadelphia, and other northern cities could vote. At first they voted for the party of Lincoln. The historic antagonisms between Negroes and the party of Jefferson and Jackson re- mained strong, at least initially. But over time, Democratic politicians in northern cities began to court the support of the black migrants, just as they had previously courted the support of the European immigrants. It was a significant change and one that would cause northern politicians to be more supportive of national civil rights measures, no matter how reluc- tant they might be to take on racial discrimination in their own states.[12]

The cities of the North also offered the children of migrants better edu- cations than were available in the legally segregated schools of the South. The cities also offered a freedom to engage in politics and protest to an ex- tent that would have been foolhardy — indeed, physically dangerous — in the Jim Crow South of the interwar years. The black neighborhoods that began to form or expand in northern cities in the 1920s and 1930s sup- ported new forms of cultural and political expression. New York had its Harlem Renaissance, which nurtured Afro-American cultural and literary expression. There were similar developments in other cities. This flourish- ing of black artistic and literary expression helped provide a critical base of support for protest against racial exclusion. This would become par- ticularly important with the onset of the Great Depression. The depression brought hard times to all Americans and perhaps particularly to those African Americans who had gained a tenuous foothold in commercial and industrial enterprises in the previous decade only to find that they were last hired and first fired as times got bad. What was often particularly galling to Negro residents of the ghettoes that had emerged in northern cities was that the very stores where they shopped often had no Negro employees. Campaigns in New York, Philadelphia, and other cities urged black consumers not to shop where they could not work. At times these campaigns were successful, at other times not, but whatever the result, they pointed out the possibilities of concerted action against the color line. The lessons would be remembered.[13]

Social change, the discrediting of scientific racism, and the movement of a significant portion of the Afro-American population to the relatively liberal cities of the North and West played an important part in setting the stage for the civil rights revolution that would occur after the Second World War. But there were other changes that were happening in the interwar years that would later prove critical to the effort to vanquish Jim Crow. Perhaps none of these changes were more critical than those that were occurring in the law. These developments included more than the simple passage of legislation or the pronouncement of judicial decisions. These were, of course, occurring in the interwar years. Some of the new legal developments were more or less favorably disposed toward the cause of racial equality. But something more would occur in the two decades between the two world wars. The law in the United States would begin to change both as a profession and as an intellectual discipline and it would do so in ways that would expand both its reach and its ability to influence social change.

The civil rights revolution of the nineteenth century had been thwarted to a striking degree by a rigid, formalistic jurisprudence that had insisted on maintaining the boundaries of the old federalism despite the enactment of the Civil War amendments. *Cruikshank* and the *Civil Rights Cases* had been sweeping pronouncements of the law's impotence, of its inability to surmount the old federalism in an effort to protect the nation's citizens. *Plessy* provided evidence of the law's blindness, of its inability to see beyond formal claims of equal treatment and recognize the law's ability to stigmatize and demean. The Supreme Court proved it could develop a quite flexible and innovative constitutional jurisprudence when it wanted to. It had demonstrated a willingness and an ability to extend itself beyond the boundaries of antebellum federalism and to use the Fourteenth Amendment quite creatively where it saw the need. In a 1905 case, *Lochner v. People of New York*, the Court held that the Fourteenth Amendment's Due Process Clause prevented the state of New York from enacting legislation restricting the number of hours a person could work. Equal treatment of the races, which had been central to the Thirty-Ninth Congress's deliberations on the Fourteenth Amendment, had been pushed to the periphery of the Court's jurisprudence. Classical liberal notions of freedom of contract had been moved to its center.

It would take some conceptual rethinking in American jurisprudence to help transform American law from a force that abetted Jim Crow into the force that would after the Second World War play a major role in ultimately defeating it. The nineteenth-century Supreme Court's narrow view of federal power played a key role in eliminating the national government's role in protecting civil rights and in ushering in the South's Jim Crow regime. The notion of robust federal power and the linking of that power to the protection of civil rights would have to be rebuilt in the twentieth century. That process would be slow, often painfully so, and would go through many detours and unanticipated byways. The connection between a robust view of federal power and the idea that national civil rights could and, of course, should be tied to that power was a long-standing one. It was certainly the vision of the Congresses that had enacted the Civil War Amendments and the accompanying civil rights legislation of the Reconstruction era. Theirs was a vision of a national law strong enough to protect the nation's citizens from violations of rights, whether the source of those violations was state governments or private citizens. That vision was not shared by the nation's leading jurists at the end of the nineteenth and beginning of the twentieth centuries. Interestingly enough, John Marshall Harlan, the great dissenter in the *Civil Rights Cases* and *Plessy*, was one who would more broadly embrace the view that the law had to have national reach in order to solve national problems. In the Supreme Court's first consideration of the 1890 Sherman Antitrust Act, *United States v. E. C. Knight* (1895), Harlan was the lone dissenter from Chief Justice Melville Fuller's majority opinion that held that the antitrust legislation could not be applied against a corporation that was monopolizing sugar refining. The Fuller opinion held that manufacturing was not commerce within the meaning of the Constitution's Commerce Clause, the provision that gives Congress the authority to regulate economic activity among the different states. Harlan's dissent, like his dissents in the two cases involving racial discrimination, anticipated a jurisprudence that would not develop until much later in the nation's legal history. In essence, he argued that congressional power could regulate manufacturing because manufacturing ultimately affected national commerce. Harlan articulated a vision of the reach of national law that would not find general acceptance on the Court for another four decades.

Egregious cases and national crises would help move the Supreme Court toward an acceptance of Harlan's vision of the need for a body of law empowered with greater national reach. Hard cases involving Negro defendants in southern states sentenced to death after trials that did not even rise to the level of mockeries pushed the Court into a reconsideration of its previous support for a narrow reading of the Fourteenth Amendment and the demands it made on state governments. These cases involved black defendants sentenced to death allegedly for the rape or murder of white victims. Their trials were hurried. The defendants received almost no opportunity to consult with their attorneys. Guilty verdicts and resulting death sentences were prompted by well-founded fears of potential lynch mobs. The more virulent racists in the towns where these trials were held made it clear that if the state's law failed to produce a guilty verdict and an execution, a mob and a rope would bring about not only the death of the accused Negro but no small amount of damage to the town's reputation as well. Cases such as *Powell v. Alabama* and *Norris v. Alabama*, the Scottsboro Boys cases, and *Brown v. Mississippi* forced the Court's hand. In the nineteenth century, immediately after the enactment of the Fourteenth Amendment, the Court rejected the notion that the new amendment made the Bill of Rights binding on the states. When faced with hard cases where defendants in capital cases were in essence denied the assistance of attorneys or were convicted based on confessions obtained through torture, the Court reconsidered. It was a step toward a body of national law, national law that could protect ordinary citizens.[14]

The New Deal would provide another set of conceptual breakthroughs that would move the United States to a more national body of law and one that would ultimately help create a strong national civil rights regime. President Franklin D. Roosevelt's New Deal was not envisioned as an attack on Jim Crow — far from it. Roosevelt was rather conservative on the issue of race. White southern Democrats formed part of his New Deal coalition, and he was careful not to offend them. He refused to support antilynching legislation. His administration maintained strict segregation in the armed forces, both the peacetime army and navy of the 1930s as well as the wartime armed forces of the Second World War. But the Great Depression — the desperate decade of the 1930s, when the nation's unemployment rolls swelled to 25 percent and unemployment among Afro-Americans in some urban areas reached a staggering 40 percent — caused many Negroes to look, often for the first time, to their historic antagonists in the Democratic Party. Relief measures provided by the New Deal administration proved literally to be lifesavers for some of the most desperately poor, even when they came with all the trappings of Jim Crow.[15]

The New Deal's most important contribution to the American civil rights movement ultimately lay not in the relief measures that it provided to the poor, black and white. Nor was its most important contribution political realignment, a realignment that over the course of the long twentieth century would turn Afro-American voters from reliable Republicans into dedicated Democrats. Instead, the importance of the New Deal was that its regulatory and relief measures forced a reconceptualization of the reach of federal power and federal law. The Supreme Court that Roosevelt inherited initially took a dim view of the New Deal architect's claim that the federal government had the constitutional authority to set wages and prices, to regulate economic activities that extended beyond interstate commerce, at least as traditionally conceived. But the Court, in response to the administration's prodding, the threat of Court packing, and some clever lawyering on the part of the administration's advocates, would ultimately come to accept the New Deal vision of a federal government of greatly expanded scope.[16]

I am spending a bit of time on this question of federalism and the reach of national authority because it has always loomed somewhat larger in the history of race and law in the United States than has been the case in other American nations. This was true from the beginning. Abolition in the United States and the extension of equal rights and citizenship to Afro-Americans came about as a result of regional conflict, not national consensus. This ensured that enforcement of civil rights law would remain a contested issue and one that was dependent on the reach of national law.

A robust view of the law's national reach would be a prerequisite to any effort to use the law as a tool to enforce racial equality.

A reconsideration of the traditional limits of federal power was critical to the development of a robust regime of civil rights law. But that reconsideration alone might not have proved sufficient. There also had to be some rethinking of what was appropriate legal reasoning. American jurists in the twentieth century would become more explicitly policy oriented. They would consult and employ the findings of the empirical sciences with greater frequency than their nineteenth-century predecessors. The growth of the legal realist movement certainly contributed to this new style of judicial decision making. The realists contributed to a shift away from the highly abstract, formalistic reasoning that dominated much of American jurisprudence in the latter part of the nineteenth century. Critics have charged that realist jurisprudence too often devolved into unprincipled judicial policymaking, devoid of meaningful legal rigor. Whether one accepts the view of those who are generally supportive or critical of legal realism, it is clear that the realists urged jurists to extend the craft of legal reasoning beyond traditional considerations of legal doctrine. They urged instead that the empirical sciences, with their examinations of economic and social conditions, were a necessary part of judicial decision making. This call for new tools and new concepts in judicial decision making would spread beyond the legal realists. It would ultimately influence even many of the realists' critics.[17]

Whether this new style of judicial decision making represented as much of a break from nineteenth-century styles of legal reasoning as some scholars have contended is subject to debate. There had long been a pragmatic, instrumental aspect to the American judiciary. Certainly antebellum jurists had quite pragmatically refashioned vast areas of the common law to meet what they saw as the economic necessities of the time. With a few notable exceptions, American jurists were practical men, not great theoreticians. The political and social consequences of their decisions were never far from their deliberations. But whether the new jurisprudence was a departure from previous styles of legal reasoning, or a repackaging of a previously existing policy-oriented judicial craftsmanship, conditions were ripe in the early twentieth century for greater and more explicit inclusion of discussions of the social and economic impact of legal rules on the broader society. The emerging social sciences, modeling themselves on the more established discipline of biology, were promising to do much in the way of explaining and predicting human behavior. The law itself was becoming more of an academic enterprise. Professors at the best law schools were proclaiming that the law should be studied as a science. The American Bar Association was pushing hard to make graduation from law school a requirement for admission to the bar. The best law schools were increasingly insisting that their students first attend undergraduate colleges, where, among other things, they would be exposed to the new thinking in disciplines such as psychology, sociology, and economics before embarking on their legal training. The more innovative members of the bar were following the example of Louis Brandeis, filing briefs that detailed the compelling policy considerations behind the cases they presented.[18]

This new legal thinking was critical to the NAACP's success in *Brown v. Board of Education. Brown* as a case has been analyzed, criticized, and at times nitpicked to a fare-thee-well by the nation's legal scholars and historians, among others. The short, unanimous opinion authored by Chief Justice Earl Warren that proclaimed state-mandated school segregation unconstitutional has been criticized for its brevity, its absence of sophisticated constitutional analysis, and the short shrift that it gave to the question of the original intentions of the authors of the Fourteenth Amendment. Advocates of a more robust judicial role in enforcing civil rights have criticized the decision's failure to order an immediate end to school segregation. The *Brown* decision famously came in two stages, *Brown I*, decided in 1954, which proclaimed school segregation unconstitutional and implicitly repudiated the Court's previous endorsement of the "separate but equal" doctrine in *Plessy*. The second stage, *Brown II*, decided in 1955, dealt with the difficult problem of implementing the high court's desegregation decision. In the 1955 decision, the Supreme Court charged the federal district courts that would have to actually issue specific orders to state governments and individual school districts to implement the Court's desegregation decision with "all deliberate speed." It would prove to be a process that would take decades.[19]

Brown was slow in implementation. It was not the Court's most elegant example of judicial reasoning or draftsmanship. It left many issues unresolved. And it was absolutely essential. The decision addressed the most fundamental contradiction in American history, the contradiction of caste in a democratic society. The issue was framed in a most compelling manner by the NAACP's lead advocate in the case, Thurgood Marshall: "Why of all the multitudinous groups of people in this country, you have to single out the Negroes and give them this separate treatment?"[20]

It had taken the NAACP a long time to get to the point where it could pose that question to the nation's highest court. The civil rights organization had been helped by important victories it had previously won against segregated graduate and profession education in state universities. The NAACP's first victory in its campaign against segregated education came in a suit against a segregated law school. The civil rights organization brought a suit against the University of Maryland because the university's law school had rejected a black applicant solely because of his race. The organization was able to convince the Maryland state courts that the absence of state law school facilities for black students was a violation of the Fourteenth Amendment's equal protection requirement. The courts held that the state's willingness to provide a scholarship that would allow Afro-Americans to attend law school out of the state was not an adequate substitute. It was a beginning. It was one that the NAACP would build on. Other suits would follow and be decided in the U.S. Supreme Court in the 1930s, 1940s, and 1950s. These suits would challenge segregation in the state law schools and graduate programs in Oklahoma, Texas, and Missouri. They were framed not as direct challenges to *Plessy*'s "separate but equal" doctrine, but as clarifications or modifications of the 1896 opinion. Could Missouri meet its obligations under the Equal Protection Clause if it failed to provide an in-state law school for black students? Could Oklahoma admit a black student to its graduate school and then require him to use separate sections of the library and cafeteria? Could Texas create a poorly resourced Jim Crow law school for Negroes and claim that it was the equivalent of the facility at the University of Texas? Increasingly the NAACP, by presenting the right cases with the right plaintiffs, was educating the Court, informing the high tribunal that separate but equal might be sound in theory but was fatally flawed in fact.[21]

That instructional program was helped along immeasurably by an event totally outside the control of the NAACP. The Second World War would change the way Americans viewed the issue of race. The nation's experience of fighting against the stark horror that was Nazi racism; the army's experience in liberating killing grounds named Buchenwald, Dachau, and Mauthausen; and the postwar Nuremberg trials all gave the nation a chance to take a cold, hard look at racism and the horrors that it could bring. The Second World War would not cause American racism to vanish, not by any means, but it did cause some rethinking. The nation became less comfortable with the casual, easy racism that prevailed earlier in the century. There was less official support for notions of inherent racial difference. Behavioral scientists had come to turn their backs on doctrines of scientific racism that had been so influential at the start of the century. Increasingly, the government would come to speak out against notions of racial supremacy, declaring them to be unpatriotic and helpful to the Nazi enemy. Racial discrimination would continue, of course — the armed forces remained segregated, and Jim Crow prevailed throughout the South, with many southern officials taking delight in rigorously enforcing Jim Crow's many indignities on Negro soldiers stationed in the region. But the ideological support that Jim Crow had had a generation earlier was being lost.

But the most important effect that the Second World War had was on the generation of Negroes who came of age during the conflict. Even before America's entry into the war, union leader A. Philip Randolph used the looming conflict and a threatened march on Washington to pressure Roosevelt into signing an executive order banning discrimination in the expanding defense industries. After the United States entered the conflict, a prominent black newspaper, the *Pittsburgh Courier*, summed up the attitude of many Negroes when it announced its "Double V" campaign — V for victory against the Axis abroad, V for victory against racists at home. The war accelerated the movement of Afro-Americans from the rural South to urban centers in the North and West. The need for workers in the wartime defense industries and the lure of greater pay and dignity in the newly opened factory jobs caused men to leave their traditional work as sharecroppers and women to abandon domestic service. The war brought other changes. One million Negroes, mostly men, served in the armed forces. With rare exceptions, they served in segregated units in the army or in menial positions as officers' servants in the navy. But the demands of global war forced the armed forces to assign them to unexpected roles. There were black combat soldiers in every theater, and enemy breakthroughs forced the army and navy to use black men who had been assigned as truck drivers, stevedores, or mess attendants in combat roles.[22]

That experience led to a new militancy on the part of those who had risked their lives for American democracy, often in military units led by white southern officers determined to maintain segregation and Negro subservience. One such man, Harry Briggs of South Carolina, served in the U.S. Navy in the South Pacific. After returning home, Briggs, who worked as a gas station attendant, and his wife, Liza, who worked as a hotel chambermaid, struggled to raise their five children yet braved economic sanctions and worse to lend their name to *Briggs v. Elliott*, a companion case to *Brown*.[23]

Brown was made possible by the courage of men like Harry Briggs and women like Liza Briggs, ordinary people who sought better lives for their children, better lives that would only be made possible if the system of segregated schooling, a system that had systematically shortchanged black children, was dismantled. But *Brown* was also made possible by broader changes that were occurring in postwar America. Racial attitudes were changing. The new president, Harry Truman, a southerner and one who had flirted with the Ku Klux Klan earlier in his political career, was more willing to challenge Jim Crow than his predecessor Franklin Roosevelt. In 1948, the former World War I artillery captain issued an executive order mandating equal opportunity in the armed forces. That order would result in the integration of the armed forces by the early 1950s. It would have far-reaching effects. Millions of American men would have their first experience with integration and with relatively equal treatment of people of different races in the Cold War–era armed forces of the 1950s, 1960s, and 1970s. Integration of the armed forces would prove to be an important step in changing the culture of race relations in postwar America.[24]

Truman's presidency also proved that the politics of race had changed. The white South had long been the anchor of the Democratic Party. Solidly Democratic, the region provided one of the key pillars of Roosevelt's New Deal. But Truman's support for civil rights angered the South. His chances for election in 1948 looked slim. The Democratic Party was split into three factions. The Democratic governor of South Carolina, Strom Thurmond, ran on a prosegregationist Dixiecrat ticket. Left-wing former vice president Henry Wallace was the candidate of the Progressive Party. Truman, the nominee of the Democratic Party, seemed to be hopelessly behind Republican Thomas Dewey. But Truman won, and by doing so he demonstrated that a national Democrat could embrace a civil rights platform and survive the defection of hard-line segregationists. The Negro vote in the North had now grown to such a point that it could compensate for the loss of the Dixiecrats. It was a lesson that emboldened advocates of racial equality.[25]

Other developments helped to pave the way for the *Brown* decision. The Court itself was reconsidering the reach of the Fourteenth Amendment. Restrictive covenants — agreements, usually mandated by neighborhood associations, that required home buyers not to resell their homes to Jews, Negroes, Asians, or other targets of racial prejudice — had long been a part of the American real estate market. These agreements were enforceable in the courts until the Supreme Court in a 1948 case, *Shelley v. Kraemer*, held that any effort to judicially enforce such agreements would require courts to violate the Fourteenth Amendment's Equal Protection Clause. The Court was taking a fresh look at race and the demands of the Constitution.[26]

The nation was doing so as well. In 1944, Swedish social scientist Gunnar Myrdal had published a massive study of American race relations, *An American Dilemma: The Negro Problem and Modern Democracy*. Myrdal's work documented the massive inequality and unfairness that was an integral part of daily life for most Negroes in Jim Crow America. Myrdal's study gave strength to those who argued that the extensive system of segregation that prevailed in America was not only unjust but also un-American. If the academic treatment of race was beginning to change in postwar America, so was the view expressed in the popular culture. Jackie Robinson played for the Brooklyn Dodgers, integrating the previously segregated national pastime. Hollywood was beginning to seriously tackle the question of racism in American life with a series of message movies condemning what had previously been routine and socially acceptable prejudices. A 1947 film, *Gentleman's Agreement*, starring Hollywood's up-and-coming leading man, Gregory Peck, explored the touchy theme of anti-Semitism in American life. In 1949, *Home of the Brave*, starring Negro actor and veteran of the Italian campaign with the 92nd Division, James Edwards, shined some light on racial prejudice in the wartime army. The nation was becoming less comfortable with its traditional caste distinctions.

None of these changes made *Brown* inevitable. Historians have debated the extent to which the desegregation decision should be seen through a Cold War lens. Was the decision helped along by the attorneys general of the Truman and Eisenhower administrations, who reminded the Court that segregation weakened the American claim to leadership of the Free World? Certainly Eisenhower's appointment of former California governor and Republican vice presidential candidate Earl Warren as chief justice played a key role in producing the unanimous Court decision. That decision was shaped by the NAACP's early determination to attack the system of caste that was inherent in Jim Crow. Warren's controversial use of social science evidence was in the decision because it directly related to the civil rights organization's central claim that segregation demeaned and stigmatized Negro children.[27]

There is neither the space nor the time to go into a more extensive discussion of *Brown,* the difficulties that occurred in implementing the decision, and the massive resistance to school desegregation that occurred in the ensuing decades. That history has been well covered and is part of an ongoing debate on the importance and legacy of the desegregation decision. But *Brown* made one thing clear: federal law had changed. The U.S. government would no longer enable the South's Jim Crow regime. If the Warren decision failed to make that clear, Eisenhower's deployment of federal troops to Little Rock, Arkansas, to stop white mobs menacing black children attempting to attend the newly desegregated Central High School in that city did. The federal government was back in the business of protecting civil rights in a big way.

The *Brown* victory energized the civil rights movement. On December 1, 1955, a courageous woman, seamstress Rosa Parks, refused to move any further to the back of a municipal bus and give her seat to a white man in Montgomery, Alabama. Her subsequent arrest would lead the black citizens of that city to boycott the city's municipal buses. Ultimately the Supreme Court would strike down the municipal ordinance requiring segregated seating on the city's buses. Freedom riders, black and white, would put their bodies on the line, risk their lives, and desegregate lunch counters and bus lines. Throughout the late 1950s and early 1960s, southern Negroes and volunteers of all races from elsewhere in the nation braved the Klan and local officials — and at times it was hard to tell the difference — to register black voters in the states of the former Confederacy. It was dangerous. Mississippi NAACP leader Medgar Evers, a veteran of the Normandy landings in June 1944, was shot in the back on his front doorstep for registering black voters. Two Jews from New York, Andrew Goodman and

are we going to do this to Clinton dns?

Michael Schwerner, and an Afro-American, James Chaney of Mississippi, were murdered with the help of local officials for their voter registration activities. The situation was desperate, yet federal officials were at first reluctant to help. Many civil rights workers only survived either because they were armed or were protected by armed citizens from African American communities.[28]

The civil rights struggles of the late 1950s and early 1960s led to comprehensive changes in federal civil rights law. The Civil Rights Act of 1964, originally introduced by President John F. Kennedy and ultimately pushed through Congress by his successor, President Lyndon Johnson, gave the federal government expanded powers to fight private discrimination. The new legislation outlawed discrimination in public accommodations and employment among other areas. The civil rights statute provides a clear example of how the new legal thinking and expanded notions of federal power played key roles in the new legal regime that would do much to vanquish Jim Crow. If the Supreme Court in 1883 had taken a narrow view of Congress's powers to attack private discrimination and invalidated key portions of the Civil Rights Act of 1875, the Court by the mid-1960s had become accustomed to sustaining far-reaching federal regulation under the Constitution's Commerce Clause. The New Deal and the expansion of the federal regulatory state had taken care of that. The Court quickly indicated that the new expanded view of Congress's power under the Commerce Clause would allow Congress to protect citizens from racial discrimination. In *Heart of Atlanta Motel v. United States*, the Court held that Congress could prohibit discrimination in public accommodations and employment. The Court's decision was handed down the same year that the legislation was enacted, 1964. Economic historian Gavin Wright has written that the new legislation had a rapid impact in some sectors. A combination of the civil rights legislation and the threat of withholding federal contracts forced the southern textile industry to go from employing almost no black workers in 1960 to having an almost 15 percent black workforce by the end of the decade. Most of that hiring came after the enactment of the civil rights legislation.[29]

The other successes of the civil rights movement of the 1950s and 1960s are well known but bear at least brief repetition. The 1965 Voting Rights Act dramatically increased the number of Afro-American voters in the South from under 20 percent of those eligible in the early 1950s to more than 60 percent by the beginning of the 1970s. Between 1968 and 1972, the number of black students in schools with 90 percent or more black enrollment declined from almost 78 percent to just under 25 percent. The new legislation made a difference not only in the behavior of whites who served customers at motels and restaurants, determined who might be hired at textile plants, or handed out voter registration cards at city hall but also among African Americans. Knowing that the law had changed, that the federal government was in the business of protecting civil rights, black people proved willing to apply to schools or for jobs or simply to sit at lunch counters that had previously been marked "Whites only." The law could make a difference, a big difference.[30]

And it did. By the early 1970s Jim Crow had been largely vanquished. There were still segregationists redoubts to be sure; there still are. Racism had not vanished, although public opinion polling indicated that fewer and fewer white Americans supported segregation and racial discrimination — or at least fewer and fewer were willing to tell pollsters that they did. The civil rights movement had helped to change minds. Television news provided indelible images of vicious police dogs attacking civil rights demonstrators or howling mobs spitting curses at black children attempting to enter previously all-white schools. These crude defenders of southern segregation left Jim Crow with few supporters in the nation at large. It even created a certain defensiveness among many white southerners. Racism, at least the open traditional kind of racism that had been so prevalent in the early part of the twentieth century, had become less and less respectable. And the most important change was that the law no longer supported discrimination. Where the law had once mandated separation of the races and indeed sanctioned and at times mandated inferior treatment for Afro-Americans, the law now prohibited racial discrimination, at least in its crudest forms. The old "Colored" and "White" signs came down from most places of public accommodation fairly quickly. Such obvious manifestations of segregation had long been something of an embarrassment to the federal government, and a vigorous program of enforcement by the Justice Department was able to largely eliminate this crude throwback to the Jim Crow era within less than a decade of passing the 1964 Civil Rights Act. The more blatant forms of employment discrimination and efforts to prevent the registration of black voters were also largely eliminated by the combined forces of the 1964 Civil Rights Act and the Voting Rights Act of

1965. By the early 1970s, even the Justice Department led by attorney general John Mitchell was attacking the more obvious remnants of Jim Crow. This was perhaps especially important. The Nixon administration had come to power in part by fanning the flames of racial resentment, using a "southern strategy" that represented a calculated effort to bring southern segregationists into the Republican Party. Nevertheless, the Nixon administration continued the work of its predecessor in attacking overt segregation. Jim Crow's day had passed.[31]

The civil rights movement's victory helped set the stage for a new and more complex phase in the effort to eliminate racial inequality in American life. Jim Crow had played an important role in mobilizing Afro-Americans and others in the fight against racial discrimination. Even before Jim Crow had been vanquished, civil rights activists had realized that the struggle for equality would have to involve more than an attack on the cruder manifestations of segregation in American life. Huge inequalities existed in American life. Not all of them were accompanied by the trappings of southern segregation or prefaced with "Colored" and "White" signs, but the inequalities were real and hard, and a victory against Jim Crow without an attack on these broader inequalities would be a hollow victory indeed. The black population increasingly was becoming a victim of hypersegregation. In many urban areas, especially in the North, African Americans were more segregated than any other American ethnic group except Indians on reservations. Black unemployment was consistently higher than white unemployment, and that gap was widening. Although black employment in the industrial workforce had grown significantly from the 1940s through 1960s, the unions that controlled employment in the skilled trades had policies that effectively kept most Afro-Americans out of more desirable blue-collar jobs. These policies might not have been overt; they might not have had the formal support of the law, but they were nonetheless real. *Brown* and the work of federal district courts in implementing the 1954 decision had largely dismantled the system of legally separate schools by the early 1970s, but segregation in education was intensifying in the North, the result of highly segregated residential patterns in many cities and more than a little manipulation on the part of some urban school boards.

The law had had tremendous success in the battle against Jim Crow. Could it be equally effective in tackling entrenched patterns of inequality caused by thousands of individual decisions not formally supported by the law but that nonetheless created barriers nearly as formidable as those maintained by the segregationist South? Could the law police real estate agents who refused to show black buyers homes in white neighborhoods or union bosses who "lost" the applications for black workers who wanted to enter apprenticeship programs? Would the law be able to bridge the educational gap between blacks and whites, a gap that left relatively few Afro-Americans prepared to enter the nation's better colleges and universities and fewer still prepared for its graduate and professional schools?[32]

These persisting inequalities would lead civil rights advocates and sympathetic lawmakers to search for a more robust set of legal tools with which to fight entrenched racial inequality. These tools, when they were initially being developed in the 1960s and 1970s, would make the United States a pioneer among multiracial and multiethnic societies of the world. While laws against racial discrimination existed in many nations, the United States in the wake of the civil rights movement's success worked to develop a set of laws and policies designed to do something more. It would not be enough that the law proclaimed discrimination illegal. Statutes in a number of northern states had prohibited discrimination in employment and housing since the 1940s, often to little avail. The law had to recognize that discrimination could take new forms, more subtle forms that would be harder to detect but in practice almost as effective as the older restrictions. The Civil Rights Act of 1964 would lead the way in creating a framework for strong antidiscrimination law. The statute did not force victims of discrimination to rely on government officials to enforce its antidiscrimination provisions; instead, it allowed complainants to bring suit. Successful complaints of racial discrimination would allow victims of discrimination to not only recover damages (lost wages for victims of employment discrimination would be one example) but attorneys' fees as well. This would give new incentive to an antidiscrimination bar. Suits against businesses that engaged in racial discrimination would come not only from longtime civil rights activists but from attorneys who were building careers in the emerging specialty of employment discrimination. The knowledge that such suits could generate fees swelled the ranks of attorneys interested in this new area of litigation.[33]

It also changed the behavior of employers and potential employers. With the passage of antidiscrimination legislation and with clear signs that both the Justice Department and the private civil rights bar would vigorously pursue cases of racial discrimination in the courts, the old ways of directly denying jobs to black applicants would stop. Only foolhardy business owners or managers would directly say that they would not hire black applicants in the new post–Jim Crow environment. It was illegal and it could bring serious penalties, costly financial penalties. Racial discrimination would have to become more subtle. Black job applicants could not be categorically rejected, even by firms that had long been reluctant to hire black employees. Some Afro-Americans would have to be hired. But their numbers could be kept down. Recruiting could occur in venues where few African Americans were likely to be found. Qualifications could be demanded that were less likely to be found in the black population, even if those qualifications had little to do with actual job performance. Managers might be hyperstrict in supervising black employees, with minor infractions that might get white employees warnings or reprimands resulting in the dismissal of black employees. A firm might not have a "Whites only" sign in front of its personnel shop, but it could find ways to mitigate the damage done by the new civil rights legislation.

It was in response to these new realities that U.S. antidiscrimination law entered an even more controversial phase. In the 1970s, using Title VII of the 1964 Civil Rights Act as a base, the courts and the Equal Employment Opportunity Commission fashioned new legal tools in the effort to combat discrimination in the workplace. The new legal doctrine was both flexible and proactive. It allowed those who claimed that they were victims of employment discrimination to prove their cases in new ways. Plaintiffs could make the case that they were victims of racial discrimination not only through direct evidence of discrimination, but by statistical inference as well. If a company employed significantly fewer minorities than were to be found in the surrounding population, a prima facie case of discrimination might be made. Disparate impact analysis would become another tool that would develop in the effort to fight discrimination in the workplace. The Supreme Court developed the doctrine in a 1971 case, *Griggs v. Duke Power Co.* It in essence required employers to demonstrate that a standardized test required for hiring or promotion was related to job performance if that test disproportionately disqualified minority applicants.[34]

The possibility that a case could be won through statistical analysis or a claim that a job qualification had a disparate impact on minority applicants by no means assured a plaintiff's victory in court or before the

EEOC. These claims could be rebutted. Such cases often became battles of the experts — fights between statistical or testing experts in the employ of plaintiffs claiming discrimination and employers defending their hiring practices. But these techniques did give at least some applicants a fighting chance to make out a case that employers engaged in discriminatory practices. They were tools that allowed the courts to consider broader patterns of exclusion without requiring improbable proof of blatant discrimination. These techniques also changed the behavior of potential employers. Aware that they could be successfully sued for discrimination based on statistical underrepresentation of minorities or because educational or testing requirements disproportionately disqualified minority applicants, employers began changing their hiring practices. Some aggressively recruited minority workers. Many took a second look at hiring requirements. Large companies and government agencies set up equal opportunity offices to make sure that managers were in compliance with the latest court decisions, EEOC rulings, and congressional enactments. The law had become a strong tool in breaking down discrimination in the workplace.[35]

These measures were controversial. Critics charged that they were radical departures from what had been agreed to in the 1964 legislation. Another measure, affirmative action, would prove even more controversial. It would be used as a tool to combat discrimination in the workplace and in government contracting, but it would prove to be most controversial in university admissions. By the early 1970s, large numbers of American universities had developed programs designed to increase the number of members of underrepresented minority groups at what had been traditionally white universities. These programs were developed for a number of different reasons. State universities in the South were under court orders to dismantle the separate university systems that had been developed for black and white students during the Jim Crow era. Universities that received federal funding, which included almost all universities of any significant size, were under federal pressure to show that they had increased the enrollment of minority students. Some university administrators wanted to increase minority enrollment because they believed doing so might help stave off urban unrest. Others wanted to increase the enrollment of historically disadvantaged minorities simply because they believed that it was the right thing to do.[36]

Whether prodded by legal or economic pressure, by the demands of black militants, or by a desire to make a contribution to a more racially egalitarian society, university administrators began fashioning affirmative action policies in the late 1960s and early 1970s. These policies took race into account in the admission of students to university programs. Sometimes race played a relatively slight role in university admissions. American universities had long taken nonacademic considerations into account in university admissions. Athletic prowess, alumni or political connections, and even geography could help convince an admissions committee to admit a candidate, even one whose academic record was somewhat below par. Some schools simply added race to that list of extra considerations that might make a difference in close cases. Other schools went further, making race a major determinant in admissions. From the beginning, opponents charged that affirmative action in the universities was unfair to white students, that it let unqualified or underqualified black and Hispanic students into universities. Supporters of affirmative action responded that affirmative action provided a necessary correction, a counterbalance to the combined burdens of racial discrimination, inferior schooling, and other social and cultural disadvantages that burdened Afro-Americans and other minorities.[37]

Affirmative action found itself under legal attack almost from the very beginning. Its critics charged that in addition to being bad policy that affirmative action policies violated the Equal Protection Clause of the Fourteenth Amendment and antidiscrimination provisions of the 1964 Civil Rights Act. Groups opposed to affirmative action in the universities would spend a considerable amount of time and effort in the 1970s and subsequent decades looking for the proper combination of plaintiffs and circumstances that might have the practice declared unconstitutional. The Supreme Court decided one such case, *Regents of the University of California v. Bakke*, in 1978.

Bakke involved a challenge by a white student, Alan Bakke, to the affirmative action program at the medical school at the University of California at Davis. The Supreme Court by a 5–4 decision held that state universities could consider race among other criteria in admissions. In what would become the operating rationale of the case, Justice Lewis Powell wrote a decision that said that while racial quotas were unconstitutional, state universities could consider race in admissions. Race could be taken into account, along with other factors, in order to enhance the diversity of the student body. Such diversity would enhance the educational experience of all students enrolled at the university in the same way that students with musical ability or from underrepresented geographical regions contributed to the educational experience. Affirmative action in higher education had survived—barely. It had survived on a rationale that was not entirely pleasing to many of its supporters. Many would have preferred the rationale proffered by Justices William J. Brennan, Byron White, Thurgood Marshall, and Harry Blackmun. Their opinion would have permitted affirmative action as a means of remedying past societal discrimination and overcoming lingering racial disadvantage. Still, *Bakke* was a win for affirmative action. It permitted the programs to continue in universities. They would be contested, challenged in courts, voted down in a few state referenda. The Supreme Court would return to the issue once again in 2003 in two cases involving affirmative action at the University of Michigan. The Court would again narrowly hold in *Gratz v. Bollinger* and *Grutter v. Bollinger et al.* that such programs, properly administered, were constitutional. It is not clear how long this judicial approval will last. I was engaged in the final writing and working with the copy editors of this volume in June 2012. The Court had previously granted certiorari in another affirmative action case involving race in university admissions, *Fisher v. University of Texas* in February of the same year. As of that final writing, the Supreme Court was scheduled to hear oral arguments in *Fisher* in the fall of 2012 and probably render a decision in June 2013. Many observers feared that the Court's conservative majority would use *Fisher* as an opportunity to sharply curtail the use of race-based affirmative action in public universities. Contested, controversial, the survivor, as of the summer of 2012, of narrow escapes in the highest court of the land, affirmative action has for some four decades played a significant role in increasing the overall number of African Americans attending universities, particularly some of the nation's stronger graduate and professional programs. Whether it will continue to do so in the future is open to question.

Affirmative action in higher education was part of a larger package of changes that would occur in the United States after the success of the civil rights movement in the 1960s. From the early 1970s on, the United States developed a set of policies and a legal framework designed to root out and eradicate entrenched patterns of racial inequality. These new policies and the legal reasoning that sustained them would go beyond simple enforcement of antidiscrimination law. They would be race-conscious. They would be premised on the controversial assumptions that despite the passage of strong civil rights legislation, a considerable amount of hidden discrimination and structural inequality remained in American life and that that discrimination had to be rooted out with measures that counted racial results and not merely the stated intentions of personnel managers and university admissions officers. Many of the architects of the new policies and legal measures also believed that there had to be a counterweight to past and indeed ongoing discrimination. Were these policies necessary? Did they play a major role in bettering the lives of Afro-Americans and other minorities in the United States over the past forty years?

Probably the best answer to these questions is that affirmative action and enhanced methods for demonstrating discrimination in the workplace made a significant difference for large sectors of the African American population that were prepared to take advantage of the new opportunities in education and employment that developed once traditional barriers were removed. From the seventies on, prodded by affirmative action and the possibilities that plaintiffs might demonstrate the existence of racial discrimination through statistical disparity or disparate impact analysis, workplaces that had previously been closed to blacks opened up. There were dramatic changes in the labor market from 1970 to 1990, with significant increases in the number of black people employed in almost every job category. African Americans could be found at the corner firehouse and the neighborhood police precinct. Black workers might be seen at the local construction site and other venues where black workers had previously been conspicuously absent. The number of Afro-Americans working in skilled positions or as managers increased dramatically. In 1966, fewer than 20 percent of black men working at firms with one hundred employees or more were classified as officials or managers. By 1980, the number was just under 47 percent. The increase in black women so classified was even more dramatic, rising from just under 23 percent in 1966 to just under 68 percent in 1980. Affirmative action in higher education helped create a pool of black professionals who increasingly in the seventies and beyond would enter the ranks of the nation's business managers, lawyers, physicians, university professors, and journalists, among other professions. Afro-Americans would remain underrepresented in these fields but would nonetheless enter these fields in sufficient numbers so that we could say that these occupational gains were real and lasting.[38]

The broadening of educational and employment opportunities made life substantially better for middle-class and working-class Afro-Americans. But the changes that have occurred over the last forty years have largely by-passed the poorest people in the black population, those whom sociologists have termed the underclass. The stark reality that a significant percentage of poor African Americans have been left behind, bypassed by more general American prosperity and by the gains of the civil rights movement, was dramatically highlighted by Hurricane Katrina as it played out in New Orleans in 2005. Poor people, most of them black, were trapped in the Crescent city, often without cars and without any viable rescue or relief plans on the part of the federal, state, and city governments. It was a telling example of the nation's neglect of inner-city communities. The nation's neglect of poor people in the inner city is more pervasive than the incidents that occurred in one dramatic episode. The problems of the underclass are familiar to every student of race in the United States. Those problems include a black poverty rate that is roughly three times that of the white population. They also include dramatically high crime rates in many black communities. Many Afro-American communities also have high percentages of female-headed, fatherless households. Close to 70 percent of black children are born out of wedlock. Most inner-city black communities have high rates of high school dropouts and unemployment. These conditions point to an underclass problem in American cities that is likely to persist for several decades into the twenty-first century if not beyond.[39]

Social scientists are engaged in a vigorous debate about the extent to which the growth of the underclass should be attributed to the persistence and extension of an underclass culture that rejects such presumably middle-class norms as a stable family life, education, and a traditional work ethic. Some observers believe that the growth of the underclass should be attributed to structural changes in the American economy, including the loss of industrial jobs, which had helped to create a blue-collar middle class in the 1950s and 1960s. Strong cases have been made for both sets of explanations. Indeed, William Julius Wilson, one of the leading sociological students of impoverished inner-city black communities, has offered persuasive evidence for both cultural and structural explanations for the paradoxical and vexing growth of the underclass over the last four decades, even as many racial barriers in education and employment were falling. Clearly the underclass phenomenon is in large part the fruit of the American history of racial exclusion. But it is also clear that what has been done since the 1960s to foster a more racially inclusive society has so far proven inadequate to address the problem of those who have been left behind by the nation's civil rights revolution.[40]

But the remarkable story of race in the United States after the civil rights revolution is not the story of the underclass, as disturbing and as critical as that story is. Nor is it the story of persistent racism and racial discrimination, even though examples of such are not hard to find. The remarkable story is not the unyielding recession that began in 2007 and that has had a devastating impact on black employment, as important as that story is. The remarkable story is the extent to which the American nation attempted to rise above its past and the extent to which it has succeeded in doing so. The United States was able to do so in part because the law had developed an adaptability and flexibility that allowed decision makers to take race into account without being overwhelmed by race. Affirmative action might be allowed, but quotas would be forbidden. Statistics might raise a presumption that a business engaged in discrimination, but they could be rebutted with contrary statistics or evidence of a good-faith effort to hire minority workers. The law remained imperfect. It was often confusing, even to the lawyers specializing in these areas. The new tools that had been developed to fight entrenched inequality were controversial. They were assailed as "preferences" and "reverse racism." The new policies were constantly in legal jeopardy and as of the final writing of this volume seem more in peril than ever. But the efforts that were made after the 1960s to develop a more inclusive society succeeded well beyond what anyone might have imagined at the beginning or even middle of the last century. Before the Second World War, the United States had been the most racially restrictive nation in the Western Hemisphere. By the end of the twentieth century, racially conscious Afro-Americans in other parts of the Americas were looking at the United States as a model of racial inclusion. It was a sea change that would reverberate throughout the hemisphere.[41]

CHAPTER EIGHT

Um País para Todos?

THE BRAZILIAN JOURNEY FROM
RACIAL DEMOCRACY TO RACIAL REFORM

THAT SEA CHANGE THAT DID SO MUCH to transform the world of race and caste in the United States was in part a product of a long-standing American discomfort with the idea of inequality. The United States was the land without class distinctions, the nation of equals, the home of Jeffersonian democracy, the republic ruled by the common man. Much of this was myth or at the very least overstatement. Class distinctions, at times quite strong ones, have always existed in American society. If the democratic ideal and a fair measure of democratic governance as well have also long existed in the United States, they have coexisted with a constitution deliberately designed to make majority rule slow and difficult. Still, democracy, equality, and the Declaration of Independence's invocation of unalienable rights are powerful ideas. They resonate deeply within the American nation. The architects of the U.S. civil rights movement were successful precisely because they could contrast the nation's lofty ideals with the shabby reality of Jim Crow. The nation's discomfort with that contradiction would finally, after decades of struggle, produce change — profound change.

But Brazil was different. It had always been a society of both deep inequality and a pronounced ambivalence concerning democracy. As both a colony and an empire, Brazil had been shaped by slavery far more profoundly than the United States, even the southern states. Slavery knew no boundaries in the Brazilian Empire. It touched every part of the emperor's domain. Unlike slavery in Jacksonian America, Brazilian slavery was not the glaring anomaly in what was otherwise thought of as a republic of equals. Instead, it was emblematic of a nation with a strong — at times

238

rigid — social hierarchy. That hierarchy went from emperor to slave, but it did not end with those distinctions. Most free Brazilians were not enfranchised. The vote was restricted to a literate, propertied few. Few free Brazilians had the opportunity to send their children to school. Fewer still had access to land and the likelihood of significantly bettering their or their children's condition. These inequalities would remain long after the empire had become a distant memory. The republic that would follow the empire retained literacy qualifications for voters, keeping a large portion of the population from the business of governance. Republican constitutions might prescribe a democratic form of government with provisions proclaiming the rights of Brazilian citizens. But republican Brazil in the twentieth century would alternate between often fragile democratic governments and relatively strong authoritarian ones. And proclamations of rights in the republic's twentieth-century constitutions were more often than not rendered useless by a weak judiciary with little ability to establish the rule of law in the Brazilian nation or even within the nation's legal system.

Deep-rooted inequalities, an ambivalent democratic tradition, and a legal system with relatively little authority all made the task of attacking racial inequality and racial discrimination difficult in twentieth-century Brazil. The national ideology also hampered the ability of Afro-Brazilians to form an effective civil rights movement. The nation's politicians and intellectuals declared that Brazil was a racial democracy. Racially linked inequality might be a reflection of the nation's strong class distinctions but it was certainly not evidence of racial discrimination. That was the official wisdom. To dare to question it was somehow un-Brazilian, even vaguely subversive — dangerous territory best avoided. Despite the official ideology, there had long been an effort on the part of many Afro-Brazilians to organize to combat racial discrimination and inequality. In the 1930s, the Frente Negra Brasileira had successfully lobbied Getúlio Vargas to end São Paulo's prohibition on Afro-Brazilian enlistment in the state's Civil Guard. In 1944, the Teatro Experimental do Negro (TEN) began as a vehicle to help black actors but soon broadened its scope, taking on the missions of teaching basic literacy and providing vocational education. The group published a journal, *Quilombo*, and sponsored the Instituto Nacional do Negro (National Black Institute), the Museu do Negro (Black Museum), and O Primeiro Congresso do Negro Brasileiro (the First National Black

Congress). The TEN group would be an advocate for black rights and black consciousness from its beginnings in the 1940s. The TEN would be one of the earlier advocates of national antidiscrimination legislation.[1]

But Brazil in the immediate postwar era was not particularly fertile soil for either a black consciousness movement or a movement seeking to use the law to fight racial exclusion. In 1946, Senator Hamilton Nogueira of Rio de Janeiro, a member of the Constituent Assembly drafting what would become the 1946 constitution, proposed a constitutional provision prohibiting racial discrimination. The provision had been formulated by the National Black Convention in 1945. It was defeated — opposed by, among others, the Brazilian Communist Party, which argued that a constitutional provision emphasizing race and the plight of Afro-Brazilians would harm working-class unity and detract from the need for class struggle. Historian Petrônio Domingues tells us that after the failure of Nogueira's proposal, the Brazilian black movement was virtually abandoned for decades, even by politicians generally considered progressive. The adoption of Lei Afonso Arinos, the nation's facially comprehensive but practically ineffective antidiscrimination legislation in 1951 came about as a result of national embarrassment over the well-publicized case of discrimination against North American dancer Katherine Dunham and not in response to concerted civil rights activity by Afro-Brazilians.[2]

The ideology of racial democracy had long inhibited the growth of a robust Afro-Brazilian movement with national support and impact. The establishment of military rule in 1964 would serve to further silence those who might raise troubling questions concerning racial inequality. Successive military governments, generally suspicious of independent political organizations, feared the growth of an independent Afro-Brazilian movement. Too much focus on race and inequality would wreak havoc with what military leaders contended was a harmonious Brazilian nation free of the plagues of racial discrimination and racial conflict. Black groups were seen as segregationist and racist. In 1967, military president Humberto Castelo Branco issued a decree prohibiting publication of material that would incite race or class prejudice. The decree's aim was to prevent racial agitation and political subversion. But presidential decrees were the least of concerns for Afro-Brazilian activists in the early 1970s. It was a bad time. Brazil's military rulers were actively searching for subversives. If the excesses of the Brazilian military regime did not reach the levels later attained by the military dictatorships of Argentina and Chile, Brazil's government could nonetheless be quite harsh. Political gatherings were restricted, dissidents tried by military tribunal. Some were imprisoned, even tortured. Many more realized that political activities would have to be circumspect, if they occurred at all. Like other Brazilian dissidents, many Afro-Brazilian political activists organized clandestinely, not daring openly to express their grievances.[3]

By the late 1970s, the Brazilian political system was beginning to liberalize. With *abertura* (political opening) came new efforts by some Afro-Brazilians to organize against the racially linked inequality that played such a major role in the nation's life. Increasingly the old bromides extolling Brazil as the land of racial democracy and racial harmony faced increasing challenges from a new generation of educated Afro-Brazilian activists. International changes were helping to precipitate this reassessment of race in the Brazilian social order. Where previous generations of Brazilians could look at the Jim Crow order that once was the United States and be comforted by the absence of rigid, codified segregation and the lack of violent racial conflict in Brazil, by the 1970s, many Afro-Brazilians were looking at the changes brought about by the U.S. civil rights movement. The United States was beginning to have in noticeable numbers black generals in the army, black diplomats in the foreign service, black representatives in Congress, black professors in largely white universities, black movie stars on the big screen, black newscasters on the small screen. Educated Afro-Brazilians, those who were aware of these new developments, were starting to ask, "Why not Brazil?" And it was not only the American example that helped prompt a new stirring of racial consciousness. Events on the other side of the Atlantic were also capturing the attention of Afro-Brazilians, as indeed they were capturing the attention of official Brazil. African independence, particularly the struggle for independence in Lusophonic Africa, especially Angola, generated interest throughout the nation. Afro-Brazilians saw an example of an African people struggling against European colonialism and racial domination. The example might not have been exactly applicable within the Brazilian context, but it nonetheless contributed to a growth of a greater racial consciousness and an awareness of racial domination on the part of at least some Afro-Brazilians. The Movimento Negro Unificado, which was founded in 1978, would be one result of this heightened racial consciousness.[4]

Throughout the early 1980s, as Brazil's last military president, João Figueiredo, made it clear that he would step down to make way for a return to civilian rule, political activists of all stripes were preparing for a new constitution. They hoped for a constitution that would address issues long suppressed by the nation's military rulers. Figueiredo left office in March 1985. That same year, another significant step toward democratization took place. Legislation was passed eliminating Brazil's long-standing literacy requirement for voters, which had prevented large numbers of Afro-Brazilians from participating in electoral politics. Brazilians were looking toward a new, democratic constitution. Between February 1, 1987, and October 5, 1988, Congress worked on the current constitution of 1988. That constitution is very much a twentieth century — indeed, late-twentieth-century — document. Americans are accustomed to a constitution that largely specifies limitations on governmental power, including the Bill of Rights, specifying freedoms on which the government is not allowed to infringe. The U.S. Constitution is, at base, a product of eighteenth-century thinking, with an overarching concern for preventing potential abuses of governmental power. Constitutions drafted in the twentieth century have frequently been concerned with ensuring positive rights, including rights to government benefits. Brazil's 1988 constitution fits this pattern, guaranteeing, at least in theory, a panoply of positive rights for Brazilian citizens, among them the right to health care, social security, education, work, housing, and access to justice.[5]

And more clearly than any of its predecessors, the 1988 constitution makes clear that freedom from racial discrimination is among the more important rights in the new Brazilian constitutional order. Title 1 of the constitution, its statement of "Fundamental Principles," indicates that one of the foundations of democratic law in the South American republic is "the promotion of the well-being of all people, without prejudice on the basis of origin, race, sex, color, age, or any other form of discrimination." That title also proclaims that the basis of Brazilian foreign policy is governed by a rejection of racism — a clear reference to the revitalized democracy's rejection of the apartheid regime in South Africa. Title 2 of the constitution goes even further. Its section on fundamental rights and guarantees proclaims the equality of all before the law. Moreover, the constitution declares racism a crime for which bail is unavailable, that cannot be defended, and that is subject to incarceration.[6]

The 1988 constitution also expresses a strong concern for the preservation of both indigenous and Afro-Brazilian cultures. The document specifies that "the state will protect manifestations of popular, indigenous, and Afro-Brazilian culture as well as those of other participants in the process of national civilization." One constitutional provision guarantees protection for documents and places connected to *quilombos*. Another recognizes *quilombo* residents as communal owners of the lands that they occupy. Anthropologist and legal scholar Jan Hoffman French informs us that by the time of the adoption of the 1988 constitution, the term *quilombo* had developed a long-standing image among Afro-Brazilian activists as a reminder of a heroic past, one that included fierce resistance to slavery and the retention of African cultures. The Quilombo Clause was proposed by Afro-Brazilian delegates to the Constituent Assembly that drafted the 1988 constitution. It would be a symbol that Brazil the revitalized democracy would remember the Afro-Brazilian past. The clause would also serve as an indication of the nation's commitment to racial justice in the future.[7]

But if the new constitution showed a robust concern for racial equality and even perhaps a measure of support for a degree of restorative justice, that new constitution also governed a nation where the older patterns of racial inequality seemed entrenched and at times unyielding. The far-reaching provisions of the new constitution designed to eradicate racism and discrimination came about in part because of pressure from Afro-Brazilian activists, activists who were increasingly bringing the unpleasant truths about racial inequality to the national consciousness. They were able to do so in part because racial inequality was becoming an embarrassment that was complicating Brazil's international efforts. Since the 1960s, a number of diplomats in Brazil's foreign ministry, Itamaraty, had urged closer contact with the newly independent nations of Africa. Brazilian officials believed that with a large population of African descent, thriving African cultures, and an international reputation for racial democracy, the South American nation was well positioned to build strong political and economic ties with the emerging states of sub-Saharan Africa. Closer ties with the newly independent nations of Africa had been supported by Presidents João Goulart and Jânio da Silva Quadros in the 1960s. Such ties also had the support of the nation's last military president, João Figueiredo, who made them a priority in his administration. But the stark facts of racial inequality and racial exclusion were making this effort to build stronger ties more difficult. African diplomats visiting Brazil as well as African lead-ers receiving Brazilian representatives at home saw an official Brazil with few Afro-Brazilians in the nation's Congress, its diplomatic corps, or the senior ranks of its armed forces. This was in marked contrast with the of-ten highly visible presence of African Americans in similar positions in the United States. Concerned Brazilian officials were often at a loss to explain the absence of Afro-Brazilians from these settings. The traditional procla-mations of racial democracy seemed less and less plausible to both foreign observers and many Brazilians as well.[8]

What did racial inequality look like in Brazil as the nation ended the twentieth century? What does it look like today in what can still be called the morning if not the dawn of the twenty-first? The answer calls for a bit of caution. Modern Brazil, the newly revitalized democracy governed by the constitution of 1988, is a nation that cannot be easily or quickly char-acterized in terms of racial stratification and racial attitudes. I am going to attempt in the next few pages to say some things about race in the new Brazil. I will not be able to do justice to the topic and I do not claim to. Brazil is a large, complex nation with a population of close to two hundred million. Much of the Brazilian world of race and inequality is changing even as I am writing this chapter and even as you are reading it. We are going to look at a sketch of the world of race, racial attitudes, and racial discrimination in Brazil. We will do this as a way of looking at the problem of racial inequality in modern Brazil and of looking at the legal and policy remedies that Brazilian administrations have begun in this new century to redress long-standing issues of race and inequality in Brazilian society.

Profound racial inequality exists. Inequality can be found in income, occupation, housing, education, health, and other important aspects of life. There is a long-standing debate over how much of that inequality is due to racial discrimination and how much might be attributed to entrenched patterns of class privilege and class disadvantage. A significant amount of research in recent decades by both Brazilian and foreign social scientists has been directed toward disentangling the different impacts of race and class in Brazilian life. If the best of this research has tended to show that race and racial discrimination have significant consequences for the lives and economic well-being of Brazilians even after taking class and income into account, the controversy over the relative importance of race and class in Brazil nonetheless continues. It is very much a part of the current debate over the direction that law and public policy should take in the fight against inequality in Brazilian life.[9]

Geography also complicates any discussion of race and inequality in Brazil. The Afro-Brazilian Northeast, particularly the states of Bahia and Pernambuco, has long been poorer and less developed than the southern states that received the bulk of large-scale European immigration in the early twentieth century. The extent to which racial inequality is a product of regional disparities in development is also part of the ongoing debate among social scientists concerned with racial stratification in Brazil.[10]

If the problems of race and inequality are often hard to unravel in Brazil, so are the racial attitudes of many Brazilians. Openly expressed prejudices, sometimes even racial slurs, often coexist with a genuine cordiality among people of different racial and ethnic groups rarely found in other nations. There are white Brazilians who refuse to hire Afro-Brazilians for certain jobs and then defend their actions and claim that they cannot be guilty of discrimination because they too are somewhat mulatto. They had or claim a black or mulatto grandparent and argue that therefore they cannot be guilty of racism. Increasingly Brazilians are becoming aware that the old view of their nation as a racial democracy is more myth than reality. There is also a growing awareness that discrimination limits opportunities for Afro-Brazilians. Nevertheless, old stereotypes persist. As late as 1995, a national survey found that 43 percent of all Brazilians agreed with the statement that Afro-Brazilians are good only in music and sports. Interestingly enough, the survey indicated that those classified as *pretos* (blacks) and *pardos* (mulattos) were as likely as those classified as *brancos* (whites) to agree with that statement.[11]

As Brazil approached the twenty-first century, most knowledgeable observers recognized the often striking inequalities between whites and Afro-Brazilians. The 2000 census indicated that Afro-Brazilians comprised approximately 45 percent of the nation's population. That figure included the population that self-identified as *preto* and *pardo* populations. Better than 86 percent of Afro-Brazilians identify themselves as *pardos*. The figures from the country's official statistical bureau, the Instituto Brasileiro de Geografia e Estatística, almost certainly underestimate the proportion of the population with some African ancestry. Many whites in Brazil have acknowledged African ancestry, and custom and courtesy still dictate that persons of mixed racial background with the proper social standing and position might be allowed to declare themselves white even if more than a trace of African ancestry might be detected in their features. Nonetheless, 45 percent of Brazil's nearly two hundred million people is a substantial figure, giving the country the second-largest population of African descent in the world, trailing only Nigeria, a demographic profile quite different from the one forecasted by the advocates of *branqueamento* at the start of the twentieth century.[12]

Brazil's official statistics documented an Afro-Brazilian population at the beginning of the twenty-first century that is significantly poorer and less well educated than its white compatriots. Afro-Brazilians earn on average less than 50 percent of the income of whites. *Pardos* and *pretos* constitute 63 percent of those classified as poor, while less than 31 percent of those classified as poor are whites. Seventy percent of those classified as among the most poor are Afro-Brazilians. Government figures indicate that roughly 20 percent of Afro-Brazilians over age fifteen are functionally illiterate, while just a little over 7 percent of the white population is so classified.[13]

If strong, racially linked disparities in wealth and income exist, so do often pronounced inequalities in education, educational opportunity, and the value of education for Brazilians of European and African descent. Less than 7 percent of the nation's population over twenty-five has university degrees. At the beginning of this century, official figures indicated that Afro-Brazilians accounted for only 2 percent of students enrolled in universities. By 2005 that figure had risen to 3 percent. Improvements in education fail to eliminate income disparities between whites and Afro-Brazilians. Even among university graduates there often is a significant gap between the incomes of whites and of Afro-Brazilians. The largest income gap between whites and Afro-Brazilians occurs among middle-class employees in the private sector, a group that presumably includes a significant number of people with strong secondary or even university educations. As is the case in other parts of the Americas, including the United States, the Afro-American middle class is disproportionately composed of government employees, reflecting strong and continuing patterns of discrimination in the private sector.[14]

If education does not overcome inequalities in income and occupation, it is hard to imagine eliminating racial disparities without it. Research indicates that much of the occupational gap between Afro-Brazilians and whites can be attributed to differences in educational levels. The Brazilian educational system shortchanges Afro-Brazilians, who have a lower rate of schooling than do whites. Regional differences in spending for education have often had a pronounced effect on Afro-Brazilians. Sociologist Edward Telles notes that in many of the nation's poorer regions, even primary education has not been widely available, contributing to the higher rates of illiteracy among Afro-Brazilians. Education is theoretically compulsory between the ages of seven and fourteen, but the law is frequently circumvented. Poor students, disproportionately *pretos* and *pardos*, are more likely to drop out of primary or secondary school in part because they have to work to supplement the family income and in part because they feel discouraged, believing that education will do little to improve their or their family's circumstances.[15]

The traditional Brazilian explanation for these disparities is that they are the results of class disadvantage, perhaps even class discrimination, but not the result of racial prejudice or animus. This assertion is not entirely without merit. Public education in Brazil has long suffered from a lack of resources, particularly in regions with strong concentrations of Afro-Brazilians. A number of critics of the Brazilian educational system have noted that Brazil has traditionally devoted its educational resources to subsidizing public universities — used overwhelmingly by students from well-to-do families — while neglecting primary and secondary education for the poor.[16]

But Brazil's very real system of class disadvantage is augmented by equally real racial prejudices and stereotypes that ensure that public schools often only increase the frustration of children labeled *preto* and *pardo.* There has been a tradition of tolerating discriminatory behavior by teachers and students in Brazilian schools that has only slowly and recently begun to change. Racial taunting and stereotyping of Afro-Brazilian children is reportedly common, as are racist remarks by teachers. Ethnographic observers have noted that teachers frequently hesitate to spend time with and pay attention to the needs of Afro-Brazilian children. Textbooks have traditionally presented students with an image of a savage Africa and a Brazil in which Afro-Brazilians contributed little to the nation's history or culture. These conditions have contributed to a sense of alienation from school on the part of many Afro-Brazilian students. This, in turn, has increased the difficulty that Afro-Brazilians have had in gaining educational parity and in preparing children for the nation's increasingly modern economy and social order.[17]

Substandard education in the public schools, combined with discrimination in admission to private schools, has led to significant racial disparities in preparing Brazilian students for university admissions. This is, to be sure, another area where it is often difficult to separate entrenched patterns of class disadvantage from patterns of racial inequality and racial discrimination. Brazil has a system of first-class public universities. Most states have both state and federal universities. They are justifiably the pride of the Brazilian system of higher education. Students who are admitted to these universities pay no tuition. Because one qualifies for professions like law and medicine in undergraduate programs in Brazil, admission to a public university can guarantee a student a free public education that provides an immediate entrée into a prestigious and hopefully lucrative career. Entrance to these public universities is governed by a set of very rigorous entrance exams called the Vestibular. The rigors of the Vestibular are legendary and are frequently the subject of national debate and occasionally cover stories in the nation's newsmagazines.[18]

Students taking the Vestibular are examined in specific subject areas, including Portuguese language, Brazilian history, foreign languages, the humanities, and the sciences. Champions of the Brazilian university system argue that the Vestibular results in a meritocratic system that fairly selects the best students for the best universities. Perhaps, but the Vestibular and the rigorous way it was traditionally applied by the public universities did something else. The entrance examination made it very hard for students from poor and working-class backgrounds to attend the nation's public universities. The Vestibular tends to test what is taught at the nation's best private secondary schools. But the class distinctions do not end there. Students who want to attend the best public universities usually spend a year taking *cursinhos,* courses specifically designed to prepare them for the university exams. Students from poor families are unlikely to finish secondary school. Those who do do not have the money to attend a *cursinho.* Brazil's "meritocratic" university entrance system has traditionally ensured that the children of the poor would rarely attend the nation's first-class public universities. Students from poor families, if they managed to finish secondary school and attend university at all, usually attended poorly funded and poorly equipped private institutions. Typically, students from poor or working-class backgrounds—backgrounds that are disproportionately Afro-Brazilian—would go to these private universities at night while working during the day.[19]

Defenders of the traditional Brazilian order—champions of the racial democracy thesis, of which there are still many—argue quite vigorously that the racial disparities revealed by social science investigations or journalistic exposés reflect the nation's entrenched class system and not racial animus or deliberate acts of racial discrimination. Yet Brazil can be a land with often open expressions of racial prejudice, expressions made all the more jarring because they frequently take place amid an atmosphere of what seems to be a genuine cordiality among Brazilians of different races. Students of race relations in Brazil have even developed a term, *racismo cordial*, to describe the paradox of discrimination and racism, at times openly expressed, in a culture that prides itself on racial harmony and seemingly amicable race relations.[20]

But cordial or not, discrimination can often be quite frank and open in Brazil, frank and open in ways that have long since become legally risky and culturally unacceptable in the United States. This kind of discrimination is seen most openly in the workplace. Black and mulatto job applicants with high test scores are frequently denied white-collar positions and offered lower-ranking jobs instead. A number of employers have traditionally used the term *boa aparência* (good appearance) in want ads as code words indicating a preference for white employees. Employers, particularly in the private sector, have also used a requirement that applicants furnish photos with their résumés as a way of identifying and discriminating against prospective Afro-Brazilian employees.[21]

Open discrimination is not confined to the workplaces. It is often felt most keenly by educated members of the Afro-Brazilian middle class. With their in-depth interviews of Afro-Brazilian professionals in Rio de Janeiro, sociologists Graziella Moraes da Silva and Elisa P. Reis have found that middle-class Afro-Brazilians most often reported discrimination and their own fears of discrimination when entering public services, theaters, restaurants, and shopping malls generally frequented by the middle class. The expectation is that an Afro-Brazilian will be poor, uneducated, and out of place in such a setting. The well-educated, middle-class *preto* or *pardo* is not expected and is often treated as an intruder. Silva and Reis report that Afro-Brazilian professionals sometimes try to compensate by exhibiting an exaggerated decorum in dress or speech beyond what might ordinarily be required of a white person in a particular public space to avoid being victim of a racial incident. As one woman journalist indicated, "The first time I went to [an upper-class mall] was four years ago. I had never been there, and since then I have only been three times. I feel highly intimidated and I do not dress like myself—with flip-flops and all—I need a crutch. I have to wear designer jeans, carry a fancy bag and whatever. . . . Hospital is the same. I have found out that, if you are not well dressed, you get bad service, even if you are with a sick child."[22]

For many Afro-Brazilians, racial prejudice can mean more than a job denied or social embarrassment suffered—far more. Racial prejudice and the association of Afro-Brazilians with crime can have even more serious and sometimes deadly consequences. The meaner streets of urban Brazil are violent, very violent. The favelas (shantytowns) in Rio, São Paulo, and a number of other cities can be quite dangerous. They have been controlled by drug gangs which have made life difficult and dangerous for residents. The government has frequently sent in the army to bring order to the favelas. President Itamar Franco did so in 1994 with a resulting high number of deaths of shantytown residents. More recently, the high degree of violence in some favelas prompted President Luiz Inácio Lula da Silva to permanently station units of the army in some favelas to augment police patrols. The policy has been continued under his successor, Dilma Rousseff.[23]

Most favela residents are Afro-Brazilian. The gangs in the favelas make the shantytowns a source of criminal activity that plagues other communities, increasing the tendency to identify poor Afro-Brazilians with criminal activity. These associations add to the difficulties of Afro-Brazilians, both those who are shantytown residents and those who are more fortunate. Police violence combined with racial prejudice is often the response. Police are known to harass Afro-Brazilians, often with an accompaniment of physical abuse and racial slurs. Extreme police violence is common in the poorer neighborhoods in many cities. According to official figures, police in Rio de Janeiro at the beginning of the twenty-first century on average killed more than 2.5 times as many people in a month than were killed by police in New York City in an entire year. Most victims are Afro-Brazilians. There is evidence that the police in many cities so closely identify Afro-Brazilians with crime that they often make little effort to distinguish law-abiding favela residents from lawbreakers when raiding the slum communities. Both groups end up being victims of violent police tactics. Favela residents end up being both underprotected and brutalized by the very police departments ostensibly charged with their safety.[24]

By the last century's end, these patterns of inequality and discrimination were increasingly causing Brazilian civil rights advocates to call for legal and policy reforms that could address deeply entrenched patterns of racial disparity in Brazilian society. Their first challenge was to see if they could develop new and effective legal tools that could overcome what had already become a heritage of nominally robust antidiscrimination laws that produced little in the way of practical results. The provisions in the new constitution governing racial discrimination followed very much in the tradition of the 1951 Lei Afonso Arinos. Racism and racial discrimination are denounced as evil. They are not merely made the subject of civil sanction but are brought within the jurisdiction of the criminal law. The criminal sanctions in the 1951 legislation had proven to be largely ineffective. A number of observers have noted that the criminalization of racism may have had the ironic effect of making the legal system less capable of dealing with the problem of discrimination. Criminal cases require stronger evidence than civil cases. Judges are, reasonably enough, far less willing to convict and imprison a defendant than they are to order back pay or require the remedial hiring of a victim of discrimination. Some commentators have suggested that strengthening civil remedies and developing greater incentives for private parties to bring suits for alleged actions of discrimination might actually strengthen the reach of Brazilian antidiscrimination law.

But Brazilian authorities, including antiracism activists who helped draft the antidiscrimination provisions in the new constitution, firmly believed that the law had to make a strong normative statement. Discrimination and racism were evil and the proper way to express the new Brazil's outrage against these wrongs was to continue the law's policy of criminalizing racial discrimination. New statutes enacted in the wake of the 1988 constitution would continue this pattern. A statute passed in 1989 declared that acts stemming from racial or color prejudice were punishable crimes. The statute, known as Lei Caó, was lengthy. Many of its critics charged that it was too vague and allowed for too many loopholes. In its original text, the statute criminalized actions motivated by racial or color prejudice, including impeding access to government agencies, employment discrimination, and discrimination in public accommodations and in the armed forces, among other areas. The statute also prohibited racial discrimination in marriage and family or social life. The 1989 law specified terms of imprisonment ranging from one to five years depending on the type of specific act involved. Lei Caó would be augmented by supplementary legislation in 1990 and 1997.[25]

Lei Caó was but one example in a series of seemingly rigorous Brazilian statutes that proved ineffective as tools in the struggle against racial discrimination. One longtime critic of the Brazilian legal system, Joaquim B. Barbosa Gomes, has suggested that it may very well be the Brazilian legal culture itself that has made the enforcement of civil rights legislation problematic. Barbosa, an Afro-Brazilian, is now a minister on the Supremo Tribunal Federal. Before his appointment to the high court by President Lula in 2003, he was a highly successful federal prosecutor and professor on the law faculty at the Universidade Federal do Rio de Janeiro. He has had extensive experience with other nations' legal systems. Barbosa received a Ph.D. in law from the University of Paris. He also taught at Columbia University and other law schools in the United States. Before his appointment to the high court, Barbosa had criticized the federal justice ministry's lack of effective enforcement of antidiscrimination statutes. He argued that the ministry's ineffectiveness was the result of systemic inefficiencies coupled with a residual reluctance to recognize the extent of racial discrimination in Brazil. That combination had thwarted the efforts of legislators who had drafted antidiscrimination legislation. Barbosa stated that the federal public ministry or prosecutor's office was plagued by a lack of organization, fiscal chaos, and even internal ideological battles. For Barbosa, the public ministry's fecklessness had been exacerbated by systemic deficiencies in the courts. According to Barbosa, the Brazilian judicial system is plagued by "exacerbated individualism, extreme formalism, lack of rationality or practicality in the great majority of instruments for action. . . . [I]t is not surprising given this context that the overall situation of public suits is so squalid that there is nothing to analyze . . . referring to protection of minorities rights by the public prosecutor's office."[26]

In the previous chapter, we looked at some of the methodological developments that have occurred in antidiscrimination law in the United States since the enactment of the Civil Rights Act of 1964. In fields like employment discrimination, American law has moved away from requiring direct evidence of discrimination — employers openly stating that they do not hire members of specific racial groups or leaving a paper trail to that effect. The traditional requirement for direct evidence of discrimination has been supplanted by additional tools — the possibility of demonstrating the likelihood of discrimination through statistical inference or disparate impact analysis, the possibility of challenging job requirements that disproportionately disqualify members of minority groups. Although many Brazilian legal scholars and civil rights attorneys are aware of these American legal innovations and some have urged their adoption in the Brazilian context, the courts have mostly remained fairly conservative in the kinds of evidence that they will accept in racial discrimination cases. They have made little use of indirect evidence in cases involving employment discrimination, although a number of courts have shown a greater willingness to use such evidence when hearing complaints by consumers alleging racial discrimination.[27]

The reluctance of Brazilian courts to accept indirect and inferential evidence of discrimination points to some important differences between the U.S. and Brazilian judiciaries. If the American courts played a significant role both in dismantling Jim Crow and in developing a robust body of antidiscrimination law, there seems little likelihood that Brazilian courts will play a similar role. Commentators have long noted the ineffectual nature of the Brazilian judiciary. Traditionally the courts have not been a robust vehicle for resolution of disputes within Brazilian society. The Brazilian judicial system is inefficient. Cases take a long time to be resolved. The nineteenth-century heritage of extreme judicial autonomy combined with the 1988 constitution's commitment to access to the justice system has made it possible for cases to take years and in extreme cases decades before final resolution. Brazilian courts have historically operated without a strong system of precedential guidance. Because of this, even if a legal issue had been previously decided in the highest courts, it could still be relitigated in subsequent cases. The highest court, the Supremo Tribunal Federal, has only recently gained discretionary power to decide which cases to review. Within the last decade, judicial reform measures have been enacted with the aim of making Brazil's courts more effective. These measures have included giving the nation's highest court discretionary review and the ability, at the court's discretion, to issue decisions with precedential weight. Whether or not these new measures will be capable of overcoming the traditional inefficiencies that have long been a part of the Brazilian legal culture remains to be seen. Despite recent reforms, the system is still often overloaded and functions with great difficulty.[28]

But it is not only the inefficiencies of the Brazilian judicial system that make the courts problematic as an effective vehicle for the enforcement of civil rights law. Barbosa has complained not only about the Brazilian legal system's inefficiencies but about its formalism and lack of contact with reality as well. Many of the great advancements in American civil rights jurisprudence came about in part because of the injection of a healthy dose of legal realism into cases involving claims of racial discrimination. A strong claim can be made that the battle for formal equality under law was largely won with the U.S. Supreme Court's decision in *Brown v. Board of Education* in 1954 and the enactment of federal civil rights legislation in the 1960s. The law prohibited racial discrimination. There were mechanisms in place to prevent the more obvious forms of racial discrimination. But the civil rights bar did not rest on these achievements. Instead, lawyers sympathetic to the antidiscrimination movement brought cases before the courts that forced the courts to consider subtle, often hidden patterns of discrimination. They could do this in part because there had been a long, if not entirely harmonious, marriage between law and the social sciences in the United States. That marriage had matured during the course of the twentieth century. The Brandeis brief, the invocation of social science evidence in *Brown*, even the structure of American legal education, with its requirement that a prospective law student first graduate from an undergraduate institution, usually with a heavy dose of social science in the curriculum, paved the way for a judiciary willing to look beyond formal legal doctrine and consider evidence in the form of often opaque disquisitions on socioeconomic inequalities or statistical disparities.

Brazilian jurists have traditionally been more attuned to formalistic legal argument — excessively so, according to their critics. This orientation begins with legal education. Brazilian law students enter law faculties directly from secondary schools. They follow a prescribed course in law for five years. The curriculum is formal and theoretical and for the most part leaves little room for exposure to the social sciences or empirical study. Much of the curriculum examines the European and classical roots of Brazilian law. Judges who are initially trained in this system usually receive additional training and experience emphasizing the ability to sift through complicated issues involving formal legal doctrine. They get little instruction in the kind of blending of legal doctrine with policy considerations that often, for better or worse, has characterized American jurisprudence for more than a century. Barbosa has been a critic of the highly formalistic nature of Brazilian jurisprudence and how it has inhibited a realistic consideration of the problem of racial inequality in the South American nation:

> Education is precisely a perfect example of the divorce between law and reality. . . . On the eve of the turn of the millennium . . . the schools that offer good-quality instruction in Brazil are in general private schools. Despite being private, these schools receive various types of government financing, including a form of direct aid for construction and repair of their facilities and through financial exemptions of various kinds. Only those families blessed with considerable financial resources have the means to enroll their children in private schools. Negroes therefore are excluded from this system by reason of the unjust artifices created by this very law.[29]

It is not just the conservative nature of the Brazilian judiciary that has made the nation's antidiscrimination laws ineffective. Brazilian law offers formidable procedural barriers that inhibit citizens from bringing allegations of racial discrimination and other complaints before the nation's courts. Brazilian-born legal scholar Antonio Gidi has noted that "Brazilian society is not very litigious because it has lost hope on the legal system." Gidi's discussion details a legal system that gives few incentives to private complainants or plaintiffs to pursue their grievances in court. Punitive damages and damages for pain and suffering are generally unavailable to Brazilian plaintiffs. Damage awards tend to be modest, while appeals tend to be frequent and lengthy. There is little incentive for parties to settle out of court. Contingency fee arrangements are rare, reducing the chances that poor complainants will find legal representation. There are, in short, few incentives for the development of a robust plaintiffs' bar that would aggressively prosecute private claims of discrimination. Indeed, Brazilian law channels individuals who believe themselves to be victims of discrimination into working through a public agency, the Ministério Público, or a recognized nongovernmental organization. Both have standing to bring class action suits. Private parties do not. A robust plaintiffs' bar played a key role in enforcing antidiscrimination law in the United States. There is little likelihood of the private bar playing a similar role in Brazil.[30]

Legal scholar Benjamin Hensler has suggested that Brazil's labor courts might prove to be a more fruitful avenue for those wishing to press claims of employment discrimination. Labor law is more highly developed than antidiscrimination law. The nation's labor code dates back to the Consolidação das Leis do Trabalho, first adopted under the administration of Getúlio Vargas in 1943. It has been extensively amended and the nation has a special system of courts responsible for hearing claims of violations of the labor code. Hensler notes that the labor courts have proven themselves to be more willing to listen to cases based on statistical and other kinds of inferential evidence than has traditionally been the case in Brazilian courts. This was particularly evident in a series of cases brought by the Ministério Público against a number of major banks that were accused of discrimination against Afro-Brazilian job applicants. Hensler's research indicates that although the labor code and the labor courts may provide some opportunities for relief in cases of employment discrimination, their employment by Afro-Brazilians is likely to be limited for three reasons. First, many Afro-Brazilian workers are employed in the informal economy and are not covered by Brazilian labor laws. Second, workers have tended to use the labor code as a means of gaining monetary compensation after they have been terminated from a job, not as a means of challenging unfair treatment on the job or the refusal of enterprises to hire them. Finally, labor courts have tended to require evidence of prejudicial motive in cases where discrimination has been alleged. Prejudicial motive is hard to demonstrate and made harder still because of the reluctance on the part of jurists to recognize the existence of very real racial prejudice in Brazilian life. If the labor courts look somewhat more promising than the rest of the Brazilian judiciary, they still provide little hope for those looking to root out discrimination in the South American nation.[31]

In part because of the traditionally unresponsive nature of the judicial system, Brazilian governments and civil rights activists have attempted to strengthen antidiscrimination policies by working through administrative agencies. The first decade of the twenty-first century would see a proliferation of government initiatives at the national level designed to remedy what was becoming fairly visible and fairly embarrassing evidence that Afro-Brazilians were not particularly well integrated into many parts of the national life. In May 2003, Congress passed legislation creating a Special Secretariat for the Promotion of Racial Equality. That agency reports directly to the president and is charged with coordinating all governmental antidiscrimination policies. The Special Secretariat is meant to have a special focus on the Afro-Brazilian population and is charged with coordinating governmental affirmative action policies and defining public actions aimed at fulfilling Brazil's international commitment to fight racial discrimination. In 2005, the Special Secretariat sponsored the National Conference on the Promotion of Racial Equality. The conference put forward a number of suggestions for reforming antidiscrimination law. Other agencies have sought to strengthen the reach of their antidiscrimination policies or to adopt affirmative action measures in their own internal hiring policies. In the last decade, the Ministry of Labor and Employment and the Human Rights Secretariat of the Ministry of Justice, among others, have adopted measures to combat employment discrimination. Whether the new emphasis on administrative initiatives to combat racial discrimination will prove an effective substitute for what has been a relatively ineffective antidiscrimination legal regime remains to be seen.

The answers to that question are not clear. The difficulties in achieving effective new policies that take into account a nation's racial history and the need to remedy the ills of the past can be seen in the Brazilian Statute of Racial Equality, which passed the Senate in June 2010 and was signed by President Lula in July of that year. The statute had been the long-term project of Afro-Brazilian senator Paulo Renato Paim from the southern state of Rio Grande do Sul. It was originally meant to be a comprehensive vehicle for resolving long-standing patterns of racial inequality in Brazil. Initially proposed in 2003, a fairly robust version of the legislation passed the Chamber of Deputies in 2009. The earlier version of the legislation included measures specifying affirmative action for Afro-Brazilians in the nation's public universities. It also mandated that Brasília take measures to reduce disparities in health care, including the greater incidence of maternal mortality in childbirth, between Afro-Brazilians and the rest of the population. These measures were stripped from the Senate version. Some of the provisions left in the Senate version of the legislation were largely symbolic or cultural — the right to follow Afro-Brazilian religions and the recognition of the Afro-Brazilian martial art capoeira as a legitimate sport. Other measures called on government agencies to take positive steps to reduce racial inequality or called for the creation of national programs to promote racial equality.[32]

It is not clear from the legislation that these provisions create enforceable mandates requiring measurable governmental action. Other provisions in the statute require either further legislation or decrees for implementation. These include grants of specific credit lines for Afro-Brazilian farmers, the creation of special ombudsmen's offices to receive complaints of racial discrimination and prejudice, and special governmental measures to promote equal opportunity in the labor market. The new statute partly reflects the Brazilian nation's desire to use the law to make a strong normative statement in favor of racial inclusion and redressing old wrongs. It also reflects the nation's deep political divisions regarding the adoption of race-conscious measures. These divisions make the adoption of effective race-conscious measures, ones that will break down deeply entrenched barriers, highly problematic.[33]

In addition to new legal and administrative initiatives, the Brazilian government, particularly since the beginning of the new century, has been particularly supportive of international initiatives to combat racial discrimination. In June 2003, Brazil recognized the competence of the International Committee for the Elimination of Racial Discrimination. The international body was empowered to receive and analyze complaints of racial discrimination. Similarly, the Ministry of Labor has recognized the authority of the International Labor Organization and has investigated complaints of racial discrimination brought before the international organization by Brazilian unions.[34]

It is still too early to tell what overall impact these domestic and international initiatives will have. They clearly reflect a growing recognition on the part of many in the Brazilian government and the Brazilian public that the problems of racial inequality and racial discrimination are severe and that they need to be directly and forcefully addressed. There are indications that the new willingness of successive Brazilian administrations to address the issue of racial discrimination has given heart to many Afro-Brazilians. It has also increased interest in affirmative action, which many Afro-Brazilian activists view as a tool that might combat well-established patterns of racial inequality. In addition to its other virtues, affirmative action has the potential to move the struggle for racial equality away from the courts, with their glacial pace and the often difficult requirement that plaintiffs or prosecutors prove bad acts and discriminatory intentions on the part of employers or others charged with discrimination. Civil rights advocates have also long believed that affirmative action had the potential to untie the Gordian knot of structural inequality. In a field such as university education, where it is difficult to determine the extent to which the underrepresentation of Afro-Brazilians is the result of class disadvantage and the extent to which it is the result of racial inequality, affirmative action had long been seen as a potential way of bypassing that debate and adding, with relative rapidity, significant numbers of Afro-Brazilians to the ranks of the nation's university students. Throughout the 1980s and 1990s, affirmative action was the subject of considerable academic debate. Its supporters pointed to the greater progress in racial inclusion that was occurring in the United States as the result of affirmative action policies. Opponents often countered that the American example was not a proper one for Brazilians to follow, arguing that Brazil lacked the history of state-mandated discrimination that had existed in the United States and that black and white were not discrete, immutable categories in Brazil as they had traditionally been in the United States.[35]

The debate took on a somewhat more concrete form in 2001. That year Brazil took its first steps toward actual affirmative action policies. A number of government agencies, including the Ministries of Agriculture and Justice, Itamaraty (the foreign ministry), and the Supremo Tribunal Federal, would issue directives ordering increased hiring of Afro-Brazilians. President Fernando Henrique Cardoso, a sociologist and longtime critic of racial inequality in Brazil, was supportive of the new more inclusive policies. Cardoso, in turn, was supported by Afro-Brazilian antidiscrimination activists who were prodding Brasília for more inclusive policies.[36]

Affirmative action has proven to be most controversial in higher education. In 2001, the legislature of the state of Rio de Janeiro passed legislation mandating quotas of 40 percent for Afro-Brazilians in the state's two public universities. The legislation had been proposed by long time Afro-Brazilian civil rights activist Benedita da Silva, who was then the state's lieutenant governor. The new policy was initially challenged in federal court by a state legislator and an association of private schools as a violation of the constitutional principle of *razoabilidade* (proportionality in the exercise of legislative discretion). The lawsuit was ruled moot when the state legislature revised the policy in 2003 to provide for more limited quotas of 20 percent for self-declared Afro-Brazilians, 20 percent for graduates of public schools, and 5 percent for indigenous and disabled students. The remedial legislation also specified that students admitted under the quotas had to meet financial eligibility requirements. The revised affirmative action policy would later also be challenged in court.[37]

The Ministry of Education has not issued a national mandate for affirmative action. Nonetheless, the federal government's recent commitment to expanding educational opportunities for Afro-Brazilians and other traditionally disadvantaged groups seems clear. In 2002, Congress passed legislation creating the University Diversity Program, designed to improve access to higher education for people from socially disadvantaged groups, particularly members of Afro-Brazilian and indigenous communities. In 2004, Congress passed legislation authorizing a new program, Universidade para Todos, to provide scholarships for students from low-income families designed to permit them to attend private universities. Despite the government's sympathy for greater access to university education for traditionally disadvantaged groups, race-based affirmative action programs continue to be controversial. More than three hundred disgruntled applicants brought court challenges to the affirmative action programs of the two state universities in Rio de Janeiro. In 2006, 114 university professors signed a "manifesto" opposing race-based affirmative action, claiming that it was unconstitutional and an engine for conflict and intolerance. A few days later, 330 intellectuals and civil rights activists signed a response arguing in favor of affirmative action. The opposing manifestos were widely discussed in the Brazilian media. The debate remains a lively one within Brazil. A national survey conducted in 2008 indicates strong and often contradictory views on the part of many Brazilians. According to the survey, 62 percent of Brazilians believe affirmative action policies are essential. But another 53 percent believe that the programs are humiliating and 62 percent of the population believe the policies can themselves cause racism.[38]

If affirmative action programs based on race are controversial, other forms of affirmative action seem to be accepted with considerably less public rancor. In the 1990s, Brazil adopted quotas requiring that a minimum of 20 percent of elected officials would be women. Legislation providing for affirmative action in education for the children of farmers dates back to 1968. The constitution of 1988 reserves a percentage of jobs for individuals with disabilities. We might speculate as to why none of these forms of affirmative action have engendered the kind of contentious debate that has accompanied race-based affirmative action. Racial animus might partially explain the difference. Equally likely is the fact that race-based affirmative action treads on very sensitive territory in Brazilian life. It is a reminder of racial inequality and that the self-image of Brazil as the land of racial democracy has not stood up very well under close scrutiny. In any event, the different reactions to different types of affirmative action are telling.[39]

Despite the controversy, race-based affirmative action programs in universities have increased dramatically in Brazil since 2001. There were no affirmative action programs at the beginning of 2001. By 2010, 70 percent of the nation's public universities had adopted some kind of affirmative action program. Forty-three percent of public universities had adopted quotas for students from Afro-Brazilian or indigenous backgrounds. The programs vary. Some target only Afro-Brazilian students from public secondary schools. Others set aside seats for public secondary school graduates regardless of race and then establish racial quotas according to the racial makeups of the states. Still other programs provide separate quotas for Afro-Brazilian students regardless of whether or not they are graduates of public or private schools. Some of these also provide separate quotas for public school graduates regardless of race. A few universities award extra points on the Vestibular to Afro-Brazilians and graduates of public schools.[40]

Brazil's moves toward affirmative action and indeed antidiscrimination measures as well have been complicated by long-standing notions of racial identity and racial mobility. Afro-Brazilian activists, starting most notably in 1990, moved to bring a measure of racial unity to the people I have, somewhat problematically, been labeling *Afro-Brazilians* by urging people who might have traditionally called themselves *preto* or *pardo* to identify as a single people, *negro* (black). Other Afro-Brazilian activists began calling for the use of *Afro-descendente* (Afro-descended) as a way of bringing about a degree of racial unity and transcending the multiplicity of color categories that had often prevented Afro-Brazilians from seeing themselves as a unified people. People began wearing T-shirts proclaiming themselves "100 percent black." Political activists used the term *Afro-descendente* with greater frequency. Afro-Brazilian activists unsuccessfully campaigned for an elimination of the *pardo* category in the census. Many urged all Afro-

Brazilians to check the *preto* category when the census came out. Even though that campaign failed, the message was clear. Afro-Brazilians should regard themselves as a unified group and should perhaps approach the question of racial identity with a mind-set closer to the traditional North American notion of the one drop rule rather than Brazilian notions of racial fluidity and negotiated racial status.[41]

This new way of thinking would immediately prove to be problematic in the new world of affirmative action in Brazilian universities at the beginning of the century. If *Afro-descendente* was to be the new term used in statutes and administrative regulations, why, then, many "whites" were *Afro-descendente*. Many whites could discover a *pardo* grandparent and then benefit from the new policies. A number of white Brazilians applied for the new quotas designed for Afro-Brazilians. It remains a dilemma for supporters of affirmative action. Some universities have developed a policy of specifying that the new considerations are reserved for those who self-identify as *negro* on the theory that while many whites are perhaps willing to admit to perhaps a mulatto grandparent, few are willing to concede that they themselves are black. Other universities have also tried to verify racial identity through photographs or interviews. The question of who might benefit from the new affirmative action programs is difficult and often highly contested and frequently receives different answers at different universities. And as late as 2012, there were still a substantial number of public universities, which generally have autonomy in determining admissions policies, where the answer is quite simple. There will be no affirmative action programs.[42]

The debate over affirmative action continues in Brazil. It is vigorous and over the last decade has moved from being a purely theoretical controversy addressed primarily in academic journals and polemical tracts to being a critical issue of concern to the nation's law- and policymakers. No event better illustrated this than the extraordinary set of hearings that were held before the Supremo Tribunal Federal on March 3–5, 2010. Brazil's highest court had agreed to hold hearings on an affirmative action case involving the affirmative action program at the Universidade Federal do Rio Grande do Sul. The ministers of the high court decided that because of the extraordinary importance of the issue, it would take presentations — essentially oral amicus curiae briefs from concerned parties. The court was in effect conducting a national debate on the issue of university quotas. Sessions of the Supremo Tribunal Federal are not only open to the public, they are televised. The proceedings from this case may still be seen on YouTube. The whole nation would be at least vicariously participating. Experts from all sides would be able to present their points of view. More than forty persons made *palestras* (presentations) putting forward their perspectives on affirmative action.[43]

The demands of time and space preclude an extensive analysis of the presentations made at the hearings. Nonetheless, the testimonies of two of the participants — Deborah Duprat, Brazil's vice attorney general, and Edson Santos de Souza, minister of the Special Secretariat for Public Policy for the Promotion of Racial Equality — made clear the Lula administration's support for affirmative action measures. Duprat argued that the 1988 constitution should be viewed as a break with Brazil's past, a past in which the legal, constitutional, and political orders all worked in harmony to preserve a hegemonic order that valued some while excluding others. As evidence that the 1988 constitution was designed to break down traditional barriers and bring about the inclusion of groups that had traditionally been excluded, Duprat pointed to provisions in the new constitution authorizing quotas for women in the labor market. Duprat also noted the prevalence of often strong discrimination in the labor market and elsewhere as a compelling reason to permit affirmative action.[44]

De Souza presented the high court with what was in effect an oral Brandeis brief. His palestra put before the court the details of social and economic inequality as faced by Afro-Brazilians. It also reviewed the history of Afro-Brazilian poverty and marginalization. The wealth of Brazil in the colonial era and the nineteenth century was created by slave labor, yet efforts to provide former slaves with land and the possibility of self-sufficiency after emancipation, although debated, were rejected. De Sousa argued that quotas, while not a panacea, would help to lessen the burdens of inequality. The minister also rejected the argument that affirmative action would bring about greater racial friction. He noted that the state universities in Rio de Janeiro had had affirmative action programs since 2002 with no ill effects on race relations. He also noted that the Pontifícia Universidade Católica do Rio de Janeiro had had an affirmative action program for fifteen years, with positive effects.[45]

In late April and early May 2012, the Brazilian high court rendered two important decisions concerning affirmative action in the nation's public universities. The first, announced on April 24, declared in a unanimous ten-to-nothing opinion, that the University of Brasilia's program of quotas for Afro-Brazilians was consistent with the equality principle in the 1988 Constitution. The program at Brasilia, which began in 2004, was the first affirmative action program at a federal university. On May 9, 2012, the Supremo Tribunal Federal declared that the affirmative action program at the Federal University of Rio Grande do Sul, the subject of the 2010 hearings, was constitutional.[46]

The decision by the Supremo Tribunal Federal, authored by minister Ricardo Lewandowski, provided a strong endorsement for the constitutionality of university affirmative action measures. The opinion stressed that the 1988 constitution was committed to equality in fact and not just formal equality. It noted that the constitution permitted affirmative action based on disability and gender and argued that extending the principle to race would be consistent with the charter's equality provisions. The Lewandowski opinion also noted that affirmative action was a way to compensate for past and continuing discrimination and that it contributed to pluralism and diversity in higher education and in the training of the nation's leaders. The high court opinion also noted with approval the U.S. Supreme Court's affirmative action jurisprudence, with an in-depth analysis of the 2003 case *Grutter v. Bollinger*. Lewandowski argued that Brazil's constitution gave public institutions even more latitude than the U.S. Constitution in adopting measures to remedy racial inequality.[47]

The hearings in 2010 and the decision by the Supremo Tribunal Federal in April 2012 indicate the profound changes that have occurred in the last two decades. Under both the Cardozo and Lula administrations, the Brazilian government made a determination to take a hard, fresh look at the issues of race and racial exclusion in Brazilian life. It was difficult; it involved confronting long-held myths concerning racial democracy and racial harmony in the South American republic. It is still not clear where this new willingness to confront the problem of racial inequality will lead. Inequality runs deep in Brazilian life. Brazil has one of the most uneven distributions of wealth and income in the world. Any attempt to deal with the issue of racial inequality that fails to address deeply entrenched patterns of class inequality is likely to produce only a hollow victory at best. Equally problematic, many Brazilians, including many Afro-Brazilians, would reject the idea that there is a serious problem of racism and racial discrimination in their nation, evidence to the contrary notwithstanding. Finally, many of the institutional mechanisms critical to any effort to implement the new egalitarian policies of modern Brazil are not particularly robust. Despite the High Court's strong endorsement of affirmative action, the Brazilian courts have proven to be a fragile vehicle for the enforcement of civil rights legislation. There have been recent efforts at judicial reform, but the extent to which they will transform the traditionally inefficient Brazilian judicial culture remains to be seen.[48]

Still, a transformation has occurred, even to the point that shortly before this volume went to press Brazil passed legislation mandating affirmative action in its public universities. If the first step in solving a problem is a recognition that there is one, then Brazil in the twenty-first century has taken the first step and perhaps a bit more. The Brazilian government has not only gotten behind the idea that it must attack the problem of racial inequality at home, it has become a supporter of efforts to attack racial discrimination and inequality throughout the American hemisphere. In 2005, the Brazilian Foreign Ministry sponsored an international conference, Exits from Slavery and Public Policy. The conference, held at the Palace of Itamaraty in Brasília, brought Afro-American scholars and activists from throughout the hemisphere to discuss ways of strengthening and improving civil rights legislation. In 2008, the Brazilian government signed a memorandum of understanding with the U.S. government agreeing that both nations would work to promote racial equality and combat racial exclusion throughout the hemisphere. It was a sign that the struggle to overcome the legacy of slavery in the Americas was increasingly becoming a matter of hemispheric concern.[49]

CHAPTER NINE

New Awakenings in Spanish America

FOR MANY CIVIL RIGHTS ACTIVISTS in the Spanish-speaking nations of the Americas, that 2008 agreement between Brazil and the United States was welcome news. Since the 1980s, Afro-Latin community activists had become increasingly vocal in their efforts to combat entrenched patterns of racial exclusion. Their efforts were being aided by growing international recognition that there were severe problems of racial inequality and racial discrimination throughout the American hemisphere. As the twentieth century was yielding to the twenty-first, international agencies were beginning to ask questions about race and whether or not racial exclusion impeded social and economic development in Latin America. The Inter-American Development Bank and the World Bank were sponsoring empirical investigations asking questions about race and social exclusion that went beyond traditional inquiries about Latin American indigenous populations. The United Nations would do much to help mobilize Afro-American community activists through their participation in two conferences — the World Conference against Racism, Racial Discrimination, Xenophobia, and Related Intolerance, held in Durban, South Africa, in September 2001, and a preparatory conference held in Santiago, Chile, in December 2000. Both congresses would have in attendance Afro-Latin activists from throughout the hemisphere including some from nations long thought not to have Afro-American populations. These and other international conferences combined with a new tool, the Internet, were giving increased visibility to peoples long ignored or simply dismissed as local curiosities. That new visibility would be enlisted in the fight against racial exclusion.[1]

It would be a difficult task. Discrimination can be strong in Spanish America, and racism at times quite open and fierce. There had been a time when Afro-Americans in Cuba, Central America, or Peru or Colombia and other venues might take comfort from the fact that they were not subject to the well-publicized rigors of formal segregation as they had existed in the United States. But by the end of the twentieth century, any comfort that such a comparison might have once brought had long since vanished. Like their Brazilian counterparts, many Afro-Americans in the Spanish-speaking nations of the hemisphere began to look at the advances that had been made by the civil rights movement in the United States and compare that progress with the relative stagnation in racial policies in their own countries.

Increasingly in the 1980s and 1990s, new voices were being heard from and new organizations were forming in Afro-American communities throughout the hemisphere. They were protesting long-standing patterns of racism and racial exclusion. Some of these civil rights activists objected to conditions long familiar to students of the American and Brazilian civil rights movements — discrimination in employment and public accommodations, police brutality, unequal access to schools, racist stereotypes in films and television, unequal distribution of government services. But in many Spanish-speaking nations, Afro-American activists faced an even more fundamental problem — the need to fight for the basic recognition of their existence, their presence in what we might call the humanscape of the nations into which they had been born, the *patrias* that their ancestors had helped create.[2]

It was a task even more difficult than the one that had been faced by the American and Brazilian civil rights movements. Formal, legal segregation in the United States had given African Americans a clear set of targets to attack. If the targets were perhaps less clear in Brazil, the sheer size of the Afro-Brazilian population and the contradiction between that nation's long celebrated support for racial democracy and the treatment accorded most Afro-Brazilians ensured that sooner or later the South American nation would have to come to address its issues of race and inequality. In many of the other nations of the hemisphere, the possibilities for organizing against racial discrimination were less clear. Afro-American populations existed throughout the Americas, to be sure. At the end of the twentieth century, they could still be found in distinct regional enclaves — Esmeraldas

Province in Ecuador, the Pacific coastal regions of Colombia, Limón and its vicinity in Costa Rica, among others. They could also be found living among the general population, usually in the poorer barrios, of most nations.

Afro-Latins faced often persistent discrimination, but unlike their American and Brazilian counterparts, they frequently lived in nations that were often uncomfortable in acknowledging their very existence, much less the very real existence of race and racial discrimination in national life. The early-twentieth-century ideologies of *blanqueamiento* and *mestizaje* had left an enduring legacy in many nations. At its most extreme, there was a reluctance to even recognize that race as such continued to exist. Government ministries might officially recognize those who were labeled *Indios*, peoples who were culturally distinct, whose first languages were the ancient indigenous tongues, who lived in distinct ethnic enclaves. But this was a recognition of ethnicity and cultural distinctiveness, not race.[3]

Racial information was often sparse in national censuses and in official statistics kept by ministries of labor, education, and public health. An antidiscrimination activist in Venezuela or Mexico might suspect that good jobs were reserved for whites or relatively light-skinned mestizos, that the phrase *buena presencia*, like *boa aparência* in Brazil, were code words meant to exclude most Afro-American applicants. Or she might believe that government agencies provided poorer services to communities with large concentrations of Afro-Americans or that those agencies discriminated in hiring blacks and dark-skinned mulattoes. She might suspect such things, but unlike her Brazilian or American counterparts, she would find little in the way of official statistics to help support her claims. It would be impossible under such circumstances to hope to do what had been done in American courts since the 1970s and use statistical evidence to demonstrate that a firm or governmental agency was engaging in employment discrimination. The possibilities of doing what Brazilian social scientists had done — using official statistics to determine the extent to which Afro-American poverty, relative lack of education, or relegation to relatively low-skilled jobs was a product primarily of racial discrimination or of entrenched patterns of class inequality — also seemed remote. Even documenting racial inequality — getting hard data that would confirm that Afro-American populations had lower levels of education, access to health care, or employment opportunities — was essentially impossible in the absence of racial data in official statistics.[4]

Because Afro-Latin civil rights activists were often faced with challenges that were more difficult than those faced by their Brazilian and U.S. counterparts, they would often find themselves more receptive to and more dependent on assistance from international organizations. Afro-American political and social organizations had long existed throughout the Americas. Political activists of African descent also had a history of being involved in national labor organizations and political protest movements and parties. But it was often hard to organize Afro-Americans to protest patterns of racial exclusion. There were many reasons for this. Certainly the unsure and intermittent nature of democracy in many of the nations in the region inhibited the growth of robust movements to combat racial exclusion. But something more was at work. The legacy of race as it had developed in the Spanish Empire and as it had been refined in the early-twentieth-century crucible that was *blanqueamiento* still shaped the racial attitudes of many Latin Americans, including many who were of African descent, at the end of the twentieth century. People of African descent, even many who were visibly Afro-American, were still often reluctant to identify themselves as such. Traditional patterns of negotiating one's racial or color classification toward a white or lighter category continued. It was a continuation of a pattern that began in the sixteenth-century world of empire and *castas* and that was still very much alive at the sunset of the twentieth century and the dawn of the twenty-first. Individual Afro-Latins might and some indeed did achieve success, sometimes spectacularly so, but they frequently did so because of strong connections to white families and patrons and frequently because of a willingness to separate themselves from others who we might call Afro-Colombians or Afro-Peruvians or other Afro-Americans.

In many ways this relative lack of racial cohesion and this felt need for successful people of African descent to separate themselves from what might be termed the Afro-American population at large was stronger in many parts of Spanish America than it had been in Brazil. The notion of racial democracy as it had worked itself out in the Lusophonic nation since the 1930s had conspicuously included the Afro-Brazilian in the national narrative. Much of this inclusion was overromanticized. Often the size of the Afro-Brazilian population was severely understated in official records.

But few Brazilians would deny that *pretos* and *pardos* were integral parts of their nation. In many parts of Spanish America, Afro-American populations were scarcely recognized. Too much attention devoted to Afro-American populations conflicted with long-standing national self-images, images that said that the nations that were the heirs of the Spanish Empire were white nations or at the very least, syntheses of the Spanish and indigenous heritages. Afro-Americans might be found in such nations, but for much of the twentieth century, there was often a strong reluctance to acknowledge their presence or to seriously study their condition.

Fighting invisibility was difficult. Ancient views that African ancestry was tainted while European and indigenous ancestries were nobler caused many Afro-Latins to be reluctant to identify as people of African descent. This view continued well into the first decade of the present century. Anthropologist Laura Lewis, while doing fieldwork in San Nicolás, an Afro-Mexican village in Guerrero on Mexico's Pacific coast, noted that many villagers had a strong reluctance to identify as Afro-Mexican. For some, this reluctance stemmed from a belief that identification as Afro-Mexicans did nothing to enhance their own well-being, that such identification would probably exacerbate prejudice against them or in any event call into question their identity as Mexicans. Similar results have been found elsewhere. One ethnographer specializing in Afro-Peruvian culture found in one setting that only a minority of visible Afro-Peruvians were willing to acknowledge that they were of African descent. Other research indicates that there may be a widespread reluctance to even discuss such topics as racism and racial discrimination. For many Afro-American activists, fighting invisibility meant fighting not only national ideologies that had traditionally relegated Afro-Latin populations to the periphery of national consciousness; it also meant a struggle against cultural norms in many Afro-Latin communities. These norms dictated that too great a willingness to identify as an Afro-American was somewhat unacceptable and might even raise doubt about an individual's or community's identification with the nation.[5]

But if long-standing traditions dictated that Afro-Latins should say little about race and mute any tendencies they might have to identify as Afro-Americans, events that were occurring elsewhere in the world and in their own societies were causing politically conscious Afro-Americans to reconsider the role of race in their individual and communal lives. The success of the civil rights movement in the United States, the achievement of independence by the nations of sub-Saharan Africa, the fight against apartheid in South Africa, and the Afro-Brazilian struggle for racial equality all contributed to this new thinking on the part of Afro-Latin civil rights activists. The old certainties about race and the inferiority of peoples of African descent — certainties that had played a decisive role in marginalizing Afro-Latins at the beginning of the twentieth century — had long since lost widespread support in the Western world. The world had changed. The Americans had come to realize that their democratic ideals and the practice of racial discrimination were incompatible. The nations of Europe had lost their colonies, no longer spoke of "the white man's burden," and remained chastened by their devastating encounter with scientific racism, the Holocaust administered by the Third Reich. The increasingly powerful and influential Brazilians were growing more and more uncomfortable with the conflict between their national ideal of racial democracy and the stark reality of racial inequality in their nation. Notions of racial hierarchy and inequality would remain strong in Spanish America, but increasingly these were notions that ran contrary to accepted international norms governing behavior. Increasingly these notions from a more racist past were less likely to be expressed in public, at least less likely in forums where they might become national and international embarrassments.

Changes in racial attitudes, or at least their public expressions, helped create a new atmosphere, one that allowed Afro-American civil rights activists to more openly organize and press the case for racial justice. But another set of developments in the late twentieth century was also helping the effort to organize against racial exclusion. The strengthening of democratic rule in a number of countries brought with it a rise of community and in many cases nationally based nongovernmental organizations that were formed to redress what had often been long-standing grievances. Often the return to democratic rule brought new leaders and new ways of thinking into the governments of many nations. Sensitive to international public opinion, very much aware of the new egalitarian thinking on race that had largely overtaken the First World, these new national leaders were far more likely to see at least the more obvious forms of racial discrimination and racial inequality as embarrassments that cast their nations in bad lights. These new leaders were far more likely to listen to complaints concerning racial discrimination and racial exclusion than their predecessors. In some countries, liberal public officials sought to redress the marginalization of their nation's Afro-American populations by working to increase the visibility of those populations in discussions of the national culture and issues of social equity. Such officials were publicly proclaiming their nations to be multicultural and multiethnic societies. Mexico provides one interesting example of this rethinking. In the 1990s, officials of that nation's National Council for Culture and the Arts began urging Mexicans to look beyond what had long been the official story — that the nation was a synthesis of the cultures of the Aztecs and the conquistadors — and to consider also the nation's "third root," the African and Afro-Mexican contribution to the nation's history and culture.[6]

And there were Afro-American activists who pushed and pushed hard to break traditional patterns of invisibility. Sometimes these activists emerged in the least likely places. Argentina, which had long considered itself not merely a white but fundamentally a European nation, found itself at the beginning of the twenty-first century facing a campaign by, among others, three quite determined Afro-Argentine women who were working to bring official and public recognition of the peoples of African descent in the Rioplatense Republic. María Magdalena Lamadrid, our friend "Pocha" from chapter 4, formed an organization, África Vive, in Buenos Aires in the 1990s. She was successful in getting the Argentine government to put up a monument to the Afro-Argentine soldiers of the nineteenth century. Lucía Dominga Molina, like Pocha a descendant of Argentine slaves, established a cultural center, La Casa de la Cultura Indo-Afro-Americana, in the province of Santa Fe. Her center has played an important role in informing residents of Santa Fe of the strong Afro-Argentine tradition in the region. Another activist, Miriam Gomes, a descendant of Cape Verdean immigrants who came to the Argentine Republic in the twentieth century, has been an active scholar documenting the history of different Afro-Argentine groups and has had a website on Afro-Argentine and Afro-Uruguayan history on the web page of Argentina's Library of Congress. Across the Río de la Plata in Montevideo, Afro-Uruguayans Romero Rodríguez and Beatriz Ramírez founded Mundo Afro in 1988. They established the organization to combat discrimination in a nation that had historically been all too willing to overlook its Afro-American population. The emergence of Afro-Argentine and Afro-Uruguayan activists toward the end of the twentieth century might have come as something of a surprising reminder to many of their fellow citizens that both nations had Afro-American populations, populations that were beginning to mobilize to combat entrenched patterns of invisibilization and marginalization. What was probably even more surprising to most Chileans was the discovery that their nation also had a modern Afro-American population, the Afro-Chilean community located in and near the northern port city of Arica. A delegation from an Arica-based group, Oro Negro, surprised many people in the Pacific coastal nation when they appeared at an international congress on racial discrimination hosted by the Chilean government in 2000.[7]

Afro-American activists in Argentina, Chile, and to a lesser extent Uruguay, had the formidable task of reminding nations that had largely forgotten or overlooked their very existence, of their continued presence, that they were still very much a part of the countries that they inhabited. They also had the task of reminding their governments and fellow citizens that they had very real and often unmet needs. This task included reminding national and at times international human rights agencies that Afro-Latins were often victims of discrimination and that they were part of the enduring problems of social exclusion and inequality in the region. They also had the difficult job of reminding their fellow citizens that they were not, as many would have wished, either invisible people or, if recognized at all, mere folkloric curiosities and historical oddities. These were problems often faced by Afro-Latin activists in nations like Argentina, Chile, and Mexico, nations where the Afro-American populations were small or so overshadowed by indigenous populations that they were frequently rendered invisible. In other nations, the problem was more direct. It was well known that Colombia, Venezuela, Panama, Peru, and other nations had large Afro-American populations. But how large? How significant? What was known about their social and economic circumstances? At the turn of this new century, the answer was, not enough. An observer traveling through Venezuela, Panama, or Peru might readily see that Afro-Americans tended to be among the poorer citizens in the region. But such information was impressionistic, not systematic, hardly sufficient for a regime of legal and policy reforms designed to tackle racial inequality and social exclusion.[8]

Recent efforts to have governments gather or improve their collection of racial data have improved our ability to understand racial inequality in the region, but official statistics still have major limitations. Some governments still do not collect racial statistics, adhering to the traditional view that counting the population by race is divisive and, given the degree of racial mixture in the population, perhaps impossible. Even where racial statistics are collected, those statistics and what they have to say about different populations in the region have to be approached with considerable caution. Census and other official records generally rely on self-reporting to determine an individual's racial or color category. Given the long history of individuals trying to deny or minimize their African ancestry in many of the countries of the region, we might properly expect a significant undercounting of what might be termed the Afro-American population of Spanish America. But even that expectation requires qualification. Who should be counted as an Afro-American? As has occurred in Brazil, Afro-American activists in many nations have advocated an expansive definition of who should be included. Many argue that the term *afrodescendiente* should be employed, a term that could include people with somewhat attenuated African ancestry. Government agencies have generally tended to be more conservative, frequently using the traditional *negro* and *mulato* in official records. These terms have historically excluded many individuals known to have some African ancestry. These difficulties have led to often sharp disagreements between national governments and Afro-Latin activists about the size of Afro-American populations. Colombia illustrates the difficulty many Latin American countries have had in gathering racial data. The 1993 census was the first since 1918 to indicate race. It showed an Afro-Colombian population of 1.5 percent, a figure that most observers agree was a severe undercount. A 1998 report prepared by a coalition of Afro-Colombian community organizations estimated that roughly 26 percent of the nation's population was of African descent. The 2005 national census shows an Afro-Colombian population of 4,311,757 — nearly 11 percent of the total. The discrepancies between the 2005 census figures and the report prepared by the Afro-Colombian organizations probably reflect both definitional differences and undercounting.[9]

Whether that undercounting serves to mask or exacerbate the level of racial inequality in the region is unclear. Nonetheless the data that we do have paints a picture of a region where race is often a decisive predictor of unequal status. The best estimates that we have indicate that the Afro-American population of Spanish America probably numbers over fifty million individuals. Statistics gathered by the governments of Colombia, Ecuador, and Uruguay, among others, show Afro-American populations that are measurably poorer, less well educated, more poorly paid, less healthy, and more likely to die prematurely than their white and mestizo counterparts.[10]

As in Brazil, it can be difficult to determine whether race or class is more important in sustaining long-standing patterns of racial inequality in Spanish America. Latin America has the most unequal distribution of wealth in the world. Many nations in the region have deeply entrenched social hierarchies. Social services for the poor are scarce, at times nonexistent, despite seemingly generous provisions in national constitutions guaranteeing the right to education, health care, and other benefits. Throughout the region, it is considered unremarkable that nepotism and clientelism will play major roles in determining who gets jobs in the private sector and in governmental agencies as well. If the civil rights movement in the United States was able to ultimately triumph in part because it could appeal to the North American nation's liberal and egalitarian traditions, advocates for racial justice in many parts of Spanish America have had a more difficult task. Liberal and egalitarian norms have certainly been part of the political ideologies of the nations of the region. These norms have at various points in history been reflected in the region's national constitutions and statutes. But those norms have had to coexist in profoundly unequal societies with significantly unequal distributions of wealth, land, and access to education and significantly different experiences with treatment or mistreatment by police and other governmental authorities. Much of this inequality has been and still is linked to race. With relatively rare exceptions, the privileged — those with access to good educations, land, governmental services, and the proper connections that lead to good jobs and relative security have been the descendants of either the Spaniards who came in the colonial era or later European settlers who were brought in to whiten a number of American nations. And with relatively rare exceptions, the poor — those with little access to education, good jobs, or government services — have been those who are the visible descendants of the displaced indigenous populations, or the Africans brought to the Americas as slaves of the Spanish Empire. Social advantage and disadvantage are racially linked, but how great a part does active racial discrimination play in sustaining inequality?[11]

According to our best evidence, it plays a significant part. Negative stereotypes of Afro-Americans are common. Films and television programs at the beginning of the twenty-first century, still present black and mulatto characters in gross racially stereotyped caricatures. High-end restaurants and nightclubs routinely refuse to serve Afro-American patrons, despite statutes prohibiting this kind of discrimination. There has been a strong tradition of discrimination in employment. Studies of hiring patterns throughout the region show that many employers have a strong reluctance to hire Afro-Americans for managerial, technical, or professional positions as well as for clerical jobs or even positions as retail sales clerks. Researchers have found significant discrimination even in jobs that require little in the way of formal education. As is the case elsewhere in the Americas, government employment is the mainstay of the relatively small Afro-Latin middle class.[12]

Our best information indicates that Afro-Latins are often severely disadvantaged by their nations' educational systems. This is in part due to the often severe underfunding of public schools in many countries. Good primary and secondary education are frequently available only to the well-to-do who can send their children to private schools. Public schools fail to prepare their students either for skilled jobs or for higher education. The victims of this system are the children of the poor, disproportionately boys and girls of visible African or indigenous ancestry. Those attending the private schools that equip their students for the modern workforce or university entrance are more likely to be those who might reasonably be categorized as white or light-skinned mestizos. Some students of underdevelopment in Latin America have argued that a major reason for the lack of social and economic progress in many parts of the region has been the failure of national governments to invest adequately in human capital, including education for large segments of the Afro-American and indigenous populations. There is also evidence that constricted educational opportunities for Afro-Latins has been the result not only of poverty and inadequate governmental investment in public education but also outright discrimination as well. Venezuelan sociologist Orlando Albornoz, in his research on education in Latin America in the 1980s and early 1990s, found evidence of racial discrimination in the hiring of teachers. He also discovered that the region's best universities frequently discriminated against applicants of African and indigenous descent.[13]

Racial discrimination hits different segments of the region's Afro-American populations in different ways. For the most desperately poor, particularly for those who live impoverished lives in remote rural areas, the burdens imposed by racial prejudice or racial discrimination can seem like somewhat distant concerns. They may endure their share and more of racial slurs and gross caricatures. But the hardships of simple survival in poor communities where the basic business of gaining a livelihood can often be in doubt frequently focuses a person's attention more on poverty and the difficulties of survival than on the question of race and racial barriers. A survey of households in Ecuador illustrates this point. The survey indicated that roughly half of Afro-Ecuadorians could not identify the term *racism*, 68 percent could not identify the term *discrimination*, and 73 percent could not identify *prejudice*. It should be added that the survey also indicated that substantial percentages of those who identified themselves as whites, mestizos, and Indians could not identify those terms. The study also indicated that those who identified themselves as *negros* or *mulatos*, like other Ecuadorians, were more likely to indicate a knowledge of the terms if they lived in urban rather than rural areas and if they had university or secondary school educations rather than simply primary school educations. Although there are quibbles that might be raised with the study, it does confirm that awareness of racial discrimination is more likely to occur among somewhat upwardly mobile individuals seeking to find their place in the modern economy and modern society than among the most desperately poor, particularly in isolated rural areas.[14]

Uruguay appears to present a case where both the educated and upwardly mobile as well as those closer to the bottom of the occupational ladder suffer from employment discrimination. The southern cone nation is something of an anomaly because of its large white population and relatively low levels of social and economic inequality. Uruguay's policy of providing universal access to education has partly paid off for Afro-Uruguayans. Ninety percent of the nation, regardless of racial identification, finishes primary school. But educational levels for Afro-Uruguayans fall significantly behind those of whites after primary schools. Nonetheless a still reasonably high 30 percent of Afro-Uruguayan youths between ages eighteen and twenty are enrolled in some form of postsecondary schooling. Fifty percent of whites of that age are in postsecondary schooling. Analysis of data gathered in 2006 indicates that Uruguay has a racial earnings gap with Afro-Uruguayan workers earning roughly 75 percent of the wages of white workers. This gap is actually significantly lower than the racial gap that has been estimated in other parts of Latin America, including Brazil and Colombia. Much of the difference in earnings is due to differences in education and other human capital considerations, but statistical analysis also indicates that racial discrimination accounts for a significant portion of the wage differential. Even Afro-Uruguayans who go beyond primary school receive measurably less in the way of occupational and wage reward than their similarly educated white compatriots, indicating racial discrimination in skilled and white-collar occupations. Interestingly enough, research also indicates that discrimination is sharpest at the low skill levels, indicating that employers are able to indulge their preference for white workers in a nation with an overwhelmingly white workforce.[15]

If Afro-Latins are subject to discrimination in employment and underrepresentation and discrimination in education and the provision of public services as well, they also rarely make it to regional and national legislatures. The reasons for this are complex. The nations of Latin America lack the history of state action designed to formally prevent Afro-Americans from voting, as was common in many parts of the United States until the passage of the Voting Rights Act of 1965. Many Latin American countries have had national political leaders of African descent in the nineteenth and early part of the twentieth centuries, despite the existence of often strong racial prejudices. But the nations of Latin America have also had a historical desire to curb the political power of the region's large poor and working-class populations. Many nations retained literacy requirements for voting well after — indeed, in many cases for a century after — independence. These requirements effectively screened out large portions of the populations, populations that were disproportionately of indigenous and African descent.[16]

But the literacy tests of the Latin American nations were not the literacy tests of the Jim Crow South. If they prevented large numbers of Afro-Latins and other poor people from voting, they also permitted suffrage and political participation by others whom we might in our North American efforts at racial construction describe as Afro-American or Indian or mestizo. Indeed, Afro-Latin participation in national politics has traditionally been high, with Afro-Americans frequently represented, particularly in the populist politics of the region. And yet the level of Afro-American political representation remains low in many nations. Many reasons might be advanced for the limited number of Afro-American elected officials in the region. Prejudice, a sense that it might somehow be unseemly to have an Afro-American representative or national leader probably plays a part. In a region where there is a traditional reluctance to hire individuals who are visibly of African descent to work in positions where they will be the public face of an enterprise, it is not surprising that many people would be reluctant to vote for such a person as the public face of either a legislative district or the nation. In 1993, Colombia took specific measures to address the underrepresentation of Afro-Colombians in the nation's Congress. That year, Congress passed legislation guaranteeing two representatives for Afro-Colombians communities in the lower house of Congress. The measure has not done much to increase the Afro-Colombian presence in Congress. Despite the provision, Afro-Colombians still make up only 1.2 percent of the nation's congressional delegation even though more than a quarter of the nation's population is Afro-American.[17]

Individual prejudices have almost certainly played a role in limiting the number of Afro-Latins who attain public office, as have formal and informal governmental prohibitions on race-based political parties. But it should also be added that any attempt to explain the low level of Afro-American representation in the political life of many nations cannot rest solely on a foundation of racial prejudice or racial barriers, at least as we might define them in the United States. Throughout this chapter I have been using the terms *Afro-American* and *Afro-Latin* somewhat interchangeably, as well as specific national terms like *Afro-Mexican*, *Afro–Costa Rican*, and *Afro-Colombian*. These terms seem pretty reasonable and unproblematic enough to North American readers, but they have a tendency to lump together all sorts of people who traditionally have not seen themselves as part of a unified group. There are Afro–Latin Americans in the nations we are discussing who see themselves as parts of reasonably unified Afro-American communities or populations — the Afro-Colombians of that nation's Pacific regions, particularly those who have lived in ethnically distinct enclaves; the *palenques* or communities originally formed by runaway slaves; the descendants of peoples from Jamaica and other parts of the British West Indies who came to Panama, Costa Rica, and other parts of Central America in the early twentieth century; the Haitians who live an often precarious existence in the Dominican Republic. But for many of the others whom we might call *Afro-Americans*, the sense of a racial identity is often conflicted. The knowledge that they are frequently victims of discrimination because of skin color and other aspects of their appearance might incline them toward a racial identification that we might term *Afro-American*, but other aspects of their lives mitigate against such. The long tradition of trying to negotiate one's way toward a lighter or whiter identity is still very much a part of the culture in many venues. Few want to be identified as *negro* or black. One's self image and even opportunities can still be improved if one can negotiate the label 'mulato' or 'moreno' or perhaps better still 'mestizo,' or even better yet 'blanco.' This kind of negotiation and the hopes that personalistic ties with powerful patrons might mitigate the damage likely to be caused by race or skin color leaves many individuals that we might term "Afro-American" with relatively weak ties to Afro-Latin communities and politics. This phenomenon has also weakened the possibilities of significant Afro-American representation in public office.[18]

Probably nowhere has this tendency to reject an Afro-American identification been stronger than in the Dominican Republic. If the late twentieth century would be a time of reawakening, of rediscovery of African pasts and Afro-American presents elsewhere in the hemisphere, for many Dominicans, little had changed. The Haitians were still the Other. They were still spilling over from the desperately poor western third of the island of Hispaniola to the relatively more prosperous eastern two-thirds that was the Dominican Republic. North Americans still had the effrontery to call Dominicans black when they went to New York when it was clear to every sensible person that they were *Indios claros* or at worst *Indios oscuros*. But the ancient problem remained — the need to make it clear that they were different from the Haitians. Too many were coming to the Dominican Republic eagerly seeking even the backbreaking work of the Dominican sugar fields. For them it was better, infinitely better, than the alternative — near starvation in impoverished Haiti. Just as many Dominicans were seeking better lives in cities on U.S. territory, New York City on the North American mainland, or Mayagüez on the nearby island of Puerto Rico, many Haitians saw the Dominican Republic as their promised land. Prejudice against Haitians would remain high — even against Dominicans of Haitian ancestry who had been on the eastern two-thirds of the island for generations, even against those who now spoke Spanish, and had long since shed the ancestral Creole or French. Their presence made many Dominicans even more determined to deny any African ancestry. It also brought about violent attacks on Haitians, Haitian-Dominicans, and even Afro-Dominicans who appeared too dark or too "Haitian." Racial prejudice in the Dominican Republic is not simply a matter of individual bigotries. It is state policy. In 2005, the Dominican government deported some two thousand people on the grounds that they "looked Haitian." In 2011, the Dominican Supreme Court issued a ruling that in effect denied birthright citizenship to children of illegal Haitian immigrants. The ruling was partly based on a 2004 statute that made a parent's legal residence a requirement for a child's Dominican citizenship. The Dominican high court upheld an administrative regulation that applied the law retroactively, depriving a number of Haitian-Dominicans of citizenship. The change in racial attitudes that appeared to be overtaking the rest of the hemisphere seemed, at the beginning of the twenty-first century, to be occurring slowly if at all in the Dominican Republic.[19]

Traditional enmity between Haitians and Dominicans has meant that long-standing patterns of racial discrimination and racial exclusion have continued in the Dominican Republic despite new ways of thinking that have developed elsewhere in the hemisphere. The end of the Cold War and the collapse of the Soviet Union have also put Cuba out of step with the racial liberalization that has been occurring in other parts of the Americas. As was discussed in chapter 4, Cuba in the early part of the twentieth century had a history that included a fairly harsh, often confrontational pattern of race relations. The island nation for most of the twentieth century was torn between its own version of racial democracy, which included a veneration of Afro-Cuban heroes in the republic's war for independence, and a strong tradition of racial segmentation and inequality, inequality that at times included segregation in public accommodations and public places. This segregation was in part — but only in part — a reflection of the island's position as a Mecca for American tourists, many of whom insisted on U.S.-style segregation in the establishments that they frequented. With Fidel Castro's assumption of power in 1959, the government made a commitment to the elimination of racial discrimination and an equalization of social services for Cubans regardless of race. The Castro government would become increasingly identified with Afro-Cubans in part because large numbers of white Cubans would leave the island nation in the early 1960s.[20]

If the Castro government initially succeeded in lessening many of the educational, medical, and economic inequalities between whites and Afro-Cubans in the 1960s, 1970s, and 1980s, most research indicates that significant racial disparities began reappearing in the 1990s after the collapse of the Soviet Union and the elimination of its subsidies to the Castro regime. By the 1990s, the Cuban government began to turn toward foreign tourism as a way to raise hard currency for the cash-strapped island. Hotels and other enterprises catering primarily to Canadian and European tourists opened up on the island. The renewed tourist industry provided an arena for obvious and observable racial discrimination that had been largely absent in the previous three decades. Hotel managers showed a reluctance to hire Afro-Cubans, fearing that their presence would offend white tourists even though Afro-Cuban culture has traditionally been one of the island's principal attractions. There were also persistent reports that the hotels would turn away black and mulatto patrons, assuming them to be Cuban and not wanting them to mingle with white foreigners. Afro-Cuban groups have attempted to organize to protest discrimination in the tourist industry and elsewhere in Cuban society. One such group, Cofradía de la Negritud, was formed in Havana in 1999, but its effectiveness has been hampered because the Cuban government has severely restricted political organizing outside of the Communist Party.[21]

If Cuba's authoritarian regime has restricted the ability of that island's Afro-American population to organize to protest racial discrimination, Afro-Latins in other nations in the region have been better able to take advantage of relatively liberal regimes and relative political pluralism to organize against racial exclusion. Their efforts, sometimes in alliances with other marginalized populations and aided by increased scrutiny from international organizations, led a number of Latin American nations to adopt new measures designed to combat racial exclusion in the 1990s and beyond. These measures might be put into four broad, overlapping categories or approaches:

1. enacting or strengthening of antidiscrimination laws;
2. treating Afro-Americans as distinct ethnic groups, an approach some observers have called *indigenization*;

3. providing greater symbolic recognition of the role of Afro-
   Americans in the nation's past and in contemporary society; and
4. affirmative action.

The first approach, the enactment or strengthening of antidiscrimination legislation actually had had a fairly long history in the
region by the 1990s. A number of nations had long-standing provisions
prohibiting discrimination, often with problematic results. The Cuban
constitution of 1940 prohibited racial discrimination. In Venezuela in
1945, an incident occurred that was something of a preview of the more
famous Katherine Dunham affair that led to the passage of Lei Afonso
Arinos in Brazil. Todd Duncan, a black singer from the United States, was
turned away from several hotels while on a tour of the South American
nation. The incident, which was featured in *Time* magazine, embarrassed
Venezuelan authorities, who, like others in Latin America, were convinced
that their nation, unlike Duncan's home country, was free of Jim Crow–
style racial discrimination. The incident led to the passage of local and
national legislation prohibiting discrimination in public accommodations.
Costa Rica, whose Afro-American population had become quite politically
active in the effort to gain citizenship, passed legislation prohibiting racial discrimination in employment. The statute would later be amended to
provide criminal penalties for racial discrimination in public accommodations and private schools.[22]

It would be fair to say that by the close of the twentieth century a number of nations had had a reasonably good record in enacting antidiscrimination legislation and an equally poor record in making such legislation
work. Discrimination in employment and public accommodations continued largely unabated despite often noble motives in enacting legislation and seemingly stern legislative language prescribing strict penalties
for violating antidiscrimination provisions. Civil rights activists pressed
for new measures, measures that would presumably put some teeth into
antidiscrimination law. Their wishes were partly fulfilled. New statutory
and constitutional provisions proclaiming the equality of all and prohibiting discrimination became commonplace throughout the region. Like
the Brazilians, lawmakers in Spanish America have seen the field of racial
discrimination as one largely belonging to the province of criminal law.
Unfortunately, the antidiscrimination measures that have been enacted

since the 1990s have had a mixed record at best in combating the problem of racial exclusion. We will return to this issue shortly.

The enactment of constitutional provisions and statutory measures designed to prohibit racial discrimination have represented an approach to the issue of racial exclusion or racial inequality rooted in the phenomenon of race. Antidiscrimination legislation operates on the assumption that Afro-Americans are part of the general society. They fall victim to discrimination usually when their phenotype or physical appearance cues a potential employer or manager of a public accommodation who possesses a certain degree of racial animus that an applicant for a job with high public visibility or a potential patron of a restaurant, hotel, or retail shop is Afro-American. This assumption enmeshes the law and, more important, those charged with its enforcement in the often disquieting realization that different races and resulting racial barriers are indeed quite real in their societies, a realization that has traditionally been resisted in many parts of the hemisphere.

If lawmakers and other public officials have traditionally been wary of giving too much in the way of public recognition to race and racial discrimination, there has been quite a long history in Spanish America of recognizing distinctive ethnic groups. From earliest colonial times, Indian populations were recognized as being a society apart, subject to a different legal regime from the population as a whole. This separation of the Indian population would continue after independence. While whites, mestizos, Afro-Americans, and in a number of countries the children of Asian immigrants would be part of the general citizenry, theoretically indistinguishable before the law, Indians were different. They lived in distinct tribal enclaves. Spanish was often their second language, sometimes a very distant second. By the 1980s, a number of Latin American nations had enacted statutory and constitutional provisions that recognized the right of Indian groups to preserve their traditional languages, to have collective land rights, or to apply customary law to group members. Could that approach work with Afro-Latin populations? Throughout Latin America, there are Afro-American enclaves whose populations are distinctive not only for reasons of race but also for reasons of language and culture as well. We have discussed the Afro–Costa Rican population of Limón on their nation's Atlantic Coast. We could also add, among others, the English-speaking Afro-Colombian population of the island of San Andreas and the Garifuna

populations of Honduras, Nicaragua, and Guatemala, to the list of ethnically distinct Afro-American populations. The latter group have a mixture
of African and indigenous ancestry and speak a distinctive language. From
the 1980s forward, new constitutions were officially recognizing—indeed,
proclaiming—the multicultural and multiethnic character of many of the
nations in the region. These constitutions included provisions that provided for land and in some cases linguistic rights for Afro-Latin populations based on the model of collective rights that had been developed for
indigenous populations. Brazil, Colombia, Ecuador, Guatemala, Honduras,
and Nicaragua all provided constitutional and statutory protection for
lands that had historically been occupied by Afro-American populations,
usually descended from *cimarrón* or maroon ancestors.[23]

The Ecuadorian constitution of 1998 provides an interesting example of
lawmakers borrowing wholesale the national approach to the indigenous
population and applying it to the Afro-American population. The first section of Chapter 5 of that constitution is devoted to the collective rights
of the "indigenous people, blacks and Afro-Ecuadorians." Article 83 of
Section 1 recognizes the indigenous and Afro-Ecuadorian populations as
integral parts of the nation. Article 84 specifies in fourteen separate provisions the communal rights of the indigenous population, including rights
to religious, cultural, linguistic, social, and political autonomy; land rights;
and rights to natural resources, among other benefits. The first section of
Chapter 5 concludes with Article 85, which provides in one sentence that
"the State will recognize and guarantee to the black and Afro-Ecuadorian
people the rights determined in the previous article that are deemed to
be applicable." The provision appears to have involved more afterthought
than careful consideration of what applying the collective rights approach
to Ecuador's Afro-American population would actually entail.[24]

The collective rights or indigenous approach has met with relatively limited success in addressing the problems of Afro-American communities in
Spanish America. Colombia has one of the region's more far-reaching legal
frameworks designed to safeguard the collective land rights of its Afro-
American population. Like other recent constitutions, Colombia's new
charter, adopted in 1991, proclaims that the state recognizes and protects
the nation's ethnic and cultural diversity. Legislation passed in 1993 specifically protects the collective land rights of Afro-Colombians who have
traditionally lived in distinctive communities on the Pacific Coast. The

purposes of the legislation have in part been thwarted by Colombia's civil war, which has brought about the displacement of many Afro-Colombians. But even in nations not plagued by civil war, the communal rights approach has proved problematic. It affects only relatively small minorities, usually those descended from *cimarrón* communities or those of relatively recent immigrant ancestry. The much larger Afro-Latin population, those who are simply part of the general population, whether in urban or rural settings, find that their needs for redress of racial grievances remain essentially unaddressed by constitutional or statutory measures designed for ethnically distinct populations. It might be added that this is also largely true for mestizo populations who are more visibly Indian than white but who lack the cultural distinctiveness of those labeled *Indian*. They, too, are often subject to a significant amount of what might be properly termed racial discrimination, a discrimination that is not addressed by measures designed to recognize and to some extent preserve distinctive cultures.[25]

The new legal measures and governmental policies that are providing recognition for some Afro-American communities as distinctive ethnic groups with communal rights are part of a new strain of official thinking that at least on the surface rejects the notion of Europeanization or *blanqueamiento*. The move toward new constitutional language specifically recognizing the multicultural and multiethnic nature of the countries in the region is part of a new way of thinking. It shows a new willingness to recognize, at least on a symbolic level, the presence of indigenous and Afro-American populations often relegated to the margins of national consciousness in the past. Provincial sponsorship of Afro-Argentine cultural festivals; the development and inclusion of curricular materials designed to present Afro-Colombian, Afro-Ecuadorian, and Afro-Peruvian history in primary and secondary schools; or discussions by Mexican officials of the nation's "third root"; and similar developments throughout the hemisphere are a hopeful sign that the often heroic and at times lonely efforts of many Afro-Latin activists to gain recognition that they and their communities are also part of the greater society are beginning to bear fruit. Such recognition will not eradicate inequality and discrimination. It would be naive to think it would. But the activists who have pushed for this greater public recognition believe, correctly in my view, that public recognition of the Afro-American population and its very real modern presence in the

Spanish-speaking nations of the hemisphere is an essential early step in tackling the problem of racial exclusion.

Closely tied to the issue of greater public recognition are the tentative steps toward affirmative action that are being undertaken in some nations. The truly tentative and preliminary nature of these steps should be emphasized. Brazil began affirmative action programs in 2001, preceded by more than a decade of debate in academic and polemical writings concerning the constitutionality and general wisdom of such measures. It can be accurately said that the national conversation over race-based affirmative action in Spanish America is really at its most preliminary stages. The absence of a significant Afro-American presence and in many cases the absence of mestizos, who are more visibly indigenous than white, in representative numbers in institutions of higher education, the higher ranks of government service, and professional and often even minor clerical positions in the private sector are glaring reminders of strong patterns of racial exclusion throughout the hemisphere. There have been recent efforts to remedy these patterns of exclusion. Ecuador's constitution of 2008, in Article 11 guaranteeing equal rights, has language authorizing affirmative action to "promote real equality in favor of the holders of rights who are found in situations of inequality." Even prior to the enactment of the 2008 Constitution, the Universidad Iberoamericana del Ecuador announced plans to develop an affirmative action program. Officials cited provisions in the 1998 constitution, arguing that the constitutional text guaranteeing equal rights and the multicultural nature of the state provided legal justification for the new policy.[26]

Colombia has probably gone furthest in developing race-based affirmative action in universities as a working concept. Beginning in the mid-1990s with financial aid programs for Afro-Colombian students enrolled in universities, a number of universities have gone further and developed programs for affirmative action or preferential admission for Afro-Colombians. The numbers enrolled have been relatively small, and administrators involved in the program have had to sort out the not always easy question of who should be counted as an Afro-Colombian for these purposes. The Colombian approach to this problem has been to rely on Afro-Colombian community organizations to make the determination. This again raises the possibility that Afro-Colombians in distinctive ethnic enclaves such as some of the communities on the Pacific coast or the

Anglophonic residents of San Andreas potentially have an advantage denied to other Afro-Colombians who might have difficulty being certified because they lack connections to recognized Afro-Colombian community organizations. Nonetheless, there have been tentative steps in the field of higher education to recognize the importance of race and the need to provide some relief for entrenched patterns of racial exclusion. In May 2009, a commission established by the Colombian government and headed by Vice President Francisco Santos recommended an extensive system of quotas in universities, government agencies, and the armed forces designed to combat structural discrimination.[27]

In moving toward affirmative action, Colombian officials are signaling that they are learning a lesson previously learned in the United States and Brazil—that simple antidiscrimination law is often a woefully inadequate tool with which to address long-standing problems of racial inequality and racial prejudice. Antidiscrimination law in Spanish America has not proven to be a particularly robust vehicle with which to combat discrimination. Many Afro-Latin civil rights activists complain that antidiscrimination law is frequently a dead letter—present on the books but nonexistent in reality. The reasons for this are varied. In a number of countries, there is a clear conflict between the new ways of thinking that emphasize the multiracial and multiethnic nature of the different nations of the hemisphere and the older ways of thinking that see various forms of racial discrimination as a natural and reasonable response to dealing with inferior peoples.

A recent study by Peruvian legal scholar Wilfredo Ardito Vega provides an insightful discussion of the problem. Peru has had a facially comprehensive framework of national antidiscrimination legislation since the late 1990s. Discrimination in employment and public accommodations is prohibited by statute, as are racial insults. As is common in Latin America, racial discrimination is treated as a criminal offense, one that is to be prosecuted by public authorities. In 2008 and 2009, some forty municipal and provincial legislatures also passed antidiscrimination legislation, in part a reflection of frustration with the ineffective nature of the national legislation. Ardito provides a framework for understanding why Peru's civil rights legislation has provided such thin protection against discrimination. His analysis can also tell us much about the broader problem of ineffective antidiscrimination legislation in the region.[28]

Historical attitudes toward race and racial discrimination play a large part in blunting the impact of antidiscrimination law. Racial discrimination is at once denied and yet seen as something that is natural and to be expected. Traditional unwillingness to acknowledge the existence or importance of race plays a key role in this process, as does a certain comfort with hierarchy — an acceptance of the notion of betters and inferiors and that such a division of the population dictates different treatment. Ardito informs us that victims of discrimination as well as the society at large seem to be participants in this widespread acceptance and negation of racial discrimination. But the difficulties in enforcing civil rights legislation do not end with cultural attitudes toward race and racial exclusion. The mechanisms for enforcement of laws prohibiting discrimination are not robust. Ardito notes that enforcement agencies are underfinanced, that there is an absence of will to enforce antidiscrimination statutes, that an inefficient bureaucracy hampers enforcement, that victims of discrimination are reluctant to complain and be forced to relive the experience, and that the Ministerio Público's office charged with prosecuting violators charged with discrimination provides little in the way of support services for victims of discrimination and indeed is hostile and often exhibits racial prejudice itself. These conditions contribute to a regime of civil rights law far more impressive on paper than in practice.[29]

Peru's experiences with antidiscrimination law as well as those of other countries in the region raise the question of how a more robust regime of antidiscrimination law might be achieved. Some observers have suggested that international law might provide relief where national law has failed. Most of the nations of Latin America are signatories to international protocols prohibiting racial discrimination. There are cases where international tribunals have intervened in egregious cases involving discrimination. In 2005, the Inter-American Court of Human Rights intervened in a Dominican case, preventing the deportation of two girls born to Haitian parents in the Dominican Republic. But the likelihood that international human rights agencies, hampered by the necessity to defer to national law and sovereignty as well as by the logistical difficulties of getting complainants to foreign venues for hearings, make it unlikely that international bodies will be able to provide the kind of sustained and continuous pressure likely to change entrenched patterns of discriminatory behavior.[30]

The quest for a legal regime capable of providing sustained and continuous pressure likely to root out centuries-old patterns of racial exclusion is likely to be elusive. Like Brazil, Spanish America treats the problem of racial discrimination as a problem in criminal law. This approach is quite popular with Afro-Latin civil rights activists as well as public officials. It makes an important normative statement confirming society's disapproval of racism and its belief in the equality of all. But this statement can have unintended consequences. Enforcement is left in the hands of public agencies, who see the prosecution of discrimination claims as a lower priority than their other concerns, including the often high rates of violent crime in the region. Criminal sanctions for discrimination also produce cases where judges are reluctant to convict. The law is placed on the books, but it frequently becomes effectively meaningless. It is part of a broader issue of the problematic nature of the rule of law in the region, a rule or unrule of law that can leave significant and at times even expected gaps between the law as it is stated and as it is actually applied.[31]

And yet if the criminal law is unlikely to produce the kind of sustained pressure that can reverse long-established patterns of racial exclusion, civil remedies seem unlikely to fill the void. The private attorney general who for considerations of profit or commitment to a cause brings cases that help enforce constitutional or civil rights norms is largely unknown in Latin America. That private attorney general — hero to some, pest to others — is sustained in the United States by a number of procedural mechanisms that encourage private litigants to bring suits that arguably redound to the public good. These mechanisms include contingency fees in suits involving private wrongs, attorneys' fees in suits involving violations of civil or constitutional rights, and class-action suits prosecuted by private parties. All of these possibilities played a role in buttressing the legal revolution that was the civil rights movement in the United States. These mechanisms are largely foreign to the legal systems of Latin America, and their wholesale importation is open to question. Changes, effective measures to fight racial exclusion, seem more likely to come from policy initiatives such as requirements for race- and class-based affirmative action measures in education and employment than effective judicial remedies stemming from antidiscrimination legislation.[32]

And it is that quest for effective measures to fight racial exclusion that will do much to shape the future of Afro-Americans in the Spanish-speaking nations of the hemisphere. There has been a new awakening in Spanish America, a new awareness that race shapes and all too often limits the lives of peoples who have long called the Americas home. This new awakening is helping to bring forth new efforts to combat long entrenched patterns of exclusion and discrimination. These new efforts are not perfect. They are being attempted in political and legal systems that have had an often troubled history of translating noble ideals into effective laws and policies. They are taking place in nations long accustomed to steep social hierarchies and encrusted notions of betters and inferiors. Much of the recent legislation designed to fight discrimination is flawed, with inadequate attention given to practical problems of enforcement. But the new awakening is nonetheless real. It has attracted the attention of national leaders. Slowly the old comforting certitudes of racial democracy and cosmic races are being shed, supplanted by new realism concerning race and its importance in the lives of many Latin Americans. Whether or not that new realism can overcome older legacies, legacies that encouraged silence on the troubling question of race, remains to be seen.

Epilogue

THE QUESTION OF HOW BEST TO ADDRESS enduring legacies of racial exclusion is not confined to the Spanish-speaking nations of the hemisphere. It is the problem of race in the Americas in the twenty-first century. The answer is by no means clear, and even our preceding discussion of race and law in the history of the Americas provides us with no sure-footed guide to the future. That history has been filled with ironies and unintended consequences, paths not taken and opportunities missed. The law can be a clumsy, often imprecise tool. At times it has produced exactly the opposite of what it was intended to achieve. Seemingly rigid and meticulous systems of *casta* categories were carefully crafted into the codes of Spain's American colonies. They were designed to rigorously separate the empire's subject peoples. Nonetheless, these fine *casta* categories played a role in producing an ideology of racial mobility, a belief, still present in much of the hemisphere, that individuals can and should strive to improve their racial status in their lifetimes or in the lifetimes of their children. The Jim Crow legislation of the American South gave African Americans a clear target against which to mobilize. That mobilization produced a civil rights revolution that transformed the United States and has been studied and copied throughout the hemisphere and indeed the world.

But unintended consequences or not, the role of law in constructing the racial order was clearest when the law specifically prescribed legal disabilities for people of African descent. Slavery was an example of such, as were statutes and judicial decisions limiting the rights of free people of color during slave regimes. Jim Crow legislation in the American South and racially restrictive immigration policies throughout the Americas were also illustrations of the law's commitment to the effort to build nations based on a belief in white supremacy. The law was mobilized in service of a hope — the hope that Afro-Americans would either disappear or be relegated to the outermost margins of national existence. The law could also show the opposite inclination. The hemisphere's first emancipation, which began in the northern states of the United States in the wake of the American war for independence, was an early example of that opposite inclination, as were the antislavery constitutions and proclamations of universal citizenship drafted in the young republics that succeeded the Spanish Empire. The Civil War amendments in the United States and the ultimate triumph of abolition in Brazil also furnish convincing evidence that the champions of equality under the law also had their triumphs in the legal history of the American hemisphere. The significant victories of the American civil rights movement after the Second World War, the adoption of strong provisions against racism in the Brazilian constitution, Brazilian jurist Ricardo Lewandowski's opinions in 2012 recognizing the constitutionality of affirmative action, and the enactment of antidiscrimination legislation throughout the hemisphere provide room for cautious optimism that we have turned a corner or at the very least a page. The law will no longer be what it historically all too often was, an overt tool of oppression, a device that would mandate or at least facilitate a system of racial subordination. Instead, new legislation, constitutional provisions, court decisions, and governmental policies give reason to believe that the law will help dismantle the system of racial hierarchy that it did so much to create.

But how will the law go about that task? And to what extent should the law take notice of race as it attempts to go about the business of trying to dismantle deeply rooted patterns of racial inequality? Should the law give Afro-Americans and other long disfavored groups a compensating preference in employment or university admissions? Should legislation or constitutional provisions reserve spaces in national or regional legislatures for racial groups that for a long time were as a matter of law, or as a matter of fact, excluded from the political process? Should legislative districts be drawn up so that long-disfavored minorities constitute a majority in at least some political districts, increasing the likelihood that some will be found among a nation's elected representatives? Is it advisable to require employers to keep statistical records of their employees by race? Should governments even be in the business of counting by race? Does counting by race mean that the government must engage in the distasteful and potentially dangerous business of defining race, determining what quantum of African, European, or indigenous heritage makes an individual black, white, Indian, or mestizo?

These are hard questions without particularly easy answers. Some students of the subject argue that the law should simply get out of the business of race altogether. They would perhaps agree that the state should have laws prohibiting discrimination, prescribing appropriate civil and criminal penalties for acts involving racial discrimination or racially motivated assault, but no more. Constant racial scorekeeping, numerical breakdowns, ministries of health, education, labor and what have you attempting to categorize the population and determine statistical imbalances among different groups are futile and perhaps even dangerous tasks. Aren't such efforts taking us further and further from where we ultimately want to go, to a color-blind society where individuals are judged on their merit and not on their skin color or ancestry? Opponents of race-conscious measures in Latin America frequently argue that such policies might perhaps be necessary in the United States, with the North American nation's history of legislated racial discrimination, but that they are inappropriate in Latin America, where the law didn't play a formal role in mandating racial discrimination and where the population is so mixed that separating people into different racial categories is difficult and indeed perhaps impossible. Such opposition is not confined to Latin America. Conservative commentators in the United States frequently remind us that race-conscious measures seem far removed from the ideal expressed by Martin Luther King Jr. in his 1963 address to the March on Washington. Opponents of affirmative action readily note that the civil rights leader expressed the hope that one day his children would live in a nation where they would be judged "not by the color of their skin but by the content of their character."[1]

I would disagree with those who argue that the law should simply ignore race. Too much damage has been done in the past. It is not unreasonable to believe that a nation's laws and public policies should play a major part in undoing deeply entrenched patterns of racial exclusion, patterns of racial exclusion that they did so much to help create in the past. Some five centuries of slavery and legally mandated or sanctioned racial exclusion have left deep marks on the Afro-American peoples of the Western Hemisphere. Traditional assertions of African and Afro-American inferiority — long repeated, amplified, and given an official imprimatur in government reports and judicial decisions, common school textbooks and university treatises and further reinforced in the public mind through novels and films, popular songs and folk sayings — have left their mark. They have contributed to popular assumptions concerning the inferiority of peoples of African descent that are often hard for even the most well meaning of people to shake off. Indeed, many individuals of African descent have also internalized these beliefs and strive hard to shed any trace of an Afro-American identity. The broader culture, backed by law and public policy, has for centuries sent a message asserting the inferiority of peoples of African descent. It is reasonable to expect that that message still affects the thoughts and behavior of Afro-Americans and non-Afro-Americans throughout the hemisphere.

That message continues to promote inequality even after the passage of antidiscrimination legislation and, yes, even after the genuine liberalization of racial attitudes. And it is not just persisting prejudice that thwarts the effort to combat racial exclusion. Very real structural barriers also stand in the way of genuine equal opportunity. Throughout the hemisphere, Afro-American children are more likely to attend underfunded schools that ill prepare them either for the workplace or to be competitive in university admissions. They are more likely to grow up in homes with low incomes, poor access to health and social services, and inadequate nutrition. There are often expectations that Afro-American children leave school as early as possible in order to augment the family's low income levels. Such conditions are often accompanied by less stable families and in many cases less of a family history of steady work in the more desirable sectors of the economy. Afro-Americans as young adults routinely begin their experience in the workforce with less in the way of human capital — education, skills, training, and familial connections — than others, ensuring that previous experiences with social and economic exclusion will continue. These problems are, of course, not limited to people of African ancestry in the Americas. They plague the poor throughout the hemisphere, particularly in nations where educational and employment opportunities have traditionally been limited for the children of the poor. But the burdens of poverty often fall harder on Afro-Americans, who must contend with traditionally restricted avenues of upward mobility in their societies, combined with the very real additional burdens of racial prejudice.

Public policies that take race into account are critical in fighting the legacy of racial exclusion that still haunts the nations of the Americas. Such measures have to be combined with a jurisprudence from the courts that recognizes that while constitutional provisions proclaiming the equality of all before the law do indeed apply to all, to the heirs of slave owners and slaves, to the descendants of dispossessed Indians and victorious conquistadors alike, such provisions should be read with a sensitivity to a nation's history and the heritage of inequality embedded in that history. That level of balance and sensitivity has not been achieved by any judicial system in the Americas to date. The United States, which has done the most to date with using race-conscious measures to combat legacies of exclusion, has done so with a jurisprudence from the nation's Supreme Court that has shown a marked reluctance to allow race-conscious policies to be based on a broad compensatory rationale. We can see this in the field of affirmative action. In university admissions as well as in governmental employment and the engaging of contractors, the court has rejected the notion that governmental entities have a legitimate role to play in remedying patterns of discrimination that were broadly and systematically engaged in by the American nation as a whole. In the field of government contracting and employment, the Court has permitted affirmative action only as a fairly narrow measure to remedy past discrimination previously engaged in by a particular governmental entity. The Court's jurisprudence with respect to admissions to public universities has been even further removed from the notion that broad compensatory measures are justified in an attempt to remedy systemic exclusion in the nation's history. Affirmative action in public universities has survived on the grounds that such measures provide for a diverse student body that enhances the overall educational mission of a university. Minority students are permitted to be at most only incidental beneficiaries in this process.[2]

The U.S. Supreme Court's reading of the demands of the Fourteenth Amendment's Equal Protection Clause in the affirmative action cases has produced a cramped although not altogether unjustifiable jurisprudence. It is an approach rooted in orthodox notions of formal equality under the law. Nonetheless, if the American approach has been cramped, if the judicial imprimatur for race-conscious measures has been thin and grudging, the use of race-conscious measures as a tool to attempt to redress historical and ongoing wrongs has made a significant difference in the lives of an important portion of the African American population over the last forty years.

But acknowledging that race-conscious policies and a jurisprudence that has, grudgingly or not, permitted those policies have made an important difference in the recent history of race in the United States is not the same as saying that such policies or a supporting jurisprudence will be easy to achieve in Latin America. The difficulties will be many. Race-conscious measures in the United States were made possible in part because of a long-standing common agreement that we knew who was black and who was white. The agreement may have been irrational; indeed, at its outer limits — the one drop rule — it was downright silly, but there was an agreed upon definition. Individuals were placed on one side or another of a fairly rigid black/white divide, advantaged or disadvantaged depending on which side of the line they had been placed. Can the nations of Latin America, with their more flexible definitions of race, their complicated racial alchemies that bring forth an often bewildering brew of phenotype, ancestry, class, culture, and familial connections in an effort to produce racial classification — can they come up with effective and meaningful efforts at race-conscious policies? Will those policies be effective at at least partially breaking down traditional patterns of racial exclusion? And will they be able to do so in societies that have traditionally had somewhat problematic records in providing possibilities for upward mobility and the elimination of social barriers for their populations as a whole?

The answers to these questions are not entirely clear. Brazil's Supremo Tribunal Federal issued a bold, possibly far-reaching decision supporting race-based affirmative action in April 2012. The Brazilian congress passed legislation mandating affirmative action programs for public universities in August 2012. Nonetheless, it is still too early to tell how many public universities will adopt effective affirmative action measures and the extent to which such measures can overcome strong structural inequalities in Brazilian life. The South American nation has developed a seemingly comprehensive framework of antidiscrimination legislation, but it has also had a history of problematic enforcement of such legislation due in no small measure to weak enforcement by public agencies and a not particularly effective judicial system. The difficulties in developing a robust regime of antidiscrimination law in Brazil are magnified severalfold in other parts of Latin America. Robust legislation and governmental policies designed to root out deeply embedded patterns of discrimination and inequality are rare in many of the Spanish-speaking nations of the hemisphere. Such policies are inhibited by a lack of basic information about the racial composition of national populations and the relative well-being or disadvantage of different racial groups. There is still, despite significant changes in recent years, a strong reluctance in many Latin American nations to acknowledge that racial discrimination is even a real issue, one that poses often formidable barriers in the lives of many people. Even the willingness to formally acknowledge that race exists and that wealth and privilege and poverty and disadvantage are frequently correlated with race is problematic in many parts of the hemisphere.

And it is not clear how long the movement for racial justice in the United States can rely on race-conscious measures in the effort to remedy the nation's legacy of racial injustice. Such measures have only survived with a somewhat tenuous warrant from the nation's judiciary. A forthcoming case, *Fisher v. University of Texas*, may very well end even the slim judicial support that affirmative action has had since *Bakke*. But it is not just their precarious legal status that portends a cloudy future for such policies. The old American consensus concerning racial definition is beginning to fray around the edges and perhaps more than around the edges. That consensus had historically produced a rigid separation of the races in the United States that was unique in the Americas. It also, over the last forty years, helped produce civil rights gains unmatched elsewhere in the hemisphere. But will that once common agreement that we knew who was black and who was white and that we could fashion race-conscious laws and policies — first for ill, later for good — survive the sociology and politics of race as it is emerging in the twenty-first century? Or are racial definition and racial identity in the United States beginning to resemble traditional patterns in Latin America, with ancestry and phenotype being but partial components of a much more complex process of racial determination, a process that also takes into account class, education, and cultural presentation?

In a very real sense the considerable successes of the American civil rights movement have been something of a two-edged sword. Barriers have fallen. Large numbers of African Americans have entered the middle and in some cases upper classes. Overt, categorical discrimination has largely become a thing of the past. Most spectacularly the nation has even elected a black president, Barack Obama. All of this has prompted a number of commentators to say that the day of race in America is over, that we have entered a new postracial phase in the nation's history. This understandable desire to bid farewell to the nation's troubled racial past has been partly reflected in the two most recent censuses. The instructions for both the 2000 and 2010 censuses allowed individuals to check off more than one racial category. This new development, something of a retreat from the nation's traditional one drop formulation and one that was not entirely pleasing to many African American activists, reflects a view held by many social commentators that a more nuanced approach to racial identification, one that reflects the multiracial character of many who traditionally would have simply been labeled black will ultimately help to break down racial barriers. Increasing rates of intermarriage and births of mixed-race children also help fuel the belief that the old binary divide of black and white is no longer viable in modern America. Immigration also calls the traditional binary divide and the possibility of race-conscious remedies into question. As new groups are added to the American racial and ethnic mix, should they be part of our efforts to develop race-conscious measures to combat continuing inequality? How should we handle the question of racial classification for immigrants from Latin American societies, societies with quite different histories of making racial determinations? These developments will all call into sharp question our ability to craft legislation and policies in the future that take race into account.

But race is still with us. Structural inequality and prejudice persist despite very real change and very real progress. There is an unwillingness on the part of many in Latin America and in the United States as well to recognize that we cannot write our laws or craft our policies on a blank slate. The past has left us with burdens to be lifted, wrongs to be set right. Doing so will require us to recognize that the legacies of more than five centuries of slavery and oppression cannot be rapidly undone with ringing proclamations announcing the equality of all or even with well-intentioned statutes declaring racial discrimination unlawful. The effort to undo the legacy of the past will take us on a difficult path. It is a journey the peoples of the American hemisphere must complete, the still unfinished journey from emancipation to equality.

Notes

INTRODUCTION

1. Tannenbaum, *Slave and Citizen*.

2. Skocpol, "Sociology's Historical Imagination."

3. Klein, *Atlantic Slave Trade*, 216–17; Bergad, García, and Barcia, *Cuban Slave Market*, 38.

4. Any discussion of Afro-Mexican studies should acknowledge the pioneering efforts of Mexican anthropologist Gonzalo Aguirre Beltrán, whose work in the 1940s and 1950s did much to lay the foundation for the field. See Beltrán, *Población negra*; Beltrán, *Cuijla*. For a recent anthology that includes valuable essays by historians and anthropologists working on Afro-Mexican themes, see Vinson and Restall, *Black Mexico*.

5. Persinal, *Presencia negra*, esp. 1–11; Pichardo, *Sobre racismo y antihaitianismo*, esp. 75–99.

6. Fuente, "Myths of Racial Democracy," 43–49.

7. Watson, *Slave Law in the Americas*.

8. Cortés López, *Esclavitud negra*, 89–91; Mauro, *Le Portugal, le Brésil, et l'Atlantique*, 165–66.

9. For a comprehensive look at slavery as a phenomenon in world history, see Patterson, *Slavery and Social Death*.

10. Andrews, *Afro-Latin America*, 55–86.

11. See generally Cottrol, "Long Lingering Shadow."

12. Brazilian historian Keila Grinberg gives us an impressive portrait of a free Afro-Brazilian of mixed racial background, Antonio Pereira Rebouças, who rose to prominence in the worlds of law and politics in the Brazilian Empire of the nineteenth century. See Keila Grinberg, *O Fiador dos Brasileiros: Cidadania, Escravidão e Direito Civil no Tempo de Antonio Pereira Rebouças*, (Rio de Janeiro: Civilização Brasileira, 2002).

13. Cottrol, "*Brown* and the Contemporary Brazilian Struggle," 123–27.

14. Friedman, *History of American Law* (1973), 10.

15. Lei No. 1.390 de Julho de 1951. Lei Afonso Arinos was Brazil's first national civil rights statute. It prohibited discrimination in public accommodations and other areas of Brazilian life.

16. Patterson, *Ordeal of Integration*, xi.

CHAPTER ONE. *Casta y Color, Movilidad y Ambigüedad*

1. Klein, *Atlantic Slave Trade*, 216–17.
2. "Desconocida comunidad Chileno-Africana."
3. Aguirre Beltrán, "Oposición de raza y cultura," 52–54.
4. Andrews, *Afro-Argentines*, 82–83; Fuente, "Myths of Racial Democracy."
5. David Brion Davis, *Problem of Slavery in Western Culture*, 42–46; Cortés López, *Esclavitud negra*, 15–16; Marzal Palacios, "Esclavitud en Valencia," 176–79.
6. *Siete partidas del Rey Don Alfonso.*
7. Ibid.; Tannenbaum, *Slave and Citizen*; Watson, *Slave Law in the Americas.*
8. *Siete partidas*, Part 4, Title 21, Law 2, 118, Part 4, Title 15, Law 4, 89. See also Berman's discussion of the humanizing influence of canonical law on Roman family law, the law of slavery, and other areas in *Law and Revolution*, 168–69.
9. *Siete partidas*, Part 4, Title 21, Law 6, Part 4, Title 22, Law 4, 120, 123.
10. Ibid., Title 22, Laws 2, 3, 122, 123.
11. Ibid., Laws 8, 9, 124–26.
12. Lane, "Captivity and Redemption."
13. Cortés López, *Esclavitud negra*, 72–75.
14. Sánchez-Albornoz, "Population of Colonial Spanish America," 19; Gibson, "Indian Societies," 401–9; Florescano, "Formation and Economic Structure," 169–71.
15. Lane, "Captivity and Redemption"; Consejo de Indias, *Recopilación*, Laws 1, 2, 6, 195.
16. Restall, "Black Conquistadors"; Herrera, "'Por Que No Sabemos Firmar,'" 259; Vinson, "Racial Profile."
17. Bennett, *Africans in Colonial Mexico*, 8–9, 51–78.
18. Schávelzon, *Buenos Aires negra*, 83.
19. Lokken, "Marriage as Slave Emancipation"; Hünefeldt, *Paying the Price*, 147–48; Consejo de Indias, *Recopilación*, Laws 2, 8, 188–89.
20. Aguirre Beltrán, *Población*, 176–77.
21. Ibid., 153–54.
22. Aguirre, *Breve historia*, 43–45; Helg, *Liberty and Equality*, 7–8, 67–68, 100–105.
23. Cope, *Limits of Racial Domination*, 49–57.
24. Almarza Villalobos, "Limpieza de sangre."
25. See Weber's discussion of the use of "ideal types" as a vehicle for clarifying comparative social research in *Economy and Society*, 20–22.
26. Watson, *Roman Slave Law*, 2–6, 23–34; Hopkins, "Novel Evidence."
27. Watson, *Roman Slave Law*, 2–6.

28. See "Resources and 'Knowledges' of a Litigant Slave Woman in the Spanish Colonial Courts: Guayaquil at the End of the Eighteenth Century," and "Slave Women's Strategies for Freedom and the Late Colonial State," both in Chaves, "Honor y libertad." See also Chaves, *María Chiquinquirá Díaz*.

29. McKinley, "Fractional Freedoms"; Fuente, "Slaves and the Creation of Legal Rights"; Lyman L. Johnson, "'Lack of Legitimate Obedience and Respect'"; Gallego, *Derecho y justicia*, 26–29.

30. Aguirre, *Breve historia*, 37–40; Helg, *Liberty and Equality*, 112–15.

31. Blanchard, "Language of Liberation."

32. Rout, *African Experience*, 212, 279.

33. Aguirre, *Breve historia*, 128–50; Helg, *Liberty and Equality*, 7–8, 22–36.

34. Helg, *Liberty and Equality*, 163–67. See also Lasso, *Myths of Harmony*.

35. Peruvian Constitution, 1823, Section 1, Chapter 4, Articles 10, 11, 17; Aguirre, *Breve historia*, 159–71, 245.

36. Klein, *Atlantic Slave Trade*, 40–41, 202, 216–17; Bergad, García, and Barcia, *Cuban Slave Market*, 25–33.

37. Knight, *Slave Society*, 95–101; Scott, *Slave Emancipation in Cuba*, 8–10.

38. Scott, *Slave Emancipation in Cuba*, 45–62, 63–83, 127–71.

CHAPTER TWO. *Terra de Nosso Senhor*

1. Araújo, "Textualidades do Brasil," 3–5.

2. Klein, *Atlantic Slave Trade*, 216–17.

3. Saunders, *Social History*, 4–11.

4. Mauro, *Le Portugal, le Brésil, et l'Atlantique*, 164–66; *Código Filipino*, 5:1218.

5. Mauro, *Le Portugal, le Brésil, et L'Atlantique*, 165; David Brion Davis, *Slavery and Human Progress*, esp. 51–62.

6. Mauro, *Le Portugal, le Brésil, et L'Atlantique*, 167–71.

7. Ibid.

8. Thornton, *Africa and Africans*, 53–57, 59–60; Amantino, "Mundo das feras," 85–90.

9. Amantino, "Mundo das feras," 90–93.

10. O'Brien, "Crime and Punishment"; *Código Filipino*, 1:xxvi; Campos, "Nas barras das tribunais," 65–67.

11. Merrick and Graham, *Population and Economic Development*, 29–30; Moura, *Rebeliões da senzala*, 205–20; Marquese, "A dinâmica da escravidão," 107–8.

12. Brazilian diplomat and historian Alberto da Costa e Silva notes that ties between Angola and Brazil were so strong that when Brazil became independent in 1822, officials in both Angola and Brazil considered having Brazil annex Angola

to create a South Atlantic empire. See Alberto da Costa e Silva, *Rio chamado Atlântico*, 12, 32, 54; Joseph C. Miller, *Way of Death*, 445–531.

13. Reis, *Slave Rebellion in Brazil*; Campos, "Nas barras dos tribunais," 18.

14. See generally Durkheim, *Rules of Sociological Method*, 65–75; Erikson, *Wayward Puritans*; Russell-Wood, *Portuguese Empire*, 72; *Codigo Filipino*, 4:1045–47.

15. Russell-Wood, *Portuguese Empire*, 31.

16. *Código Filipino*, 4:863.

17. Boxer, *Golden Age of Brazil*, 164–67; Lewin, *Surprise Heirs*, 20–22, 102.

18. Marquese, "A dinâmica da escravidão," 109–11.

19. Nabuco, *Abolicionismo*, 102; Emília Viotti da Costa, *Brazilian Empire*, 7–23.

20. *Diário da assembléia*, Book 1, Vol. 1, Diário 3 (May 3, 1823), 17–19.

21. Ibid., Diário 21 (June 7, 1823), 177–79.

22. Ibid., Book 3, Vol. 2, Diário 10 (September 30, 1823), 133–40.

23. Ibid., Book 1, Vol. 1, Diário 28 (June 19, 1823), 249.

24. Ibid., Book 3, Vol. 2, Diário 7 (September 23, 1823), 90–93, Diário 10 (September 30, 1823), 132–36.

25. Emília Viotti da Costa, *Brazilian Empire*, 58–62.

26. Grinberg, *Fiador dos Brasileiros*, 153–54, 174, 201–2.

27. Ibid., 24–30, 153–54, 201–2; Emília Viotti da Costa, *Brazilian Empire*, 132–39, 181–201.

28. Grinberg, *Fiador dos Brasileiros*, 24–26, 69–78, 102–3, 153–54, 186, 201–2, 238–42.

29. Ibid.

30. *Código Filipino*, 4:863–66.

31. Grinberg, *Fiador dos Brasileiros*, 108–9, 117–18.

32. Afro-Brazilian legal scholar Eunice Prudente notes that Brazilian slaveholders were quite successful at using the constitution's provision protecting private property as a tool to fend off abolitionist attacks. See Prudente, *Preconceito racial e igualdade*, 30–31; Brazilian Constitution, 1824, Title 8, Article 179, xxii.

33. Emília Viotti da Costa, *Da monarquia à república*, 61–69, 87–88; Nabuco, *Abolicionismo*, 105, 182.

34. Elciene Azevedo, "Direito dos escravos," 15, 74–89.

35. Grinberg, *Fiador dos Brasileiros*, 216–39.

36. Klein and Luna, *Slavery in Brazil*, 253–54.

37. Elciene Azevedo, "Direito dos escravos," 28, 34–35, and 43–48.

38. Lei No. 2040 de 28 de setembro de 1871; Nabuco, *Abolicionismo*, 53–54.

39. Scisínio, *Dicionário da escravidão*, 21–22.

40. Nabuco, *Abolicionismo*, 69–73.

41. Ibid., 82–83.

42. Klein and Luna, *Slavery in Brazil*, 295–319.

CHAPTER THREE. Race, Democracy, and Inequality

1. See Graber, *Dred Scott*; Finkelman, "Was Dred Scott Correctly Decided?"

2. *Dred Scott v. Sandford*, 417.

3. Genovese, "Treatment of Slaves," 202–10.

4. J. H. Baker, *Introduction to English Legal History*, 536.

5. Catterall, *Judicial Cases*, 9; *Somersett v. Stewart*, 20 How. St. Tr. 1 (1772).

6. J. H. Baker, *Introduction to English Legal History*, 540–41.

7. Blackstone, *Commentaries*, 411–13.

8. See Dunn, *Sugar and Slaves*.

9. Friedman, *History of American Law*, 3rd ed., 3–16.

10. Ibid.

11. Cottrol, *Afro-Yankees*, 13–14; Breen and Innes, *"Myne Owne Ground"*; Higginbotham, *In the Matter of Color*, 36–37.

12. Galenson, "Settlement and Growth," 173–75. See also Wood, *Black Majority*.

13. Steinfeld, *Invention of Free Labor*, 15–54.

14. Cottrol, *Afro-Yankees*, 18–20; Lois E. Horton, "From Class to Race," 629–34; James Oliver Horton and Horton, *Slavery and the Making of America*, 40–41.

15. Berlin, *Generations of Captivity*, 36–39.

16. Jordan, *White over Black*; Philip D. Morgan, *Slave Counterpoint*, 2–3.

17. Edmund S. Morgan, *American Slavery, American Freedom*, 327–37.

18. Tucker, "Note H," 58; Higginbotham and Kopytoff, "Racial Purity and Interracial Sex."

19. Tucker, "Note H," 45–46, 56–60; McManus, *Black Bondage*, 90–91.

20. Philip D. Morgan, *Slave Counterpoint*, 11–13.

21. Wood, *Black Majority*, 124–26.

22. David Brion Davis, *Inhuman Bondage*, 127–30; Hoffer, *Great New York Conspiracy*, 159–64.

23. McManus, *Black Bondage*, 149–50; Cottrol and Diamond, "Second Amendment," 325–27; Greene, *Negro in Colonial New England*, 294–97, 303; Higginbotham, *In the Matter of Color*, 85.

24. Higginbotham, *In the Matter of Color*, 48.

25. Ibid., 293–99.

26. Berlin, *Generations of Captivity*, 103–4; Newman, *List of Black Servicemen*. War Department records indicate that although the northern states had only 10 percent of the nation's black population, they furnished 75 percent of the Continental Army's black soldiers.

27. Higginbotham, *In the Matter of Color*, 49, 372.

28. See, e.g., *Commonwealth v. Jennison*; Goldin, "Economics of Emancipation," 67–68.

29. Tucker, "Note H," 66; Whitman, *Price of Freedom*, 63–69.

30. Tucker, "Note H," 31.

31. Ibid., 78.

32. Ibid., 56–58.

33. Cottrol, "Law, Politics, and Race," 504–5.

34. Bogen, "Maryland Context of Dred Scott," 383–85, 388–400.

35. Berlin, *Slaves without Masters*, 91; Genovese, *Roll, Jordan, Roll*, 398–412; Shugg, "Negro Voting."

36. *Dred Scott v. Sandford*, 572–76.

37. 1 Stat. 271 (1792); Wesley, "Negro's Struggle," 64–66.

38. Morris, *Southern Slavery*, 170–74. Laura Edwards's research suggests that being within the law's peace often provided protection for slaves despite limitations on slave testimony; see Edwards, "Status without Rights."

39. Berlin, *Slaves without Masters*, 347–49.

40. Kawashima, "Adoption in Early America."

41. Atack and Passell, *New Economic View*, 300–303; Fogel and Engerman, *Time on the Cross*, 86–89; Gavin Wright, *Political Economy*, 13–15; Fogel, *Without Consent or Contract*, 35, 41–42, 107–9.

42. James Hammond, "'Mud-Sill' Speech," in *Slavery Defended*, ed. McKitrick, 121–25; Fredrickson, *Black Image*, 78.

43. Berlin, *Slaves without Masters*, 79–107, 138–41; Fredrickson, *Black Image*, 50–51; Stampp, *Peculiar Institution*, 215–17.

44. See Cole, "Capitalism and Freedom."

45. *Heirn v. Bridault and Wife*, 232–33.

46. Ford, "Making the 'White Man's Country' White," 731–34.

47. Gross, *What Blood Won't Tell*, 1–72.

48. Curry, *Free Black in Urban America*, 19–22, 90–92, 147–73; James Oliver Horton and Horton, *Black Bostonians*, 70–76; Cottrol, "Law, Politics, and Race," 520.

49. Cottrol, "Law, Politics, and Race," 503–5; Finkelman, "Prelude to the Fourteenth Amendment," 424–25.

50. *Hobbs et al. v. Fogg*, 558; Winch, *Philadelphia's Black Elite*, 138–42.

51. Fox, "Negro Vote," 254, 256–62; Strum, "Property Qualifications," 357–63.

52. Foner, *Free Soil, Free Labor, Free Men*, 230–31, 237–40; *Roberts v. City of Boston*, 59 Mass. 198 (1850); *Plessy v. Ferguson*, 163 U.S. 537 (1896); *Brown v. Board of Education*, 347 U.S. 483 (1954).

53. Field, *Politics of Race*, 85–113, 126–47, 61–63.

54. Ibid.; Benson, *Concept of Jacksonian Democracy*, 166, 179–80.

55. See Finkelman, "Prelude to the Fourteenth Amendment."

56. *Dred Scott v. Sandford*, 407–8.

57. Ibid., 572–76.

58. See Maltz, "Unlikely Hero"; Stampp, "Comment on Earl Maltz."

59. Confederate States of America Constitution, Article 1, Section 9, Clause 4, in Lee, *Confederate Constitutions*, 171–200; Stephens, "Cornerstone Speech," 717–29.

CHAPTER FOUR. *Blanqueamiento*

1. Kinigsberg, "Mujer denunció."

2. Castro, *Afro-Argentine*, 2.

3. Andrews, *Blackness in the White Nation*, 2–4; Cottrol, "Beyond Invisibility," 139–40.

4. Martínez-Echazábal, "Mestizaje and the Discourse of National/Cultural Identity," 23–24; Carroll and Lamb, "Mexicanos negros."

5. Winthrop R. Wright, *Café con Leche*, 2, 62, 65, 78; Soto Quirós, "Desafinidad con la población nacional," 2, 4; Bronfman, *Measures of Equality*, esp. 6–7, 23–41; Fuente, *Nation for All*, 74–76.

6. Fuente, *Nation for All*, 6–10.

7. Helg, "Race in Argentina and Cuba," 37–38.

8. Stepan, *Hour of Eugenics*, 27–28; García Jordán, "Reflexiones."

9. Andrews, *Afro-Argentines*, 47–49, 57.

10. Schávelzon, *Buenos Aires negra*, 6–8; Andrews, *Afro-Argentines*, 91, 113–37.

11. Andrews, *Afro-Argentines*, 91, 113–37; Andrews, *Afro-Latin America*, 136.

12. Argentine Constitution, 1853, Article 25.

13. Andrews, *Blackness in the White Nation*, 8; Castro, *Afro-Argentine*, 2.

14. Andrews, *Afro-Argentines*, 83–87; Frigerio, "Candombe Argentino."

15. Cottrol, "Beyond Invisibility," 140–42. See, e.g., Chamosa, "Indigenous or Criollo."

16. Argentine researcher and historian M. Cristina de Liboreiro is of the opinion that the Afro-Uruguayan and Afro-Argentine populations are basically of similar size, a view she expressed to me in a conversation in 2006. In a study she published in 1999, she placed the Afro-Argentine population at 150,000. See Liboreiro, *No hay negros argentinos?*, 47.

17. Andrews, *Blackness in the White Nation*, 2–6, 22–23.

18. Ibid., 38–42.

19. Castro, *Afro-Argentine*, 114–19; Cáceres, *Tango negro*.

20. Monkevicius and Maffia, "Memoria y límites étnicos"; Rout, *African Experience*, 366; Solomianski, *Identidades secretas*, 231–32.

21. See, e.g., Helg, "Black Men, Racial Stereotyping, and Violence"; Sanchez, "Black Mosaic," 21–23.

22. Rodríguez Pastor, *Herederos del dragón*.

23. Bonfiglio, *Presencia europea*, 11–33, 44–47.

24. Cuche, *Poder blanco y resistencia negra*, 37, 68, 103–6.

25. Ibid., 147; Sanchez, "Black Mosaic," 34.

26. Sanchez, "Black Mosaic," 44–45.

27. Ibid., 27–30.

28. Haak, "Raza y etnicidad."

29. Andrews, *Afro-Latin America*, 140.

30. Panamanian Constitution, 1941, Title 2, Articles 12–14; Pearcy, "Panama's Generation of '31," 696, 704–8.

31. Putnam, "Eventually Alien"; Senior Angulo, "Incorporación social," 145–46.

32. Putnam, "Eventually Alien," 289; Senior Angulo, "Incorporación social," 153–63, 145–46.

33. Harpelle, "Social and Political Integration," 104, 111.

34. Turits, "World Destroyed."

35. Sánchez-Albornoz, *Population of Latin America*, 167.

36. Bronfman, *Measures of Equality*, 67–117.

37. Pignot, "Asociacionismo negro en Cuba," 841–42.

38. Fuente, *Nation for All*, 27, 36–40.

39. Helg, "Black Men, Racial Stereotyping, and Violence," 586–87.

40. Chomsky "'Barbados or Canada?,'" 427–30; Helg, "Black Men, Racial Stereotyping, and Violence," 586–87.

41. Fuente, "Race and Inequality," 146–56; Moreno Vega, "Interlocking African Diaspora Cultures."

42. Whitney, "Architect of the Cuban State"; Cuban Constitution, 1940, Title 4, Article 20, Title 7, Article 102.

43. Daniel J. Davis, "Nationalism and Civil Rights," 39–41; Fuente, "Race and Inequality," 155–57.

44. Wade, *Blackness and Race Mixture*, 295–97.

45. Andrews, *Afro-Latin America*, 158–60.

CHAPTER FIVE. *No País do Futuro*

1. Prudente, *Preconceito racial*, 129–31.

2. Cottrol, "Long Lingering Shadow," 13, esp. n. 4.

3. Oliven, "A invisibilidade social"; Leite, "Descendentes de africanos"; Hutchinson, "Race Relations," 28.

4. Oliven, "A invisibilidade social," 27; Oro and de Bem, "A discriminação."

5. Bastide, *African Religions*, 164; Fry, Carrara, and Martins-Costa, "Negros e brancos," 259; Butler, *Freedoms Given, Freedoms Won*, 185.

6. Decreto N. 847 — De 11 de outubro de 1890, Chapter 3, Dos Crimes Contra a Saúde Pública, Articles 156, 157, 158, Chapter 13. The 1890 code also outlawed capoeira, a martial art that had been used by slaves as a means of resistance and self-defense. See Decreto N. 847 — De 11 de outubro de 1890, Chapter 3, Dos Vadios e Capoeiras, Art. 402.

7. Netto, "Africanos no Brasil."

8. Borges, "Puffy, Ugly, Slothful, and Inert," 235–36.

9. See Oda, "Alienação mental e raça"; Schwarcz, "Quando a desigualdade é diferença," 48–49.

10. Skidmore, *Black into White* (1993), 55–62.

11. Senado Federal, Subsecretaria de Informações, *Decreto No. 528*, Chapter 1, Da Introducção de Immigrantes, Articles 1, 6, 7, 12, 18, Chapter 3, Da Venda dos Lotes e Modo de Pagamento — Auxílios aos Immigrantes — Título de Propriedade, Articles 24–26.

12. Domingues, *História não contada*, 60–66, 89–91.

13. Ibid., 67–71; Andrews, *Blacks and Whites*, 54–60; Domingues, *História não contada*, 68–70.

14. Prudente, *Preconceito racial*, 153–54; Makabe, "Ethnic Hegemony."

15. Lesser, "Immigration and Shifting Concepts"; Meade and Pirio, "In Search of the Afro-American 'El Dorado'"; Act to Limit the Immigration of Aliens into the United States, 5–7; Act to Limit the Immigration of Aliens into the United States and for Other Purposes," 153–69.

16. Loveman, "Race to Progress," 450–51.

17. Ibid., 460–67; Nobles, *Shades of Citizenship*, 88–96.

18. Leite, "Descendentes de africanos," 38.

19. Andrews, *Blacks and Whites*, 68–69; Domingues, *História não contada*, esp. 83–132.

20. Elisa Larkin Nascimento, "Aspects of Afro-Brazilian Experience," 206; Paul Christopher Johnson, "Law, Religion, and 'Public Health,'" 23; Meade, *"Civilizing" Rio*, 83–85.

21. Domingues, *História não contada*, 157–62; Maciel, "Discriminações raciais," 10–12.

22. Domingues, *História não contada*, 157–62; Maciel, "Discriminações raciais," 10–12.

23. Brazilian Constitution, 1891, Title 2, Title 4, Section 1, Article 70, Subsection 2; Title 4, Section 2, Article 72, Subsection 2; Love, "Political Participation," 8.

24. Domingues, "'Templo de luz,'" 519.

25. Ibid., 520.

26. See Gilmar Luiz de Carvalho, "Imprensa negra paulista."

27. Horbach, *Memória jurisprudencial.*

28. Love, "Political Participation," 9–13; Domingos, "Powerful in the Outback"; Degler, *Neither Black nor White.*

29. Skidmore, "Raízes de Gilberto Freyre," 4.

30. Ibid., 4–7; Braudel, "Través de un continente de historia," 168.

31. Andrews, "Brazilian Racial Democracy," 488; Lehman, "Gilberto Freyre," 209–10.

32. Andrews, "Brazilian Racial Democracy," 486–87; Maram, "Urban Labor and Social Change"; Maram, "Labor and the Left"; Decreto 20.921, 13:552–58.

33. Burns, *History of Brazil*, 396–99; John D. French, *Drowning in Laws.*

34. Brazilian Constitution, 1934, Article 121, Section 6, Article 138, Section b; Skidmore, *Politics in Brazil*; Fernando de Azevedo, *Brazilian Culture*, 33, 40–41; Lowrie, "Negro Element."

35. Darien J. Davis, "Mechanism of Forging," 230, 249–60.

36. Brazilian Constitution, 1934, Chapter 2, Article 113, Section 1, Article 121, Section 1, Subsection a.

37. Weinstein, "Racializing Regional Difference," 247.

38. Andrews, *Blacks and Whites*, 232–34; Garfield, "'Roots of a Plant,'" 748–49; Andrews, "Brazilian Racial Democracy," 488.

39. Morison, *History of United States Naval Operations*, 376–91; Sander, *Brasil na mira de Hitler*; Ivy, "Study in Leadership," 60. See also McCann, "Brazil and World War II."

40. Rosenheck, "Olive Drab in Black and White."

41. Ibid.; Maximiano and Oliveira, "Raça e forças armadas"; Hargrove, *Buffalo Soldiers*, 23–24, 30–31, 169–71; Vilela, "Brasil na Segunda Guerra."

42. Barcellos and Fernandes, "Jornal *A Notícia*"; Santos, "Construção do inimigo."

43. Naiara Magalhães, "Nisseis."

44. Brazilian Constitution, 1946, Title 4, Chapter 2, Article 141, Section 5.

45. Cottrol, "*Brown* and the Contemporary Brazilian Struggle," 123–29; "Caso Grafite."

46. Wagley, introduction, 7.

47. Maio, "Projeto UNESCO," 153; Fernandes, *Negro in Brazilian Society*, 134–44.

CHAPTER SIX. Jim Crow

1. Fox-Genovese and Genovese, *Mind of the Master Class*, 35–39.

2. Douglas, *Jim Crow Moves North*.

3. Sundstrom, "Color Line"; Andrews, *Blacks and Whites*, 75, 102, 137–38, 160–71.

4. See Woodward, *Strange Career*; Mack, "Law, Society, Identity."

5. Phillips, "Central Theme," 31.

6. Foner, *Reconstruction*, 198–200; Stampp, *Era of Reconstruction*, 80; Fleming, *Documentary History*, 280–91.

7. Cottrol, "Static History," 365–67.

8. Ibid.; Cottrol, "Thirteenth Amendment."

9. Cottrol, "Static History," 371–73.

10. Hyman and Wiecek, *Equal Justice under Law*, 395–400, 467–72, 497–500.

11. Ibid.

12. Blassingame, *Black New Orleans*, 112–22; Franklin and Moss, *From Slavery to Freedom*, 205–7.

13. *Civil Rights Cases*, 36.

14. Woodward, *Strange Career*, 102.

15. Ibid., 67–69.

16. Sharfstein, "Crossing the Color Line"; Hickman, "Devil and the One Drop Rule."

17. Berlin, *Slaves without Masters*, 108–32.

18. Golub, "Plessy as 'Passing'"; Scott, "Public Rights."

19. *Plessy v. Ferguson*, 551.

20. Ibid., 559.

21. Newby, *Jim Crow's Defense*, 137–39.

22. Woodward, *Strange Career*, 72–74.

23. Dunning, *Reconstruction*; Bowers, *Tragic Era*.

24. Cooper, *Woodrow Wilson*, 203–6; Wolgemuth, "Woodrow Wilson."

25. Dudziak, "Oliver Wendell Holmes."

26. Sumner, *Folkways*, 48, 64, 77–78, 90, 267, 304–7.

27. Ransom and Sutch, *One Kind of Freedom*, 162–70.

28. Goluboff, "'We Live's in a Free House,'" 2002–5; Lichtenstein, *Twice the Work*; Oshinsky, *Worse Than Slavery*.

29. See Forbath, *Law and the Shaping*.

30. Carter, *Scottsboro*, 1–10, 161–63, 184–269.

31. *Wolfe v. Georgia Railway and Electric Co.*, 505.

32. *Watson v. Stone*, 524.

33. *State v. Petit*.

34. McMath, "C. Vann Woodward."

CHAPTER SEVEN. An American Sea Change

1. See, e.g., Page, *"Hopes Are High"*; Bumiller, *"Obama Elected President"*; Arana, "Outlook"; M. Alex Johnson, "Barack Obama Elected."

2. See, e.g., Capdevila, "Obama cambió la historia"; "Victoire de Barack Obama"; "U.S. Election Night Victory Celebrations"; "Obama Win Sparks Global Praise."

3. Richburg, "Now the World Has to Rethink."

4. *Membership of the 110th Congress*, 5.

5. Thernstrom and Thernstrom, *America in Black and White*, 499–501.

6. Hall, "Long Civil Rights Movement."

7. Berlin, *Generations of Captivity*, 243.

8. Cottrol, Diamond, and Ware, *Brown v. Board of Education*, 34–48.

9. Brigham, *Study of American Intelligence*, 205–7.

10. Herbert S. Lewis, "Passion of Franz Boas"; Lee D. Baker, "Columbia University's Franz Boas."

11. Temin, "Great Depression," 303; Douglas, *Jim Crow Moves North*, 65–99; Spear, *Black Chicago*, 6–8; Katzman, *Before the Ghetto*, 88–98; Pleck, *Black Migration and Poverty*, 29–31.

12. Sugrue, *Sweet Land of Liberty*, 10–15, 20, 180–82, 194–96, 270–73.

13. Ibid., 28–30.

14. Klarman, *From Jim Crow to Civil Rights*, 117.

15. Ibid., 168; Weiss, *Farewell*, 209–35; Temin, "Great Depression," 301; Sundstrom, "Last Hired, First Fired?," 417–20.

16. Horwitz, *Transformation*, 213–46.

17. Ibid., 200–205; Kalman, *Legal Realism*, 17–20, 42–47.

18. See Friedman, *American Law*, 33–39; Horwitz, *Transformation*, esp. 188–89; Hovenkamp, "Social Science and Segregation."

19. Cottrol, Diamond, and Ware, *Brown v. Board of Education*, 208–33.

20. Ibid., 1.

21. Ibid., 59–76.

22. Franklin and Higginbotham, *From Slavery to Freedom*, 449–72.

23. Cottrol, Diamond, and Ware, *Brown v. Board of Education*, 120.

24. Moskos, "American Dilemma."

25. Cottrol, Diamond, and Ware, *Brown v. Board of Education*, 99.

26. *Shelley v. Kraemer*.

27. Cottrol, Diamond, and Ware, *Brown v. Board of Education*, 214; Dudziak, "Desegregation."

28. Hill, *Deacons for Defense*.

29. Gavin Wright, "Civil Rights Revolution."

30. Ibid.

31. Cottrol, Diamond, and Ware, *Brown v. Board of Education*, 224–45, 230–31; McAndrews, "Politics of Principle," 187–88.

32. William Julius Wilson, *Truly Disadvantaged*, 31; Massey and Denton, *American Apartheid*, 10, 74–78.

33. Sugrue, "Affirmative Action from Below," 150–51; Bloch, "Discrimination"; Kittner and Kohler, "Conditioning Expectations," 278.

34. Gastwirth, "Issues Arising."

35. Epstein, *Forbidden Grounds*, 182–204.

36. Ibid., 193–204; Thernstom and Thernstrom, *America in Black and White*, 393–422.

37. See, e.g., Thernstrom and Thernstrom, *America in Black and White*, 393–422; Patterson, *Ordeal of Integration*, 9–11, 147–69.

38. King, "Are African Americans Losing Their Footholds"; Smith and Welch, "Affirmative Action and Labor Markets."

39. Bumiller and Kornblut, "Black Leaders"; William Julius Wilson, *Truly Disadvantaged*.

40. William Julius Wilson, *Truly Disadvantaged*.

41. Weller and Fields, *Black and White Labor Gap*.

CHAPTER EIGHT. *Um País para Todos?*

1. Domingues, "Movimento negro brasileiro," 107–10.

2. Ibid., 110–11.

3. Lei No. 5.250; Domingues, "Movimento negro brasileiro," 111–12.

4. Domingues, "Movimento negro brasileiro," 111–12.

5. Comparato, "Economic Order"; Gonçalves, "Políticas," 69–91.

6. Brazilian Constitution, 1988, Title 1, Article 4, No. 8, Title 2, Article 5, No. 42.

7. Ibid., Article 215, Section 1, Article 216, Section 5; Jan Hoffman French, *Legalizing Identities*, 92–95.

8. Alberto, "Para Africano Ver"; Dzidzienyo, "Triangular Mirrors"; Sundiata, "Late Twentieth Century Patterns."

9. See, e.g., Heringer, "Desigualdades racias," 57–65; Kilsztajn et al., "Concentração e distribuição."

10. Kilsztajn et al., "Concentração e distribuição"; Souza, *Case Study Brazil*.

11. Racusen, "Making the 'Impossible' Determination," 805–7; Telles, *Race in Another America*, 42–44, 153–56, 261; Bailey, "Race Construct."

12. Instituto Brasileiro de Geografia e Estatística, *Séries estatísticas e séries históricas*; Schwarcz, "Previsões são sempre traiçoeiras."

13. Rodrigues, "Igualdade racial," 38–40; Telles, *Race in Another America*, 129–30.

14. Alânia Magalhães, "Trabalho e educação"; José Alcides Figueiredo Santos, "Efeitos de classe," 48, 51.

15. Telles, *Race in Another America*, 124–31.

16. Ibid.; Gomes, "Discriminação racial."

17. Telles, *Race in Another America*, 156–59; Hédio Silva Jr., *Discriminação racial*, 34–38.

18. See, e.g., "Vestibular: Mudou e agora?"

19. "Cresce o número."

20. Owensby, "Toward a History"; Lima and Vala, "Novas formas de expressão," 407–8.

21. Caldwell, *Negras in Brazil*, 66–67; Graziella Moraes da Silva and Reis, "Perceptions of Racial Discrimination," 69.

22. Graziella Moraes da Silva and Reis, "Perceptions of Racial Discrimination," 71–72.

23. See, e.g., "Lula garante"; Gaier, "Lula." See also Arias, "Faith in Our Neighbors."

24. Arias, "Faith in Our Neighbors"; Vargas, "When a Favela Dares," 56.

25. Paim and Thobias, "Exposição dos motivos"; Lei No. 7.716; Lei No. 8.081; Lei No. 9.459; Gomes, "Discriminação racial."

26. Gomes, "Discriminação racial."

27. Justice Studies Center of the Americas, "Judicial System and Racism."

28. Verissimo, "Brazilian 1988 Constitution."

29. Gomes, "Discriminação racial."

30. Gidi, "Class Actions," 317–20, 333, 342–46, 365–66, 372–73.

31. Hensler, "Não Vale a Pena?"

32. Brazil, Secretaria Especial, *Conferência nacional*; "Lula sanciona"; "Estatuto da Igualdade Racial aprovado no Senado acaba com cotas para negros nas universidades,"; Maldonado, "Estatuto racial"; Estatuto da Igualdade Racial.

33. "Estatuto da Igualdade Racial aprovado no Senado acaba com cotas para negros nas universidades"; Maldonado, "Estatuto racial"; Estatuto da Igualdade Racial.

34. Organization of American States, Inter-American Commission on Human Rights, *Report on the Situation of Human Rights*, chapter 9.

35. Alexandre do Nascimento, "Movimentos sociais."

36. Htun, "From 'Racial Democracy' to Affirmative Action."

37. Cottrol, "*Brown* and the Contemporary Brazilian Struggle," 126–27; Hernandez, "To Be Brown."

38. Brazil, Ministério de Educação, *Programa universidade para todos*; Gois, "Brasileiros."

39. Brazilian Constitution, 1988, Article 37, No. 8; Lei No. 9.100, Article 11; Lei No. 9.504; Lei No. 5.456; Lei No. 8.112; Lei No. 8.213.

40. "Ação afirmativa."

41. José Alberto Magno de Carvalho, Wood, and Andrade, "Estimating the Stability"; Sanjek, "Brazilian Racial Terms"; Telles, "Racial Ambiguity."

42. Racusen, "Fictions of Identity."

43. *Audiência pública.*

44. "Palestra da Senhora Deborah Duprat (Vice-Procuradora Geral da República)," in ibid.

45. "Palestra de Edson Santos de Souza," in ibid.

46. Argüição de Descumprimento de Preceito Fundamental 186 Distrito Federal, Ricardo Lewandowski (Relator).

47. Ibid.

48. Informe Regional, *Actuar sobre el futuro*, 25–28.

49. Cardoso, "Fundação Palmares"; U.S. Department of State, *Joint Action Plan*.

CHAPTER NINE. New Awakenings in Spanish America

1. See, e.g., Giuffrida, *Racial and Ethnic Disparities*; Cunningham and Jacobsen, *Earnings Inequality.*

2. For an anthology discussing the efforts of Afro-Latins in a number of American societies to emerge from invisibility, see *No Longer Invisible.*

3. Hooker, "Indigenous Inclusion/Black Exclusion."

4. Sociologist Edward Telles notes that as late as 2006, Nicaragua, Panama, Peru, and Uruguay completely lacked census information on their Afro-American populations. Costa Rica and Ecuador collected such information for the first time in 2000, while Honduras did so in 2001. See Telles, *Incorporating Race and Ethnicity*, 1. The Inter-American Development Bank helped sponsor conferences in 2000 and 2002 urging Latin American governments to include racial data in their censuses. See Inter-American Development Bank, *Todos contamos*; Inter-American Development Bank, *Todos Contamos II*, 3–5.

5. Laura A. Lewis, "'Afro' Mexico," 183–87; Golash-Boza, *Yo Soy Negro*, 45–49; Beck, Mijeski, and Stark, "¿Qué Es Racismo?"

6. N'Djoli, "Need to Recognize Afro-Mexicans," 226–29.

7. Cottrol, "Beyond Invisibility," 139–45; Andrews, *Blackness in the White Nation*, 146–48, 152. See Oro Negro Foundation, *Afro Descendants Organize Themselves*.

8. Telles, *Incorporating Race and Ethnicity*, 1.

9. Rodríguez Garavito, Sierra, and Adarve, "Cifras de la discriminación racial," esp. 22–23.

10. See, e.g., *Plan plurinacional*, 10–11; Rodríguez Garavito, Sierra, and Adarve, "Cifras de la discriminación racial," 19–32; Bucheli and Porzecanski, "Racial Inequality."

11. Hoffman and Centeno, "Lopsided Continent"; Rosenn, "Success of Constitutionalism," 26; Gargarella, "Towards a Typology," 149–52.

12. See, e.g., Molina Bustamante, *Propaganda racista*; Inter-American Development Bank, *Outsiders*, 24–26.

13. Zoninsein, "Economic Case"; Albornoz, *Education and Society*, 21, 141.

14. Beck, Mijeski, and Stark, "¿Qué Es Racismo?" One potential quibble with the study is that the researchers appeared to ask the respondents if they knew the terms *racism, discrimination,* and *prejudice* without then proceeding to determine if respondents were familiar with the concepts even if they were unfamiliar with the terms. One can easily imagine follow-up questions for those who indicated that they were unfamiliar with the term *racism* — for example, "Are there people who believe blacks are not as intelligent as whites?"

15. Cabella, "Panorama de la infancia y la adolescencia," 119–22, 135–36; Bucheli and Porzecanski, "Racial Inequality." Comparative figures for Latin American racial wage gaps can be seen in Busso, Cicowiez, and Gasparini, *Ethnicity and Millennium Development Goals*, Graph 2.9, "Whites and Non-Whites Mean Incomes," 97.

16. Engerman and Sokoloff, "Evolution of Suffrage Institutions," 909–15.

17. Cottrol, "Long Lingering Shadow," 77; Wade, "Etnicidad, multiculturalismo, y políticas sociales."

18. Wade, *Blackness and Race Mixture*, 121, 127–28, 295–97, 325–34.

19. Howard, "Development, Racism, and Discrimination,"; *República Dominicana, Suprema Corte de Justicia, Sentencia No. 460.*

20. Blue, "Erosion of Racial Equality"; Hernandez, "Exploration of the Efficacy."

21. Blue, "Erosion of Racial Equality"; Hernandez, "Exploration of the Efficacy."

22. Winthrop R. Wright, "Todd Duncan Affair"; Ley No. 2694, Article 1; Decreto No. 4230.

23. Hooker, "Indigenous Inclusion/Black Exclusion," 285–86; Wade, "Etnicidad, multiculturalismo, y políticas sociales," 64.

24. Ecuadoran Constitution, 1998, Title 3, Chapter 5, De los Derechos

Colectivos, Section 1, De los Pueblos Indígenas y Negros o Afroecuatorianos, Articles 83–85.

25. Colombian Constitution, 1991 with 2005 reforms, Title 1, Article 7, Law 70 of 1993 (August 27).

26. Ecuadoran Constitution, 2008, Article 11, Section 2.

27. See, e.g., León and Holguín, "Acción afirmativa"; Castro Heredia, Giraldo, and López, "Breve acercamiento"; "Debating Quotas."

28. Ardito Vega, *Ordenanzas*.

29. Ibid., 5, 12–13.

30. Organization of American States, Inter-American Court of Human Rights, *Case 130*.

31. Méndez, O'Donnell, and Pinheiro, *(Un)Rule of Law*; Domingo, "Rule of Law."

32. Oquendo, *Latin American Law*, 797–800.

EPILOGUE

1. See, e.g., Spalding, "King's Conservative Mind."

2. See, e.g., *Richmond v. J. A. Croson Co.*; Harold S. Lewis Jr. and Elizabeth J. Norman, *Employment Discrimination Law*, 384–86. See also *Regents of the University of California v. Bakke*; *Grutter v. Bollinger et al.*

Glossary of Spanish and Portuguese Terms

abertura. Political opening; a series of liberal reforms by the Brazilian military government during the period of 1974–1985 that gradually allowed limited political organization and paved the way for Brazil's return to democratic rule

Acción Democrática. Democratic Action; Venezuelan political party

Afro-descendente. Afro-descended; term for a person of African descent (*Portuguese*)

afrodescendiente. Afro-descended; term for a person of African descent (*Spanish*)

alforria. Manumission of a slave under Portuguese law

audiencia. Regional territory in Spanish America

bacharel. Graduate of the equivalent of a university-level undergraduate program in law, economics, or the arts. Graduation from such a program was usually expected of men who wanted to practice law or work in policy-making positions in the Brazilian Empire in the nineteenth century.

bandeirantes. Roving bands of frontiersmen and freebooters from São Paulo who ventured into unmapped regions of South America to capture indigenous slaves and search for mineral wealth during the sixteenth through eighteenth centuries

blanco. White (*Spanish*)

blanqueamiento. Policy aimed at whitening the populations of Spanish American nations through European immigration

boa aparência. Good appearance; term often used in want ads as a code indicating a preference for white applicants (*Portuguese*) *bozal.* Slave recently brought to a colony from Africa

branco. White (*Portuguese*)

branco da terra. Racial term used in Bahia, Brazil, to describe a person acknowledged as white but who has perceivable or known African ancestry

branqueamento. Policy aimed at whitening the Brazilian population through European immigration

buena presencia. Good appearance; term often used in want ads as a code indicating a preference for white applicants (*Spanish*)

caboclo. Racial term used in Brazil to describe a person of indigenous descent

calpa mulatto. Colonial Spanish racial category describing a person of approximately three-eighths African, three-eighths indigenous, and one-fourth Spanish descent

cambujo. Colonial Spanish racial category describing a person with a dark complexion, of approximately three-fourths African and one-fourth Spanish descent

candombe. Type of dance originated by descendants of black slaves in the Río de la Plata region

casta. Human racial or color category specified in the Colonial Spanish codes

castizo. Colonial Spanish racial category describing a person of three-fourths Spanish and one-fourth indigenous descent

chino. Colonial Spanish racial category describing a person of seven-eighths Spanish and one-eighth African descent

cimarrón. Runaway slave community in Spanish America

Código Negro. Code of laws governing slavery in the Spanish Empire

Consolidação das Leis do Trabalho. Consolidation of Labor Laws; Brazilian decree issued by President Getúlio Vargas in 1943 that governs labor relations *conventillo.* Tenement in Argentina or Uruguay, especially in Buenos Aires or Montevideo

cursinho. Course specifically designed to prepare students for the *Vestibular*, the Brazilian university entrance exam

dictanegra. Black dictatorship; term used by opposition to refer to Brazilian President Getúlio Vargas's regime

encomendero. Spanish settler who was granted free indigenous labor

encomienda. Legal system in colonial Spanish America that regulated the use of indigenous labor

Estado Novo. Period of Brazilian history from 1930 to 1945, when the country was under the leadership of Getúlio Vargas

estancia. Cattle ranch

favela. Brazilian shantytown

fazenda. Large land holding or plantation in Brazil

Frente Negra Brasileira. Brazilian Black Front; racially conscious political party organized in 1930 and abolished in 1937

gaúcho. Inhabitant of the Brazilian state of Rio Grande do Sul

gibaro. Colonial Spanish racial category describing a person of approximately five-eighths Spanish, two-eighths African, and one-eighth indigenous descent

gracias al sacar. Legal mechanism by which persons with attenuated African ancestry could purchase a document declaring them legally white

hacienda. Large land holding or plantation in Spanish America

Hora do Brasil. Brazilian Hour; daily radio program used by Brazilian President Getúlio Vargas

Indio. Indian; ethnic term used in Spanish America to describe a person of indigenous descent, usually one who has maintained his or her indigenous culture

Indio claro. Racial term used in the Dominican Republic. Although its literal meaning is "light Indian," it is often used by people of mixed African and European ancestry to deny African ancestry.

Indio oscuro. Racial term used in the Dominican Republic. Although its literal meaning is "dark Indian," it is often used by people who are predominately of African ancestry to deny African ancestry.

ingênuo. Child born to a slave mother in Brazil after the passage of "The Law of the Free Womb" legislation of September 1871; such a child who was forced to labor for his master as an indentured servant until the age of twenty-one.

Instituto Brasileiro de Geografia e Estatística. Brazilian Institute of Geography and Statistics; Brazil's official statistical bureau

Itamaraty. Brazil's Ministry of Foreign Relations

La Casa de la Cultura Indo-Afro-Americana. Indo-Afro-American Cultural Center

La Raza Cósmica. The Cosmic Race; Mexican ideology referring to the blend of indigenous, African, and European races in the country

la reducción de los indios. Spanish program aimed at civilizing and converting the indigenous population to Christianity

Las siete partidas. Castilian statutory code and reception of Roman law. It was first compiled in the thirteenth century under the reign of Alfonso the Wise with the intent of establishing a uniform body of normative rules for the Spanish kingdom.

Lei Afonso Arinos. Brazilian law passed in 1951 that outlawed racial discrimination

Lei Áurea. Brazilian law passed in 1888 that abolished slavery

Lei Caó. Brazilian law passed in 1989 that criminalized acts stemming from racial or color prejudice

lei da boa razão. Portuguese law establishing criteria for jurists to base their decisions on multiple sources of law and their own best judgment or reasoning

Lei Rio Branco (also known as Lei do Ventre Livre or Law of the Free Womb). Brazilian law that provided for the freedom of children born of slave mothers after September 28, 1871

liberto. A freed slave

limpieza de sangre. Spanish practice that ensured that persons of Jewish or Moorish ancestry did not achieve high civil or ecclesiastical office; also Spanish American practice that kept persons with indigenous and African ancestry out of prestigious offices and schools

mestiço. Racial term used in Brazil to describe a person of mixed descent

mestizaje. Physical and cultural mixing of the three races (indigenous, African, European) in Latin America

mestizo. Racial term used in Spanish America to describe a person of mixed descent; also a colonial Spanish racial category describing a person of indigenous and Spanish descent

milonga. Form of music and dance that originated in the Río de la Plata region and preceded the tango

Ministério Público. Attorney General's Office (*Portuguese*)

Ministerio Público. Attorney General's Office (*Spanish*)

moreno. Racial term used in Brazil and Spanish America to describe a person with a dark complexion

morisco. Colonial Spanish racial category describing a person of three-fourths Spanish and one-fourth African descent

Movimento Negro Unificado. Unified Black Movement; Brazilian organization founded in 1978

mulato. Racial term describing a person of mixed African and Spanish descent *negro.* Black (*Spanish and Portuguese*)

negros del congreso. Afro-Argentines who served as doormen and servants in Congress

Ordenações Filipinas. Compilation of Portuguese laws especially meant for colonies or overseas territories. Continued to be an authoritative source of law in Brazil after independence. A Brazilian version was published in Rio de Janeiro in 1870.

palenque. Runaway slave community in Spanish America

palestra. Speech or presentation

pardo. Racial term describing a person of mixed African and European descent

Partido Independiente de Color. Independent Party of Color; Cuban political party

Partido Liberación Nacional. National Liberation Party; Costa Rican political party

patria. Fatherland

peliculum. Property or allowance that a slave could use to purchase manumission

Pontifícia Universidade Católica do Rio de Janeiro. Pontifical Catholic University of Rio de Janeiro

preto. Black (*Portuguese*)

procurador. Government attorney

Programa Universidade para Todos. Program created by the Brazilian government in 2004 that provides scholarships to students from low-income families to attend private universities

quilombo. Runaway slave community in Brazil

racismo cordial. Cordial racism; term used by students of race relations to describe the Brazilian paradox of discrimination and racism in a culture that prides itself on racial harmony

razoabilidade. Brazilian constitutional principle requiring proportionality in the exercise of legislative discretion

sainete. Comic sketch performed in Buenos Aires's La Boca neighborhood

Santeria. Afro-Caribbean religion based on Yoruba beliefs and traditions, with some Roman Catholic elements added

sertão. Backlands; sparsely populated wilderness in the interior of Brazil

Supremo Tribunal Federal. Supreme Federal Court; highest court of law in Brazil

Teatro Experimental do Negro. Black Experimental Theater; Brazilian group established in 1944 that advocated for black rights and black consciousness

trigueño. Racial term describing a person of mixed descent with a light complexion

Turco. Turk; term used in Brazil to describe an immigrant or descendant of an immigrant from lands that once formed the Ottoman Empire

Universidade Federal do Rio de Janeiro. Federal University of Rio de Janeiro

Universidade Federal do Rio Grande do Sul. Federal University of Rio Grande do Sul

Velha República. Period of Brazilian history from 1889 to 1930

Vestibular. Brazilian university entrance exam

zambaigo. Colonial Spanish racial category describing a person of approximately one-half indigenous, three-eighths African, and one-eighth Spanish descent

zambo. Racial term describing a person of mixed African and indigenous descent

Bibliography

PRIMARY SOURCES

U.S. CASES

Berea College v. Kentucky, 211 U.S. 45 (1908).

Briggs v. Elliot, 98 F. Supp. 529 (U.S.D.C. East. Div. of S.C., Charleston Div., 1951).

Brown v. Board of Education, 347 U.S. 483 (1954).

Brown v. Board of Education II, 349 U.S. 294 (1955).

Buchanan v. Warley, 245 U.S. 60 (1917).

Civil Rights Cases, 109 U.S. 3 (1883).

Clyatt v. United States, 197 U.S. 207 (1905).

Commonwealth v. Jennison, in *Proceedings of the Massachusetts Historical Society, 1873–1875*. Boston: Massachusetts Historical Society, 1875.

Dred Scott v. Sandford, 60 U.S. (19 How.) 393 (1857).

Fisher v. University of Texas, No. 11-345, S.C., 80 U.S.L.W. 3476.

Giles v. Harris, 189 U.S. 475 (1903).

Gratz v. Bollinger, 539 U.S. 244 (2003).

Griggs v. Duke Power Co., 401 U.S. 424 (1971).

Grutter v. Bollinger et al., 539 U.S. 306 (2003).

Guinn v. United States, 238 U.S. 347 (1915).

Heart of Atlanta Motel, Inc., v. United States, 379 U.S. 241 (1964).

Heirn v. Bridault and Wife, 37 Miss. 209 (1859), in *Reports and Cases Argued and Determined in the High Court of Errors and Appeals for the State of Mississippi*, vol. 37. Philadelphia: Johnson, 1860.

Hobbs et al. v. Fogg, 6 Watts 553 (1837).

Lochner v. New York, 198 U.S. 45 (1905).

Loving v. Virginia, 388 U.S. 1 (1967).

McCabe v. Atchison, Topeka, and Santa Fe Railway Company, 235 U.S. 151 (1914).

Norris v. Alabama, 294 U.S. 587 (1935).

Plessy v. Ferguson, 163 U.S. 537 (1896).

Powell v. Alabama, 287 U.S. 45 (1932).

Regents of the University of California v. Bakke, 438 U.S. 265 (1978).

Richmond v. J. A. Croson Co., 488 U.S. 469 (1989).
Roberts v. City of Boston, 59 Mass. 198 (1850).
Shelley v. Kraemer, 334 U.S. 1 (1948).
Somersett v. Stewart, 20 How. St. Tr. 1 (1772).
State v. Davis, 52 N.C. 52 (1859).
State v. Petit, 119 La. 1013 (1907).
Strauder v. West Virginia, 100 U.S. 303 (1879).
United States v. Cruikshank, 92 U.S. 542 (1875).
United States v. E. C. Knight Co., 156 U.S. 1 (1895).
Watson v. Stone, 148 Fla. 516 (1941).
Wolfe v. Georgia Railway and Electric Co., 2 Ga. App. 499 (1907).
Yick Wo v. Hopkins, 118 U.S. 356 (1886).

NON-U.S. CASES

Suprema Corte de Justicia de la República Dominicana, *Sentencia No. 460*, Rec.:
Emildo Bueno Oguis, November 2, 2011.
Supremo Tribunal Federal do Brasil, *Argüição de Descumprimento de Preceito
Fundamental 186*, April 26, 2012.

COMPILATIONS, TREATISES, AND CONSTITUTIONAL ASSEMBLIES

Código Filipino ou Ordenações e leis do reino do Portugal, decima quarta edição.
Ed. Cândido Mendes de Almeida. Rio de Janeiro: Tipografia do Instituto
Filomático, 1870.
Consejo de Indias. *Recopilación de leyes de los reynos de las Indias.* Vol. 2, Book
6, Title 1, *De los Indios*, Title 2, *De la libertad de los Indios*. Madrid: Antonio
Perez de Soto, 1774.
Diário da assembléia geral constituinte e legislativa do império do Brasil. Books 1,
3. Rio de Janeiro: Imprensa Nacional, 1823.
Lei No. 5.250, de 9 de fevereiro de 1967. In *Anti-racismo: Coletânea de leis brasilei-
ras (federais, estaduais, municipais)*, ed. Hédio Silva Jr. São Paulo: Editora
Oliveira Mendes, 1998.
Newman, Debra L., comp. *List of Black Servicemen Complied from the War
Department Collection of Revolutionary War Records.* Washington, D.C.:
National Archives and Record Service, 1974.
*Las siete partidas del rey Don Alfonso el Sabio cotejadas con varios códices antiguos
por la Real Academia de la Historia.* Madrid, 1807. http://bib.us.es/derecho
/recursos/pixelegis/index-ides-idweb.html.

DECREES, STATUTES, AND CONSTITUTIONS

An Act to Limit the Immigration of Aliens into the United States. *Statutes at Large*, vol. 19, chap. 8 (1921): 5–7.

An Act to Limit the Immigration of Aliens into the United States and for Other Purposes. *Statutes at Large*, vol. 43, pt. 1, chap. 190, secs. 2–5 (1924): 153–55.

Anais da Câmara dos Deputados de São Paulo. Vol. 1, 1928.

Argentine Constitution. 18.

Brazilian Constitutions. 1824, 1891, 1934, 1946, 1967, 1988.

Colombia Corte Constitucional. *Sentencia T-025*. 2004.

Colombian Constitution. 1991, with 2005 reforms.

Confederate States of America Constitution. 1861. In Charles Robert Lee Jr., *The Confederate Constitution*. Chapel Hill: University of North Carolina Press, 1963.

Cuban Constitution. 1940.

Decreto No. 847 de 11 de outubro de 1890: Código penal dos Estados Unidos do Brasil.

Decreto No. 1122. Colombia, June 18, 1998.

Decreto No. 4230. Costa Rica, November 19, 1969.

Decreto 20.921. *Diário oficial dos Estados Unidos do Brasil*. August 25, 1931.

Ecuadoran Constitutions. 1998, 2008.

Enforcement Act of 1870. 16 Stat. 140. United States, 1870.

Estatuto da Igualdade Racial. Brazil, 2010.

Lei No. 1.390 de 3 de julho de 1951: Lei Afonso Arinos. Brazil, 1951.

Lei No. 5.456. Brazil, 1968.

Lei No. 7.716. Brazil, 1989.

Lei No. 8.081. Brazil, 1990.

Lei No. 8.112. Brazil, 1990.

Lei No. 8.213. Brazil, 1991.

Lei No. 9.100. Brazil, 1995.

Lei No. 9.459. Brazil, 1997.

Lei No. 9.504. Brazil, 1997.

Lei No. 2040 de 28 de setembro de 1871. Brazil, 1871.

Ley No. 2694. Costa Rica, 1960.

Ley No. 7711. Costa Rica, 1997.

Panamanian Constitution. 1941.

Peruvian Constitution. 1823.

Regulamento para o serviço de imigração da província de São Paulo. São Paulo: Tipografia do Correio Paulistano, 1887.

Senado Federal, Subsecretaria de Informações. *Decreto No. 528 de 28 de junho de 1890*. Brazil, 1890.

Tribunal de Justiça do Estado de São Paulo. 2a, Câmara Criminal; Proceso No. 272.907. Brazil, 1999.

NEWSPAPER AND MAGAZINE ARTICLES

"Ação afirmativa privilegia ensino público e não raça." *Folha.com* (Brazil), August 30, 2010. http://www.folha.com.br/sa790861.

"Aprodeh señala que hay más discriminación racial en Lima, Cusco y Arequipa." *El Comercio* (Peru), March 10, 2005.

Arana, Marie. "Outlook, First Multi-Racial President." *Washington Post*, December 1, 2008.

Ardito Vega, Wilfredo. "Discriminación en los servicios turísticos." *La Insignia* (Peru), December 5, 2006.

Bumiller, Elisabeth. "Obama Elected President as Racial Barrier Falls." *New York Times*, November 5, 2008.

Bumiller, Elisabeth, and Anne E. Kornblut. "Black Leaders Say Storm Forced Bush to Confront Issues of Race and Poverty." *New York Times*, September 18, 2005.

Capdevila, Inés. "Obama cambió la historia: Será el primer presidente negro de Estados Unidos." *La Nación* (Argentina), November 5, 2008.

"O caso Grafite tem conteúdo emblemático." *O Globo* (Brazil), April 17, 2005.

"Cresce o número de universitários que trabalham." *Folha.com* (Brazil), December 14, 2009. http://www1.folha.uol.com.br/folha/educacao/ult305u666204.shtml.

"Debating Quotas: Affirmative Action in Colombia." *The Economist*, July 30, 2009.

"La desconocida comunidad Chileno-Africana: Chile también tiene la piel negra." *El Mercurio.com* (Chile), June 8, 2008. http://www.mapuche.info/docs/merco80608.html.

Downes, Patricio. "Casi dos millones de argentinos tienen sus raíces en el África negra." *Clarín* (Argentina), June 9, 2006.

"Estatuto da Igualdade Racial aprovado no Senado acaba com cotas para negros nas universidades." *Blog do Marcelo* (Brazil), June 16, 2010. http://www.blogdomarcelo.com.br/v2/2010/06/16/estatuto-da-igualdade-racial-aprovado-no-senado-acaba-com-cotas-para-negros-nas-universidades/ (citing "CCJ do senado aprova Estatuto da Igualdade Racial, mas retira cotas para ingresso na universidade," *O Globo*, June 16, 2010, and Claudia Andrade, "Senado aprova Estatuto Racial sem cotas para negros," *Terra*, June 16, 2010).

Gaier, Rodrigo Viga. "Lula: Ação no Alemão mostra que Estado pode vencer o tráfico." *O Globo* (Brazil), December 7, 2010.

Gois, Antônio. "Brasileiros vêem cota como essencial e humilhante, revela Datafolha." *Folha.com* (Brazil), November 23, 2008. http://www1.folha.uol.com.br/folha/brasil/ult96u470649.shtml.

Johnson, M. Alex. "Barack Obama Elected 44th President, 'Change Has Come to America,' First African-American Leader Tells Country." *msnbc.com*, November 5, 2008. http://www.msnbc.msn.com/id/27531033/ns/politics-decision_08/t/barack-obama-elected-th-president/#.T3dQutUw3ec.

Kinigsberg, Yanina. "Una mujer denunció que la discriminaron por ser negra." *Clarín Edición Sábado* (Argentina), August 24, 2002.

"Lula garante permanência do Exército e diz que governos anteriores fizeram acordo com bandidos." *O Globo* (Brazil), December 7, 2010.

"Lula sanciona Estatuto de Igualdade Racial." *Jornal do Brasil* (Brazil), July 20, 2010.

Maldonado, Raquel. "Estatuto racial perdeu 'espinha dorsal', diz representante do Movimento Negro." *UOL Notícias em São Paulo* (Brazil), July 26, 2010.

Marotto, Telma. "Brazilian Secret 93 Million Don't Want to Talk about Is Racism." *Bloomberg.com*, June 26, 2008. http://www.bloomberg.com/apps/news?pid=newsarchive&sid=a1ezjRWRd5Tk.

Menezes, Maiá. "Vítimas de racismo perdem 57,7% das ações." *O Globo* (Brazil), November 20, 2008.

"Obama Win Sparks Global Praise, Cheers." *msnbc.com*, November 5, 2008. http://www.msnbc.msn.com/id/27542176/ns/world_news-watching_america_vote/t/obama-win-sparks-global-praise-cheers/.

Page, Susan. "Hopes Are High for Race Relations." *USA Today*, November 7, 2008.

Petry, André. "O Brasil nunca teve um ministro como ele." *Veja* (Brazil), September 5, 2007.

Richburg, Keith. "Now the World Has to Rethink Its Image of a Racist US." *Observer* (United Kingdom), November 8, 2008.

Secco, Alexandre, and Sérgio Ruiz Luz. "Somos Todos Reféns." *Veja* (Brazil), February 7, 2001.

"U.S. Election Night Victory Celebrations around the Globe." *Guardian* (United Kingdom), November 5, 2008.

"Vestibular: Mudou e agora?" *Veja* (Brazil), April 15, 2009.

"La victoire de Barack Obama porte un nouveau rêve américain." *Le Monde* (France), November 5, 2008.

NOVELS AND FILMS

Birth of a Nation. David W. Griffith Corporation, 1915.

Dixon, Thomas. *The Clansman: An Historical Romance of the Ku Klux Klan.* Intro. Thomas D. Clark. Lexington: University Press of Kentucky, 1970.

Gentleman's Agreement. Twentieth Century Fox, 1947.

Gone with the Wind. Selznick International Pictures, 1939.

Home of the Brave. Screen Plays Corporation, 1949.

OTHER PRIMARY SOURCES

Audiência pública: Argüição de descumprimento de preceito fundamental 186, recurso extraordinário 597.285. Brasília: Supremo Tribunal Federal, 2010.

Brazil, Ministério de Educação. *Programa universidade para todos (PROUNI).* 2004. http://siteprouni.mec.gov.br/.

Brazil, Secretaria Especial de Políticas de Promoção da Igualdade Racial. *I Conferência Nacional de Promoçao da Igualdade Racial: Estado e sociedade promovendo a igualdade racial, relatório final.* 2005.

Bucheli, Marisa, and Wanda Cabella. *Perfil demográfico y socioeconómico de la población uruguaya según su ascendencia racial.* Montevideo: Instituto Nacional Estadística, 2006.

Cardoso, Oscar Henrique. "Fundação Palmares promove seminário internacional em Brasília." *Ministério da Cultura Online,* February 28, 2005. http://www.cultura.gov.br/site/2005/02/28/fundacao-palmares-promove-seminario-internacional-em-brasilia/.

Comisión Económica para América Latina y el Caribe. *Pueblos indígenas y afrodescendientes de América Latina y el Caribe: Información sociodemográfica para políticas y programas.* 2006.

Cunningham, Wendy, and Joyce P. Jacobsen. *Earnings Inequality within and across Gender, Racial, and Ethnic Groups in Four Latin American Countries.* Policy Research Working Paper 4591. Washington, D.C.: World Bank, 2008.

D'Ou, Lino. "El fantasma histriónico." *Labor Nueva,* February 20, 1916.

Galton, Francis. *Hereditary Genius: An Inquiry into Its Laws and Consequences.* London: Macmillan, 1869.

———. *Inquiries in Human Faculty and Its Development.* London: Dent, 1883.

Giuffrida, Antonio, ed. *Racial and Ethnic Disparities in Health in Latin America and the Caribbean.* Washington, D.C.: Inter-American Development Bank, 2007.

Informe Regional sobre Desarrollo Humano para América Latina y el Caribe

2010. *Actuar sobre el futuro: Romper la transmisión intergeneracional de la desigualdad*. New York: United Nations, 2010.

Instituto Brasileiro de Geografia e Estatística. *Séries estatísticas e séries históricas: População residente, por cor ou raça*. 2009.

———. *Síntese de indicadores socias: Uma análise das condições de vida da população brasileira*. 2006.

Inter-American Development Bank. *Outsiders: The Changing Patterns of Exclusion in Latin America and the Caribbean*. Washington, D.C.: IADB, 2007.

———. *Todos contamos: Los grupos étnicos en los censos*. Cartagena: IADB, 2000.

———. *Todos Contamos II: National Censuses and Social Inclusion Back to Office Report*. Lima: IADB, 2002.

Justice Studies Center of the Americas. *The Judicial System and Racism against People of African Descent: The Cases of Brazil, Colombia, the Dominican Republic and Peru*. 2004.

Manning, Jennifer E. *Membership of the 111th Congress: A Profile*. http://assets .opencrs.com/rpts/R40086_20100204.pdf.

Membership of the 110th Congress: A Profile. Washington, D.C.: Congressional Research Service, 2008.

Organization of American States, Inter-American Commission on Human Rights. *Annual Report: Peru*. 2000. http://www.cidh.oas.org/annualrep/2000eng /annex.htm.

———. *Case 130*. September 8, 2005. http://www.corteidh.or.cr/docs/casos /artìculos/seriec_130_esp.pdf.

———. *IACHR Releases Report on Afro-Descendants in Colombia*. May 15, 2009. http://www.cidh.org/comunicados/English/2009/28-09eng.htm.

———. *Preliminary Observations of the Inter-American Commission on Human Rights after the Visit of the Rapporteurship on the Rights of Afro-Descendants and against Racial Discrimination to the Republic of Colombia*. March 27, 2009. http://www.cidh.org/countryrep/ColombiaAfrodescendientes.eng /ColombiaAfros2009Toc.eng.htm.

———. *Report on the Situation of Human Rights in Brazil*. 1997. http://www.cidh .oas.org/countryrep/brazil-eng/index%20-%20brazil.htm.

———. *Rules of Procedure of the Inter-American Commission on Human Rights*. 2009. http://www.cidh.oas.org/basicos/English/Basic18 .RulesOfProcedureIACHR.htm.

Plan plurinacional para eliminar la discriminación racial y la exclusión étnica y cultural. Quito: Ministerio Coordinador de Patrimonio Natural y Cultural del Ecuador, 2009.

Schkolink, Susana, and Fabiana del Popolo. *Los censos y los pueblos indígenas en*

América Latina: Una metodología regional. Santiago de Chile: United Nations Economic Commission for Latin America and the Caribbean, 2005.

Souza, Celina. *Case Study Brazil: Evaluation of the National Human Development Report System.* New York: United Nations Development Program Evaluation Office, 2006.

Stephens, Alexander H. "Cornerstone Speech," March 21, 1861. In *Alexander H. Stephens, in Public and Private: With Letters and Speeches, before, during, and since the War,* by Henry Cleveland. Philadelphia: National, 1886.

United Nations International Convention on the Elimination of All Forms of Discrimination. *Reports Submitted by States Parties under Article 9 of the Convention: Eighteenth Periodic Reports of States Parties Due in 2004: Addendum, Costa Rica.* May 31, 2006.

U.S. Department of State. *Joint Action Plan Between the Government of the Federative Republic of Brazil and the Government of the United States of America To Eliminate Racial and Ethnic Discrimination and Promote Equality.* 2008.

U.S. Department of State, Bureau of Democracy, Human Rights, and Labor. *2005 Country Reports on Human Rights Practices: Costa Rica.* March 8, 2006.

———. *2006 Country Reports on Human Rights Practices: Costa Rica.* March 6, 2007.

SECONDARY SOURCES

Aguilar, Luis E. "Cuba, c. 1860–c. 1930." In *Cuba: A Short History,* ed. Leslie Bethell. Cambridge: Cambridge University Press, 1993.

Aguirre, Carlos. *Breve historia de la esclavitud en el Perú: Una herida que no deja de sangrar.* Lima: Fondo Editorial del Congreso del Perú, 2005.

Aguirre Beltrán, Gonzalo. *Cuijla: Esbozo etnográfico de un pueblo negro.* Mexico City: Fondo de Cultura Económica, 1958.

———. "Oposición de raza y cultura en el pensamiento antropológico mexicano." *Revista Mexicana de Sociología* 31, no. 1 (January–March 1969): 51–71.

———. *La población negra de México, 1519–1810: Estudio etnohistórico.* 1946; Mexico City: Fondo de Cultura Económica, 1972.

Alberto, Paulina. "Para Africano Ver: African-Bahian Exchanges in the Reinvention of Brazil's Racial Democracy, 1961–1963." *Luso-Brazilian Review* 45, no. 1 (June 2008): 78–117.

Albornoz, Orlando. *Education and Society in Latin America.* Pittsburgh: University of Pittsburgh Press, 1993.

Almarza Villalobos, Ángel Rafael. "La limpieza de sangre en el Colegio de

Abogados de Caracas a finales del siglo XVIII." In *Fronteras de la historia*. Bogotá: Instituto Colombiano de Antropología e Historia, 2005.

Alonso, Ana María. "Conforming Disconformity: 'Mestizaje,' Hybridity, and the Aesthetics of Mexican Nationalism." *Cultural Anthropology* 19, no. 4 (November 2004): 459–90.

Álvarez de Flores, Raquel. "Evolución histórica de las migraciones en Venezuela: Breve recuento." *Aldea Mundo* 11, no. 22 (November 2006–April 2007): 89–93.

Amantino, Marcia. "O mundo das feras: Os moradores do Sertão Oeste de Minas Gerais século XVIII." Ph.D. diss., Federal University of Rio de Janeiro, 2001.

Andrews, George Reid. *The Afro-Argentines of Buenos Aires, 1800–1900*. Madison: University of Wisconsin Press, 1980.

———. *Afro-Latin America, 1800–2000*. New York: Oxford University Press, 2004.

———. *Blackness in the White Nation: A History of Afro-Uruguay*. Chapel Hill: University of North Carolina Press, 2010.

———. *Blacks and Whites in São Paulo, Brazil, 1888–1988*. Madison: University of Wisconsin Press, 1991.

———. "Brazilian Racial Democracy, 1900–1990: An American Counterpoint." *Journal of Contemporary History* 31, no. 3 (July 1996): 483–507.

Andújar Persinal, Carlos. *La presencia negra en Santo Domingo: Un enfoque etno-histórico*. Santo Domingo, D.R.: n.p., 1997.

Araújo, Rodrigo da Costa. "Textualidades do Brasil: Literatura, música e imagens em aulas do ensino médio." Círculo Fluminense de Estudos Filológicos e Linguísticos, IX Fórum de Estudos Lingüísticos. 2007. http://www.filologia .org.br/ixfelin/trabalhos/pdf/67.pdf.

Ardito Vega, Wilfredo. *Las ordenanzas contra la discriminación*. Lima: Pontificia Universidad Católica del Perú, 2009.

Arias, Enrique Desmond. "Faith in our Neighbors: Networks and Social Order in Three Brazilian Favelas." *Latin American Politics and Society* 46, no. 1 (Spring 2004): 1–38.

Atack, Jeremy, and Peter Passell. *A New Economic View of American History*. New York: Norton, 1994.

Augustine-Adams, Kif. "Making Mexico: Legal Nationality, Chinese Race, and the 1930 Population Census." *Law and History Review* 27, no. 1 (Spring 2009): 113–44.

Azevedo, Elciene. "O direito dos escravos: Lutas jurídicas e abolicionismo na província de São Paulo na segunda metade do século XIX." Ph.D. diss., State University of Campinas, 2003.

Azevedo, Fernando de. *Brazilian Culture: An Introduction to the Study of Culture in Brazil*. Trans. William Rex Crawford. New York: Macmillan, 1950.

Bailey, Stanley R. "The Race Construct and Public Opinion: Understanding Brazilian Beliefs about Racial Inequality and their Determinants." *American Journal of Sociology* 108, no. 2 (September 2002): 406–39.

Baily, Samuel L. "The Adjustment of Italian Immigrants in Buenos Aires and New York, 1870–1914." *American Historical Review* 88, no. 2 (April 1983): 281–305.

Baker, J. H. *An Introduction to English Legal History.* 3rd ed. London: Butterworths, 1990.

Baker, Lee D. "Columbia University's Franz Boas: He Led the Undoing of Scientific Racism." *Journal of Blacks in Higher Education* 22 (Winter 1998–1999): 89–96.

Barbosa Gomes, Joaquim B. "Discriminação racial: Um grande desafio para o direito brasileiro." http://www.adami.adv.br/artigos/artigo28.asp.

———. "O Ministério Público e os efeitos da discriminação racial no Brasil: Da indiferença à inércia." Boletim dos Procuradores da República, 2, no. 15 (July 1999): 15–25.

Barcellos, Bruna Luíza, and Mário Luis Fernandes. "Jornal *A Notícia* e o discurso nazista em Santa Catarina." *Cenários da Comunicação* 7, no. 2 (October 2008): 127–35.

Barra, Felipe de la. *Invasiones militares de Lima: Desde la Conquista hasta la República.* Lima: Fundación de Lima, 1959.

Bastide, Roger. *The African Religions of Brazil: Toward a Sociology of the Interpenetration of Civilizations.* Trans. Helen Sebba. Baltimore: Johns Hopkins University Press, 1978.

Beck, Scott H., Kenneth J. Mijeski, and Meagan M. Stark. "¿Qué Es Racismo? Awareness of Racism and Discrimination in Ecuador." *Latin American Research Review* 46, no. 1 (2011): 102–25.

Bennett, Herman L. *Africans in Colonial Mexico: Absolutism, Christianity, and Afro-Creole Consciousness, 1570–1640.* Bloomington: Indiana University Press, 2005.

———. *Colonial Blackness: A History of Afro-Mexico.* Bloomington: Indiana University Press, 2009.

Benson, Lee. *The Concept of Jacksonian Democracy: New York as a Test Case.* Princeton: Princeton University Press, 1961.

Bergad, Laird W., Fe Iglesias García, and María del Carmen Barcia. *The Cuban Slave Market, 1790–1880.* New York: Cambridge University Press, 1995.

Berlin, Ira. *Generations of Captivity: A History of African American Slaves.* Cambridge: Harvard University Press, 2003.

———. *Slaves without Masters: The Free Negro in the Antebellum South.* New York: Random House, 1974.

Berman, Harold J. *Law and Revolution: The Formation of the Western Legal Tradition*. Cambridge: Harvard University Press, 1983.

Blackstone, William. *Commentaries on the Laws of England*. Vol. 1, *Of the Rights of Persons*. Intro. Stanley Katz. Chicago: University of Chicago Press, 1979.

Blanchard, Peter. "The Language of Liberation: Slave Voices in the Wars of Independence." *Hispanic American Historical Review* 82, no. 3 (August 2002): 499–523.

Blassingame, John W. *Black New Orleans, 1860–1880*. Chicago: University of Chicago Press, 1973.

Bloch, Herman D. "Discrimination against the Negro in Employment in New York, 1920–1963." *American Journal of Economics and Sociology* 24, no. 4 (October 1965): 361–82.

Blue, Sarah A. "The Erosion of Racial Equality in the Context of Cuba's Dual Economy." *Latin American Politics and Society* 49, no. 3 (Fall 2007): 35–62.

Bodnar, Yolanda. *Colombia: Apuntes sobre la diversidad cultural y la información sociodemográfica disponible en los pueblos indígenas*. Chile: United Nations Economic Commission for Latin America and the Caribbean, 2005.

Bogen, David Skillen. "The Maryland Context of Dred Scott: The Decline in the Legal Status of Maryland Free Blacks, 1776–1810." *American Journal of Legal History* 34, no. 4 (October 1990): 381–411.

Bonfiglio, Giovanni. *La presencia europea en el Perú*. Lima: Fondo Editorial del Congreso del Perú, 2001.

Borges, Dain. "Puffy, Ugly, Slothful, and Inert: Degeneration in Brazilian Social Thought, 1880–1940." *Journal of Latin American Studies* 25, no. 2 (May 1993): 235–56.

Bowers, Claude G. *The Tragic Era: The Revolution after Lincoln*. Cambridge, Mass.: Houghton Mifflin, 1929.

Boxer, C. R. *The Golden Age of Brazil, 1695–1750: Growing Pains of a Colonial Society*. Berkeley: University of California Press, 1962.

Braudel, Fernand. "A través de un continente de historia: Brasil y la obra de Gilberto Freyre." *Revista Mexicana de Sociología* 61, no. 2 (April–June 1999): 167–87.

Breen, T. H., and Stephen Innes. *"Myne Owne Ground": Race and Freedom on Virginia's Eastern Shore, 1640–1676*. New York: Oxford University Press, 1980.

Brigham, Carl. *A Study of American Intelligence*. Princeton: Princeton University Press, 1923.

Bronfman, Alejandra. *Measures of Equality: Social Science, Citizenship, and Race in Cuba, 1902–1940*. Chapel Hill: University of North Carolina Press, 2004.

Bryan, Maurice, and Margarita Sanchez. *Afro-Descendants: Discrimination and Economic Exclusion in Latin America*. London: Minority Rights Group, 2003.

Bucheli, Marisa, and Rafael Porzecanski. "Racial Inequality in the Uruguayan Labor Market: An Analysis of Wage Differentials between Afro-Descendants and Whites (Research Note)." *Latin American Politics and Society* 53, no. 2 (Summer 2011): 113–50.

Burdick, John. *Blessed Anastácia: Women, Race, and Popular Christianity in Brazil*. New York: Routledge, 1998.

Burkhardt, Richard W. *The Spirit of the System: Lamarck and Evolutionary Biology*. Cambridge: Harvard University Press, 1977.

Burns, E. Bradford. *A History of Brazil*. New York: Columbia University Press, 1980.

Busso, Matías, Martín Cicowiez, and Leonardo Gasparini. *Ethnicity and Millennium Development Goals*. Bogotá: UNDP, 2005.

Butler, Kim D. *Freedoms Given, Freedoms Won: Afro-Brazilians in Post-Abolition São Paulo and Salvador*. New Brunswick, N.J.: Rutgers University Press, 1998.

Buvinić, Mayra, Jacqueline Mazza, and Ruthanne Deutsch. *Social Inclusion and Economic Development in Latin America*. Washington, D.C.: Inter-American Development Bank, 2001.

Cabella, Wanda. "Panorama de la infancia y la adolescencia en la población afrouruguaya." In *Población afrodescendiente y desigualdades étnico-raciales en Uruguay*, ed. Lucía Scuro Somma. N.p.: PNUD Uruguay, 2008.

Cáceres, Juan Carlos. *Tango negro, la historia negada: Orígenes, desarrollo y actualidad del tango*. Buenos Aires: Editorial Planeta, 2010.

Caldwell, Kia Lilly. *Negras in Brazil: Re-Envisioning Black Women, Citizenship, and the Politics of Identity*. New Brunswick, N.J.: Rutgers University Press, 2006.

Campos, Adriana Pereira. "Nas barras das tribunais: Direito e escravidão no Espírito Santo do século XIX." Ph.D. diss., Federal University of Rio de Janeiro, 2003.

Carroll, Patrick J., and Jeffrey N. Lamb. "Los mexicanos negros, el mestizaje, y los fundamentos olvidados de la 'Raza Cósmica': Una perspectiva regional." *Historia Mexicana* 44, no. 3 (March 1995): 403–38.

Carter, Dan T. *Scottsboro: A Tragedy of the American South*. Baton Rouge: Louisiana State University Press, 1969.

Carvalho, Gilmar Luiz de. "A imprensa negra paulista entre 1915 e 1937: Características, mudanças, e permanências." Master's thesis, University of São Paulo, 2009.

Carvalho, José Alberto Magno de, Charles Wood, and Flávia Cristina Drumond Andrade. "Estimating the Stability of Census Based Racial/Ethnic Classifications: The Case of Brazil." *Population Studies* 58, no. 3 (November 2004): 331–43.

Casal, Lourdes, and Anani Dzidzienyo. *The Position of Blacks in Brazilian and Cuban Society.* London: Minority Rights Group, 1979.

Castro, Donald. *The Afro-Argentine in Argentine Culture: El negro del acordeón.* New York: Mellen, 2001.

Castro Heredia, Javier Andrés, Fernando Urrea Giraldo, and Carlos Augusto Viáfara López. "Un breve acercamiento a las políticas de acción afirmativa: Orígenes, aplicación, y experiencia para grupos étnico-raciales en Colombia y Cali." *Revista Sociedad y Economía* 16 (2009): 161–72.

Catterall, Helen T., ed. *Judicial Cases Concerning American Slavery and the Negro.* Vol. 1, *Cases from the Courts of England, Virginia, West Virginia, and Kentucky.* New York: Octagon, 1968.

Chamosa, Oscar. "Indigenous or Criollo: The Myth of White Argentina in Tucumán's Calchaquí Valley." *Hispanic American Historical Review* 88, no. 1 (February 2008): 71–106.

Chaves, María Eugenia. "Honor y libertad: Discursos y recursos en la estrategia de libertad de una mujer esclava (Guayaquil a fines del período colonial)." Ph.D. diss., University of Göteborg, 2001.

———. *María Chiquinquirá Díaz, una esclava del siglo XVIII.* Guayaquil: Archivo Histórico del Guayas, 1998.

Chomsky, Avia. "'Barbados or Canada'? Race, Immigration, and Nation in Early Twentieth Century Cuba." *Hispanic American Historical Review* 80, no. 3 (August 2000): 415–62.

Cole, Shawn. "Capitalism and Freedom: Manumission and the Slave Market in Louisiana, 1725–1820." *Journal of Economic History* 65, no. 4 (December 2005): 1008–27.

Comparato, Fábio Konder. "The Economic Order in the Brazilian Constitution of 1988." *American Journal of Comparative Law* 38, no. 4 (Autumn 1990): 753–71.

Conrad, Robert Edgar. *The Destruction of Brazilian Slavery, 1850–1888.* Berkeley: Krieger, 1972.

Cook, Rebecca J. "Overcoming Discrimination: Introduction." In *The (Un)Rule of Law and the Underprivileged in Latin America,* ed. Juan E. Méndez, Guillermo O'Donnell, and Paulo Sérgio Pinheiro. Notre Dame, Ind.: University of Notre Dame Press, 1999.

Cooper, John M., Jr. *Woodrow Wilson: A Biography.* New York: Random House, 2009.

Cope, R. Douglas. *The Limits of Racial Domination: Plebian Society in Mexico City, 1660–1720.* Madison: University of Wisconsin Press, 1999.

Correa Sutil, Jorge. "Judicial Reforms in Latin America: Good News for the Underprivileged." In *The (Un)Rule of Law and the Underprivileged in Latin America,* ed. Juan E. Méndez, Guillermo O'Donnell, and Paulo Sérgio Pinheiro. Notre Dame, Ind.: University of Notre Dame Press, 1999.

Cortés López, José Luis. *La esclavitud negra en la España peninsular del siglo XVI.* Salamanca: Ediciones Universidad de Salamanca, 1989.

Costa, Emília Viotti da. *The Brazilian Empire: Myths and Histories.* Rev. ed. Chapel Hill: University of North Carolina Press, 2000.

———. *Da monarquia à república: Momentos decisivos.* São Paulo: Editora UNESP, 1998.

———. *Da senzala à colônia.* São Paulo: Editora UNESP, 1997.

Cottrol, Robert J. *The Afro-Yankees: Providence's Black Community in the Antebellum Era.* Westport, Conn.: Greenwood, 1982.

———. "Beyond Invisibility: Afro-Argentines in Their Nation's Culture and Memory." *Latin American Research Review* 42, no. 1 (February 2007): 139–56.

———. "*Brown* and the Contemporary Brazilian Struggle against Racial Inequality: Some Preliminary Comparative Thoughts." *University of Pittsburgh Law Review* 66, no. 1 (Fall 2004): 113–29.

———. "Law, Politics, and Race in Urban America: Towards a New Synthesis." *Rutgers Law Journal* 17, nos. 3–4 (Spring–Summer 1986): 483–536.

———. "The Long Lingering Shadow: Law, Liberalism, and Cultures of Racial Hierarchy and Identity in the Americas." *Tulane Law Review* 76 (November 2001): 11–79.

———. "Static History and Brittle Jurisprudence: Raoul Berger and the Problem of Constitutional Methodology." *Boston College Law Review* 26, no. 2 (March 1985): 353–87.

———. "The Thirteenth Amendment and the North's Overlooked Egalitarian Heritage." *National Black Law Journal* 11, no. 2 (Summer 1989): 198–211.

Cottrol, Robert J., and Raymond T. Diamond. "The Second Amendment: Toward an Afro-Americanist Reconsideration." *Georgetown Law Journal* 80, no. 2 (December 1991): 309–61.

Cottrol, Robert J., Raymond T. Diamond, and Leland B. Ware. *Brown v. Board of Education: Caste, Culture, and the Constitution.* Lawrence: University Press of Kansas, 2003.

Cuche, Denys. *Poder blanco y resistencia negra en el Perú.* Lima: Fondo Editorial del Congreso del Perú, 2001.

Curry, Leonard P. *The Free Black in Urban America, 1800–1850: The Shadow of the Dream*. Chicago: University of Chicago Press, 1981.

Curtin, Philip D. *The Atlantic Slave Trade: A Census*. Madison: University of Wisconsin Press, 1969.

Dávila, Jerry. *Diploma of Whiteness: Race and Social Policy in Brazil, 1917–1945*. Durham, N.C.: Duke University Press, 2003.

Davis, Daniel J. "Nationalism and Civil Rights in Cuba: A Comparative Perspective." *Journal of Negro History* 83, no. 1 (Winter 1998): 35–51.

Davis, Darien J. "The Mechanism of Forging a National Consensus: A Comparative Approach to Modern Brazil and Cuba, 1930–1964." Ph.D. diss., Tulane University, 1992.

Davis, David Brion. *Inhuman Bondage: The Rise and Fall of Slavery in the New World*. New York: Oxford University Press, 2006.

———. *The Problem of Slavery in the Age of Revolution, 1770–1823*. Ithaca: Cornell University Press, 1975.

———. *The Problem of Slavery in Western Culture*. Ithaca: Cornell University Press, 1966.

———. *Slavery and Human Progress*. New York: Oxford University Press, 1984.

Degler, Carl. *Neither Black nor White: Slavery and Race Relations in Brazil and the United States*. Madison: University of Wisconsin Press, 1986.

Domingo, Pilar. "Rule of Law, Citizenship, and Access to Justice in Mexico." *Mexican Studies/Estudios Mexicanos* 15, no. 1 (Winter 1999): 151–91.

Domingos, Manuel. "The Powerful in the Outback of the Brazilian Northeast." Trans. Laurence Hallewell. *Latin American Perspectives* 31, no. 2 (March 2004): 94–111.

Domingues, Petrônio. *Uma história não contada: Negro, racismo, e branqueamento em São Paulo pós-abolição*. São Paulo: Editora Senac, 2004.

———. "Movimento negro brasileiro: Alguns apontamentos históricos." *Tempo* 12, no. 23 (July 2007): 100–122.

———. "Um 'templo de luz': Frente Negra Brasileira (1931–1937) e a questão da educação." *Revista Brasileira de Educação* 13, no. 39 (September–December 2008): 517–96.

Douglas, Davison M. *Jim Crow Moves North: The Battle over Northern School Segregation, 1865–1954*. New York: Cambridge University Press, 2005.

Dudziak, Mary. "Desegregation as a Cold War Imperative." *Stanford Law Review* 41, no. 3 (November 1998): 61–120.

———. "Oliver Wendell Holmes as a Eugenic Reformer: Rhetoric in the Writing of Constitutional Law." *Iowa Law Review* 71, no. 3 (March 1986): 833–67.

Dunn, Richard S. *Sugar and Slaves: The Rise of the Planter Class in the English West Indies, 1624–1713*. Chapel Hill: University of North Carolina Press, 1972.

Dunning, William A. *Reconstruction, Political and Economic, 1865–1877*. New York: Harper, 1907.

Durkheim, Émile. *The Rules of Sociological Method*. 8th ed. Trans. Sarah A. Solovay and John H. Mueller. Ed. George E. G. Catlin. New York: Free Press, 1938.

Dzidzienyo, Anani. "Triangular Mirrors and Moving Colonialisms." *Etnográfica* 6, no. 1 (2002): 127–40.

Edwards, Laura. "Status without Rights: African Americans and the Tangled History of Law and Governance in the Nineteenth Century U.S. South." *American Historical Review* 112, no. 2 (April 2007): 365–93.

Engerman, Stanley L., and Kenneth L. Sokoloff. "The Evolution of Suffrage Institutions in the New World." *Journal of Economic History* 65, no. 4 (December 2005): 891–921.

Epstein, Richard A. *Forbidden Grounds: The Case against Employment Discrimination Laws*. Cambridge: Harvard University Press, 1992.

Erikson, Kai T. *Wayward Puritans: A Study in the Sociology of Deviance*. New York: Allyn and Bacon, 1966.

Fernandes, Florestan. *The Negro in Brazilian Society*. New York: Atheneum, 1971.

Field, Phyllis. *The Politics of Race in New York: The Struggle for Black Suffrage in the Civil War Era*. Ithaca: Cornell University Press, 1982.

Figueroa, Luis A. *Sugar, Slavery, and Freedom in Nineteenth-Century Puerto Rico*. Chapel Hill: University of North Carolina Press, 2005.

Finkelman, Paul. "Prelude to the Fourteenth Amendment: Black Legal Rights in the Antebellum North." *Rutgers Law Journal* 17, nos. 3–4 (Spring–Summer 1986): 415–82.

———. "Was Dred Scott Correctly Decided? An 'Expert Report' for the Defendant." *Lewis and Clark Law Review* 12, no. 4 (2008): 1219–52.

Fix Zamudio, Hector. "The Writ of Amparo in Latin America." *Lawyer of the Americas* 13, no. 3 (Winter 1981): 361–91.

Fleming, Walter L., ed., *Documentary History of Reconstruction: Political, Military, Social, Religious, Educational, and Industrial, 1865 to the Present Time*. Vol. 2. Gloucester, Mass.: Smith, 1960.

Florescano, Enrique. "The Formation and Economic Structure of the Hacienda in New Spain." In *The Cambridge History of Latin America*, vol. 2, *Colonial Latin America*, ed. Leslie Bethell. New York: Cambridge University Press, 1984.

Fogel, Robert W. *Without Consent or Contract: The Rise and Fall of American Slavery*. New York: Norton, 1989.

Fogel, Robert W., and Stanley L. Engerman. *Time on the Cross: The Economics of American Negro Slavery*. Boston: Little, Brown, 1974.

Foner, Eric. *Free Soil, Free Labor, Free Men: The Ideology of the Republican Party before the Civil War*. New York: Oxford University Press, 1970.

———. *Reconstruction: America's Unfinished Revolution, 1863–1877*. New York: Harper and Row, 1988.

Foote, Nicola. "Race, State, and Nation in Early Twentieth Century Ecuador." *Nations and Nationalism* 12, no. 2 (April 2006): 261–78.

Forbath, William E. *Law and the Shaping of the American Labor Movement*. Cambridge: Harvard University Press, 1991.

Ford, Lacy K., Jr. "Making the 'White Man's Country' White: Race, Slavery, and State-Building in the Jacksonian South." *Journal of the Early Republic* 19, no. 4 (Winter 1999): 713–37.

Fox, Dixon Ryan. "The Negro Vote in Old New York." *Political Science Quarterly* 32, no. 2 (June 1917): 252–75.

Fox-Genovese, Elizabeth, and Eugene Genovese. *The Mind of the Master Class: History and Faith in the Southern Slaveholders' Worldview*. New York: Cambridge University Press, 2005.

Franklin, John Hope, and Evelyn Brooks Higginbotham. *From Slavery to Freedom: A History of African Americans*. 9th ed. New York: McGraw-Hill, 2011.

Franklin, John Hope, and Alfred A. Moss Jr. *From Slavery to Freedom: A History of Negro Americans*. 6th ed. New York: Knopf, 1988.

Fredrickson, George M. *The Black Image in the White Mind: The Debate on Afro-American Character and Destiny, 1817–1914*. New York: Irvington, 1971.

French, Jan Hoffman. *Legalizing Identities: Becoming Black or Indian in Brazil's Northeast*. Chapel Hill: University of North Carolina Press, 2009.

French, John D. *Drowning in Laws: Labor Law and Brazilian Political Culture*. Chapel Hill: University of North Carolina Press, 2004.

Freyre, Gilberto. *Casa-grande e senzala: Formação da família brasileira sob o regimen do economia patriarchal*. Rio de Janeiro: Schmidt-Editor, 1938.

———. *Maîtres et esclaves*. Trans. Roger Bastide. Paris: Gallimard, 1952.

———. *The Masters and the Slaves: A Study in the Development of Brazilian Civilization*. Trans. Samuel Putnam. New York: Knopf, 1956.

Friedman, Lawrence M. *American Law in the Twentieth Century*. New Haven: Yale University Press, 2002.

———. *A History of American Law*. New York: Simon and Schuster. 1973.

———. *A History of American Law*. 3rd ed. New York: Simon and Schuster, 2005.

Frigerio, Alejandro. "El candombe Argentino: Crónica de una muerte anunciada." *Revista de Investigaciones Folklóricas* 8 (1993): 50–60.

Fry, Peter, Sérgio Carrara, and Luíza Martins-Costa. "Negros e brancos no carnaval da Velha República." In *Escravidão e a invenção da liberdade: Estudos sobre o negro no Brasil*, ed. João José Reis. São Paulo: Editora Brasiliense with Conselho Nacional de Desenvolvimento Científico e Tecnológico, 1988.

Fuente, Alejandro de la. "Myths of Racial Democracy: Cuba, 1900–1912." *Latin American Research Review* 34, no. 3 (Fall 1999): 39–73.

———. *A Nation for All: Race, Inequality, and Politics in Twentieth-Century Cuba.* Chapel Hill: University of North Carolina Press, 2001.

———. "Race and Inequality in Cuba, 1899–1981." *Journal of Contemporary History* 30, no. 1 (January 1995): 131–68.

———. "Slaves and the Creation of Legal Rights in Cuba: Coartación and Papel." *Hispanic American Historical Review* 87, no. 4 (November 2007): 659–92.

Galenson, David W. "The Settlement and Growth of the Colonies: Population, Labor and Economic Development." In *The Cambridge Economic History of the United States*, vol. 1, *The Colonial Era*, ed. Stanley Engerman and Robert E. Gallman. New York: Cambridge University Press, 1996.

Gallego, José Andrés. *Derecho y justicia en España y la América prerrevolucionarias.* Madrid: Fundación Mapfre Tavera y Fundación Ignacio Larramendi, 2001.

García, Iliana París. *Ideología y proceso de blanqueamiento: Una aproximación construccionista a su posible influencia en la identidad y la auto imagen de tres mujeres negras venezolanas.* Caracas: Universidad Central de Venezuela, 2002.

García Jordán, Pilar. "Reflexiones sobre el Darwinismo social: Inmigración y colonización, mitos de los grupos modernizadores peruanos (1821–1919)." *Bulletin de l'Institut Français d'Études Andines* 21, no. 3 (1992): 961–75.

Garfield, Seth. "'The Roots of a Plant That Today Is Brazil': Indians and the Nation-State under the Brazilian Estado Novo." *Journal of Latin American Studies* 29, no. 3 (October 1997): 747–68.

Gargarella, Roberto. "Towards a Typology of Latin American Constitutionalism, 1810–60." *Latin American Research Review* 39, no. 2 (June 2004): 141–53.

Garro, Alejandro M. "Access to Justice for the Poor in Latin America." In *The (Un)Rule of Law and the Underprivileged in Latin America*, ed. Juan E. Méndez, Guillermo O'Donnell, and Paulo Sérgio Pinheiro. Notre Dame, Ind.: University of Notre Dame Press, 1999.

Gastwirth, Joseph L. "Issues Arising in the Use of Statistical Evidence in Discrimination Cases." In *Statistical Science in the Courtroom*, ed. Joseph L. Gastwirth. New York: Springer, 2000.

Genovese, Eugene. *Roll, Jordan, Roll: The World the Slaves Made*. New York: Vintage, 1974.

———. "The Treatment of Slaves in Different Countries: Problems in the Applications of the Comparative Method." In *Slavery in the New World: A Reader in Comparative History*, ed. Laura Foner and Eugene Genovese. Englewood Cliffs, N.J.: Prentice-Hall, 1969.

Gibson, Charles. "Indian Societies under Spanish Rule." In *The Cambridge History of Latin America*, vol. 2, *Colonial Latin America*, ed. Leslie Bethell. New York: Cambridge University Press, 1984.

Gidi, Antonio. "Class Actions in Brazil: A Model for Civil Law Countries." *American Journal of Comparative Law* 51, no. 2 (Spring 2003): 311–408.

Golash-Boza, Tanya Maria. *Yo Soy Negro: Blackness in Peru*. Gainesville: University of Florida Press, 2011.

Goldin, Claudia Dale. "The Economics of Emancipation." *Journal of Economic History* 33, no. 1 (March 1973): 66–85.

Goldstein, Donna M. *Laughter Out of Place: Race, Class, Violence, and Sexuality in a Rio Shantytown*. Berkeley: University of California Press, 2003.

Golub, Mark. "Plessy as 'Passing': Judicial Responses to Ambiguously Raced Bodies in *Plessy v. Ferguson*." *Law and Society Review* 39, no. 3 (September 2005): 563–600.

Goluboff, Risa L. "'We Live's in a Free House Such as It Is': Class and the Creation of Modern Civil Rights." *University of Pennsylvania Law Review* 151, no. 6 (June 2003): 1977–2018.

Gonçalves, Cláudia Maria da Costa. "Políticas dos direitos fundamentais sociais na constituição federal de 1988: Releitura de uma constituição dirigente." Ph.D. diss. Federal University of Maranhão, São Luís, 2005.

González Navarro, Moisés. "Mestizaje in Mexico during the National Period." In *Race and Class in Latin America*, ed. Magnus Mörner. New York: Columbia University Press, 1970.

Gott, Richard. *Cuba: A New History*. New Haven: Yale University Press, 2005.

Graber, Mark A. *Dred Scott and the Problem of Constitutional Evil*. New York: Cambridge University Press, 2006.

Greene, Lorenzo Johnston. *The Negro in Colonial New England*. New York: Atheneum, 1968.

Grinberg, Keila. *O fiador dos Brasileiros: Cidadania, escravidão, e direito civil no tempo de Antonio Pereira Rebouças*. Rio de Janeiro: Civilização Brasileira, 2002.

Gross, Ariela J. *Double Character: Slavery and Mastery in the Antebellum Southern Courtroom*. Princeton: Princeton University Press, 2000.

——. *What Blood Won't Tell: A History of Race on Trial in America.* Cambridge: Harvard University Press, 2008.

Guevara, Gema R. "Founding Discourses of Cuban Nationalism: La Patria, Blanqueamiento, and La Raza de Color." Ph.D. diss., University of California, San Diego, 2000.

——. "Inexacting Whiteness: Blanqueamiento as a Gender-Specific Trope in the Nineteenth Century." *Cuban Studies Journal* 36, no. 1 (2005): 105–28.

Haak, David Sulmont. "Raza y etnicidad desde las encuestas sociales y de opinión: Dime cuántos quieres encontrar y te diré qué preguntar . . . ." Paper presented at conference, La Discriminación Social en el Perú: Investigación y Reflexión, Centro de Investigación de la Universidad del Pacífico-Lima, Peru, June 24, 2010; revised September 11, 2010.

Hall, Jacquelyn Dowd. "The Long Civil Rights Movement and the Political Uses of the Past." *Journal of American History* 91, no. 4 (March 2005): 1233–63.

Hargrove, Hondon B. *Buffalo Soldiers in Italy: Black Americans in World War II.* Jefferson, N.C.: McFarland, 1985.

Harpelle, Ronald N. "Ethnicity, Religion, and Repression: The Denial of African Heritage in Costa Rica." *Canadian Journal of History* 29, no. 1 (April 1994): 95–112.

——. "The Social and Political Integration of West Indians in Costa Rica: 1930–50." *Journal of Latin American Studies* 25, no. 1 (February 1993): 103–20.

Hasenbalg, Carlos A., and Nelson do Valle Silva. "Race and Educational Opportunity in Brazil." In *Race in Contemporary Brazil: From Indifference to Inequality*, ed. Rebecca Reichmann. Philadelphia: University of Pennsylvania Press, 1999.

Helg, Aline. "Black Men, Racial Stereotyping, and Violence in the U.S. South and Cuba at the Turn of the Century." *Comparative Studies in Society and History* 42., no. 3 (July 2000): 576–604.

——. *Liberty and Equality in Caribbean Colombia, 1770–1835.* Chapel Hill: University of North Carolina Press, 2004.

——. *Our Rightful Share: The Afro-Cuban Struggle for Equality, 1886–1912.* Chapel Hill: University of North Carolina Press, 1995.

——. "Race and Black Mobilization in Colonial and Early Independent Cuba: A Comparative Perspective." *Ethnohistory* 44, no. 1 (Winter 1997): 53–74.

——. "Race in Argentina and Cuba, 1880–1930: Theory, Politics, and Popular Reaction." In *The Idea of Race in Latin America, 1870–1949*, ed. Richard Graham. Austin: University of Texas Press, 1990.

Hensler, Benjamin. "Não Vale a Pena? (Not Worth the Trouble?): Afro-Brazilian Workers and Brazilian Anti-Discrimination Law." *Hastings International and Comparative Law Review* 30, no. 3 (Spring 2007): 267–346.

Heringer, Rosana. "Desigualdades raciais no Brasil: Síntese de indicadores e desafios no campo das políticas públicas." *Cadernos Saúde Pública* 18, Supplement (2002): S57–S65.

Hernandez, Tanya K. "Comparative Judging of Civil Rights: A Transnational Critical Race Theory Approach." *Louisiana Law Review* 63, no. 3 (Spring 2003): 875–86.

——. "An Exploration of the Efficacy of Class-Based Approaches to Racial Justice: The Cuban Context." *UC Davis Law Review* 33, no. 4 (Summer 2000): 1135–71.

——. "To Be Brown in Brazil: Education and Segregation Latin American Style." *New York University Review of Law and Social Change* 29, no. 4 (2005): 683–717.

Herrera, Robinson A. "'Por Que No Sabemos Firmar': Black Slaves in Early Guatemala." *The Americas* 57, no. 2 (October 2000): 247–67.

Hickman, Christine. "The Devil and the One Drop Rule: Racial Categories, African Americans, and the U.S. Census." *Michigan Law Review* 95, no. 5 (March 1997): 1161–1265.

Higginbotham, A. Leon, Jr. *In the Matter of Color: Race and the American Legal Process: The Colonial Period.* New York: Oxford University Press, 1978.

Higginbotham, A. Leon, Jr., and Barbara K. Kopytoff. "Racial Purity and Interracial Sex in the Law of Colonial and Antebellum Virginia." *Georgetown Law Journal* 77, no. 6 (August 1989): 1967–2029.

Hill, Lance. *The Deacons for Defense: Armed Resistance and the Civil Rights Movement.* Chapel Hill: University of North Carolina Press, 2004.

Hoetink, Harry. "The Dominican Republic in the Nineteenth Century: Some Notes on Stratification, Immigration, and Race." In *Race and Class in Latin America*, ed. Magnus Mörner. New York: Columbia University Press, 1970.

Hoffer, Peter Charles. *The Great New York Conspiracy of 1741: Slavery, Crime, and Colonial Law.* Lawrence: University Press of Kansas, 2003.

Hoffman, Kelly, and Miguel Angel Centeno. "The Lopsided Continent: Inequality in Latin America." *Annual Review of Sociology* 29 (June 2003): 363–90.

Hooker, Juliet. "Indigenous Inclusion/Black Exclusion: Race, Ethnicity, and Multicultural Citizenship in Latin America." *Journal of Latin American Studies* 37, no. 2 (May 2005): 285–310.

Hopkins, Keith. "Novel Evidence for Roman Slavery." *Past and Present* 138 (February 1993): 3–27.

Horbach, Carlos Bastide. *Memória jurisprudencial: Ministro Pedro Lessa.* Brasília: STF, 2007.

Horton, James Oliver, and Lois E. Horton. *Black Bostonians: Family Life and*

Community Struggle in the Antebellum North. New York: Holmes and Meier, 1979.

———. *Slavery and the Making of America*. New York: Cambridge University Press, 2005.

Horton, Lois E. "From Class to Race in Early America: Northern Post-Emancipation Racial Reconstruction." *Journal of the Early Republic* 19, no. 4 (Winter 1999): 629–49.

Horwitz, Morton J. *The Transformation of American Law, 1780–1860*. Cambridge: Harvard University Press, 1977.

———. *The Transformation of American Law, 1870–1960*. New York: Oxford University Press, 1992.

Hovenkamp, Herbert. "Social Science and Segregation before *Brown*." *Duke Law Journal* 1985, nos. 3–4 (June–September 1985): 624–72.

Howard, David. *Coloring the Nation: Race and Ethnicity in the Dominican Republic*. Oxford: Signal, 2001.

———. "Development, Racism, and Discrimination in the Dominican Republic." *Development in Practice* 17, no. 6 (November 2007): 725–38.

Htun, Mala. "From 'Racial Democracy' to Affirmative Action: Changing State Policy on Race in Brazil." *Latin American Research Review* 39, no. 1 (February 2004): 60–89.

Hünefeldt, Christine. *Paying the Price of Freedom: Family and Labor among Lima's Slaves, 1800–1854*. Berkeley: University of California Press, 1994.

Hutchinson, Harry W. "Race Relations in a Rural Community of the Bahian Recôncavo." In *Race and Class in Rural Brazil: A UNESCO Study*, ed. Charles Wagley. New York: UNESCO, 1963.

Hyman, Harold M., and William M. Wiecek. *Equal Justice under Law: Constitutional Development, 1835–1875*. New York: HarperCollins, 1982.

Ivy, Leonora A. "A Study in Leadership: The 761st Tank Battalion and the 92nd Division." Master's thesis, U.S. Army Command and General Staff College, Ft. Leavenworth, Kans., 1995.

Johnson, Lyman L. "'A Lack of Legitimate Obedience and Respect': Slaves and Their Masters in the Courts of Late Colonial Buenos Aires." *Hispanic American Historical Review* 87, no. 4 (November 2007): 631–57.

Johnson, Paul Christopher. "Law, Religion, and 'Public Health' in the Republic of Brazil." *Law and Social Inquiry* 26, no. 1 (Winter 2001): 29–33.

Jordan, Winthrop. *White over Black: American Attitudes toward the Negro, 1550–1812*. Chapel Hill: University of North Carolina Press, 1968.

Kalman, Laura. *Legal Realism at Yale, 1927–1960*. Chapel Hill: University of North Carolina Press, 1986.

Katzman, David M. *Before the Ghetto: Black Detroit in the Nineteenth Century.* Urbana: University of Illinois Press, 1973.

Kawashima, Yasuhide. "Adoption in Early America." *Journal of Family Law* 20, no. 4 (1981–82): 677–96.

Kilsztajn, Samuel, Manuela Santos Nunes do Carmo, Gustavo Toshiaki Lopes Sugahara, et al. "Concentração e distribuição do rendimento por raça no Brasil." *Revista de Economia Contemporânea* 9, no. 2 (May–August 2005): 367–84.

King, Mary C. "Are African Americans Losing Their Footholds in Better Jobs?" *Journal of Economic Issues* 32, no. 3 (September 1998): 641–68.

Kittner, Michael, and Thomas C. Kohler. "Conditioning Expectations: The Protection of the Employment Bond in German and American Law." *Comparative Labor Law and Policy Journal* 21, no. 2 (Winter 2000): 263–330.

Klarman, Michael. *From Jim Crow to Civil Rights: The Supreme Court and the Struggle for Racial Equality.* New York: Oxford University Press, 2004.

Klein, Herbert S. *The Atlantic Slave Trade.* New York: Cambridge University Press, 2010.

———. "The Integration of Italian Immigrants into the United States and Argentina: A Comparative Analysis." *American Historical Review* 88, no. 2 (April 1983): 306–29.

Klein, Herbert S., and Francisco Vidal Luna. *Slavery in Brazil.* New York: Cambridge University Press, 2010.

Knight, Franklin W. *Slave Society in Cuba during the Nineteenth Century.* Madison: University of Wisconsin Press, 1970.

Lacombe, Américo Jacobina, Francisco de Assis Barbosa, and Eduardo da Silva. *Rui Barbosa e a queima dos arquivos.* Rio de Janeiro: Fundação Casa de Rui Barbosa, 1988.

Lane, Kris. "Captivity and Redemption: Aspects of Slave Life in Early Quito and Popayán." *The Americas* 57, no. 2 (October 2000): 225–46.

Lasso, Marixa. *Myths of Harmony: Race and Republicanism during the Age of Revolution, Colombia, 1795–1831.* Pittsburgh: University of Pittsburgh Press, 2007.

Lehman, David. "Gilberto Freyre: The Reassessment Continues." *Latin American Research Review* 43, no. 1 (2008): 208–18.

Leite, Ilka Boaventura. "Descendentes de africanos em Santa Catarina: Invisibilidade histórica e segregação." In *Negros no sul do Brasil: Invisibilidade e territorialidade*, by Ilka Boaventura Leite, Ruben George Oliven, et al. Ilha de Santa Catarina: Letras Contemporâneas, 1996.

León, Magdalena, and Jimena Holguín. "La acción afirmativa en la Universidad de los Andes: El caso del programa 'Oportunidades para Talentos Nacionales.'" *Revista de Estudios Sociales* 19 (December 2004): 57–70.

Lesser, Jeffrey. "Immigration and Shifting Concepts of National Identity in Brazil during the Vargas Era." *Luso-Brazilian Review* 31, no. 2 (Winter 1994): 23–44.

Lewis, Harold S., Jr., and Elizabeth J. Norman. *Employment Discrimination Law and Practice.* 2nd ed. St. Paul, Minn.: West, 2001.

Lewis, Herbert S. "The Passion of Franz Boas." *American Anthropologist* 103, no. 2 (June 2001): 447–67.

Lewis, Laura A. "'Afro' Mexico in Black, White, and Indian: An Anthropologist Reflects on Fieldwork." In *Black Mexico: Race and Society from Colonial to Modern Times,* ed. Ben Vinson III and Matthew Restall. Albuquerque: University of New Mexico Press, 2009.

Lewin, Linda. *Surprise Heirs.* Vol. 1, *Illegitimacy, Patrimonial Rights, and Legal Nationalism in Luso-Brazilian Inheritance, 1750–1821.* Stanford: Stanford University Press, 2003.

Liboreiro, M. Cristina de. *No hay negros argentinos?* Buenos Aires: Editorial Dunken, 1999.

Lichtenstein, Alex. *Twice the Work of Free Labor: The Political Economy of Convict Labor in the New South.* London: Verso, 1996.

Lima, Marcus Eugênio Oliveira, and Jorge Vala. "As novas formas de expressão do preconceito e do racismo." *Estudos de Psicologia* 9, no. 3 (December 2004): 401–11.

Lokken, Paul. "Marriage as Slave Emancipation in Seventeenth Century Rural Guatemala." *The Americas* 58, no. 2 (October 2001): 175–200.

Love, Joseph L. "Political Participation in Brazil, 1881–1969." *Luso-Brazilian Review* 7, no. 2 (December 1970): 3–24.

Loveman, Mara. "The Race to Progress: Census Taking and Nation Making in Brazil (1870–1920)." *Hispanic American Historical Review* 89, no. 3 (August 2009): 435–70.

Lowrie, Samuel H. "The Negro Element in the Population of São Paulo, a Southernly State of Brazil." *Phylon* 3, no. 4 (4th Quarter 1942): 398–416.

Macieal, Cleber da Silva. "Discriminações raciais: Negros em Campinas (1888–1926) alguns aspectos." Master's thesis, State University of Campinas, 1985.

Mack, Kenneth. "Law, Society, Identity, and the Making of the Jim Crow South: Travel and Segregation on Tennessee Railroads, 1875–1905." *Law and Social Inquiry* 24, no. 2 (Spring 1999): 377–409.

Mac-Lean y Estenos, Roberto. "La eugenesia en América." *Revista Mexicana de Sociología* 13, no. 3 (September–December 1951): 359–87.

Magalhães, Alânia. "Trabalho e educação: Os efeitos de educação sobre o processo de estratificação social entre brancos e não-brancos no Brasil." *Sociologia e Política: I Seminário Nacional Sociologia e Política* (2009): 1–17. http://www .humanas.ufpr.br/site/evento/SociologiaPolitica/GTs-ONLINE/GT5%20online /EixoI/trabalho-educacao-AlaniaMagalhaes.pdf.

Magalhães, Naiara. "Os nisseis." *Revista Veja*, December 12, 2007.

Maio, Marcos Chor. "O projeto UNESCO e a agenda das ciências sociais no Brasil dos anos 40 e 50." *Revista Brasileira de Ciências Sociais* 14, no. 41 (October 1999): 141–58.

Makabe, Tomoko. "Ethnic Hegemony: The Japanese Brazilians in Agriculture, 1908–1968." *Ethnic and Racial Studies* 22, no. 4 (July 1999): 702–23.

Maltz, Earl M. "The Unlikely Hero of *Dred Scott*: Benjamin Robbins Curtis and the Constitutional Law of Slavery." *Cardozo Law Review* 17, no. 6 (May 1996): 1995–2016.

Maram, Sheldon L. "Labor and the Left in Brazil, 1890–1921: A Movement Aborted." *Hispanic American Historical Review* 57, no. 2 (May 1977): 254–72.

———. "Urban Labor and Social Change in the 1920s." *Luso-Brazilian Review* 16, no. 2 (Winter 1979): 215–23.

Marinho, Cláudia Margarida Ribas. "O racismo no Brasil: Uma análise do desenvolvimento histórico do tema e da eficácia da lei como instrumento de combate á discriminaçao racial." Undergraduate thesis, Federal University of Santa Catarina, 1999.

Marquese, Rafael de Bivar. "A dinâmica da escravidão no Brasil: Resistência, tráfico negreiro, e alforrias, séculos XVII a XIX." *Novos Estudos* 74 (2006): 107–23.

Martínez, Frédéric. "Apogeo y decadencia del ideal de la inmigración europea en Colombia, siglo XIX." *Boletín Cultural y Bibliográfico* 34, no. 44 (1997): 3–45.

Martinez, Samuel. "From Hidden Hand to Heavy Hand: Sugar, the State, and Migrant Labor in Haiti and the Dominican Republic." *Latin American Research Review* 34, no. 1 (1999): 57–84.

Martínez-Echazábal, Lourdes. "Mestizaje and the Discourse of National/Cultural Identity in Latin America, 1845–1959." *Latin American Perspectives* 25, no. 3 (May 1998): 21–42.

Marzal Palacios, Francisco Javier. "La esclavitud en Valéncia durante la baja edad media (1375–1425)." Ph.D. diss., University of Valéncia, 2006.

Masferrer, Marianne, and Carmelo Mesa-Lago. "The Gradual Integration of the Black in Cuba: Under the Colony, the Republic, and the Revolution." In *Slavery and Race Relations in Latin America*, ed. Robert Brent Toplin. Westport, Conn.: Greenwood, 1974.

Massey, Douglas S., and Nancy A. Denton. *American Apartheid: Segregation and the Making of the Underclass*. Cambridge: Harvard University Press, 1993.

Mauro, Frédéric. *Le Portugal, le Brésil, et l'Atlantique au XVIIe siècle (1570–1670): Étude économique*. Paris: Fondation Calouste Gulbenkian, 1983.

Maximiano, Cesar Campiani, and Dennison de Oliveira. "Raça e forças armadas: O caso da campanha da Itália (1944/45)." *Estudos de História Franca* 8, no. 1 (2001): 157–84.

McAndrews, Lawrence J. "The Politics of Principle: Richard Nixon and School Desegregation." *Journal of Negro History* 83, no. 3 (Summer 1998): 187–200.

McCann, Frank D. "Brazil and World War II: The Forgotten Ally: What Did You Do in the War, Zé Carioca?" *Estudios Interdisciplinarios de América Latina y el Caribe* 6, no. 2 (July–December 1995). http://www.tau.ac.il/eial/VI_2/mccann.htm.

McKinley, Michelle. "Fractional Freedoms: Slavery, Legal Activism, and Ecclesiastical Courts in Colonial Lima, 1593–1689." *Law and History Review* 28, no. 3 (July 2010): 749–90.

McKitrick, Eric L., ed. *Slavery Defended: The Views of the Old South*. Englewood Cliffs, N.J.: Prentice-Hall, 1963.

McManus, Edgar J. *Black Bondage in the North*. Syracuse, N.Y.: Syracuse University Press, 1973.

McMath, Robert C., Jr. "C. Vann Woodward and the Burden of Southern Populism." *Journal of Southern History* 67, no. 4 (November 2001): 741–68.

Meade, Teresa A. *"Civilizing" Rio: Reform and Resistance in a Brazilian City, 1889–1930*. University Park: Pennsylvania State University Press, 1997.

Meade, Teresa A., and Gregory Alonso Pirio. "In Search of the Afro-American 'Eldorado': Attempts by North American Blacks to Enter Brazil in the 1920s." *Luso-Brazilian Review* 25, no. 1 (Summer 1988): 85–110.

Méndez, Juan E., Guillermo O'Donnell, and Paulo Sérgio Pinheiro, eds. *The (Un) Rule of Law and the Underprivileged in Latin America*. Notre Dame, Ind.: University of Notre Dame Press, 1999.

Merrick, Thomas W., and Douglas H. Graham. *Population and Economic Development in Brazil: 1810 to the Present*. Baltimore: Johns Hopkins University Press, 1979.

Miller, Joseph C. *Way of Death: Merchant Capitalism and the Angolan Slave Trade, 1730–1830*. Madison: University of Wisconsin Press, 1988.

Miller, Marilyn Grace. *The Rise and Fall of Cosmic Race: The Cult of Mestizaje in Latin America*. Austin: University of Texas Press, 2004.

Molina Bustamante, Sergio. *La propaganda racista contra los afrodescendientes en el Perú: Estudio de caso sobre un programa de humor.* Lima: Coordinadora Nacional de Derechos Humanos y LUNDU, 2008.

Monkevicius, Paola C., and Marta M. Maffia. "Memoria y límites étnicos entre los caboverdeanos de Argentina." *Boletín de Antropología* 24, no. 41 (August 2010): 115–33.

Morgan, Edmund S. *American Slavery, American Freedom: The Ordeal of Colonial Virginia.* New York: Norton, 1975.

Morgan, Philip D. *Slave Counterpoint: Black Culture in the Eighteenth Century Chesapeake and Low Country.* Chapel Hill: University of North Carolina Press, 1998.

Morison, Samuel Eliot. *History of United States Naval Operations in World War II.* Vol. 1, *The Battle of the Atlantic, September 1939–May 1943.* Boston: Little, Brown, 1951.

Morris, Thomas D. *Southern Slavery and the Law, 1619–1860.* Chapel Hill: University of North Carolina Press, 1996.

Moskos, Charles C., Jr. "The American Dilemma in Uniform: Race in the Armed Forces." *Annals of the American Academy of Political and Social Science* 406, no. 1 (March 1973): 94–106.

Moura, Clóvis. *Rebeliões da senzala: Quilombos, insurreições, guerrilhas.* Porto Alegre: Livraria editora ciências humanas, 1988.

Mustelier, Gustavo Enrique. *La extinción del negro: Apuntes político-sociales.* Havana: Rambla, Bouza, 1912.

Myrdal, Gunnar. *An American Dilemma: The Negro Problem and Modern Democracy.* New York: Harper, 1944.

Nabuco, Joaquim. *O abolicionismo, com introdução de Izabel A. Marson e Célio R. Tasinafo.* Brasília: Kingdon, 2003.

Nascimento, Abdias do, and Elisa Larkin Nascimento. "Dance of Deception: A Reading of Race Relations in Brazil." In *Beyond Racism: Race and Inequality in Brazil, South Africa, and the United States,* ed. Charles V. Hamilton, Lynn Huntley, Neville Alexander, Antonio Sérgio Alfredo Guimarães, and Wilmot James. Boulder, Colo.: Rienner, 2001.

Nascimento, Alexandre do. "Movimentos sociais, educação e cidadania: Um estudo sobre os cursos pré-vestibulares populares." Master's thesis, State University of Rio de Janeiro, 1999.

Nascimento, Elisa Larkin. "Aspects of Afro-Brazilian Experience." *Journal of Black Studies* 11, no. 2 (December 1980): 195–216.

———. "It's in the Blood: Notes on Race Attitudes in Brazil from a Different Perspective." In *Beyond Racism: Race and Inequality in Brazil, South Africa, and the United States,* ed. Charles V. Hamilton, Lynn Huntley, Neville

Alexander, Antonio Sérgio Alfredo Guimarães, and Wilmot James. Boulder, Colo.: Rienner, 2001.

──── . *The Sorcery of Color: Identity, Race, and Gender in Brazil.* Philadelphia: Temple University Press, 2007.

N'Djoli, Jean-Philibert Mobwa Mobwa. "The Need to Recognize Afro-Mexicans as an Ethnic Group." In *Black Mexico: Race and Society from Colonial to Modern Times,* ed. Ben Vinson III and Matthew Restall. Albuquerque: University of New Mexico Press, 2009.

Netto, José Apóstolo. "Os africanos no Brasil: Raça, cientificismo, e ficção em Nina Rodrigues." *Revista Espaço Acadêmico* 44 (2005). http://www .espacoacademico.com.br/044/44netto.htm.

Newby, Idus A. *Jim Crow's Defense: Anti-Negro Thought in America, 1900–1930.* Baton Rouge: Louisiana State University Press, 1965.

Nobles, Melissa. *Shades of Citizenship: Race and the Census in Modern Politics.* Stanford: Stanford University Press, 2000.

No Longer Invisible: Afro-Latin Americans Today. London: Minority Rights Group, 1995.

O'Brien, Patricia. "Crime and Punishment as Historical Problem." *Journal of Social History* 11, no. 4 (Summer 1978): 508–20.

Oda, Ana Maria Galdini Raimundo. "Alienação mental e raça: A psicopatologia comparada dos negros e mestiços brasileiros na obra de Raimundo Nina Rodrigues." Ph.D. diss., State University of Campinas, 2003.

Oliven, Ruben George. "A invisibilidade social e simbólica do negro no Rio Grande do Sul." In *Negros no sul do Brasil: Invisibilidade e territorialidade,* by Ilka Boaventura Leite, Ruben George Oliven, et al. Ilha de Santa Catarina: Letras Contemporâneas, 1996.

Oquendo, Angel R. *Latin American Law.* 2nd ed. New York: Foundation Press, 2011.

Oro Negro Foundation. *Afro Descendants Organize Themselves.* http://www .nuestro.cl/eng/stories/people/oronegro.htm.

Oro, Pedro, and Daniel F. de Bem. "A discriminação contra as religiões afro-brasileiras ontem e hoje." *Ciências e Letras Porto Alegre* 44 (July–December 2008): 301–18.

Oshinsky, David. *Worse Than Slavery: Parchman Farm and the Ordeal of Jim Crow Justice.* New York: Simon and Schuster, 1996.

Owensby, Brian. "Toward a History of Brazil's 'Cordial Racism': Race beyond Liberalism." *Comparative Studies in Society and History* 47, no. 2 (April 2005): 318–47.

Paim, Paulo Renato, and Thiago Thobias. "Exposição dos motivos que levaram à apresentação do Estatuto da Igualdade Racial: O Estatuto da Igualdade Racial, a dor da esperança: 20 anos de sangue, suor, e lágrimas." In *Estatuto da Igualdade Racial: Comentários doutrinários*, ed. Calil Simão. São Paulo: Mizuno, 2011.

Palma, Héctor, and Eduardo Wolovelsky. "Tecnologías biopoliticas: El caso de la eugenesia." In *Ciências da vida: Estudos filosóficos e históricos*, ed. Lilian A. Pereira Martins, Ana C. Regner, and Pablo Lorenzano. Campinas: Associação de Filosofia e História da Ciência do Cone Sul, 2006.

Patterson, Orlando. *The Ordeal of Integration: Progress and Resentment in America's "Racial" Crisis*. New York: Civitas/Counterpoint, 1997.

———. *Slavery and Social Death: A Comparative Study*. Cambridge: Harvard University Press, 1982.

Pearcy, Thomas L. "Panama's Generation of '31: Patriots, Praetorians, and a Decade of Discord." *Hispanic American Historical Review* 76, no. 4 (November 1996): 691–719.

Pérez, Louis A., Jr. "Politics, Peasants, and People of Color: The 1912 'Race War' in Cuba Reconsidered." *Hispanic American Historical Review* 66, no. 3 (August 1986): 509–39.

Phillips, Ulrich B. "The Central Theme of Southern History." *American Historical Review* 34, no. 1 (October 1928): 30–43.

Pichardo, Franklin Franco. *Sobre racismo y antihaitianismo y otros ensayos*. Santo Domingo, D.R.: n.p., 1997.

Pignot, Elsa. "El asociacionismo negro en Cuba: Una vía de integración en la sociedad republicana (1920–1960)." *Revista de Indias* 70, no. 250 (September–December 2010): 837–62.

Pinheiro, Paulo Sérgio. "The Rule of Law and the Underprivileged in Latin America: Introduction." In *The (Un)Rule of Law and the Underprivileged in Latin America*, ed. Juan E. Méndez, Guillermo O'Donnell, and Paulo Sérgio Pinheiro. Notre Dame, Ind.: University of Notre Dame Press, 1999.

Plank, David N. *The Means of Our Salvation: Public Education in Brazil, 1930–1995*. Boulder, Colo.: Westview, 1996.

Pleck, Elizabeth Hafkin. *Black Migration and Poverty, Boston 1865–1900*. New York: Academic, 1979.

Prudente, Eunice. *Preconceito racial e igualdade jurídica no Brasil*. Campinas: Julex Livros, 1989.

Putnam, Lara. "Eventually Alien: The Multi-Generational Saga of British West Indians in Central America, 1870–1940." In *Blacks and Blackness in Central America: Between Race and Place*, ed. Lowell Gudmundson and Justin Wolfe. Durham, N.C.: Duke University Press, 2010.

Racusen, Seth. "Fictions of Identity and Brazilian Affirmative Action." *National Black Law Journal* 21, no. 3 (2009). http://journals.cdrs.columbia.edu/nblj /index.php/nblj/article/view/29.

———. "Making the 'Impossible' Determination: Flexible Identity and Targeted Opportunity in Contemporary Brazil." *Connecticut Law Review* 36, no. 3 (Spring 2004): 787–29.

———. "A Mulatto Cannot Be Prejudiced: The Legal Construction of Racial Discrimination in Contemporary Brazil." Ph.D. diss., Massachusetts Institute of Technology, 2002.

Rama, Carlos M. "The Passing of the Afro-Uruguayans from Caste Society into Class Society." In *Race and Class in Latin America*, ed. Magnus Mörner. New York: Columbia University Press, 1970.

Ransom, Roger L., and Richard Sutch. *One Kind of Freedom: The Economic Consequences of Emancipation*. 2nd ed. New York: Cambridge University Press, 2001.

Reis, João José. *Slave Rebellion in Brazil: The Muslim Uprising of 1835 in Bahia*. Trans. Arthur Brakel. Baltimore: Johns Hopkins University Press, 1993.

Restall, Matthew. "Black Conquistadors: Armed Africans in Early Spanish America." *The Americas* 57, no. 2 (October 2000): 171–205.

Rodrigues, Eder Bomfim. "A igualdade racial no estado democrático de direito." In *Estatuto da igualdade racial: Comentários doutrinários*, ed. Calil Simão. São Paulo: Mizuno, 2011.

Rodríguez Garavito, César, Tatiana Alfonso Sierra, and Isabel Cavelier Adarve. "Las cifras de la discriminación racial y la situación de la población afroco-lombiana." In *El derecho a no ser discriminado: Primer informe sobre discrimi-nación racial y derechos de la población afrocolombiana (Version resumida)*. Bogotá: Universidad de los Andes, 2008.

Rodríguez Pastor, Humberto. *Herederos del dragón: Historia de la comunidad China en el Perú*. Lima: Fondo Editorial del Congreso del Perú, 2000.

Rosenheck, Uri. "Olive Drab in Black and White: The Brazilian Expeditionary Force, the us Army, and Racial National Identity." Paper Presented at Latin American Studies Association, October 8, 2010.

Rosenn, Keith S. "The Success of Constitutionalism in the United States and its Failure in Latin America: An Explanation." *University of Miami Inter-American Law Review* 22, no. 1 (Fall 1990): 1–39.

Rout, Leslie B., Jr. *The African Experience in Spanish America, 1502 to the Present Day*. New York: Cambridge University Press, 1976.

Russel-Wood, A. J. R. *The Portuguese Empire, 1415–1808*. Baltimore: Johns Hopkins University Press, 1992.

Safford, Frank. "Race, Integration, and Progress: Elite Attitudes and the Indian in Colombia, 1750–1870." *Hispanic American Historical Review* 71, no. 1 (February 1991): 1–33.

Sagrera, Martín. *Los racismos en las Américas: Una interpretación histórica.* Madrid: IEPALA, 1998.

Sanchez, Robert. "Black Mosaic: The Assimilation and Marginalization of Afro-Peruvians in Post-Abolition Peru, 1854–1930." Ph.D. diss., University of Illinois, Urbana-Champaign, 2008.

Sánchez-Albornoz, Nicolás. "The Population of Colonial Spanish America." In *The Cambridge History of Latin America*, vol. 2, *Colonial Latin America*, ed. Leslie Bethell. New York: Cambridge University Press, 1984.

————. *The Population of Latin America: A History.* Trans. W. A. R. Richardson. Berkeley: University of California Press, 1974.

Sander, Roberto. *O Brasil na mira de Hitler: A história do afundamento de navios brasileiros pelos nazistas.* Rio de Janeiro: Objetiva, 2007.

Sanjek, Roger. "Brazilian Racial Terms: Some Aspects of Meaning and Learning." *American Anthropologist* 73, no. 5 (October 1971): 1126–43.

Santos, Fabiane dos. "A construção do inimigo: É tempo de guerra, medo, e silêncio." *Revista Santa Catarina em História* 1, no. 2 (2007): 62–72.

Santos, José Alcides Figueiredo. "Efeitos de classe na desigualdade racial no Brasil." *Dados: Revista de Ciências Socias* 46, no. 1 (January–March 2005): 21–65.

Saunders, A. C. de C. M. *A Social History of Black Slaves and Freedmen in Portugal, 1441–1555.* New York: Cambridge University Press, 1982.

Schávelzon, Daniel. *Buenos Aires negra: Arqueología histórica de una ciudad silenciada.* Buenos Aires: Emecé Editores, 2003.

Schwarcz, Lilia Katri Moritz. "Previsões são sempre traiçoeiras: João Baptista de Lacerda e seu Brasil branco." *História, Ciências, Saúde-Manguinhos* 18, no. 1 (January–March 2001): 225–42.

————. "Quando a desigualdade é diferença: Reflexões sobre antropologia criminal e mestiçagem na obra de Nina Rodrigues." *Gazeta Médica da Bahia* 140, no 76, supplement 2 (2006): 47–53.

Scisínio, Alaôr Eduardo. *Dicionário da escravidão.* Rio de Janeiro: Christiano, 1997.

Scott, Rebecca J. "Public Rights, Social Equality, and the Conceptual Roots of the Plessy Challenge." *Michigan Law Review* 106, no. 5 (March 2008): 777–804.

————. *Slave Emancipation in Cuba: The Transition to Free Labor, 1860–1899.* Pittsburgh: University of Pittsburgh Press, 1985.

Senior Angulo, Diana. "La incorporación social en Costa Rica de la población afrocostarricense durante el siglo XX, 1927–1963." Master's thesis, Rodrigo Facio City University, Costa Rica, 2007.

Sharfstein, Daniel J. "Crossing the Color Line: Racial Migration and the One-Drop Rule, 1600–1860." *Minnesota Law Review* 91, no. 3 (February 2007): 592–656.

Sheriff, Robin E. *Dreaming Equality: Color, Race, and Racism in Urban Brazil.* New Brunswick, N.J.: Rutgers University Press, 2001.

Shugg, Roger Wallace. "Negro Voting in the Ante-Bellum South." *Journal of Negro History* 21, no. 4 (October 1936): 357–64.

Sieder, Rachel. "Conclusions: Promoting the Rule of Law in Latin America." In *Rule of Law in Latin America: The International Promotion of Judicial Reform*, ed. Pilar Domingo and Rachel Sieder. London: University of London, Institute of Latin American Studies, 2001.

Silva, Alberto da Costa e. *Um rio chamado Atlântico: A África no Brasil e o Brasil na África.* Rio de Janeiro: Nova Fronteira, 2003.

Silva, Graziella Moraes da, and Elisa P. Reis. "Perceptions of Racial Discrimination among Black Professionals in Rio de Janeiro." *Latin American Research Review* 46, no. 2 (2011): 55–78.

Silva, Hédio, Jr. *Discriminação racial nas escolas: Entre a lei e as práticas sociais.* Brasília: UNESCO, 2002.

Skidmore, Thomas E. *Black into White: Race and Nationality in Brazilian Thought.* Durham, N.C.: Duke University Press, 1993.

———. *Politics in Brazil, 1930–1964: An Experiment in Democracy.* New York: Oxford University Press, 1967.

———. "Raízes de Gilberto Freyre." *Journal of Latin American Studies* 34, no. 1 (February 2002): 1–20.

Skocpol, Theda. "Sociology's Historical Imagination." In *Vision and Method in Historical Sociology*, ed. Theda Skocpol. New York: Cambridge University Press, 1984.

Smith, James P., and Finis Welch. "Affirmative Action and Labor Markets." *Journal of Labor Economics* 2, no. 2 (April 1984): 269–301.

Solomianski, Alejandro. *Identidades secretas: La negritud argentina.* Buenos Aires: Viterbo, 2003.

Soto Quirós, Ronald. "Desafinidad con la población nacional: Discursos y políticas de inmigración en Costa Rica, 1862–1943." *Istmo*, July 24, 2003. http://istmo.denison.edu/n06/articulos/desafinidad.html.

Spalding, Matthew. "King's Conservative Mind." *National Review Online.* January 21, 2002. http://old.nationalreview.com/comment/comment-spalding012102.shtml.

Spear, Allen H. *Black Chicago: The Making of a Negro Ghetto, 1890–1920*. Chicago: University of Chicago Press, 1967.

Stampp, Kenneth. "Comment on Earl Maltz." *Cardozo Law Review* 17, no. 6 (May 1996): 2017–22.

———. *The Era of Reconstruction, 1863–1877*. New York: Knopf, 1965.

———. *The Peculiar Institution: Slavery in the Ante-Bellum South*. New York: Vintage, 1964.

Steinfeld, Robert J. *The Invention of Free Labor: The Employment Relation in English and American Law and Culture, 1350–1870*. Chapel Hill: University of North Carolina Press, 1991.

Stepan, Nancy Leys. *The Hour of Eugenics: Race, Gender, and Nation in Latin America*. Ithaca: Cornell University Press, 1991.

———. "The Pan American Experiment in Eugenics." In *Science and Empires: Historical Studies about Scientific Development and European Expansion*, ed. Patrick Pettijean, Catherine Jami, and Anne Marie Moulin. Dordrecht, the Netherlands: Kluwer Academic, 1992.

Strum, Harvey. "Property Qualifications and Voting Behavior in New York, 1807–1816." *Journal of the Early Republic* 1, no. 4 (Winter 1981): 347–71.

Sugrue, Thomas J. "Affirmative Action from Below: Civil Rights, the Building Trades, and the Politics of Racial Equality in the Urban North, 1945–1969." *Journal of American History* 91, no. 1 (June 2004): 145–73.

———. *Sweet Land of Liberty: The Forgotten Struggle for Civil Rights in the North*. New York: Random House, 2009.

Sumner, William Graham. *Folkways: A Study of the Sociological Importance of Usages, Manners, Customs, Mores, and Morals*. Boston: Ginn, 1907.

Sundiata, I. K. "Late Twentieth Century Patterns of Race Relations in Brazil and the United States." *Phylon* 48, no. 1 (1st Quarter 1987): 62–76.

Sundstrom, William A. "The Color Line: Racial Discrimination in Urban Labor Markets, 1910–1950." *Journal of Economic History* 54, no. 2 (June 1994): 382–96.

———. "Last Hired, First Fired? Unemployment and Urban Black Workers during the Great Depression." *Journal of Economic History* 52, no. 2 (June 1992): 415–29.

Tannenbaum, Frank. *Slave and Citizen: The Negro in the Americas*. New York: Vintage/Random House, 1946.

Telles, Edward E. *Incorporating Race and Ethnicity into UN Millennium Development Goals*. Washington, D.C.: Inter-American Dialogue, 2007.

———. *Race in Another America: The Significance of Skin Color in Brazil*. Princeton: Princeton University Press, 2004.

———. "Racial Ambiguity among the Brazilian Population." *Ethnic and Racial Studies* 25, no. 3 (May 2002): 414–41.

Temin, Peter. "The Great Depression." In *The Cambridge Economic History of the United States*, vol. 3, *The Twentieth Century*, ed. Stanley L. Engerman and Robert E. Gallman. New York: Cambridge University Press, 2000.

Thernstrom, Stephan, and Abigail Thernstrom. *America in Black and White: One Nation, Indivisible.* New York: Simon and Schuster, 1997.

Thornton, John. *Africa and Africans in the Making of the Atlantic World, 1400–1680.* New York: Cambridge University Press, 1992.

Toplin, Robert Brent. *The Abolition of Slavery in Brazil.* New York: Atheneum, 1972.

Torres-Saillant, Silvio. "The Tribulations of Blackness: Stages in Dominican Racial Identity." *Latin American Perspectives* 25, no. 3 (May 1998): 126–46.

Tucker, St. George. "Note H: On the State of Slavery in Virginia." In *Blackstone's Commentaries: With Notes of References to the Constitution and Laws, of the Federal Government of the United States, and of the Commonwealth of Virginia,* by St. George Tucker, vol. 4. Clark, N.J.: Lawbook Exchange, 2008.

Turits, Richard Lee. "A World Destroyed, a Nation Imposed: The 1937 Haitian Massacre in the Dominican Republic." *Hispanic American Historical Review* 82, no. 3 (August 2002): 589–635.

Twine, France Winddance. *Racism in a Racial Democracy: The Maintenance of White Supremacy in Brazil.* New Brunswick, N.J.: Rutgers University Press, 1998.

Using the Inter-American System for Human Rights: A Practical Guide for NGOs. Washington, D.C.: Global Rights: Partners for Justice, 2004.

Vandiver, Marylee Mason. "Racial Classifications in Latin American Censuses." *Social Forces* 28, no. 2 (December 1949): 138–46.

Vargas, João H. Costa. "When a Favela Dares to Become a Gated Community: The Politics of Race and Urban Space in Rio de Janeiro." *Latin American Perspectives* 33, no. 4 (July 2006): 49–81.

Vasconcelos, José. *The Cosmic Race: A Bilingual Edition.* Trans. Didier T. Jaén. Baltimore: Johns Hopkins University Press, 1997.

Vázquez, Mario C. "Immigration and *Mestizaje* in Nineteenth-Century Peru." In *Race and Class in Latin America*, ed. Magnus Mörner. New York: Columbia University Press, 1970.

Vega, Marta Moreno. "Interlocking African Diaspora Cultures in the Work of Fernando Ortiz." *Journal of Black Studies* 31, no. 1 (September 2000): 39–50.

Velho, Yvonne Maggie Alves. *Medo do feitiço: Relações entre magia e poder no Brasil.* Rio de Janeiro: Arquivo Nacional, Orgão do Ministério da Justiça, 1992.

Verissimo, Marcos Paulo. "The Brazilian 1988 Constitution Twenty Years On: Supreme Court and Activism in a 'Brazilian Mode.'" *Revista Direito GV* 4, no. 2 (July–December 2008): 407–40.

Vianna, Oliveira. "O povo brasileiro e sua evolução." In *Recenseamento do Brasil, 1920.* Rio de Janeiro: Ministério da Agricultura, 1922.

Vilela, Túlio. "Brasil na Segunda Guerra—FEB na Itália: Brasileiros receberam treinamento intensivo." *UOL Educação.* N.d. http://educacao.uol.com.br /historia-brasil/brasil-na-segunda-guerra-feb-na-italia.jhtm.

Vinson, Ben, III. "The Racial Profile of a Rural Mexican Province in the 'Costa Chica': Igualapa in 1791." *The Americas* 57, no. 2 (October 2000): 269–82.

Vinson, Ben, III, and Matthew Restall, eds. *Black Mexico: Race and Society from Colonial to Modern Times.* Albuquerque: University of New Mexico Press, 2009.

Wade, Peter. *Blackness and Race Mixture: The Dynamics of Racial Identity in Colombia.* Baltimore: Johns Hopkins University Press, 1995.

———. "Etnicidad, multiculturalismo, y políticas sociales en Latinoamérica: Poblaciones afrolatinas (e indígenas)." *Tabula Raza* 4 (January–July 2006): 59–81.

Wagley, Charles. Introduction to *Race and Class in Rural Brazil: A UNESCO Study,* ed. Charles Wagley. New York: UNESCO, 1963.

Watson, Alan. *Roman Slave Law.* Athens: University of Georgia Press, 1987.

———. *Slave Law in the Americas.* Athens: University of Georgia Press, 1989.

Weber, Max. *Economy and Society.* Vol. 1. Ed. Guenther Roth and Claus Wittich. Berkeley: University of California Press, 1978.

Weinstein, Barbara. "Racializing Regional Difference: São Paulo versus Brazil, 1932." In *Race and Nation in Modern Latin America,* eds. Nancy P. Appelbaum, Anne S. Macpherson, and Karin Alejandra Rosenblatt. Chapel Hill: University of North Carolina Press, 2003.

Weiss, Nancy J. *Farewell to the Party of Lincoln: Black Politics in the Age of FDR.* Princeton: Princeton University Press, 1983.

Weller, Christian E., and Jaryn Fields. "The Black and White Labor Gap in America: Why African Americans Struggle to Find Jobs and Remain Employed Compared to Whites." July 2011. http://www.americanprogress.org /issues/2011/07/black_unemployment.html.

Werneck, Jurema. "O belo ou o puro? Racismo, eugenia, e novas (bio)tecnologias." In *Sob o signo das bios: Vozes críticas da sociedade civil, reflexões no Brasil,* vol. 1, ed. Alejandra Rotania and Jurema Werneck. Rio De Janeiro: E-Papers Serviços Editoriais, 2004.

Wesley, Charles H. "The Negro's Struggle for Freedom in Its Birthplace." *Journal of Negro History* 1, no. 1 (January 1945): 62–81.

Whitman, T. S. *The Price of Freedom: Slavery and Manumission in Baltimore and Early National Maryland.* Lexington: University Press of Kentucky, 1997.

Whitney, Robert. "The Architect of the Cuban State: Fulgencio Batista and Populism in Cuba, 1937–1940." *Journal of Latin American Studies* 32, no. 2 (May 2000): 435–59.

Wilson, William Julius. *The Truly Disadvantaged: The Inner City, the Underclass, and Public Policy.* Chicago: University of Chicago Press, 1987.

Wilson, Woodrow. *Division and Reunion.* New York: Longmans, Green, 1921.

Winch, Julie. *Philadelphia's Black Elite: Activism, Accommodation, and Struggle for Autonomy, 1787–1848.* Philadelphia: Temple University Press, 1988.

Wolgemuth, Kathleen L. "Woodrow Wilson and Federal Segregation." *Journal of Negro History* 44, no. 2 (April 1959): 158–73.

Wood, Peter H. *Black Majority: Negroes in Colonial South Carolina from 1670 through the Stono Rebellion.* New York: Knopf, 1974.

Woodward, C. Vann. *The Strange Career of Jim Crow.* New York: Oxford University Press, 2001.

———. *Tom Watson: Agrarian Rebel.* New York: Oxford University Press, 1963.

Wright, Gavin. "The Civil Rights Revolution as Economic History." *Journal of Economic History* 59, no. 2 (June 1999): 276–81.

———. *The Political Economy of the Cotton South: Households, Markets, and Wealth in the Nineteenth Century.* New York: Norton, 1978.

Wright, Winthrop R. *Café con Leche: Race, Class, and National Image in Venezuela.* Austin: University of Texas Press, 1990.

———. "The Todd Duncan Affair: Acción Democrática and the Myth of Racial Democracy in Venezuela." *The Americas* 44, no. 4 (April 1988): 441–59.

Zoninsein, Jonas. "The Economic Case for Combating Racial and Ethnic Exclusion in Latin America and the Caribbean Countries." In *Social Inclusion and Economic Development in Latin America,* ed. Mayra Buvinić, Jacqueline Mazza, and Ruthanne Deutsch. Washington, D.C.: Inter-American Development Bank, 2001.

Index

Made in the USA
Middletown, DE
24 August 2023

37289902R00234